A Century of Restaurants

This book, and the two-plus years it took to accomplish it, is dedicated to some very special people who believed in me and in this ambitious endeavor to capture the essence, history, and soul of one hundred of America's oldest restaurants. They generously supported me with their hearts and minds, and many of them with their pocketbooks. I am deeply indebted to each and every one of the following for their contribution to *A Century of Restaurants*: Lynn Johnson, Steve Marsden (LHS '64), Dennis and Melinda Young (LHS '64), Janet Stafford Myers (LHS '64), Kathy Baker (LHS '64), Dan Macey, Clare and Ken Adair, James Barggren, Chris Peterson, John and Kathy Angood, Jim and Barb Smith, Dr. Thomas Kovaric, and Chris Browne.

Additionally, my heartfelt thanks and gratitude go to Andrews McMeel publisher Kirsty Melville, to my patient editor and fellow barbecue aficionado Jean Lucas, editor Lane Butler, and to Sandy Frye, who designed this beautiful book. I've reserved a special hug and a plate-load of thanks for my agent and dear friend Dennis Hayes, who was key in making this happen.

And finally, a banquet of thanks to my family, especially my wife, Kate, who is my unofficial editor, traveling companion, co-foodie, and love of three-plus decades. Also there to support and encourage me were our daughters Kara and Tricia, their husbands Stephen and Reed, and our sons Christopher and Kevin.

Mom and Dad: This is what comes of your taking me to Schuler's in 1962 and starting me on the delicious road I've wandered ever since.

Andrews McMeel Publishing, LLC
an Andrews McMeel Universal company
1130 Walnut Street, Kansas City, Missouri 64106
www.andrewsmcmeel.com

13 14 15 16 17 TEN 10 9 8 7 6 5 4 3 2 1

ISBN: 978-1-4494-0781-0
Library of Congress Control Number: 2011944563

Photography by Rick Browne
Design by Sandy Frye

ATTENTION: SCHOOLS AND BUSINESSES

Andrews McMeel books are available at quantity discounts with bulk purchase for educational, business, or sales promotional use. For information, please e-mail the Andrews McMeel Publishing Special Sales Department: specialsales@amuniversal.com

A Century of Restaurants

STORIES AND RECIPES FROM 100 OF AMERICA'S MOST HISTORIC AND SUCCESSFUL RESTAURANTS

Rick Browne

Andrews McMeel Publishing, LLC

Kansas City • Sydney • London

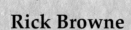

∽ Contents ∽

∽ Introduction ∽

This book celebrates one hundred of the country's oldest restaurants. Scattered from coast to coast and border to border, they have been continuously serving patrons for at least one hundred years. The oldest opened in 1673, the youngest dates back to 1911.

My research turned up more than 240 centenarian restaurants, which is an unworkable number for a book, and it would have been impossible for me to personally visit each one. Instead I weighed the geographical, historical, and culinary significance of each, and selected what I feel are some of the most representative of America's historic restaurants. The 300-year-old and 200-year-old establishments were "grandfathered in," with the balance of the centenarians I profile being a mere 100-plus years old.

In an industry where 70 percent of all restaurants fail after ten years, these establishments have beaten the odds. *A Century of Restaurants* will take you on a culinary road trip through history, guiding you to every corner of the country while exploring the culture, history, and gastronomic traditions of American cuisine.

These gathering places have played a vital part in shaping the nation's culinary culture for the past three centuries. They represent the best of family traditions, have provided jobs for millions of people and have entertained and fed many millions more, and in many ways they define American cuisine and hospitality.

The dining places in this book are found in America's smallest towns and in its biggest cities. Some are found in historic homes, others in tiny inns, rustic taverns, or weather-beaten saloons. They're on sleepy back roads and bustling boulevards. Some are homespun plain and simple, while others rival the palatial opulence of kings and queens. In some ways, they all have helped to build America.

Griswold Inn, Essex, Connecticut

Guests at these restaurants may eat inside, outside, under a chandelier, or under the stars, overlooking a rushing river, or watching a desert sunset. The table may be bare Formica or covered with a white linen; the glassware may be crystal wineglasses or mason jars; the dinnerware may be fine china or pie plates; the chairs perfectly matched antiques, wooden benches, or mismatched hand-me-downs.

The oldest restaurant we'll visit and profile is the White Horse Tavern in Newport, Rhode Island, which began serving hungry folks Stewed Pompion and Roast Beefe-Stake in 1673. The youngest eatery on our list is the iconic Pleasant Point Inn in Lovell, Maine. A classic Down East resort on a magnificent lake, it offers an eclectic mixture of Mediterranean, New England, and Continental cuisines, and that iconic Maine dessert, fresh wild blueberry pie.

When I started this project, I wasn't looking for the secrets to the longevity of the restaurants— the magic that has kept people coming into their

Mark Twain's seventieth birthday party at Delmonico's, 1905.
Copyright © Museum of the City of New York. Used with permission.

dining rooms for most of our nation's history. But after a while, there seemed to be a number of "truths" shared by the establishments I visited, some commonalities that these historic burger joints, taverns, inns, and restaurants share. And all of them are truly historic, not just because they are old, but because they have been important to the history of their state, the nation, and to their owners, customers, and the communities they're located in, and because of the major historical events that have taken place in or near them.

Over tens of decades, these restaurants have perfected a few techniques that keep their doors open, their customers happy, and their dining rooms full. The most common success factor is the continuation of ownership within one or two families. Restaurants that have been in one family for decades, passing from generation to generation, are to be in the majority in this book. Some of these establishments began in the late nineteenth or twentieth century and are operated today by the third generation, while many others have kept ownership within the family for six, seven, or eight generations. Even when ownership has been transferred to outsiders, there is usually a familial tie, or the new owners are personal or business acquaintances of the previous owners or customers.

Almost equally as important for a lengthy life in the restaurant business is the passion of the proprietors for their livelihood. Cosmo Torrigno, the former owner of the Centerton Inn in New Jersey, says "I loved my restaurant. I used to get up early every morning and go down there, and my day was made when I could serve up great meals that my customers loved. My restaurant was the beginning, middle, and end of my days. I was doing what I was meant to do, and by gosh, I think, doing it damn well."

The third most common factor, and perhaps the most important, is that without exception these elders of the restaurant world make people feel welcome, at home, and special. "We have customers who come here every day and sit at the same table," says Casselman Inn's Merve Benneman. "They say we make them feel like they are welcome guests in our home, and they wouldn't feel right unless they started

Barbetta's signature scallops and bok choy.

their day here, which they've been doing for forty-plus years!"

Some other indicators of long-term success kept cropping up as well, such as chefs and cooks who make everything from scratch, and waitstaffs and kitchen staffs who have happily worked there for decades. At Galatoire's in New Orleans, guests are encouraged to ask for a waiter they know, and some people even call ahead to schedule reservations for times when "their waiter" will be working.

One piece of advice for restaurant owners who want to join this fraternity of historic establishments: Do not radically change your menu! If you must add a new dish or two every now and then, fine. But do not throw out the signature dishes that you've been serving for years and think you're going to dazzle your regulars. Those dishes are a huge reason why people come back time and again. And if their favorite dishes vanish, so will they. Customers like the familiar foods they are comfortable with, that bring back memories of previous visits with their father, mother, grandfather, uncle, son, daughter, or friends. Certain dishes, like one restaurant's chicken and biscuits, a tavern's lobster salad, or the inn's warm apple pie with cheddar cheese can vividly call to mind a memorable anniversary, birthday, or other celebration.

Philadelphia City Tavern servers wear custom-tailored eighteenth-century attire.

By sharing the phenomenal success stories of these one hundred restaurants, inns, taverns, public houses, and saloons, I hope to have captured some of their soul, and through words and photographs provide a better understanding and appreciation for three centuries of American dining.

In addition to the historical chronicles here, each of the restaurants generously shared with me, and with you, the reader, some of their favorite recipes. They range from appetizers to entrees, soups to salads, side dishes to desserts, and they provide a variety of historic recipes that makes this a most unique cookbook.

Dear readers, please remember that restaurant menus are seasonal and thus based on the availability of certain items at certain times. If you go to one of these wonderful places and they don't have dishes I've described, don't be deterred. They no doubt have many excellent alternatives. After all, they have survived more than one hundred years in business, so they must know what they are doing.

So please pull up a comfortable chair and break out your napkin, knife, and fork, because we're going to take you to some of America's oldest and best dining rooms—and we've reserved a special table for you.

Rick Browne

A Century of Restaurants ~ Menu

APPETIZERS
~~~

Number of restaurants in America: 960,000

Number of fast food restaurants: 160,000

Number of fast food restaurants that failed in 2009: 164

Number of independent restaurants that failed in 2009: 2,685

FIRST COURSES
~~~

Amount spent daily in U.S. restaurants: $1.7 billion

Amount spent yearly in U.S. restaurants: $604.2 billion

Overall impact of restaurant industry on U.S. economy: $1.7 trillion

Number of people employed in the U.S. restaurant industry: 12.8 million

ENTREES
~~~

Length of my project.. 3 years, 2 months, 12 hours
First restaurant visited... June 2009
Last restaurant visited .... August 2011
Number of states visited... 44*, plus the District of Columbia
Miles flown.. 26,162
Miles driven... 19,904
Total miles traveled... 46,066
Longest single trip .... 8,232 miles in June/July 2011
List of states visited on that trip (in order of travel) .... Washington, Idaho, Montana, Wyoming, Nebraska, Iowa, Minnesota, Wisconsin, Michigan, Indiana, Illinois, Missouri, Kansas, Oklahoma, Texas, New Mexico, Colorado, Oregon
Entrees eaten..163 (in more than a few places I "tried" two or three)
Most expensive entree .... $99: Orca Platter, Old Ebbit Grill, Washington, D.C.
Least expensive entree....................$2.50: Smoked Pork Sandwich, Jones' Bar-B-Q Diner, Marianna, Arkansas
Largest restaurant ....Columbia (Tampa, Florida) seats 1,700
Smallest restaurant .... Jones' Bar-B-Q Diner (Marianna, Arkansas) seats 8

SIDE DISHES
~~~

Photographs taken: 14,455
Words written: 126,000
Hours spent writing: 1,600
Hours spent editing images: 1,400
New friends made: Hundreds

*I was unable to find century-old restaurants in two states: Hawaii and Alaska, and in four states I felt the places I did find weren't of the same quality and standard as establishments in the 44 states I did visit.
   Restaurant statistics provided by the National Restaurant Association 2010 Year-End Report. Restaurant failure statistics from a joint survey by Michigan State University and Cornell University business schools.

DESSERTS
~~~

Favorite desserts: Raspberry Pie (Breitbach's, Iowa), Warm Brown Sugar Cakes (Red Lion Inn, Massachusetts), Blueberry Cream Pie (The Publick House, Massachusetts), Cannoli (Ferrara, New York), Boston Cream Pie (Omni Parker House, Massachusetts), Brandy Ice (Wilmot Stage Stop, Wisconsin), Moravian Gingerbread (Old Salem Tavern, North Carolina)

The Bright Star
BESSEMER, AL ~ EST. 1907

In the early 1900s, Bessemer was a booming steelmaking town and Alabama's eighth largest city. Between 1901 and 1910, more than 9 million people, many from Eastern and southern Europe, arrived in the United States to seek their fortune. Over 150,000 were from Greece, and among them was young Tom Bonduris, who joined one hundred or so of his countrymen already living in Birmingham. He began baking pies in a suburban restaurant called the Bright Star. A year later, he moved to Bessemer and opened a small restaurant of the same name, consisting of a horseshoe-shaped bar and a row of iron barstools—there were no tables or booths.

Two years later, two other Greek immigrants, Bill and Pete Koikos, bought the restaurant and ran it until 1966, when their two sons, Jim and Nick, took over. They have managed it for the past forty-four years. Jimmy greets the customers, and Nicky supervises the kitchen.

When asked why he thought the restaurant has survived, despite the demise of the steel industry when its raw materials were mined out, and the subsequent loss of the town's population, Nick said, "We do everything to please our customers and make sure they have a great meal and a good time. I have to admit that early on we didn't pay as much attention to food costs as we should have. We just wanted our customers to have a great experience and come back."

They have certainly achieved that goal. Bright Star has grown from a twenty-five-seat café to a restaurant that seats 350, with a bar, a large banquet room, and several smaller dining rooms.

From left: Wanda Little, Marie Jackson, Evelyn Rembert, and Anita Moore have a combined 75 years in the Bright Star kitchen.

The main dining room is a relic of the early 1900s, with its leather booths, dark wood wainscoting, large mirrors, dramatic lighting, and WPA-era murals of the Old Country that are nicotine-stained from the early years.

At the back of the main dining room are several tiny curtained-off booths, one decorated with a portrait of Alabama football coach

Paul "Bear" Bryant. It seems he loved to come here for dinner after the football season, when he always ordered the Greek salad and the fourteen-ounce K.C. extra-cut rib-eye steak. There are many photos and Bryant memorabilia scattered around the restaurant, as both Koikos brothers graduated from the University of Alabama, and like many folks in the state are die-hard Crimson Tide fans.

Co-owner Nick says he thinks one of the reasons for the restaurant's success over the years is their emphasis on seafood. They used to drive down to Florida twice a week to pick up fresh seafood but now have it shipped in every day. Oysters, shrimp, flounder, grouper, catfish, stone crabs, and red snapper all are regularly featured on the restaurant's lunch and dinner menus. The red snapper, cooked "Greek style," is one of their signature dishes, so popular that they sell an unbelievable twenty-four hundred pounds of it every week.

Nick credits Bright Star's kitchen staff and cooks with a large part of its longevity and success. "Many of our employees have been here more than seven years, and a dozen or so have been working with us for more than twenty years. They certainly have helped maintain the consistency and excellence of what we serve, and we're lucky to have so many loyal people."

Bright Star's menu is a delicious mix of Southern and Greek cooking, featuring Greek Salad, Beef Tenderloin Greek Style, Broiled Chicken Greek Style, Greek-Style Broiled Shrimp, and Greek-Style Broiled Snapper. You get the picture. Alongside the Hellenic-influenced items are regional standbys like gumbo, turnip greens with bacon, fried okra, macaroni and cheese, carrot and raisin salad, lima beans, and buttered squash. The desserts are pure Southern, such as lemon icebox, coconut cream, pineapple cheese, and peanut butter pies.

When Tom Bonduris, the original owner, opened The Bright Star in Bessemer, it consisted of a horseshoe-shaped bar and a row of iron barstools — with no tables or booths.

A private booth favored by Alabama football coach Paul "Bear" Bryant whose picture hangs at the back. The coach loved to come here for dinner after the football season and always ordered the Greek salad and the 14-ounce K.C. extra cut rib-eye steak.

Bright Star Greek-Style Snapper

∿ SERVES 6 ∿

Juice of 3 lemons

1 teaspoon dried oregano

Salt and freshly ground black pepper

1 cup plus 2 tablespoons plus 1 teaspoon extra-virgin
olive oil

½ cup (1 stick) unsalted butter, melted

6 (8-ounce) red snapper fillets

½ cup all-purpose flour, for dusting

In a small bowl, whisk the lemon juice, oregano, and
salt and pepper to taste together. Gradually whisk the
1 cup plus 2 tablespoons of the olive oil into the lemon
mixture until emulsified. Set aside.

Brush the melted butter on each fillet, coating evenly.
Lightly dust each fillet with flour on both sides.
In a heavy skillet or on a griddle, heat the 1 teaspoon
olive oil over medium heat. Sauté the fish until lightly
browned and cooked through, about 2 ½ minutes per
side. Do not overcook.

Place the fillets on a platter and pour the lemon sauce
over them. Serve immediately.

This restaurant, which began life as a tiny, humble café, was honored by the James Beard Foundation in 2010 with an America's Classic award, which is given to "restaurants with timeless appeal, beloved for quality food that reflects the character of their community." The Foundation also specifically lauded the Bright Star for its Greek-meets-Southern cuisine. It is the first Alabama restaurant to ever receive this award.

When their father, Bill, was ninety-two years old, he called the brothers into his office and, as Jimmy recalls, told them, "This is a special place; I want you to take care of it." So Jimmy said, "Daddy, we'll do the best we can." I think they've fulfilled that promise.

The Bright Star dining room in 1938.
The restaurant today still has the same murals on the wall.

Golden Rule Bar-B-Q and Grill
IRONDALE, AL ~ EST. 1891

The Golden Rule, the only chain restaurant in this book, has twenty-nine franchise locations scattered around the South. What started in tiny Irondale back in the late 1800s has turned into the second-largest barbecue-restaurant chain in the United States.

The original wooden building was a gathering place for locals and a roadside stop for travelers journeying between Birmingham and Atlanta on a two-lane dirt road. The eatery served plates of smoked pork and beer, sold cigarettes, and even did some automobile work, which gives a whole new meaning to the phrase "greasy spoon."

The tiny restaurant didn't change for forty years until new owners constructed a building closer to the county line on the edge of the Atlanta Highway. Like its predecessor, the kitchen had a dirt floor, but the dining area had a wooden floor built right on the ground like a backyard deck. The place served much the same menu, but it didn't do car repairs anymore.

The 1960s brought yet another new building, as the restaurant had to move again so the highway could be widened. They added neon signs (a big deal in that part of the country in the 1950s), metal awnings, and new kitchen equipment.

Owner Michael Matsos recalls, "I used to go to the Rule. I loved their barbecue sandwich and their sauce. I used to talk to Jabo Stone, the owner, and tried to learn about how he worked his pits and how he cooked up such great barbecue. At the time, I owned a steakhouse and was always looking for new things to serve. So when he wanted to retire he called me and asked if I wanted to take over his restaurant, and after some haggling I assumed ownership in 1969."

With his ownership came a new, slightly larger menu: pork plates, pork sandwiches, fresh-cut French fries, and a green salad with a spoonful of mayonnaise as the dressing. You could wash down the barbecue with beer, water, or bottled Coke, as they had no soda fountain in those days. Over the years, the Golden Rule added other menu items: chicken, loin back ribs, beef brisket, homemade pies, and more side dishes. But one thing hasn't changed: They still hand-cut their fries. "If we tried to use frozen potatoes, our customers would mutiny," Michael says, laughing.

The flagship Irondale location changed again to make way for highway construction and was built right by Interstate 20. It is an extremely popular spot for locals, as well as for folks driving over from Georgia, who like to pick up the

Rule's popular ribs and side dishes on the way to Crimson Tide tailgate parties in Tuscaloosa.

As with most century-old restaurants, many of the Golden Rule's staff have been working there for decades. Bernice Kelly, who started as a teenager, celebrated her seventy-fifth birthday in 2011 but is still in charge of cooking the signature

Veteran servers and cooks (from left): Bernice Kelly, Peggy Martin, Michael Booker and Willie Morgan have put in a staggering total of 164 years of service at the Golden Rule.

baked beans. Pit master Michael Booker has been in charge of the pits for more than thirty-six years, and Peggy Martin has been baking the pies for more than thirty-three years. "We're just a big happy family," says Michael.

The Golden Rule cooks six hundred pounds of pork butt at a time in a smoker behind the open pit, then finishes off the roasts and ribs in the dining room pit where everyone can see and smell the charcoal, roasting meat, and bubbling barbecue sauces. Customers can order sandwiches made with "outside meat," "inside meat," or any

Golden Rule Bar-B-Q Famous Baked Beans

∼ SERVES 10 TO 12 ∼

6 slices hickory smoked bacon, chopped

¼ cup chopped yellow onion

½ teaspoon ground cinnamon

½ teaspoon ground nutmeg

½ teaspoon ground allspice

¼ pound firmly packed light brown sugar

1 (No. 10) can Bush's Baked Beans (see Note)

¼ cup yellow prepared mustard

¼ cup ketchup

1 cup Golden Rule Original Bar-B-Q Sauce (see Note)

4 ounces barbecued pork, finely chopped

Preheat the oven to 350°F. In a large soup pot, sauté the bacon and onion over medium heat for about 5 minutes, or until the bacon is soft and the onion is translucent.

Add the spices and brown sugar. Mix well. Decrease the heat to low and simmer for another 5 minutes. Add the beans, mustard, ketchup, barbecue sauce, and pork. Mix well.

Pour into a large casserole dish. Cover with aluminum foil and bake for 15 to 20 minutes, until the beans are bubbling. Let cool for 5 minutes before serving.

NOTE: It's very important that you use Bush's beans. The No. 10 can holds 115 ounces, or a little more than 7 pounds. The barbecue sauce is available online at www.goldenrulebbq.com.

combination thereof. "We spoil our customers, giving them exactly what they want, and that includes sauces," says Michael. They have five varieties, including the iconic mayonnaise-based white sauce that seems to crop up only in Alabama.

You can stand by and watch the pit master pull ribs fresh from the pit and chop the sizzling, moist slabs into single bones. The famous rib platter is huge, with two small bowls of potato salad and marinated coleslaw surrounded by fifteen ribs. The meat is smoky, moist, and tender (but chewy at the same time), and comes off the bone with a slight tug. If I were judging a barbecue contest (and I've judged a few in my day), I would give the Golden Rule ribs a perfect score.

The Palace Restaurant & Saloon

PRESCOTT, AZ ~ EST. 1877

The Palace could easily have been called the Phoenix, after the mythical bird that burned to a crisp and rose from the ashes. Destroyed by two major fires, which wiped out most of the buildings on Prescott's Whiskey Row (aka Montezuma Street), the oldest frontier saloon in America was rebuilt both times and stands proudly today as a tribute to the Old West.

After the first fire in 1883, owner Bob Brow promised the new saloon would be "fireproof" and constructed the building from pressed ornamental bricks and native gray granite, with an iron roof and iron shutters. But it was destroyed in the second major Row fire in 1901. During that fire, patrons carried the ornate Brunswick bar to safety

across the street. It's said that before the fire was out, the bartenders were pouring drinks from the relocated bar, and people were gulping down whiskey and rye as the firemen vainly fought the flames.

The bar itself was unlike no other in the West at the time: twenty-four-feet long and made from solid oak and polished cherry, the back bar had intricate carvings on huge soaring columns and was topped with superb oval French mirrors. Today, it's the most striking feature of the large bar area of the restaurant.

Once upon a time, beer was five cents a glass, there were bands and dancing, and a retinue of female hostesses entertained patrons with songs and dances—and in more intimate and financially profitable ways upstairs. There was also plenty of action in the saloon, which offered faro, craps, roulette, poker, and keno. It's reported that Little Egypt wowed patrons with the same belly dance she introduced at the 1890s World's Fair, and Wyatt, Virgil, and Marshall Earp and Doc Holliday were regularly seen throwing down whiskeys and enjoying thick steaks. The Palace also included a Chinese restaurant and a very popular barbershop. It functioned as sort of a frontier community center. Men came to check on available work, it became headquarters for several local political races, and it was a clearinghouse for mineral claims that were sold from the bar.

Prohibition saw the bar business decline, but the Palace soldiered on as one of the best places in town to get a good meal and enjoy the congenial, if slightly less personal, atmosphere provided by the saloon gals. But over the years, the owners let the place slide and it began to deteriorate, the walls and ceilings becoming thick with brown goo from years of smoking in the saloon.

In 1996, Dave and Marilyn Michelson took over the Palace, vowing to restore it to the glory days of the early 1900s. The walls and ceiling were scraped and cleaned, the floors sanded and finished to their former gleam, and the skylights opened up to reveal the sparkle of that Parisian glass. The Michelsons researched the saloon's history at a local museum and re-created the elegance of the early Palace. They did, however, replace the gaming tables with dining tables and wood booths.

In honor of the Steve McQueen movie *Junior Bonner*, which was filmed at the Palace, a huge wall mural dominates the dining area of the saloon, lit by a beautiful skylight, and you can sit in one of the four booths named for the three Earp brothers and Doc Holliday. I suggest starting with a cup of the Palace's signature corn chowder, then digging

The Palace Corn Chowder

∽ SERVES 4 TO 6 ∽

8 ounces bacon, diced

1 tablespoon minced garlic

1 small yellow or white onion, diced

3 to 4 stalks celery, chopped

2 cups all-purpose flour

7½ cups water

¼ cup chicken base

¼ cup dry white wine

¼ tablespoon hot sauce

¼ teaspoon Worcestershire sauce

¼ teaspoon dried thyme

1 teaspoon ground white pepper

¼ teaspoon ground nutmeg

4¾ cups heavy cream or half-and-half

½ cup (1 stick) unsalted butter

3 to 4 baking potatoes, peeled and diced

3 cups fresh or thawed frozen corn
  kernels (about 6 ears)

Milk for thinning, if desired

In a large stockpot, cook the bacon over medium-high heat and until it renders its fat, 6 to 8 minutes. Add the garlic, onion, and celery and sauté until soft, about 10 minutes.

Gradually stir in the flour to make a roux, then gradually whisk in the water, chicken base, and wine. Cook for 10 minutes. Add the hot sauce, Worcestershire sauce, thyme, white pepper, and nutmeg. Lower the heat to a simmer and stir in the cream and butter. Continue to cook, stirring frequently, until thickened to a chowder consistency, about 12 minutes. Add the potatoes and corn and cook for 15 to 20 minutes, until the potatoes are tender, stirring constantly. Add the milk if the consistency is too thick. Serve hot.

into a 1½-inch-thick prime rib accompanied with crisp onion strings, a loaded baked potato, an assortment of sautéed fresh veggies, and a glass of California cabernet. I doubt the Earp brothers had grub this good, because the Palace has refined the menu from one hundred years ago, adding dishes such as Fried Calamari Steak Strips, Grilled Prawns and Prosciutto, Mile High Caesar Salad, Montezuma's Chicken Linguini, and Fresh Citrus Grilled Salmon.

On Sunday nights, a ragtime pianist performs, and occasionally there are other live

performers, including a concert pianist, an Irish singing group, and the great-grand-nephew of Wyatt Earp, who re-creates life on the frontier in a one-act play. In the summer, the restaurant and saloon are jammed with tourists seeking the Old West experience of Whiskey Row, and this restored shrine to the days of the Earps and Doc Holliday fills that niche pretty well. Kids love to sit in the booths named after those famous gunslingers. And just in case some of you buckaroos are wondering, those upstairs rooms, where the ladies frolicked the night away with local cowpokes, have been turned into offices for the Palace owners and staff.

Jones' Bar-B-Q Diner
MARIANNA, AR ~ EST. 1910

The air was hot and sticky and uncomfortable. There was no wind or breeze to cool the Arkansas Delta. Only that fiery round sun baking me nearly to death. But I had driven 150 miles to visit a local barbecue legend, and no blazing sun was going to stop me.

I had heard and read about the legendary pulled-pork sandwiches sold at the historic Jones' Bar-B-Q Diner in tiny Marianna, Arkansas—a restaurant that had survived more than a century in one of the poorest counties in the state. But the Diner, a two-story white house, seemed to be losing its battle with time. The paint was peeling, the windows were so dirty you couldn't see in, and the wrought-iron door squealed in protest as it was opened.

I stepped to the small inside window and ordered two sandwiches, feeling as if I were in a culinary confessional booth. "Two, please." I didn't have to say what meat I wanted, as pork is the only meat the Diner serves. I watched as the clerk made a few motions below my line of sight, handed me a brown paper lunch bag, took my wrinkled five-dollar bill, and looked past me at the next person in line. The tiny dining room was filled, with eight customers at its two tables, so I went out to the car, turned the air conditioning to high, and eagerly unwrapped my treasures.

The sandwich was good—no, damn good. The Wonder bread fought a losing battle with the sauce and drippingly moist pork, the chunks and strands tender and steaming and sopping wet with a thin cayenne-paprika-vinegar sauce. Every bite was an epiphany, the mustardy slaw wrapping its arms around the smoky meat. I hurried through the second sandwich, worried that the bread and I would both lose the battle— me suffering the most by having most of my lunch drop in my lap.

Only $2.50 for this manna from heaven? In Atlanta or Denver or Los Angeles, a pulled-pork sandwich costs five or six dollars, and in New York I'd shelled out $11.50 for one that wasn't half as good as this. Of course, they'd served it on a "homemade brioche bun." But here the Wonder bread did right by the juicy filling, as long as I ate quickly. The pork sandwich was simply the best I've ever eaten.

The Jones family has been serving barbecue since around 1910, when Walter and his brother

The tiny, somewhat crowded kitchen, turns out magnificent slow-smoked pork that is dripping with Jones' rich barbecue sauce.

Joe started selling barbecue hogs from a screened porch. Walter's son, Hubert, was the next to supply locals with smoky meat, raising his own hogs and selling the cooked pork by the pound from a laundry tub until he built and opened the Diner in 1964. James, sixty-five, who's been here for more than thirty years, works in the long, narrow kitchen making sandwiches until the Diner runs out of meat, which is often as early as 10:30 in the morning. The rest of his day is spent piling huge logs into an open fireplace, then later shoveling the coals into the two pits in the low smoke-filled building next door.

The pits have seen the ravages of time as well. Covered with a thick jet-black patina from the thousands of whole hogs, hams, and pork shoulders cooked in them, the cement-block pits are covered with tin lids that are raised by a system of pulleys that would make Rube Goldberg proud. The nights James cooks up shoulders, he naps in a small room upstairs, getting up once or twice during the wee small hours to replenish the coals. I asked James for a recipe, and he politely but firmly denied the request. "Just can't do it," he grinned.

The pits often contain other meats, mostly wild game and turkeys, smoked for a nominal fee for local hunters, but the pork is for the Diner. For $6 you can get a pound; $12 gets you two pounds. You get the idea. Cheap, yes. Wonderful, too. But since the county has an unemployment rate upward of 25 to 30 percent the Diner really couldn't charge much more. "We're doin' alright," he says, adjusting his St. Louis Cardinals baseball hat, "but I really don't have time to talk today. Gotta check the pits."

In a story published in the *Oxford American* magazine, food columnist John T. Edge, who is also the director of the Southern Foodways Alliance, wrote, "If a firm opening date could be established, a task at which this writer has failed, Jones might prove to be the oldest black-owned restaurant in the South, and, perhaps, one of the oldest family-owned black restaurants in the nation." I don't know if the Jones family tree will produce another generation as dedicated as Walter, Hubert, and James. After all, this is hard work, with long hours and not a lot of money, and rumor has it that James's son wants to do something else with his life. But today I salute James Jones, a quiet, hard-working, humble, and passionate man, who has dedicated his life to cookin' up some of the best barbecue in the South.

Some of the South's best barbecue, smoked for hours in long wide pits over hickory, is dished up at the rather spartan, no-frills Jones' Bar-B-Q Diner.

James sits watching a ball game as logs blaze in the open fireplace soon to turn to fiery coals, which will be shoveled into the cement-block pits to work their culinary magic.

Williams Tavern Restaurant
WASHINGTON, AR ~ EST. 1832

In the early days in Arkansas, many people who lived on or near the wagon trails or primitive roads opened their homes to travelers in need of food, drink, and sometimes overnight accommodations. Most travelers came on horseback or in wagons, and they often had additional horses or cattle with them as they traveled—animals that needed to be fed and watered as well. When the travelers couldn't find a welcoming home or ranch, they often camped right by the road, buying feed for their stock from local farmers.

John Williams had built his home along the Southwest Trail in the small village of Marlbrook, and because he was so close to the busy trail often provided for man and beast overnight—one time allegedly feeding, and we can assume housing, sixty men and their horses

in one night. In those days, such homes were referred to as "stands" and charged a small amount for their hospitality. Sam Williams, John's nephew, wrote that his uncle "kept open house, where, for pay, he entertained travelers, and perhaps there was no plate between Memphis and Red River better known."

In 1824, the nearby town of Washington was founded, not coincidentally the same year that George Washington was inaugurated as the nation's first President, and the small collection of houses and businesses soon became the economic and social center of the region. Anyone on the way to Texas passed through the town, including some famous pioneers like Sam Houston, Davy Crockett, and Jim Bowie (the latter two went on to fight and die in the Battle of the Alamo). In 1831, a local blacksmith forged the famous "Bowie knife" and presented it to the knife's namesake during one of his visits.

Washington is now a National Historic Landmark on the National Register of Historic Places, and a popular Arkansas State Park. Thirty of its buildings have been restored as examples of the Southern Greek Revival, Gothic Revival, Italianate, and Federal architectural styles, and the buildings stand as a living museum to life in the small Arkansas town from 1824 to 1900. Guides in period attire lead tours through their collections of antiques, farm tools, guns, and knives; answer questions about the town's history; and give tourists surrey rides around the town.

Surrey rides often end at the quaint Williams Tavern Restaurant, where visitors can enjoy traditional regional cuisine in one of the three small dining rooms. The simple, nutritious comfort food meals (lunch only) are unbelievably inexpensive. The chicken and dumplings, with two corn muffins and a thick chunk of jalapeño corn bread, a side dish of

The main dining room here is certainly not fancy; nor is their simple menu. But the home style cooking will fill your belly for amazingly low prices, just as they have for 180 years.

Chicken and Dumplings

SERVES 4

½ pound chicken legs and thighs, separated

½ cup chicken base

1 cup self-rising flour

2 tablespoons vegetable shortening

¼ cup boiling water

Chopped fresh flat-leaf parsley, for garnish

Place the chicken in a large stockpot and add water to cover. Boil over medium-high heat until the chicken is tender, about 30 minutes. Remove the chicken from the pot and set it aside to cool to the touch.

Add the chicken base to the broth in the pot and maintain the liquid at a simmer. Remove and discard the chicken skin, then pull the meat from the bones. Cover the meat and set it aside.

In a medium bowl, combine the flour and shortening, Using a pastry cutter or two dinner knives, cut in the shortening until the mixture forms pea-sized pieces. Stir the boiling water in a little at a time until the dough forms a ball but is not too wet. Roll the ball of dough out on a floured board, then cut it into 2-inch-square pieces.

Drop the dumplings into the simmering chicken broth and cook until tender, 10 to 12 minutes.

Place the chicken pieces in a large serving bowl and pour the broth and dumplings over the chicken. Garnish with the parsley and serve immediately.

black-eyed peas, and a serving of green beans, comes to just $5.99. The most expensive dish is the shrimp plate, which is priced at $8.99.

Enthusiastic character actors play roles of historic people from the tavern's early days, answering questions about what life was like in the late 1880s. Other pretend pioneers drive carriages up to the front of the tavern, dropping off people after a buggy ride through the park. If you find yourself in Washington, take a few moments to explore the historic buildings, experience the Washington of the 1800s, and take a trip back in time at one of the oldest "stands" on what was once the Southwest Trail.

They serve a pretty good plate themselves.

George Staples in costume as Abraham Block, the patriarch of the first Jewish family to move to Arkansas. Right: Jon Orr, a state historical park guide and buggy driver.

A local blacksmith forged the original "Bowie Knife" and presented the first one to Jim Bowie when he visited the Tavern the year it was opened.

Cold Spring Tavern
SANTA BARBARA, CA ~ EST. 1865

Opened in 1865 as a stagecoach stop where passengers could relax and have a meal, and where a stable of horses was ready to supply fresh mounts to pull the heavy coaches over steep San Marcos Pass, the Cold Spring Relay Station, now the Cold Spring Tavern, has been a welcome haven for travelers for almost 150 years. In fact, if you look closely you can still see stagecoach tracks nearby.

In 1865, Chinese laborers were brought in to construct a "turnpike" over the pass, as the old roads were dusty, treacherous, and a nightmare for anyone traveling in a coach. The workers were bunked in the old Road Gang House, still situated on the property. The rustic (meaning the walls, floors, and ceilings all cant this-a-way and that-a-way) log cabin restaurant, with its moss-covered planked roof, wood-paneled dining room and bar, stone-hearth fireplaces, and mounted animal heads, looks like the set of a Western movie starring John Wayne.

The old Ojai jail, moved from a nearby community, has been turned into a delightful cocktail bar on the large shaded deck. The four storage buildings at the back of the property, the only remains of the ghost town of Gopherville, add to the Old West atmosphere. "We feel like we bought the whole town, ghosts and all," says restaurant manager John Locke.

The tavern has been featured on many TV shows and was once a movie set, and over the years has hosted celebrities whose visits the owners do not publicize because "that's why they come here." A regular visitor recently brought his an open firewood grill. The nearby town of Santa Maria is famous for the recipe for sirloin top roast, and once you've tasted Tom's tri-tip sandwich, you'll want to ask your butcher for this cut, which is also known as a triangle cut. Sliced thin and served with grilled peppers and onions on a hearty sourdough roll, this is one of America's best sandwiches. But sadly much of the country ignores this delicious cut of meat.

Cold Spring's buffalo burgers, wild-game chili, whole wheat–molasses bread, charbroiled venison steak sandwich, medallions of rabbit, and rum-walnut chocolate chip pies are other huge favorites that keep people coming back. You can start your lunch with a Chili Sampler, featuring cups of

The Cold Spring Tavern in the Santa Ynez Mountains near Santa Barbara, approximately 1830s when it was part of Ovington's Brewery. The sign at right says "Cold Beer at Cold Springs."

ninety-two-year-old father, who claimed the place hadn't changed a whit since his first visit sixty-two years earlier. "It's the same," said another man who met his wife here twenty-eight years ago. They were revisiting for the first time since they left California fifteen years ago. "The moss on the roof is a little thicker, but that's about it." Even the employees don't change. Three out of the current twenty-five have been here more than twenty years.

Adelaide Ovington and her daughter, Audrey, bought the place for $2,000 in 1941 and ran it for sixty-five years. The Tavern is operated today by Audrey's daughter, Joy, and her husband, Wayne, who took over in 2006 when Audrey passed away. "We intend to carry on the traditions of the old tavern and will endeavor to preserve it for the enjoyment of future generations," Joy says.

Only on Sundays, Tom Perez, a giant of a man with a smile you can feel in your hip pocket, cooks up a dozen or so Santa Maria–style tri-tips over

On Sundays, Tom Perez barbecues tri-tip roasts and serves them sliced thinly, with grilled onions and the tavern's barbecue sauce.

Cold Spring Tavern's Wild-Game Black Bean Chili

Texas-style beef chili, a pork and chicken chile verde, and their most popular wild-game black bean chili, which contains venison, rabbit, and buffalo meat. It has great flavor, a chewy texture, and just the right amount of fresh chiles. The large buffalo burger is served with a large slice of melted Jack cheese and a generous portion of panfried onions, topped with barbecue sauce.

Despite the relatively isolated location and the fact that it doesn't advertise, this folksy log cabin restaurant has stayed in business for 150 years, and was recently voted the most romantic place for a daytime getaway in California. Although it isn't far off the "turnpike," which is now called Highway 154, it's hidden a mile or so up the mountain. Driving the fifteen miles from Santa Barbara literally takes you back in time to a gentler, more romantic, quieter, and less frenzied age. And, once you get there, if you're the adventurous type that needs to find the "cold spring" the place is named for, you won't have any trouble. There are actually fifty-two of them in the woods surrounding the tavern.

Wild-Game Black Bean Chili
∽ MAKES ABOUT 1 GALLON ∽

3½ cups dried black beans, rinsed and picked over

3 tablespoons canola oil

2½ pounds mixed chopped or ground venison, buffalo, and rabbit meat (see Note)

1½ pounds poblano chiles

1½ pounds yellow onions

12 ounces tomatoes, diced

¼ cup chili powder

2½ tablespoons cumin seeds

Salt and freshly ground black pepper

Sour cream, for serving

Minced jalapeños, for serving

Sweet or sourdough French bread, for serving

In a large pot, soak the beans overnight in water to cover by 2 inches. Drain and add fresh water to cover by 2 inches. Bring to a low boil over medium heat, then reduce the heat to a simmer and cook for about 2 hours, or until tender. Drain.

In a large skillet, heat the oil over medium heat and sauté the meat until browned. Using a slotted spoon, transfer the meat to a dish but leave the pan on the heat. Sauté the poblano chiles and onions in the pan for about 5 minutes, or until the onions are translucent. Combine the beans, meat, onions, chiles, and tomatoes in a stockpot over medium heat. Stir in the chili powder, cumin seeds, and salt and pepper to taste. Lower the heat and simmer, uncovered, for at least 1 hour.

Ladle the chili into bowls and top each serving with a dollop of sour cream and a sprinkling of jalapeños. Serve with sweet or sourdough French bread.

NOTE: You could use pork or chicken in this dish. But the wild game adds the rich taste that has made this one of the most popular dishes at the tavern.

Cole's
LOS ANGELES, CA ~ EST. 1908

A customer walks into a restaurant and orders a sliced beef sandwich, but having sore gums because of a recent dentist visit, asks the cook to dip the bread in some of the au jus to soften it, then goes away happy. Thus the legacy of "French dip" sandwiches at Cole's in Los Angles began, though it's a heritage disputed by another LA restaurant that claims it is the birthplace of this particular sandwich (see Philippe's, page 34).

Founded in 1908, Cole's had an ideal downtown location: the basement of the Pacific Electric Building, the center of the Pacific Electric Red Car customers who have been coming here for more than thirty years. In addition to the beef on a roll, which you dip yourself, they provide a comfort-food list of side dishes, including potato bacon salad, coleslaw, pickled eggs, macaroni salad, and pickled beets, as well as a few pies for dessert.

The chefs hand-cut their roasts, ensuring slices that vary in thickness, and they sometimes prepare as many as two hundred sandwiches a day. Cole's cooks up their beefy broth in large stew pots using beef bones, vegetables, and spices, cooking the tasty "au jus" gravy for twenty-four hours. Their bread rolls are delivered by a local bakery.

The sandwich roll is served with sides such as coleslaw and salad, and a small cup of their au jus. Its rich, subtle, curiously spicy tang might have you dipping so often that you will need to request more. The beef is tender, perfectly medium-rare, cut into thick slices, and very flavorful. The roll

At Cole's, customers can stand in the entryway and watch through the glass as the chefs prepare their French dip sandwiches.

is crunchy outside but soft and moist inside, and holds together well, unless you boldly attempt a triple dip. Their "atomic" yellow mustard and "atomic" pickles are not for the faint of heart; fans of heat will love them.

Cole's was closed for renovations for almost two years, from 2007 to 2008, and it has been re-created as a saloon of the early 1900s, with a massive forty-foot mahogany bar and historic photos of the neighborhood and the long-defunct Red Car electric train line. The original lighting has Tiffany shades, the floors are penny tile, and the tables are old oak (some of them made from the sides of the famed Red Cars), and the booths are upholstered in rich leather.

There is both booth and table seating, and the waitstaff will happily take your order and speedily deliver your food and libations. Cole's is very much about bringing back the golden age of saloons, with individual service and hand-sliced

The main terminal building of the Pacific Electric Red Car streetcar, light rail, and bus system. In 1925 it was the largest electric railway in the world, and was also the original location of Cole's restaurant.

Cole's Potato Bacon Salad

∽ SERVES 8 TO 10 ∽

5½ pounds Yukon Gold potatoes, peeled

10 slices bacon, chopped

¼ cup cider vinegar

½ cup minced green onion, including green parts

¼ cup minced fresh thyme

½ cup minced fresh flat-leaf parsley

2¾ cups mayonnaise

¼ cup Dijon mustard

Smoked salt

Kosher salt

Freshly ground black pepper

Place the potatoes in a large saucepan and add water to cover by 2 inches. Bring to a boil, lower the heat to a rapid simmer, and cook until tender, 15 to 20 minutes. Drain and let cool to the touch.

In a large skillet, cook the bacon over medium heat until crisp. Using a slotted spoon, transfer to paper towels to drain. Reserve the bacon fat.

In a large bowl, gently toss the potatoes with 4 tablespoons of the reserved bacon fat and the vinegar until well mixed. Add the bacon, green onion, thyme, parsley, mayonnaise, and mustard and gently mix. Add the salts and pepper to taste and stir once more. Cover and refrigerate until ready to serve.

sandwiches. As to whether they're the "originator" of LA's French dip sandwich, in the long run, who cares? The sandwiches are delicious, and Cole's is part of the history of Los Angeles, serving good food to customers for over a century.

Below: Cole's had an ideal downtown location: the basement of the Pacific Electric Building. During the 1950's gangster Mickey Cohen used an intimate corner booth at Cole's as his "hangout."

Duarte's Tavern
PESCADERO, CA ~ EST. 1894

"Whiskey. 10¢ A Shot." That began it all for this rustic tavern in a small, sleepy former fishing village forty-five miles south of San Francisco, which was once mostly inhabited by fishermen, whalers, and a few farmers.

In 1894, Frank Duarte, a Portuguese immigrant, bought a small wooden tavern in the tiny rural town of Pescadero for the princely price of $12 in gold. Then he set up a whiskey barrel in the bar, and folks would stop by to fill their own bottles with the potent amber liquid. As the sign said, you could also buy whiskey by the shot; two bits (25¢) would get you three shots. To make ends meet, Frank would occasionally cut people's hair in a shop next door.

One of the most popular taverns and restaurants on the Northern California coast today, Duarte's (pronounced Doo-arts) is beloved by locals and culinary-savvy tourists who venture down from the city by the Bay or up from Santa Cruz. It serves about thirteen thousand folks a week, or seven hundred a day on busy weekends.

A family business right from the start, Duarte's is run today by Frank's great-grandson Ron and great-great grandchildren Kathy and Tim. "I guess I started kinda early," Ron says, smiling. "At twelve, I was a counter waiter in the summer, and at fifteen, I moved into the kitchen helping where I could." Today, his favorite activity is supervising a large garden behind the restaurant, where he grows many of their herbs and everything from cabbage to peas, and garlic to pumpkins. When asked by a reporter if he "ran the tavern," Tim laughingly replied, "I'm the owner until my Dad comes around."

Emma Duarte, Ron's mother, was the one who began baking the tavern's famed pies back in the early 1930s. The pies are still one of the reasons many folks come back here, and they include olallieberry, peach, apricot, and blueberry. Olallieberries are two-thirds loganberry and one-third youngberry (a blackberry hybrid). They are similar in flavor to the blackberry but are larger in size and generally are sweeter.

"Back in the thirties, we had a fountain, sold sandwiches and ice cream. Today, we have an extensive menu that features a wide variety of artichoke dishes and fresh local seafood, and we have over one hundred wines in our cellar,"

Early 1900s customers arrive for lunch at Duarte's dressed in the finery of the day.

The ambiance in this tavern is warm, folksy, hospitable, and utilitarian, featuring simple wooden tables and chairs.

Duarte's Crab Cioppino

∽ SERVES 4 ∽

CIOPPINO SAUCE

1 yellow onion, finely chopped

4 stalks celery, finely chopped

1 tablespoon minced garlic

1 bay leaf

1 teaspoon dried oregano

1 teaspoon dried basil

1 teaspoon Italian seasoning

1 teaspoon ground cumin

½ teaspoon red pepper flakes

1 (28-ounce) can diced tomatoes

1 (15-ounce) can tomato sauce

7 cups water

2 teaspoons salt

½ cup chopped fresh flat-leaf parsley

3 Dungeness crabs, cleaned and cracked

12 jumbo shrimp, in shells or shelled

12 clams, scrubbed

8 ounces white fish fillet such as snapper

⅓ cup dry white wine

Fresh sourdough French bread, for serving

For the sauce: Combine all the ingredients except the parsley in a large nonreactive pot. Bring to a boil over high heat, then decrease the heat and simmer for 1 hour. Just before serving, add the parsley. Taste and adjust the seasoning.

In a large stockpot, place the crabs, then top with the shrimp, then the clams, and finally the fish. Ladle the cioppino sauce over the fish, then add the white wine. Cover and bring it to a boil over high heat. Lower the temperature to medium-high and cook until the clams have opened and the fish is opaque throughout, about 10 minutes. Discard any clams that do not open. Serve with bread to sop up all those wonderful seafood juices.

says Kathy. Her father, Ron, is responsible for the other two of the restaurant's most popular dishes: artichoke soup and crab cioppino. Since the Northern California coast is considered by most the center of U.S. artichoke production (nearby Castroville calls itself the "Artichoke Capital of the

World"), and many of the fields around Pescadero grow the spiky globes, Ron decided they should make good use of that local product. And there is probably no locally caught seafood that is more famous or favored than Dungeness crab.

These days, 150 to 200 pounds of crab, 110 olallieberry pies, and a staggering 1,200 pounds of artichokes a week are ravenously consumed by the legions of Duarte's customers—customers who come back, some as often as two or three times a week. The ambiance is warm, folksy, hospitable, and utilitarian, featuring simple wooden tables and chairs tucked into 2½ small dining rooms with well-worn wood paneling. There is also a counter at the back (in the half–dining room) with seven rotating stools, and an adjoining tavern that is the usual haunt of many of their most loyal and local customers. Customers who, by the way, don't much like any changes. "One time they moved a door ten feet to widen the entrance," says Ron Cicorniao, who has been coming here for forty years. "Everyone was ticked off and a bunch of folks thought the end of the place was near," he laughs. "Thank God they haven't changed," says one customer visiting from South Dakota, "It's like coming home."

For me, sitting down to the trio of Duarte's fame——a bowl of artichoke soup, a large bowl of crab cioppino, and a slice of olallieberry pie (not to mention their house-made sourdough bread)—rekindles memories of many a foggy, damp coastal day spent here when I lived in nearby Santa Cruz. The soup is creamy and filling; the cioppino, piled high with half a crab and a half-dozen shrimp and clams, and bathed in garlic, tomatoes, and cumin, is messy and heavenly to eat; and the pie is sweet, juicy, and tangy.

In 2003, the James Beard Foundation said it best when they named Duarte's an America's Classic, describing it as one of five "beloved neighborhood landmarks, casual places with distinct menus and singular atmospheres. Collectively and individually, these restaurants are a slice of American culinary history. They have withstood the test of time."

Fenton's Creamery
OAKLAND, CA ~ EST. 1894

When E. S. (Elbridge Seth) Fenton opened his creamery in Oakland, California, 119 years ago, I'm sure he never thought his small business would become known worldwide, including being featured in an Academy Award–winning movie. But the famed Bay Area ice cream parlor and restaurant was not only mentioned in the film by name but the director and the producer of the successful animated movie *Up* also showed a stylized version of the place on screen. Both had taken their families there for ice cream for years, and since Fenton's is just down the street from Pixar, it was natural to include it. In fact, a cast party for the movie was also held here.

Long a favorite stop in the East Bay, Fenton's began as a creamery run by E. S. and his thirteen children, and it was eventually taken over by three sons when E. S. retired. When they left the business, they passed it on to eight of their children, one of whom, Melvin, persuaded his grandfather to begin producing ice cream. Melvin later became the chief ice cream maker at the parlor and invented their most popular flavors: Toasted Almond, Swiss Milk Chocolate, and Rocky Road.

When the brothers sold the dairy / creamery / ice cream store to Golden State Dairy (which then became Foremost), it still stayed somewhat in the family as one of the new owners was married to Virginia Fenton, one of E. S.'s granddaughters. Then in 1987, present owner Scott Whidden, a self-described ice cream fanatic who had been making his own ice cream since the age of

sixteen, finally brought the business back
to single-family ownership.

The present-day Fenton's also is a restaurant
serving hot and cold sandwiches, burgers and
hot dogs, salads, French fries, and onion rings.
But it's the ice cream that most people go there for.
In a glassed-in section at the back of the parlor,
you can watch ice cream being made every day.
Each flavor is made from scratch and, for quality
control, in small batches. I had the pleasure of
pouring crumbled Oreo cookies into a vat of
churning cream as they whipped up a batch of
Cookies n' Cream, then got to taste it. I have to
say it tasted pretty good, for an amateur anyway.

Fenton's makes their ice cream about fifty feet
from where it's served, unlike most parlors that
have their products trucked in anywhere from
several dozen to several hundred miles away. The
ice cream here moves twenty feet from the mixers

*The counter at Fenton's when it was moved to Piedmont Avenue
in Oakland in the early 1960s. At that time, it was operated
by Foremost Creamery.*

Rocky Road Ice Cream

∽ MAKES SLIGHTLY MORE THAN 1 QUART ∽

6 ounces milk chocolate, chopped

2 cups heavy cream

1 cup half-and-half

1 large egg, beaten

⅓ cup sugar

Pinch of salt

2 teaspoons vanilla extract

½ cup chopped English walnuts

½ cup milk chocolate chunks

½ cup mini marshmallows

Place the chopped milk chocolate in the top of a double boiler and melt over barely simmering water. Set aside and keep warm.

In a small saucepan, heat the cream, half-and-half, egg, sugar, and salt over medium-low heat, stirring until the sugar dissolves. Remove from the heat and set the saucepan in a bowl of cold or ice water to cool to room temperature. Strain.

Pour the chocolate into a blender or food processor and add the vanilla. Process until smooth. Chill or refrigerate until ready to freeze. Pour the chocolate and cream mixtures into an ice cream maker and freeze according to the manufacturer's instructions.

About a minute before the ice cream is finished (it will be fairly stiff in appearance and touch), add the walnuts and chocolate chunks and freeze another minute. Using a rubber spatula, fold in the marshmallows. Eat immediately or freeze and enjoy later. You are now an (un)official Fenton's ice cream maker!

NOTE: Prior to the Great Depression, most ice creams were smooth. In reaction to the "rocky times," Fenton's created an ice cream with chunks of chocolate, walnuts, and pieces of marshmallow: Rocky Road.

to the blast chiller freezer, where fans quickly freeze it at −20 to −90°F, ensuring no ice crystals in the final product. Then the frozen tubs are trucked another fifty feet or so to the display freezers at the front of the store, preventing the "temperature abuse" that competitors' products suffer during

transfer from factory to warehouse to grocery or ice cream store. And with a relatively high butterfat level of between 14 to 16 percent, Fenton's ice creams are considered "super premium."

Even in mild-wintered California, they sell more ice cream in the summer and early fall, and in a busy month hand-craft upward of 500 to 650 gallons of ice cream in small individual flavor batches. The current menu lists fifty-two varieties, including the ubiquitous vanilla, chocolate, and strawberry, but also some not-so-common flavors, such as Cream Caramel Almond Crunch, Dark Chocolate Raspberry Twist, Pomegranate, and Apple Pie.

Having fifty-two flavors is great, but it's the sundaes that draw crowds. The Banana Special is the size of Rhode Island, the Fenton's Special sundae (a tall glass filled with alternating layers of pineapple, strawberry, chocolate, and caramel sauces, with vanilla, strawberry, chocolate, and toasted almond ice cream, topped with sherbet slices, almonds, whipped cream, and a cherry) serves four people.

Fenton's most famous creation, the Black and Tan, captured my attention: generous (meaning huge) scoops of their handmade toasted almond and creamy vanilla ice cream (made with 100 percent Madagascar vanilla) floating in and covered with hot chocolate fudge and caramel sauce, the tall glass so full that the fudge and caramel dripped down the sides. The wondrous mass of super-creamy ice cream was topped with freshly whipped cream, a handful of toasted almonds, and a cherry.

-80° F

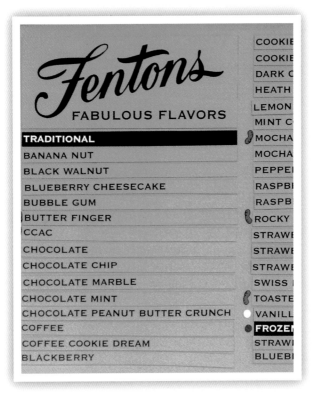

Fenton's Facts

- Fenton's makes 350 gallons of ice cream a day.
- Every day, they make or scoop about a ton of ice cream.
- In a normal week, they'll whip up 2,000 gallons.
- They store 600 tubs (1,800 gallons) in their super-cold blast freezer.
- Another 200 tubs (600 gallons) is in the "ready-to-eat" freezer in the main part of the store.

Fior d'Italia
SAN FRANCISCO, CA ~ EST. 1886

Fior d'Italia (the Flower of Italy) is the oldest continuously running Italian restaurant in the United States, and in its early days was one of the most elegant restaurants in San Francisco. It has hosted the social elite and sophisticated, including athletes (Joe Montana, Jerry Rice, Ty Cobb, Joe DiMaggio, Tommy Lasorda, Maury Wills, and Willie Mays), entertainers (Enrico Caruso, Luciano Pavarotti, Mary Pickford, Douglas Fairbanks, and Rudolph Valentino), politicians and financial giants (A. P. Giannini, and every San Francisco mayor and California governor since its opening), and just plain famous folks like Guillermo Marconi.

In its early days it served quite another class of customers. Opened in the North Beach district of San Francisco in 1886 by Angelo Del Monte and "Papa" Marianetti, the original intent was to serve the customers of the brothel upstairs in the same building. It became so popular that other clients began frequenting the restaurant. At that time, San Francisco had a fairly large population of miners, would-be-miners, and miners who had given up their searches for treasure in the '49 Gold Rush. It has been said that the population of the city almost tripled in those years with men heading to or coming back from gold country, so there were a lot of customers for both the upstairs and street-level businesses in the two-story building on Broadway.

In 1893, the bordello and restaurant burned down, not an uncommon occurrence in fire-prone San Francisco, but the owners managed to reopen the Fior later that same year. Nine years later, that new building was destroyed in the 1906 quake and fire, but Angelo and Papa wouldn't give up. Within a week they put up a tent, fired up huge cauldrons of minestrone, and fed the hungry locals for about a year until they once again had a building to house them.

The restaurant moved again in 1930 as a result of a dispute with the landlord, and they stayed on Kearny Street for twenty-three years. After several more moves, the restaurant was again destroyed by a fire in 2005. After a brief closing in 2012, Chef Audieri and his wife Trudy took over the restaurant and reopened it in its location on Mason Street near Fisherman's Wharf, thus keeping one of San Francisco's signature restaurants alive and kicking.

The past few decades of customers included just about every celebrity in the world of entertainment, sports, politics, or business, including Frank Sinatra, Eva Gabor, Vic Damone, Gregory Peck, Robert Preston, Raymond Burr, Phil Harris, and Clint Eastwood. The restaurant honored Tony Bennett in the 1970s by naming one of their small dining rooms after him, filling it with portraits and historic photographs of his career.

Over the years, the Fior has had a succession of waiters and chefs, many of whom worked there for ten years or more, as well as a large and devoted customer base who followed the restaurant from location to location. From *The Fabulous Fior*, her book about the history of the Fior, author Francine Brevetti

The dining room at Fior in the late 1800s

Milan-born chef and Fior owner, Gianfranco Audieri

WORLD'S MOST LOYAL CUSTOMER

Anyone who's dined at the Fior will have seen a copy, much enlarged, of an entry from the long-lived cartoon, Ripley's "Believe It or Not." The portrayal features the likeness of Luigi Scaglione, who ate at the Fior every day for 54 years. He sat at the same table and same chair every day. Nobody else would dare sit in that seat. He sat at a round table that seated maybe eight people. He was there by himself every evening, but eventually the table would fill and they would seat single people at the same table. He [Scaglione] worked as a tailor at the fine gentlemen's haberdashery Bullock and Jones, and put most of his funds into stocks. When the 1929 crash came, he lost almost everything. He asked the owner, then Papa Marianetti, if he could charge his meals and pay at the end of the month. Papa obligingly kept a record, entering vague marks on a pad to satisfy his customer, but charging only a very modest sum when payment day came around. The last three years, he wouldn't allow Scaglione to pay at all, reassuring him with an offhanded "Pagherà" ("You'll pay some day").

tells the story of one of the restaurant's most loyal customers who ate two meals a day in the restaurant for 54 consecutive years!

The restaurant is not huge, seating one hundred people, and the kitchen is tiny compared to many restaurants of its size, but quite functional. Somehow, chef Gianni and his staff manage to turn out an amazing 250 to 300 dinners on busy nights.

Make sure you try one of their most popular dishes, Petto di Pollo Ligure, a broiled breast of chicken served with sautéed-dried tomatoes, zucchini, and artichoke hearts. The portion is huge—so much so that you could easily have half packaged to go—and it is delicious, the chicken tender and moist, the vegetables al dente and crisp. A Banfi Chianti Riserva (from Tuscany) from their extensive wine list pairs beautifully with the tangy tomato, garlic, and chicken dish.

Throughout its long history, the Ristorante Fior d'Italia has opened its doors to hundreds of thousands of customers, all while being managed by just three sets of owners. From humble beginnings on the ground floor of a bordello, Angelo Del Monte created a culinary empire that has withstood fires, earthquakes, the Depression, Prohibition, and all the trials, troubles, and tribulations that have caused thousands of other restaurants to close their doors. The Fior today stands as a delicious tribute to his insight and the hard work and dedication of his family, the succeeding owners, chefs, line cooks, waitstaff, and other employees who have "left their hearts" in San Francisco.

Petto di Pollo Ligure
(Ligurian Chicken)
∽ Serves 4 ∽

½ cup small dry-packed sun-dried tomatoes

4 tablespoons olive oil

4 (6-ounce) boneless, skinless chicken breasts

Salt and freshly ground black pepper

All-purpose flour, for dusting

4 small zucchini, cut into 1-inch slices

4 cooked artichoke hearts, quartered

4 shallots, chopped

2 cloves garlic, minced

2 cups chicken broth

1 pound linguine, cooked, buttered, and kept warm, for serving

In a small bowl, combine the tomatoes with just enough water to cover. Soak until soft and pliable, about 20 minutes. Drain well, thinly slice, and set aside.

Preheat the oven to 400°F. In a large ovenproof sauté pan, heat 2 tablespoons of the olive oil over medium-high heat. Generously season the chicken with salt and pepper. Dust lightly with flour and shake gently to remove any excess.

Arrange the chicken in a single layer in the hot pan and cook until golden, about 5 minutes per side. Using tongs, transfer the chicken to a plate and keep warm. In the same pan, heat the remaining 2 tablespoons olive oil. Add the zucchini, artichoke hearts, shallots, and garlic; cook until just tender, about 5 minutes. Add the broth and sun-dried tomatoes and bring to a boil. Season to taste with salt and pepper.

Return the chicken to the pan, along with any juices that have accumulated, and transfer to the oven. Bake until the juices run clear when the chicken is pierced with a knife (or until an instant-read thermometer inserted in the breast and not touching bone registers 160°F), about 10 minutes.

To serve, divide the pasta evenly among 4 warmed serving plates. Arrange the chicken over the pasta and spoon the sauce over the top. Serve immediately.

Philippe the Original
LOS ANGELES, CA ~ EST. 1908

Philippe's, which claims to be the inventor of the French dip sandwich, says the whole thing was a fortuitous mistake. Founder Philippe "Frenchy" Mathieu (he was born in France) took an order from a policeman for a beef sandwich and accidentally dropped the roll into a pan of roast beef juice as he was preparing it. The cop was in a hurry and told him he'd eat it anyway; he loved the taste, and thus began the legacy.

Founded in 1908, Philippe's is located right outside LA's Union Station, an ideal spot to lure in thousands of arriving and departing train passengers who travel to the city from all over the West and as far east as New Orleans and Chicago. The station, opened in 1936, helped Philippe's keep going and at one time sent more than forty-two hundred passengers a day by the restaurant.

No one knows for sure if Philippe's was indeed first to serve the French dip sandwich. Another restaurant, Cole's (page 20), also claims the honor. The subject has been debated for years, but most folks we talked to, including Philippe's employees, couldn't care less, including manager Mark Massengill, who notes, "No one ever asks any of my carvers who invented the dip; they just order and enjoy them."

Philippe's "dipped-for-you" beef roll is a great value. The chefs slice their beef on a machine to ensure consistency in the size of each portion, and they pile on so much you won't care how it's cut. Philippe's customized mustard, a fixture in the restaurant for much of its history, is described on the menu as "hot," and it will sear your tonsils. They offer a variety of side dishes, including potato

Philippe Facts

On a normal Saturday, Philippe serves:

- 3,800 to 4,000 bread rolls
- 1,000 pounds of beef
- 40 New Zealand legs of lamb
- 180 pounds of pork shoulder
- 13 to 14 ten-pound roast turkeys

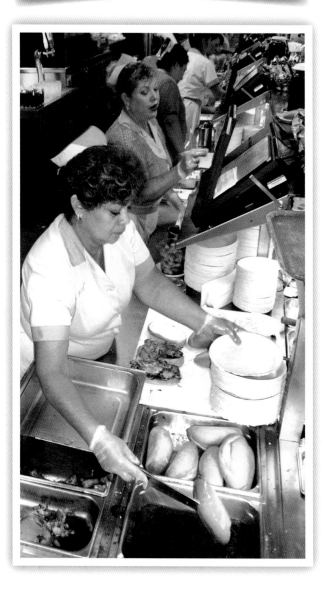

salad, coleslaw, pickled eggs, macaroni salad, and pickled beets, as well as pies baked at a local bakery. A cup of coffee to go with your pie will cost you ten cents. Yes, a dime, and although there are no free refills, at ten cents you could drink twenty cups for the price of one cuppa joe elsewhere.

The gang of women carvers at Philippe's serves thousands of beef, lamb, and pork sandwiches every day, averaging over four thousand on Saturdays. Philippe's makes their au jus from scratch, cooking vegetables, large chunks of beef, and spices in huge stainless-steel pots for three hours. There's always a new batch cooking so they won't run out at a critical time.

Philippe's main dining rooms are bustling, with long communal tables, worn wooden stools, lazily churning ceiling fans, paper plates, and sawdust floors. The walls are covered with old clippings, historic train pictures, and memorabilia. A visit often necessitates standing in a long line for up to twenty minutes to order food from one of the ten to twelve carvers who take your order and prepare your sandwich right in front of you.

Even in its early years Philippe's served up a large variety of cream and fruit pies, sweet treats to top off a meal of their French dip sandwiches.

You can have the rolls dipped, double-dipped, or, if you like a really soggy sandwich, "wet."

Philippe's is about volume and quickly serving the fast food of the 1900s. Yes, fast, because once you get to your carver, your order is handed to you in less time than it takes a burger-joint server to grab already prepared fries, burgers, and drinks. And, oh yes, cash only please, but they have an ATM on the premises.

I had lunch at Philippe's on a busy Saturday (remember the 20-minute standing-in-line thing). Not a wise day for a first-timer's visit. I ordered the "single dip" and, passing on an incendiary adventure with their hot mustard, settled into enjoying my sandwich. Philippe's bakes their rolls every day, then warms them in an oven for a couple of minutes just before serving to crisp them up a bit and better absorb the dip. A single dip is crunchy on the outside and deliciously sopping wet inside, the beef medium-rare, tender, moist, flavorful, lightly spiced, and piled high. The coleslaw is also fantastic: sweet, tangy, creamy, and crunchy. It's a filling, tasty, and satisfying lunch. You might even consider going back for seconds, but, oh, that line...

Philippe Pickled Beets
∾ MAKES ABOUT 3 CUPS ∾

1 pound beets

6 cups water

2 cups distilled white vinegar

1 tablespoon pickling spice

3 tablespoons salt

1 cup cider vinegar

1 cup sugar

White onion slices, for garnish

This recipe takes 4 days to make but is well worth the effort. Cut down the stems of the beets, leaving about 2 inches. In a medium saucepan, place the beets and add water to cover by 2 inches. Bring to a boil, reduce the heat to a low boil, and cook for about 45 minutes, or until tender. Drain and fill the pan with cold water to cool the beets. When cool to the touch, cut off the remaining beet stems and tails. Peel the beets and cut them into slices.

Combine 5 cups of the water, the white vinegar, pickling spice, and salt in a medium nonreactive saucepan. Bring to a simmer and remove from the heat once the salt has dissolved. Add the beets to the pickling mixture. Let cool to room temperature, cover, and refrigerate for 3 days.

In a medium nonreactive bowl, combine the remaining 1 cup water, the cider vinegar, and sugar. Stir until the sugar is dissolved. Pour into a 4-cup plastic container. Remove the beets from the pickling mix and drain well. Add the drained beets to the sugar mixture. Toss, cover, and refrigerate for at least 1 day or up to 1 month. Garnish with the onion slices and serve.

From left: Amy Mora, Barbara Boley, Gale Ward, Pam Hop, and Suzy Bozeman celebrate Gale's upcoming move to Alaska with their "first time" visit to Philippe's.

Below: Takeout is a large part of Philipe's, especially on days the Dodgers play at home; this large order is destined to be taken to nearby Chavez Ravine.

The Tadich Grill

SAN FRANCISCO, CA ~ EST. 1849

Tadich Grill evidently has the strongest will to live of any of the restaurants in this book, having survived for over 150 years despite six devastating fires and three major earthquakes, each of which destroyed sections of San Francisco. Between 1849 and 1851, much of the city was devastated, with more than three thousand buildings burned to the ground in five different fires. In 1868, 1906, and 1989, major earthquakes rocked the city, the '06 quake causing a citywide conflagration that all but totally destroyed the downtown area.

In 1849, the year the California gold rush began, three Croatian immigrants opened a simple coffee stand beside the New World Market building on the city's wharf. It was a popular stop for merchants, sailors, and the thousands who passed through the city on the way to the gold hidden in the mountains to the east. In 1871, the New World Coffee Stand made its first move away from the wharf, and that same year sixteen-year-old John Tadich arrived from Croatia seeking his fortune. After landing in New York, he took a train west, ending up at his uncle's home in San Francisco, and five years later began working as a bartender at the New World. In 1885, he bought the place, which he owned until it was destroyed in the earthquake and fire of 1906.

Like the city itself, the restaurant was reborn several blocks away when Tadich partnered with another restaurant owner. That partnership lasted six years, and when it broke apart Tadich opened a new restaurant that bore his name, a name that has been in the forefront of San Francisco's restaurant culture ever since. The Grill stayed at that location for fifty-five years before it moved to its present spot on busy California Street, right in the heart of San Francisco's financial district. In 1928, Tadich sold the restaurant to then head chef Mitch Buich and his brother Louis, who were also Croatian

immigrants, for a paltry $8,000, and the Grill has been in the Buich family ever since.

The restaurant has maintained the charm and ambiance of its earlier days, with its long bar and lunch counters, dark-wood-paneled booths, white-clothed tables, Deco-style lighting, an open kitchen, and waiters who are dressed as they have been here for many years: starched white jackets, short white aprons, white shirts, and conservative ties. You almost feel as if you've walked into a gentleman's club, and indeed for many years that's what Tadich's was, as early photographs show a clientele almost 100 percent male.

The founders of Tadich Grill revolutionized cooking in the city when they brought the technique of grilling fish over wood from their

Adriatic seaside villages. Their chefs still grill over open flames, having bought mesquite charcoal from one local supplier for over one hundred years, but they also offer dishes that are deep- and panfried, poached, sautéed, broiled, or steamed. As in the beginning, seafood is the main protein served here; in fact, of the more than eighty dishes on the menu, more than fifty are fish or shellfish.

As one of the most popular restaurants in a city with almost forty-five hundred restaurants, long lines are a normal feature of the Grill as people line up along California Street for a chance to eat at this historic city icon. Waiting times of more than an hour are standard in the summer, when tourists vie with locals for spots at the counter or in one of the booths.

I've eaten at Tadich Grill many times, and their cioppino is outstanding. Their version of this

In the 1940s and 1950s Tadich's lunchtime crowd was mostly men from nearby banks and other financial institutions, and cigarette smoking was de rigueur, even during meals.

Tadich Cioppino
∾ SERVES 2 TO 4 ∾

1 cup (2 sticks) unsalted butter

1 cup extra-virgin olive oil

1 yellow onion, chopped

2 carrots, peeled and chopped

1 stalk celery, chopped

1 green bell pepper, seeded, deribbed, and chopped

1 leek, white part only, rinsed and chopped

½ small fennel bulb, trimmed, cored, and chopped

2 (28-ounce) cans crushed Italian tomatoes

2 tablespoons tomato paste

4 cups water

4 bay leaves

1 teaspoon dried oregano

1 teaspoon dried thyme

1 teaspoon dried basil

2 pinches cayenne pepper

Salt and freshly ground black pepper

2 cloves garlic, minced

1½ pounds halibut fillets, cut into large pieces

16 sea scallops

16 large shrimp, peeled, deveined

8 ounces bay shrimp

1 to 2 cups all-purpose flour

12 ounces lump crabmeat, preferably Dungeness, picked over for shells

2 cups dry white wine

16 Manila clams, scrubbed

½ bunch flat-leaf parsley, stemmed and chopped

Toasted garlic bread, for serving

In a large pot, melt ½ cup (1 stick) of the butter with ½ cup of the oil over medium heat. Add the onion and cook, stirring often, for about 2 minutes. Add the carrots, celery, bell pepper, leek, and fennel and cook, stirring often, for about 5 minutes. Add the tomatoes, tomato paste, water, bay leaves, oregano, thyme, basil, and cayenne and season to taste with salt and pepper. Bring to a boil, decrease the heat to low, and simmer, stirring occasionally, for 2 hours.

In a large, heavy skillet, melt the remaining ½ cup (1 stick) butter with the remaining ½ cup oil and the garlic over high heat until the garlic is fragrant, 1 to 2 minutes. Working in two batches, dredge the halibut, scallops, and shrimp in the flour, shaking off the excess, and sauté until golden, 1 to 2 minutes. Using a slotted spoon, transfer the seafood to the pot with the tomato mixture. Reserve the skillet. Add the crabmeat to the pot, cover, and simmer for 10 to 15 minutes.

Add the wine to the reserved skillet over high heat, stirring to scrape up the browned bits on the bottom of the pan. Add the clams, cover, and cook until the shells open, about 5 minutes. (Discard any clams that don't open.) Add the clams and broth to the pot; taste and adjust the seasoning. Ladle the soup into large bowls, garnish with parsley, and serve with garlic bread.

popular San Francisco seafood dish mixes crabmeat, clams, prawns, scallops, and white fish with a slightly spicy tomato broth and serves it with thick slices of toasted garlic bread. A hundred other restaurants offer cioppino, but somehow here, in the center of the city by the bay, it tastes better, and, well, historic. It is, by the way, one of the oldest dishes on the menu, sharing a genealogy with the grilled sole, clam chowder, Dungeness crab cocktail, and sautéed sand dabs. The bread for the garlic toast is cut from loaves of the famed San Francisco sourdough provided to the restaurant for over 150 years by the local Parisian Bread company.

In 1950, food critic Salvatore P. Lucia wrote of the Tadich Grill, "It's a place for the more sophisticated fancier of fish dishes." The five generations of Croatian owners, who struggled through massive fires, destructive earthquakes, two world wars, Prohibition, the Depression, and the ravages of history would agree. But if you go, please remember: Wear comfortable shoes, bring a jacket for San Francisco's chilly breezes, and prepare yourself for a long wait standing on California Street. Because never in their 162 years has the restaurant taken reservations.

The Buckhorn Exchange
DENVER, CO ~ EST. 1893

If you are a staunch vegetarian or vegan or a member of P.E.T.A. (People for the Ethical Treatment of Animals), you may want to skip the Buckhorn Exchange, for the walls, ceiling, staircases, and bookcases throughout the restaurant feature the largest collection of taxidermy in any restaurant in the world. At last count, there were over five hundred wild animal heads and bodies perched around the rooms, many of them looking down on diners eating—you guessed it—wild animals!

The mounted animals include elk, moose, deer, and antelope, of course, but also bighorn sheep, zebra, cape buffalo, wild boar, reindeer, eland, gazelles, ibex, kudu, caribou, foxes, wolves, bears, cougars, badgers, mink, coyotes, rabbits, raccoons, gophers, lynx, and bobcats. In display cases rest dozens of waterfowl (ducks, loons, and geese), as well as upland game birds (pheasant, quail, grouse, doves, partridge, and so on). To top it off, the second-floor bar displays 125 Colt .45s, derringers, and other antique rifles and shotguns, and an entire wall displays historic photographs of hunters with their game.

Buckhorn founder Henry H. Zietz, one of the most colorful characters in the Old West, bought the saloon a year after it moved from Market Street to its present location in 1892. At age ten, Zietz had met Colonel William "Buffalo Bill" Cody, and two years later (yes, at twelve) he became a full-fledged member of Cody's scout band. After years of working with Cody and his Wild West group, including Chief Sitting Bull, Zietz moved to Colorado and began his career as a saloon owner. Sitting Bull called him "Shorty Scout," as while he was big in character and reputation, he was a small man in stature.

But even in a small package, Shorty was not a man to be messed with. There's the tale of a would-be robber who burst into the saloon in 1900 brandishing a huge .45 caliber pistol and demanded that the dozen or so patrons put their valuables on the bar. When one waitress screamed in fright, the man pistol-whipped her, then he grabbed the loot and mounted a horse and rode off. That was a mistake. Shorty grabbed a rifle and ran outside, and even though the rider was a half block away, riding at full speed, Shorty dropped him with one shot.

Henry Zietz, who was a scout for General Custer, stands in front of the Buckhorn in 1893.

Several years later, President Theodore Roosevelt came to the restaurant and took the diminutive saloon owner as a guide for a very successful antelope and buffalo hunt in the Colorado Rockies. Afterward, the President commented, "I've hunted all over the world and, by Jove, Shorty is one of the best guides I ever had." In 1938, Sitting Bull's nephew Chief Red Cloud and a delegation of thirty Blackfeet Sioux Indians in full battle regalia rode up Osage Street to the Buckhorn and presented Shorty Scout with the military saber taken from General George Armstrong Custer when he was killed at Little Big Horn. Sadly, there are no pictures of this amazing historical event.

Jamieson Fuller, from Cincinnati, reacts to hearing the "Rocky Mountain Oyster" he's eating came from a steer, not the ocean.

Like many saloonkeepers and restaurant owners, Zietz squeaked through Prohibition, reportedly hiding homemade hooch in hollowed-out loaves of pumpernickel bread and a hollow baluster in the staircase. When Prohibition ended, he applied for and received Colorado Liquor License No. 1, which still hangs in the bar. The white-oak bar itself and several of the tavern tables were made in Essen, Germany, in 1857 and brought to the United States by the Zietz family. The bar was later brought to the saloon and moved to the second floor, where it sits today, right next to the Victorian Lounge.

When Shorty died in 1949, his son took over, adding many animal mounts from his own hunting expeditions to the existing collection. In failing health, he sold the restaurant to a group of investors, who still own it today. Happily, the new owners

Elk Strip Steak Sauce

∼ MAKES 8 CUPS ∼

3 cups cranberry juice

1½ cups orange juice

3 cups dry red wine

2 tablespoons juniper berries

2 tablespoons freshly ground black pepper

2 tablespoons chicken base

1 pound dried sweet cherries

¼ cup cold water

¼ cup cornstarch

In a medium saucepan, combine the juice, wine, berries, pepper, and chicken base, stirring to combine. Heat over medium heat for 10 minutes, or until it just begins to bubble. Add the dried cherries, lower the heat to medium, and continue cooking, stirring often, for 25 to 30 minutes, until the cherries are soft and the liquid is reduced by one-third.

Combine the water and cornstarch in a small bowl and stir to blend. Gradually stir into the cherry mixture and cook, stirring, until thickened enough to coat the back of a spoon.

NOTE: This sauce is also great with venison, buffalo, antelope, beef, or any other red meat.

have taken great care to not only keep the Old West charm of the Buckhorn alive, but have preserved the memorabilia and taxidermy pieces and maintained the basic exterior of the historic building. They have also stayed true to the culinary history of the Buckhorn. "We scoured old Western cookbooks and researched chuck wagon legends to bring our customers the finest in authentic Western cuisine and exotic meats," says general manager Bill Dutton. "The cuisine is kept traditional," he continues, "not only with the recipes we use but by using ingredients like spring onions, dried fruits, juniper berries, and chiles that were around at the turn of the century. In fact, much of our cuisine can be directly traced to 1893 and the recipes Henry Zietz brought with him from his German and Pennsylvania Dutch heritage."

If you love the taste of wild game, a meal here will surely satisfy you. A partial list of the game dishes on the menu includes alligator tail, rattlesnake, buffalo, elk, duck, and quail. Of course, being located in Denver, the Buck also features USDA Prime T-bones, beef tenderloin, and New York strip steaks (in sizes from 1½ to 4 pounds), which share the menu with Colorado lamb, salmon, Grandma Fanny's pot roast, and calf fries, also known as Rocky Mountain oysters (which, of course, come from the nether parts of cattle instead of the briny deep).

The Buckhorn Special combines farm-raised elk medallions with a buffalo strip steak enhanced by an order of calf fries. The elk is firm in flavor, very tender, and slathered with a cherry-juniper berry sauce, and the buffalo is fork-tender and blanketed with a garlic-butter sauce. The meat almost melts in your mouth. The calf fries are chewy, with a crunchy breading, and nicely livened up with a horseradish dipping sauce.

When the owners of the Buckhorn were doing some renovations in 1978, they discovered the original doors to the restaurant in an upstairs storage room, completely refinished them, and installed them in the main entrance. So today, as you enter this fascinating building loaded with memorabilia from the Old West, you are truly walking through the doors of history.

Hotel Jerome
ASPEN, CO ~ EST. 1893

With the coming of the railroad in the fall of 1887, Aspen, Colorado, became a boomtown almost overnight. In a little over a year, it grew from a collection of log shacks, tents, and false-front wooden structures to rows of brick buildings with streetcar lines, dance halls, theaters, skating rinks, a racetrack, six newspapers, fifty lawyers, and twenty-five bawdy houses.

Part of the boom was because Jerome Wheeler, a former president of Macy's and a key investor in local silver mines, had fallen in love with Aspen and so did everything he could to financially help the small town grow. In 1888, amid the explosion of building and growth, he agreed to finance both an opera house and a great hotel. There was already a wooden hotel in town, but Wheeler

and two Kansas innkeepers wanted to build an establishment the equal of a grand European hotel—quite an ambition for a small town in the Rocky Mountains. Nonetheless, after loans from Wheeler, the Jerome was constructed at the huge cost (in those days, anyway) of $150,000.

The Jerome was truly impressive. There were ninety rooms, fifteen baths, indoor hot and cold plumbing, steam heat, electricity, and even a primitive paging system so guests could summon service to their suites. There was also an elevator with a settee for ladies, a hothouse, stables, parlors, a barbershop, a ballroom, offices, a steam laundry, and a French chef in the kitchen.

The hotel became the gathering spot of local and visiting guests, grande dames, cattle and

The Hotel Jerome in 1889; note the stagecoach just leaving the coach entrance. Remarkably the hotel exterior has virtually remained unchanged in 123 years.

silver barons, Eastern bankers, congressmen, and senators. Opera stars and stage actors visited, along with artists and poets, and the hotel became the social center not just of Aspen but of the state itself.

Then, in 1893, President Grover Cleveland oversaw the repeal of the Sherman Silver Purchase Act, which had required the U.S. government to purchase millions of ounces of silver in exchange for paper money, which many people then used to buy and seriously deplete the government's gold reserves. When the act was repealed, the silver boom of Aspen ended, and the town all but fell apart. Wheeler went bankrupt, his mines caught fire or flooded, his palatial home was sold to pay creditors, and his beloved hotel was sold for back taxes to an immigrant bartender who had worked at the hotel for eleven years and had apparently saved every

penny he had earned. The hotel, under his and his son's tutelage, struggled on through the war and the Depression, and the bar turned into a soda fountain during Prohibition. To support the local community, they offered a Sunday chicken dinner for fifty cents a head.

During the next few decades, the hotel began to come to life again, and the Hotel Grille, decorated with the ubiquitous deer heads of Western eateries, became known as the place for a good, inexpensive meal. The list of celebrity clients grew larger as Gary Cooper, Lana Turner, Lex "Tarzan" Barker, Hedy Lamarr, Norma Shearer, John Wayne, and even Albert Schweitzer (on his only trip to the United States) all visited. Hunter S. Thompson, the creator of gonzo journalism, once ran unsuccessfully for local sheriff, and was a regular at the Jerome. In 1985, yet another new owner brought the grand old hotel back to life, giving it a face-lift with refurbished fittings and opening the Silver Queen Dining Room. Today, hotel guests flock there for breakfast. Morning favorites include the Lemon Soufflé Pancakes with fresh raspberries and blueberries, topped with pine nuts and confectioners' sugar and served with

house-made raspberry syrup, and the hearty Corn Meal Pancakes served with blueberries, sliced bananas, and maple syrup.

The new owners also reopened the famed J-Bar, the only hotel area maintained over its one-hundred-year history in its original style, although it was moved to its present location on the opposite side of the building. Many local residents pop in to enjoy a local brew with a Jerome Burger (beef, cheese, caramelized onions, mushrooms, and applewood-smoked bacon) or the equally popular Reuben. Both come with an order of their house-made truffle fries, served vertically in a paper cone, Belgian style. It takes a big eater to finish half of the popular three-inch-thick Reuben, as yummy and tasty as it is. The fries are scrumptious and indulgent. The Aspen Crud, a bourbon-laced milk shake first developed during Prohibition, is still wildly popular, as are the thirty-one pre-Prohibition cocktails the Jerome actively promotes.

As when it burst on the scene in 1888, the Jerome is still the unannounced center of town, not only geographically but socially. The place seems to have captured or created part of the soul of this small mountain town, and although it's now fancy, expensive, and owned by a major U.S. hotel corporation, it retains the charm that has captivated guests over the decades. Once the home of "swells" and the richest members of society, today the old girl welcomes everyone who enters the ornate lobby: cowboys and skiers, backpackers and businessmen, Levi's and Gucci sets alike. The Jerome is a bit of the Old West, restored with all the comfort and convenience of the present day.

Jerome Bar Reuben Sandwich

⌒ SERVES 2 ⌒

4 teaspoons Thousand Island dressing, plus more for serving

4 slices marble rye bread

¼ cup sauerkraut

4 slices Gruyère cheese

8 ounces corned beef, sliced thin

Salt and freshly ground black pepper

¼ cup clarified butter, for cooking (recipe follows)

Preheat the oven to 350°F. Spread 1 teaspoon of the dressing on each slice of bread. Spoon one-quarter of the sauerkraut on each slice of bread, followed by the Gruyère. Top the cheese with the corned beef and season lightly with salt and pepper.

In a large ovenproof skillet, heat the butter over medium heat and toast the sandwiches until lightly browned on each side. Place the skillet in the oven to heat the sandwiches through for 2 to 3 minutes.

Cut each sandwich in half and serve with a side of Thousand Island dressing.

Clarified Butter: In a heavy saucepan, melt unsalted butter over very low heat. Pour the clear yellow liquid into a glass container, leaving the milk solids in the bottom of the pan. Cover and store the clarified butter in the refrigerator indefinitely. One stick (½ cup) of butter makes about 6 tablespoons clarified butter.

The Griswold Inn
ESSEX, CT ~ EST. 1776

In 1775, Sala Griswold purchased property and began construction of the Griswold Inn, which opened its doors a year later. The inn was sold twice in the next half-century, changing from a stagecoach stop to a steamboat stop to an important country inn. For a short time, it was run as a "first-class temperance hotel." It changed hands only twice more, in the 1970s and 1990s. In over 220 years of operation, it has been under the direction of just six families. Since everyone who comes here almost immediately feels like a member of the historic Griswold family, let's dispense with formality and call it the Gris, as the locals do.

The Gris was the first three-story frame structure built in Connecticut, and with the exception of the second-floor gallery it has remained pretty much the same as the day it was opened. Several buildings and rooms have been added to the inn over the years. The Tap Room, behind the main lobby, used to be one of the first schoolhouses in Essex. The Covered Bridge, the largest dining room in the Gris, was constructed from an abandoned New Hampshire covered bridge.

At its founding, the inn was located on the waterfront, near the steamboat docking area. In those years, steamboats provided regular service between Hartford and New York and included a stop in Essex. This "golden era" of steamboating is remembered well in the Gris's outstanding collection of marine art and artifacts. They have one of the most comprehensive and important collections of original Currier & Ives and Endicott & Company steamboat lithographs in the nation.

Antonio Jacobsen, a world-renowned marine artist known as the "Audubon of steam vessels" is also honored, with sixteen of his original canvases on exhibition—the largest private collection of his works in the United States—which draws fans from all over the world. Also on display are fifty-five pistols and rifles that trace the development of firearms from the fifteenth century.

every night of the week, and it's an extremely popular local watering hole. You can still stay at the inn, too, in rooms decorated with traditional New England fixtures, period and reproduction furniture, and colorful Turkish carpets.

During its tenure, the Gris has been known for more than just its art collections, rescued historic buildings, and antique-filled rooms. People love

In the Tap Room, you can enjoy a lunch of (what else) fish and chips and a caramel-citrus-tinged Revolutionary Ale. In the evenings, you can catch a performance by the Jovial Crew, who delight a jam-packed house with traditional sea chanteys that grow more ribald as the evening wears on. The irreverent lyrics often draw loud applause and more than a few standing ovations. Various other local groups entertain there almost

the food, whether it's the famed hunt breakfasts on Sundays, which include traditional English fare and American classics in an expansive buffet; lunches that feature their 1776-brand sausages; or wonderful dinners of New England favorites such as crab, lobster, and flounder, and "historic dining" entrees of beef short ribs and chicken potpie.

Speaking of potpies, the Gris's lobster version must contain at least a whole lobster,

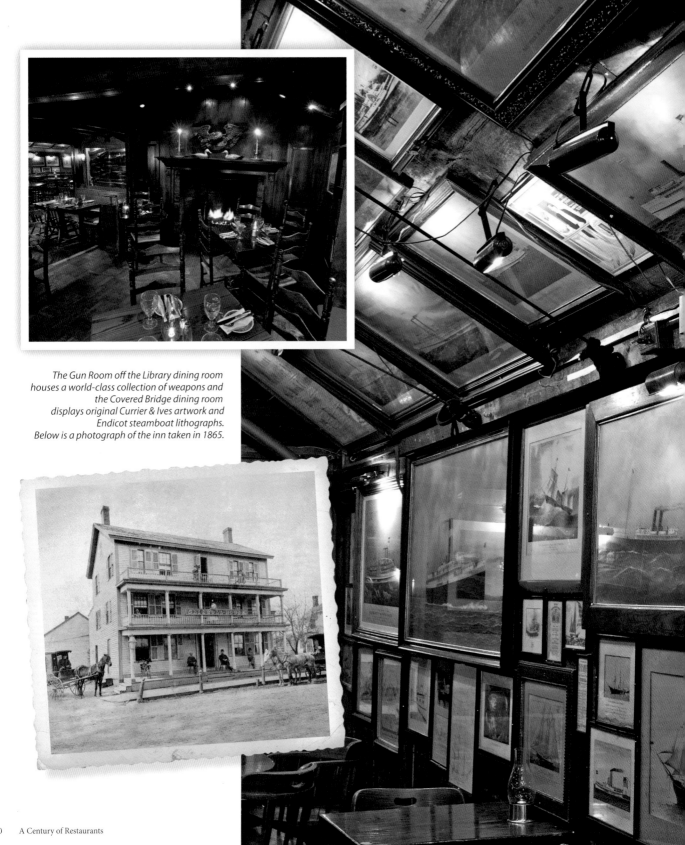

The Gun Room off the Library dining room houses a world-class collection of weapons and the Covered Bridge dining room displays original Currier & Ives artwork and Endicot steamboat lithographs. Below is a photograph of the inn taken in 1865.

with large, rich chunks of the crustacean meat in a creamy sauce dotted with carrots and topped with an inch-thick, flaky crust. It may be the best potpie you will ever eat.

With a lengthy history of family involvement in every phase of innkeeping, the present owners, Gregory, Douglas and wife, Joan, and Geoffrey Paul, all of whom grew up in Essex, are committed to preserving the atmosphere, reverence for history, sophisticated cuisine, and rich hospitality of the Gris into the next century. From the antique potbelly stove in the Tap Room to the brand-new potbelly you can get from a week of gourmet meals here, the Gris is one of the most hospitable places to dine in this part of the world.

The Griswold Inn Signature New England Lobster Potpie

∞ SERVES 2 ∞

1 (1½-pound) live New England lobster

1 medium carrot

2 large stalks celery

1 large white onion

1 fennel bulb, trimmed and cored

1 tablespoon olive oil

2 cloves garlic, minced

1 tablespoon tomato paste

2 cups chardonnay wine

3 cups water or lobster broth

2 large potatoes, peeled and cut into ½-inch dice

6 cups corn kernels (about 3 ears)

2 cups heavy cream

1 tablespoon chopped fresh tarragon

1 tablespoon chopped fresh basil

Salt and freshly ground white pepper

1 large sheet thawed frozen puff pastry

1 egg, beaten with ½ cup water

Bring a large pot of salted water to a boil and add the lobster, head first. Cook for 10 minutes. Remove the lobster from the pot and plunge it into ice water to stop the cooking process. Crack the tail, claws, and knuckles and remove the meat. Reserve the head for garnish. Cut the lobster meat into ½-inch chunks. Cut the carrot, celery, onion, and fennel into ½-inch chunks as well.

Preheat the oven to 400°F. Butter a large soufflé dish.

In a medium sauté pan, heat the olive oil over medium heat and sauté the diced vegetables and the garlic until the vegetables start to brown, about 8 minutes. Stir in the tomato paste. Add the wine and stir to scrape up the browned bits from the bottom of the pan. Continue to cook until the liquid is reduced by half. Stir in the water, then the potatoes and corn, and cook again to reduce the liquid by half. Add the cream and cook to reduce by half again. Add the tarragon and basil. Season with salt and pepper to taste.

Stir the lobster meat into the vegetable mixture, then pour this mixture into the prepared dish. Cut the puff pastry sheet to fit over the top of the baking dish and place it on top of the filling. Brush the pastry sheet with the egg and water mixture. Cut a small hole in the center of the pastry just large enough to fit the lobster head.

Bake the pie for 5 to 7 minutes, or until golden brown. Insert the lobster head on top for garnish and enjoy.

Louis' Lunch
NEW HAVEN, CT ~ EST. 1895

The story goes that in 1900, a customer, supposedly a busy office worker, arrived at the tiny Louis' Lunch wagon in downtown New Haven, Connecticut, and told Louis that he was in a hurry and needed something that he could take with him to eat on the run. Louis thought for a minute, then placed a ground-meat patty onto two slices of toasted bread and sent the man happily on his way. Thus began the long history of the hamburger, and the reason many consider Louis' Lunch its birthplace.

There are claims that the iconic burger was also invented by a Texas café, two Ohio sausage vendors, or a vendor in Wisconsin who flattened a large meatball and stuffed it between two slices of bread. But according to an article in the *New York Times* in 1975, and seconded by no less an authority than the United States Library of Congress, Louis indeed made America's first hamburger.

Thankfully, we can still sample his invention at a tiny lunch spot near Yale University. The place may have moved four times, but they still cook the burgers on the same gas grill that they used back in the late 1800s, and they still serve their burgers on toast. The city of New Haven declared the building a landmark in 1967, recognizing its importance to local history and to the generations of Yale students the place made feel at home, even when they committed the colossal faux pas of asking for ketchup on their burgers.

Lassen's son Ken became locally famous by standing up to City Hall and the forces of urban renewal, who wanted to tear Louis's second building down, but thanks to Ken's lobbying, the city packed up the building and moved it lock, stock, and burger to its present location in 1975. The east wall was left behind, still attached to the tannery, so Ken had workmen construct a new wall out of recycled bricks from the tannery and other bricks and stones and rocks, including tiny chunks of the Great Wall of China, St. Phillip's Palace in London, a barn in Norway, and the homes of Presidents Buchanan and Coolidge, sent to the hamburger joint by fans from all over the world.

Ken's son Jeff Lassen, grandson of the founder, mans the well-worn and carved-on counter today and hustles up many dozens of burgers amid a frenzy of customers who show up just before the lunch hour and proceed to jam the small eatery five days a week. "We're usually filled to the rafters," he says. "Tuesdays and Wednesdays, there's the

Louis Lassen in the original Louis' Lunch wagon around 1897. Below: grandson Ken uses the same vertical broilers to cook his burgers.

lunch and late-lunch rushes, and of course there's a huge rush on Thursday, Friday, and Saturday when we stay open until 2 A.M."

When asked how many burgers would constitute a "busy day," Jeff laughed. "Well, the most I can remember is a day when we went through 500 pounds of meat, but usually we cook up 100 to 150 pounds a day." Don't ask him for the burger formula, though; the only thing he'll share is that the burgers are composed of five different cuts of beef. We've heard a rumor that sirloin and chuck steak are involved, but we can't tell for certain. It is a daunting fact to note that Jeff cooks up all that meat in the 3 by 5-foot "working part" of a 3 by 9-foot kitchen.

The freshly formed patties are placed in a specially designed gridiron that holds them vertically in the unique, hundred-year-old Bridge & Beach Company cast-iron gas broilers, which cook them on both sides at the same time. Each burger is cooked to order, and Jeff times them all by instinct and feel. If you want yours well done, you'd better tell him before he begins cooking; otherwise, you get what everybody gets: medium-rare.

Two things you don't ask for here are ketchup or mustard. Louis's burgers are only served with tomato and/or cheese and/or onion slices, and they are incredibly juicy, beefy, and absolutely delicious. Why add condiments when you've got a great-flavored burger? You might fear that the Pepperidge Farm toast (the only bread they'll use) could get a bit soggy near the end, but the whole burger probably won't last long enough for that to matter.

You can also supplement your meal with potato chips or the house-made potato salad, which is creamy with slightly al dente chunks of potato and a hint of green onion. The only desserts are the pies made by Jeff's mom, Lee, with two choices per day at $4 a slice.

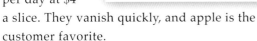

They vanish quickly, and apple is the customer favorite.

Since Louis' Lunch is such a tiny place, many of their customers just grab their burgers and, like that harried office worker more than a century ago, run off to work or school. But they still get a little bite of Louis's history to take with them.

Louis' Lunch Apple Pie

∾ MAKES 1 (9-INCH) PIE ∾

Pastry for a two-crust 9-inch pie

⅓ cup granulated sugar

⅓ cup firmly packed brown sugar

2 tablespoons all-purpose flour

½ teaspoon ground cinnamon

¼ teaspoon ground nutmeg

⅓ teaspoon grated lemon zest

1 to 2 teaspoons freshly squeezed lemon juice

6 to 7 cups thinly sliced cooking apples (about 2½ pounds)

1 tablespoon unsalted butter, cut into small bits

Vanilla ice cream or fresh whipped cream, for serving (optional)

Preheat the oven to 425°F. On a floured board, roll out half of the pastry to an 11-inch round. Fit into a 9-inch pie pan and trim the overhang to ½ inch. Roll out the other half of the pastry to the same size and set aside.

In a small bowl, combine the sugars, flour, cinnamon, nutmeg, lemon zest, and juice. Stir to blend. Put half of the apple slices in the pastry-lined pan and sprinkle with half of the sugar mixture. Add the remaining apples and sprinkle with the remaining sugar mixture. Dot with the butter. Place the top crust over the apples and trim to ¾ inch. Fold the edges of the top crust under the bottom crust and flute the edges. Cut steam vents in the top of the pie.

Bake for 40 to 45 minutes, or until golden and bubbling. Let cool and serve with ice cream or whipped cream, if you like.

Jessop's Tavern
NEW CASTLE, DE ~ EST. 1674

The town of New Castle began its life in 1650, when ships from Holland, Sweden, England, and Finland brought trade and settlers to the New World. A year later, Peter Stuyvesant, the governor of New Netherlands (today, New York, New Jersey, Delaware, Connecticut, and parts of Pennsylvania and Rhode Island), began building a castle where New Castle now lies. Then William Penn, who had been given the provinces of Pennsylvania and Delaware by King James II of England when he was the mere Duke of York, came to New Castle to survey his holdings in 1682. After the local citizenry pledged allegiance to their new proprietor, Penn headed up the Delaware River and founded Philadelphia.

But trouble was brewing back in Delaware. Penn's Quaker government had riled up the Dutch, Swedish, and English settlers so much that they began petitioning for their own Assembly. When the three southernmost colonies of Pennsylvania were permitted to split off they became Lower Delaware, and New Castle was incorporated in 1875 to become the capital. The small town's early importance was soon overshadowed by the larger and better-known towns of Dover and Wilmington, and New Castle faded into near obscurity as a simple colonial river town of Dutch, English, and American farmers and fishermen.

As in many colonial towns, the center of action was the tavern, in New Castle's case the

Green Frog Tavern, a dark and moody smoke-filled place that featured drinking, gossip, local news, and barmaid chasing. It was built by Joseph Alsop as a cooperage, then taken over by Abraham Jessop, who continued the process of making barrels, eventually obtaining a license and opening the Green Frog. At the time, the Crown sought to enhance commerce in the colonies by the establishment of licensed inns and public houses. The resulting travel and trade generated by these community gathering places not only promoted local prosperity, they also helped to fill English bank accounts back home via the levied tax revenues on goods and services.

The food served at the Green Frog was supposedly barely tolerable, while the wine, rum, and ales were very popular. Nearly every citizen of the day knew that drinking water could make you deathly ill. Ale drinkers were spared this affliction, and therefore most people soon substituted the frequent imbibing of ale for polluted water. In 1790, United States government figures showed that annual per-capita alcohol consumption for everybody over fifteen amounted to thirty-four gallons of beer and cider, five gallons of distilled spirits, and one gallon of wine. With that much booze on board, it's surprising they even knew the food was bad.

When traders, immigrants, seamen, and visitors left their ships at the public landing and walked up the heavily shaded brick walkways and cobblestone streets of New Castle, one of the first buildings they spotted was the Green Frog. There they could enjoy some thirst-quenching pints or tankards of local handcrafted ales, a filling if less-than-gourmet-quality meal, and hours of conversation, pipe smoking, belching, and other attributes of male-dominated taverns. Taverns that served meals and drinks at a fixed price were called "ordinaries."

Not much is recorded about the Green Frog during the subsequent centuries, but somehow it survived two wars, Prohibition, and the Depression. In 1998 the tavern was taken over by Dick Day and his wife, Tika, was renamed Jessop's Tavern, and the new owners set about to make the food as good as the locally brewed beers. The fare served in the tavern today includes classics such as shepherd's pie and fish and chips, as well as some top-drawer entrees. The menu lists soups as "From the Ladle," salads as "On the Green," entrees as "Center of the Plate," and sandwiches as "Between Bread." Hutspot Dutch Pot Roast, Thirteen Colonies Chowder, a Smorgas-Bord of cheeses, Pilgrim's Feast (roast turkey), Olde Dutch Tilehouse Chicken, and Dutch Pastrami Reuben are all popular dishes, but the real winner is the Imperial Stuffed Flounder. A large fillet is stuffed (to the gills, you might say) with a filling loaded with lump crabmeat. The fish is then cooked to moist perfection and served with a sherry-chive cream sauce so rich you really don't need any dessert.

Imperial Stuffed Flounder

∾ SERVES 4 ∾

CRAB IMPERIAL

1 cup mayonnaise

½ cup Dijon mustard

2 tablespoons freshly squeezed lemon juice

2 tablespoons Worcestershire sauce

1 tablespoon Old Bay Seasoning

1 teaspoon minced fresh chives

½ tablespoon Tabasco sauce

1 pound fresh lump crabmeat, picked over for shell

¼ to ⅓ cup fresh or dried bread crumbs

SHERRY-CHIVE CREAM SAUCE

¾ cup dry sherry

2 tablespoons minced shallots

¾ cup heavy cream

2 tablespoons minced fresh chives

4 tablespoons unsalted butter, melted

4 (7-ounce) flounder fillets

Salt, white pepper, and Old Bay Seasoning, for sprinkling

For the Crab Imperial: In a large bowl, combine the mayonnaise, mustard, lemon juice, Worcestershire sauce, Old Bay, chives, and Tabasco sauce. Whisk until smooth. Add the crabmeat and fold in gently. Fold in the bread crumbs until just combined. Set aside.

For the sauce: In a small, heavy saucepan, bring the sherry to a boil over medium heat. Add the shallots and cook for 1 minute. Add the cream and cook again for 1 minute. Stir in the chives. Set aside and keep warm.

Preheat the broiler. In a large ovenproof skillet, spoon 3 tablespoons of the melted butter. Lay a fillet flat in the pan and spoon ½ cup of the crab imperial mixture on top of the fish. Roll and tie closed with kitchen twine. Cut a small slit in the top of the roll to expose the filling. Repeat with the remaining fish and filling.

Pour the remaining butter over the flounder fillets. Sprinkle with salt, white pepper, and Old Bay. Place under a broiler 4 to 6 inches from the heat source until golden brown, 6 to 8 minutes. Pour the sauce over the flounder rolls just before serving.

Old Ebbitt Grill
WASHINGTON, D.C. ~ EST. 1856

The original Ebbitt House was a simple boardinghouse created by combining several existing Federal-style town houses in what was once Washington's Chinatown. Centered in the middle of the nation's capital, the boardinghouse was popular with the politicians who flocked to the city, including President McKinley, who lived here while he was a Congressman. It was the city's first saloon and restaurant, and Presidents Grant, Andrew Johnson, Cleveland, Theodore Roosevelt, and Harding frequented the popular stand-up bar and grill. A menu from 1866 featured items such as Leg of Mutton with Caper Sauce, Boiled Capons with Pork Sauce, and Wild Red Head Duck Broiled with Currant Jelly Sauce.

Old Ebbitt later housed military officers, earning the nickname "the Army and Navy Headquarters," then was torn down and reborn in a small Victorian storefront before being moved into a converted haberdashery. By the 1950s, it had disintegrated into a rundown hotel. In the 1970s, the hotel was put up for auction to pay back taxes. Two local restaurant owners went to the auction to buy the Ebbitt's collection of antique beer steins to display at their Georgetown restaurant, but ended up buying the entire saloon for the paltry sum of $11,200. In 1983, Old Ebbitt was moved to its present location when the old building was torn down, and today it is one of Washington's most popular restaurants, known locally as a "saloon Smithsonian."

With its marble stairs, antique gas chandeliers and fixtures, an antique clock over the revolving door, engraved glass panels and mirrors, and

historic paintings lining the walls, the place could easily be a museum. Each of the four bars and several of the dining rooms are decorated in a Victorian style reminiscent of Washington saloons at the turn of the century. Rich mahogany wood and plush velvet-lined booths, engraved beveled-glass panels, brass fittings, and dozens of large, elaborately framed commissioned paintings of Washington, D.C., scenes complete the luxurious ambiance of days long past. Even the dining room chairs are copies of those used in early NYC railroad dining cars.

The 1920s-style mahogany bar in the Old Bar is topped with those famous beer steins,

carved wooden bears imported by Alexander Hamilton, and some of the mounted animal trophies donated to the Grill by Teddy Roosevelt when he left office. Speaking of Presidents, you must visit Grant's Bar, one of the most intimate, romantic, and beautiful lounges in the country. With a ceiling mural reminiscent of a European cathedral, colorful paintings on the walls, and soft lavender and beige tones throughout, no wonder it's the favorite haunt of many of Washington's most private people: off-duty Secret Service agents who work just up the street at a really big white house. A framed painting by Peter Egeli and inspired by Mathew Brady's famed black and white portrait of General Ulysses S. Grant stands guard over the room, a painting I'm told that the Smithsonian would love to have in their presidential collection.

The Oyster Bar, considered by most to be the city's best provider of the tasty bivalves, hosts an annual Oyster Riot, an all-you-can-eat-and-drink event featuring great wines paired with an impressive list of fresh oysters. The menu features "high-end American food in large portions," and includes a large variety of seafood and shellfish entrees, including their famous crab cakes, salmon, halibut, and at least five or six daily varieties of fresh oysters. The prices, considering Old Grill has the look, feel, and service of a very expensive restaurant, are extremely reasonable, about half what you'd pay in New York or other major U.S. cities.

I asked chef Robert McGowan what he considered their signature dish, and he offered up the Orca Platter, which is popular as an appetizer for small groups. Note: There is no killer whale on this platter, merely lobster, oysters, clams, shrimp, and huge stone crab claws.

The New Ebbitt, Washington, Army and Navy Headquart

In 1912 the Grill was part of the Ebbitt House, the Army and Navy Headquarters, which was later torn down. The Grill was then relocated just blocks from the White House.

The Trout Parmesan is also a favorite. A flash-fried crusted rainbow trout with a golden brown Parmesan coating, it is served on a bed of roasted potatoes next to a generous pile of bright green beans. The trout is perfectly crunchy and buttery—cheesy outside, and tender, flaky and moist inside, sparingly dolloped with tangy hollandaise sauce. The kitchen is a study in organized chaos, with orders flying in by the dozens and stove tops crowded with sizzling skillets and bubbling saucepans as cooks toast bread and rolls, whip up fresh salads, fill skillets with seafood and sauces, grill steaks, remove lobsters from the steamers, and pile steaming vegetables on hot plates awaiting the addition of any number of entrees.

And then there are the "long-arm" waiters, with their uncanny ability to pile five dishes on

one arm, while carrying a sixth one in their other hand. These consummate professionals open the door to the dining room with a hip bump and wind their way through the dining room like hockey players crossing the blue line, weaving through customers, other waiters, and busboys, arriving at the tables to the wonderment of their customers. One of the long-armed guys swears he could actually carry five dishes on each arm, but that's against the rules. Six plates per waiter is the limit.

With all the presidents, politicians, celebrities, and famous folk who dine here regularly, the waiters are pretty immune to the oohs, aahs, and whispered comments as customers realize who is sitting at the next table or across the aisle. But having dealt with many such glitterati, I figured I could take it all in stride. After all, they're just people, right? During my dinner, U.S. Attorney General Eric Holder and his stunning wife, Sharon, passed by my table, and when they caught me looking up, gracefully acknowledged me with a pleasant "Good evening." At which point, I found myself buttering a dinner roll with hollandaise sauce. So much for cool.

Old Ebbitt Trout Parmesan

∾ SERVES 2 ∾

SIMPLIFIED HOLLANDAISE SAUCE

3 egg yolks

⅛ teaspoon Tabasco sauce

2 tablespoons lemon juice

¼ teaspoon kosher salt

Black pepper

8 tablespoons (1 stick) butter, clarified (Note page 47)

Vegetable oil, for frying

1 (10-ounce) rainbow trout, butterflied (see Note)

1 cup all-purpose flour

1 teaspoon kosher salt

½ teaspoon freshly ground black pepper

2 large eggs, lightly beaten

Grated Parmesan cheese

For the hollandaise sauce: In a mixing bowl, use a hand or immersion blender to whip the egg yolks together. Leaving the blender on, add the Tabasco, lemon juice, kosher salt, and some black pepper, then slowly drizzle the melted clarified butter into the mixture and blend until the sauce emulsifies and thickens.

Pour the vegetable oil to a depth of 3 to 4 inches in a straight-sided deep sauté pan or Dutch oven wide enough to accommodate the butterflied trout laid flat. Heat the oil over medium heat.

Dry the trout thoroughly with paper towels. Set up three flat shallow bowls: one with flour, salt, and pepper; another with the eggs; and the third with the Parmesan. Test the temperature of the oil by dropping in a pinch of flour. The flour should sizzle, sink, and then immediately rise to the surface.

Dredge the trout in flour, then shake off the excess; next, dip it into the egg mixture, and then into the Parmesan. The most efficient method is to keep one hand dry for the flour and use the other hand for the other bowls.

Slip the coated trout into the hot oil. Fry until golden and the trout floats, 5 to 10 minutes.

Serve immediately, topped with hollandaise sauce.

NOTE: You can purchase the trout already cleaned, or scale it, remove the head, and debone it yourself. To butterfly it, cut down the underside so that the fish lies flat.

Columbia
YBOR CITY, FL ~ EST. 1905

Casimiro Hernandez opened Columbia as a small sixty-seat street corner café in 1905. Famous for its Cuban coffee and authentic Cuban sandwiches, the restaurant is located in the Tampa suburb of Ybor (pronounced EE-bore) City, called by some "America's Havana," where the main industry at the turn of the twentieth century was the hand rolling of Cuban cigars.

After fifteen years, Columbia expanded into a small restaurant next door, doubling its size. Ten years later, Casimiro's son built the first air-conditioned dining room in Tampa, and years later still, Casimiro's granddaughter Adela and husband Cesar took over the Columbia and kept it alive through the fifties and sixties when Ybor City was in a state of decay. They brought in some of the top Latin talent of the era to perform, a musical side dish that continues today with Spanish flamenco dancers who perform every night but Sunday.

It is said that after one particularly dismal day during the Depression, when eight customers netted the restaurant a measly $12.42, the owner called a staff meeting and placed a box of nails on the table. "Another twelve-dollar day and I nail up the damned joint," he promised. But they pulled through, and he never had to make that threat again.

During World War II, because of generous rationing based on business levels at the beginning of the war (December, the month war was declared, is high season in Florida), their high allocations helped them get just about any kind of food they

wanted. In fact, they ran newspaper ads that promised: "We have it all at La Fonda" (their main dining room then).

Over the years, Columbia has amassed many restaurant honors, but the two most treasured are the Distinguished Restaurants of North America Award of Excellence, and Outstanding Spanish Restaurant in North America, which was awarded by the government of Spain.

The largest Spanish restaurant in the world, Columbia takes up an entire city block, seating seventeen hundred people in fifteen dining rooms. Each room is decorated in authentic Spanish and Moorish style, with original art, vibrant tile murals, natural stone, stained glass, and stately wrought iron. The wine cellar holds a staggering fifty thousand bottles of wine, and has been recognized by leading winemakers in Spain as the world's greatest assemblage of Spanish

Columbia was opened in 1905 as a sixty-seat street corner café. Here (in 1920) it doubled in size, but today it takes up a full city block and seats over 1,700. At left is the popular Patio dining room.

wines. Their kitchen alone is bigger than many restaurants. Chef Geraldo Bayona jokes that it's so vast that he needs to get everyone cell phones so he can communicate with them. The practiced grace and efficiency of the dining room waitstaff is repeated in the gargantuan kitchen, and despite the hundreds of orders pouring into the kitchen, and two dining rooms packed with over 450 customers, there is no chaos, no dashing about, no waiters shouting or screaming at the chefs, or vice versa. The professionals in white tunics and chef's hats or tuxedos efficiently do what they've done at Columbia for a century.

When dining at the Columbia, I suggest trying two of their most historic dishes: the "1905" Salad and the Red Snapper Alicante. Both are assembled at your table, offering a culinary floor show for the surrounding diners. The waiter skillfully tosses the ingredients for the salad (a scrumptuous combination of lettuce, tomatoes, julienned Swiss cheese and ham, Romano cheese, Worchestershire, and lemon juice) in a large wooden bowl, then with a flourish drizzles on their "1905" dressing. This mixture of olive oil, minced garlic, oregano, red wine vinegar, and black pepper is simply fantastic.

I love salads and until I'd tasted this dish thought that Caesar salad was the end-all and be-all of salads. But I'd have to say this was one of the best I've ever enjoyed. Created by one of their waiters in 1940 it is one of Columbia's most popular dishes.

The Red Snapper Alicante consists of snapper baked with onions and peppers and topped with eggplant, shrimp, onions, and peppers. The waiter

places them on your plate, then ladles some brown beef sauce over the fish. Brown "beef" sauce!? On fish? Believe it or not, it's a great combination. The sauce perfectly enhances the tender and

The Don Quixote dining room features a stage where Flamenco dancers perform in the evening, six days a week.

moist snapper, and the beefy flavor is gently mellowed by the Madeira wine, tomato, and cream incorporated in the sauce.

Columbia's future is bright and it includes the possibility that for the first time in family history a woman may take over the reins.

It seems likely that one of CEO Richard Gonzmart's two daughters, either Andrea or Lauren, will break through that glass ceiling in the Patio Room and carry the family values of their great-grandfather into the future. Boy would Great-Grandpa Casimiro be delighted!

Above: Their legendary "1905" Salad.
Left: The fifth generation of Columbia owners. Adults (left to right): Casey Jr., Casey, Jessica, Cassandra, Richard, Andrea, and Lauren. Children: Christian, Marlena, Charlie, Isabella, and Michael.

Red Snapper Alicante

~ SERVES 4 ~

COLUMBIA SEASONING

5 teaspoons garlic powder

2½ teaspoons salt

1¼ teaspoons freshly
ground black pepper

8 jumbo shrimp, peeled, tails left on

4 slices bacon, halved crosswise

4 cups extra-virgin Spanish olive oil

1 cup freshly squeezed lemon juice

½ cup minced garlic

4 cups all-purpose flour

4 large eggs, beaten

1 globe eggplant, peeled and cut
into 1-inch-thick crosswise slices

2 cups dried bread crumbs

2 Spanish onions, cut into ¼-inch
thick slices

4 (7-ounce) snapper fillets

2 green bell peppers, seeded,
deribbed, and cut into ¼-inch
thick slices

Alicante Sauce

Splash of dry white wine

¼ cup sliced almonds

1 lemon, thinly sliced

For the Columbia Seasoning: In a small bowl, combine the garlic powder, salt and pepper and stir to blend.

Wrap each shrimp with ½ slice of bacon and secure with a toothpick. In a medium bowl, combine 2 cups of the olive oil, the lemon juice, garlic, and 2 tablespoons of the Columbia Seasoning. Stir to blend. Add the shrimp, cover, and refrigerate for 2 to 3 hours.

Preheat the oven to 550°F. Combine the flour with 6 tablespoons of the remaining Columbia Seasoning in a shallow bowl. Stir with a whisk to blend. One at a time, dip the shrimp in the seasoned flour, the beaten eggs, and then in the seasoned flour again to coat evenly. Set aside. Dip the eggplant slices in the seasoned flour, the beaten eggs, and then the bread crumbs to coat evenly.

Place 8 onion slices in the bottom of a shallow casserole dish. Season the fish with the remaining ¾ tablespoon Columbia Seasoning and place on top of the onions. Lay 2 slices of green pepper on top of each fillet and then top with Alicante Sauce. Bake in the oven for 20 minutes, or until opaque throughout.

While the fish is cooking, heat the remaining 2 cups of olive oil to 350°F on a deep-fat thermometer in a large, heavy skillet. In batches, add the breaded eggplant and fry until golden brown. Using a wire-mesh skimmer, transfer to paper towels to drain. Next, fry the shrimp in batches until golden brown. Transfer to paper towels to drain. Remove the toothpicks. Set the eggplant and shrimp aside and keep warm.

Remove the fish from the oven. Add the white wine to the pan, then transfer the fish to serving plates and top with the almonds. Serve at once with the shrimp, eggplant, lemon slices, and the remaining Alicante Sauce.

Alicante Sauce

2 tablespoons unsalted butter

¾ cup olive oil

2 yellow onions, chopped

2 stalks celery, chopped

2 carrots, peeled and chopped

2 bay leaves

1 teaspoon dried thyme

½ cup all-purpose flour

2 cups tomato puree

5 peppercorns

12 cups beef broth

¼ cup coarsely chopped fresh flat-leaf parsley

½ cup Madeira wine

¼ cup heavy cream

¼ cup dry white wine

Salt to taste

In a medium saucepan, melt the butter with the olive oil over medium heat. Add the onions, celery, carrots, bay leaves, and thyme and sauté until the onions are translucent, about 3 minutes. Add the flour and stir until the flour is lightly browned.

Add the tomato puree, peppercorns, 8 cups of the beef broth, and the parsley. Reduce the heat to low, cover, and cook for 2 hours.

Add the remaining 4 cups beef broth and the Madeira wine and simmer over medium heat until reduced by one-third. Strain the sauce and stir in the heavy cream and white wine. Season with salt to taste.

Lakeside Inn
MT. DORA, FL ~ EST. 1883

Soon after the tiny Florida town of Royallou in the center of Florida's Lake Country changed its name to Mt. Dora, four investors built a two-story, ten-room hotel overlooking nearby Lake Dora. Travelers had to really, really want to go there, as the only means of transportation at the time was horseback or progressively smaller steamboats and finally rowboats across numerous small lakes.

It is no wonder that once guests arrived, the average stay was from several weeks to several months. During these long stays, guests fished, went bird watching or snake hunting, and enjoyed picnics. There wasn't much else to do. The women, often in full-length gowns which was the custom of the time, sat and sipped a new beverage that was becoming popular locally: freshly squeezed orange juice.

Several years later, the railroad came to town, making it slightly easier to get here. That is, if you didn't mind cinders, sparks, and the thick black smoke coming into the railroad cars, cows and pigs on the tracks, and storms that would often wash away those tracks.

But once past those hazards, the guests enjoyed the casual, relaxed atmosphere and gentle ambiance, and most especially the breakfast buffets and hearty lunches and dinners cooked up by the hotel's cook, Tempy. Wearing a white dust cap and a huge apron, she worked in the small kitchen creating simple but filling meals that included fried chicken, raised biscuits, and her very popular lemon meringue pie.

In the next few decades, the hotel added rooms, a wrap-around front porch, and a new name: the Lakeside Inn. During Prohibition, the inn was the most popular spot in that part of Florida, as northerners abandoned their winters for Florida sunshine. Around this time, Mt. Dora became known as a boating mecca after the hotel sponsored the Mt. Dora Annual Sailing Regatta. Over the years, that gathering of sailing enthusiasts and boat fanciers has brought thousands of guests to the town and the inn.

In the following three decades, the inn added an Olympic-sized swimming pool, a three-story annex, extensive landscaping, and a large boathouse, and continued the gentle custom of serving guests an evening glass of orange juice squeezed from oranges picked from a grove on the property. When President Calvin Coolidge retired in 1930, he and his wife, Grace, enjoyed a month-long vacation at the inn. They are counted in a long list of notable guests, including Thomas Edison, Henry Ford, and President Dwight Eisenhower, as well as governors, senators, and more than a few Hollywood stars, all seeking a quiet place to relax.

Through much of the twentieth century, the inn operated on a seasonal basis, and even today, like most Florida resorts it is most heavily booked during the winter high season.

Today, the inn has eighty-five guest rooms and suites in a cluster of five buildings decorated with gables, porches, balconies, and Victorian ornaments, along with a plethora of antiques shops—one of the reasons people drive to Mt. Dora from Orlando, a mere forty-five minutes away. The original hotel has been turned into the lobby, the Beauclaire restaurant, and Tremain's lounge, and the inn is perched on acres of green lawn and is surrounded by stately oaks hung with lacy curtains of Spanish moss.

Chef Patrick Deblasio, along with chef Myrtle Hawthorne, has been cooking here for more than two decades. Their signature Georgia Chicken is a dish of sautéed chicken breasts in a peach sauce with bourbon, pecans, and honey that is dramatically flambéed at the table.

Above: The striking etched glass panel, added in 1950, lends a Roaring Twenties elegance to the romantic Tremain lounge. The floor-to-ceiling panel certainly adds romance, especially at night, when candles and the glow from the lighted glass panel illuminate the lounge.

Georgia Chicken

∾ SERVES 4 ∾

¼ cup honey

1 (12-ounce) can sliced peaches

¼ cup whole pecans

2 tablespoons bourbon

4 (5-ounce) skinless, boneless chicken breast halves

Flour, for dusting

4 tablespoons unsalted butter

Chopped fresh flat-leaf parsley, for garnish

In a small saucepan, combine the honey, peaches, pecans, and bourbon. Cook, stirring gently, over medium-low heat until the peach slices are heated through. Set aside and keep warm.

Lightly dust the chicken breasts with flour. In a large sauté pan, melt the butter over medium heat. Add the chicken and sauté until golden on both sides.

Add the sauce and, averting your face, use a long match or a charcoal lighter to ignite the sauce, swirling the pan until the fire dies down. Divide the chicken and sauce among warmed plates, garnish with the parsley, and serve immediately.

The inn is also known for its Sunday brunches featuring cinnamon-dipped French toast, strawberry-spinach salad, delicate chicken potpie, homemade scones, and a deep-dish pecan pie.

You can enjoy an after-dinner drink in the Tremain lounge that was added in 1950 where a floor-to-ceiling engraved-glass panel adds a Roaring Twenties elegance, especially at night, when candles and the glow from the lighted glass panel illuminate the romantic lounge. You can almost see the bobbed hair, flapper dresses, top hats and spats on the customers around you. Well, almost. The mood may be shattered, as it was for me, by a more contemporary young couple wearing sneakers, college sweatshirts, and super tight jeans. But like Gatsby, you can dream.

The Pirates' House
SAVANNAH, GA ~ EST. 1753

Twenty years after Savannah was settled by a small band of English colonists, the town was a bustling seaport with newly constructed houses and maritime businesses springing up everywhere. A boardinghouse built on the ten-acre site of a failed experimental botanical garden became the Seafarer's Inn and welcomed visiting sailors and soldiers, providing them with drink, food, lodging, and the "services" of the tavern's retinue of young women.

But after a few years, the inn became a refuge and favorite gathering spot of bloodthirsty pirates and cold-blooded privateers who prowled the seas along the Georgia and Carolina coasts. The area was the hunting grounds of many infamous pirates, including Edward Teach (Blackbeard),

Calico Jack, William Kidd, Black Bart, and Edward England. Privateers, who were even worse than pirates, raided enemy shipping, massacred the crews, and sold the captured ships, all with permission of the English government. French privateer Jean Lafitte did so well that he had a nice home in Savannah, and reputedly frequented the Seafarer's.

When Robert Louis Stevenson visited the inn, he learned about its tarnished history and the various pirates and privateers who had caroused there. After he wrote *Treasure Island,* many suggested that he had modeled Long John Silver, Captain Flint, and Billy Bones on the seedy characters he had heard about at the Seafarer's.

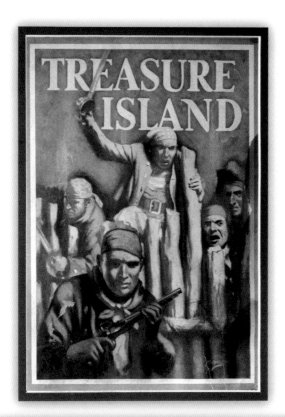

Through the years, there have been stories of pirate-like ghosts on the inn's stairways, crying out in the night and peeking through windows. Even Stevenson's mythical Captain Flint has been spotted climbing the stairs in the Herb House dining room. One of the managers closing at night saw flickering in the Herb House and discovered a twelve-year-old boy, who had died in that room in the 1800s, standing in the locked and closed restaurant. Waitperson Pam Kennedy, an eleven-year veteran, took another waiter with her into the cellar to take pictures with a customer's camera. When she pressed the shutter, a small, angry face came at her with the speed of a fastball, causing her to panic and jump back, knocking the waiter to the floor. They both ran out of the cellar and didn't go back down for months.

At one time, the inn helped to illegally supply unwilling crewmen to ship captains who were shorthanded when they arrived in port. People

The Captain's Room, and several of the other dining rooms, are allegedly prowled by ghosts of Blackbeard, Captain Flint, and other pirate spirits.

Honey-Pecan Fried Chicken

∞ SERVES 4 ∞

HONEY-PECAN GLAZE

1 cup (2 sticks) unsalted butter

½ cup honey

½ cup coarsely chopped pecans

1 (3- to 3½-pound) frying chicken, cut into 8 pieces

2 cups buttermilk

½ teaspoon salt

Pinch of cayenne pepper

½ teaspoon garlic powder

SEASONED FLOUR

1 cup self-rising flour

¾ teaspoon salt

¼ teaspoon cayenne pepper

¼ teaspoon garlic powder

Vegetable oil, for frying

For the glaze: In a medium saucepan, melt the butter over low heat. Whisk in the honey until well blended. Add the pecans and simmer, stirring frequently, for 15 to 20 minutes. Set aside and keep warm.

Rinse and dry the chicken and place in a sealable plastic bag. In a medium bowl, combine the buttermilk, salt, cayenne, and garlic powder. Pour the mixture into the bag, seal, and refrigerate for at least 2 hours or up to 24 hours.

Drain the chicken and let stand at room temperature for 20 minutes. Combine the seasoned flour ingredients in a shallow bowl and stir with a whisk. Coat the chicken in the seasoned flour, dredging both sides of each piece evenly. Cover and set aside for another 20 minutes.

In a deep cast-iron skillet or an electric frying pan, heat 1½ inches oil to 375°F on a deep-fat thermometer. In batches if necessary to prevent crowding, add the chicken to the hot oil. Cover, leaving the lid slightly ajar. Lower the temperature to 325°F and cook for 10 minutes. Using tongs, carefully turn the chicken pieces and cook another 10 minutes. Large, thick breasts may take a couple of minutes more.

Transfer the chicken to paper towels to drain and keep warm while cooking the remaining chicken. Place the chicken on a serving platter, pour the sauce over the chicken, and serve.

would come to the tavern and, after being served a drink spiked with laudanum (a powerful knockout drug) or being knocked unconscious with a club, would be carried through a tunnel from the old rum cellar to the nearby riverbank, only to wake up hours later at sea having been "shanghaied." They then faced either a two- to three-mile swim back to shore, or a punishing six- to eight-month cruise on the high seas. One story related the woes of a policeman

who came to investigate some wrongdoing and ended up being loaded on a boat headed to China. It took him two years to find his way home.

This kind of lawlessness finally caused the local police to close the tavern, and for quite a few years it was shuttered and empty. But the inn was eventually sold, renovated, and converted into one of Savannah's most unique restaurants. Owner Bob Turner has turned nine former houses into a rambling eatery with fifteen dining rooms—with six more upstairs under construction—that can seat as many as 650 customers. And although they have a modern kitchen, a sometimes-amusing and pseudo-nautical décor in each of the scattered dining rooms, and a gift shop that sells tons of kitschy pirate stuff, they have preserved an unmistakable air of mystery inside their storied walls. The only pirates today, other than the ghostly ones, are pictured on the walls, in a life-sized carving in the lobby, or are imitated by one of several local actors who "aaarrrr" their way through the crowded rooms, delighting children and adults alike.

The only booty or treasures hereabouts are the "gold" souvenir coins on the bar and on the tables, for as the place mats claim: "Our most precious treasure is our food." The menu includes golden Shrimp and Grits, golden Pineapple and golden Rum Glazed Salmon, and their signature buttermilk-marinated fried chicken, bathed in a golden sauce of honey and pecans. This dish features half of a large chicken, a large baked potato, and a generous portion of perfectly grilled veggies. The chicken is fried in a light coating, then covered with a succulent honey and pecan sauce.

Admittedly, I was disappointed that I'd failed to see any pirate spirits, and I didn't hear any moaning, creaking stairs, or crying from the basement while at the Pirate House. But I did overhear a young boy asking his parents some questions. "How much did the pirates pay to have their ears pierced, and how much did it cost to buy the hook or wooden peg leg some of them had?" he asked seriously. I leaned closer to their table.

When his father dutifully answered, "I don't know. How much?" The boy answered, giggling, "A buck an ear—and an arm and a leg!"

Captain Flint must have rolled over in his grave.

Strange noises and apparitions have been heard and seen on the staircase of the Herb House dining room and in the tunnels of the basement.

Hudson's Hamburgers
Coeur d'Alene, ID ~ Est. 1907

It began life simply as the "Missouri Lunch." The year was 1907, and Harley Hudson figured that people in the booming timber town of Coeur d'Alene would be hungry for his burgers. The name, by the way, wasn't for the state of Missouri; it was his brother's nickname. Harley was right. Today, the lumber mills are gone, and the city is no longer booming, but millions of customers later, his hamburger joint is still thriving.

Harley's tiny cooking tent had a very tiny menu, but everyone's favorite was the ten-cent hamburger sandwich. Today's Hudson's is a bit larger, with a somewhat larger menu, but it's still the burger everyone craves. Brothers Steve and Todd split the duties of running the place

today, the fifth generation of Hudsons to do so. During the summer (June through August), they're open seven days a week; the rest of the year they close on Sunday.

With a mere eighteen stools at a long counter, it's not a big restaurant, but there's seldom an open stool, and usually a long line forms out the door as folks from far and near head downtown for a "Huddy," the nickname for the simple but delicious burgers. The restaurant had competition a few years back when one of those Golden Arches places opened up the street—but it only lasted a year!

You can order a single or double hamburger, or a single or double cheeseburger. That's it! No fries, coleslaw, potato salad, chips, onion rings, or

side salad. You get meat and cheese and a bun, a dill pickle, and onion slices. No tomato, relish, mayonnaise, lettuce, or bacon. And condiment wise, things are just as basic. Hudson's gives customers a spartan choice of their famed spicy ketchup, mustard, or (only in recent years) regular ketchup.

The spicy ketchup has become almost as famous as the burgers. It seems that Great-Grandfather Harley figured he was losing too much money during the Depression when customers came in and doused their burgers with an inch or so of ketchup, figuring that would help fill their tummies. So he spiced up the ketchup to prevent that from happening. It is quite spicy, and in any amount would be a bit much to take.

Riley Wasson, 9, and biker Roger Smith enjoy their first "Huddies."

Harley Hudson, founder, stands in the original cooking tent in the summer of 1907. Four generations later, Hudson's is a street front restaurant.

Sitting at the counter watching owners Todd or Steve, or Tessa Weston, one of their employees, grill up burgers is like watching a Vegas blackjack dealer in a busy casino. They grab a handful of 14 to 16 percent fat ground beef from a tub beside the grill, hand-form a burger, mash it down with a well-used

Flo's Huckleberry Cobbler

∽ SERVES 4 TO 6 ∽

2 to 3 cups fresh or thawed frozen huckleberries

1 tablespoon freshly squeezed lemon juice

BATTER MIX

3 tablespoons margarine or butter, at room temperature

¾ cup sugar

½ cup milk

1 cup all-purpose flour

1 teaspoon baking powder

¼ teaspoon salt

TOPPING

½ to 1 cup sugar

1½ tablespoons cornstarch
for fresh berries, 2½ tablespoons
for frozen

¼ teaspoon salt

1 cup boiling water

Whipped cream or ice cream,
for serving

Preheat the oven to 350°F and butter a 9 by 13-inch baking pan. In a medium bowl, combine the huckleberries and lemon juice; stir to blend. Pour into the prepared pan.

In a medium bowl, combine the butter, sugar, milk, flour, baking powder, and salt. Stir with a whisk to blend, then pour over the berries.

For the topping: In a small bowl, mix together the sugar, cornstarch, and salt and sprinkle the mixture over the batter.

Pour the boiling water over the top of the cobbler and bake for 1 hour. Serve with freshly whipped cream or a favorite flavor of ice cream.

Note: Todd Hudson can't give out his burger secrets, but longtime customer Flo Harris shared this recipe for a cobbler she often brings to the restaurant to share with other diners.

spatula, slap it on the grill, arrange buns like a hand of cards, add cut-to-order slices of pickle and onion, drop slices of cheese on singles and make them into doubles, all the while carrying on a conversation with the customers seated behind them.

Other than a pinch of salt there is nothing special added to the burgers while cooking—no pepper or secret sauce or magical spice mixture. As Todd proudly puts it, "They are simply good-quality beef burgers, from local ranches, hand-formed and cooked to supreme juiciness." There is one cooking secret, though. When they add cheese to a sizzling burger on the Depression-era flattop grill, the cook often drags it through the hot grease first. That way the cheese begins to melt even before it hits the burger.

"We make so many of them every day I could do it in my sleep," says Tessa. Her knife work is almost surgical as she grabs a large dill pickle (they go through one hundred or so per day) and cuts seven thin slices, then follows with two wafer-thin slices of onion (forty to fifty pounds a day) as the only non-protein additions to the quarter-pound burgers.

An odd fact: They cut so many onions and pickles every day on the wooden cutting board that they are actually wearing through it. "We haven't changed the current one since 1982," Todd says, "we just turn it over occasionally and have it planed down every other year or so, but it's been getting thinner and thinner. I guess it's time for a new one."

The Huddy is crisp and nicely browned on the outside and very juicy inside, the spicy ketchup adding mouth-tingling warmth, the cheese melting into the meat. It is a very good burger. In fact, it's so good that next time I'm going to get a double.

The Berghoff
CHICAGO, IL ~ EST. 1898

All Herman J. Berghoff wanted to do was sell his beer. He had immigrated to the United States from Dortmund, Germany, in 1870, at the ripe old age of seventeen. After a dozen years or so roaming the country he worked as a farm laborer, a pastry chef on a small freighter, with Buffalo Bill's Wild West Show, as a railroad laborer, and finally as a salesman for a jewelry company in Ft. Wayne, Indiana. In 1887 Herman and brothers Henry, Hubert, and Gustav started a small brewery in town, finally fulfilling their dream of brewing German-style beers. And while their beer was very popular locally, Herman wanted to expand and brought his suds to the 1893 Chicago World's Fair, where his Dortmunder-style beer was a huge success.

After that, Herman applied to city officials in Chicago for a wholesale license so he could sell to hotels, restaurants, and saloons but they turned him down, not wanting to facilitate an "out-of-town beer" competing with the thirty existing local brewing companies. Not giving up, he went after a retail license, which would allow him to open a restaurant where he could sell food and his beers. When this was granted, he opened a storefront bar, furnished it very simply, and began selling his light and dark Berghoff beers for five cents a glass, ten cents a stein. With the stein you also got your choice of a free frankfurter, corned beef, or boiled ham sandwich.

The restaurant and bar prospered and was humming along quite well until Prohibition. But instead of closing up shop, Herman began brewing near-beer (which was legal) as well as a line of soda pop, including a root beer that is still popular in the area today. He also began to expand the food service, enlarging the menu over the next decade as the Berghoff became one of the Windy City's most popular restaurants.

The next hurdle for the Berghoffs was surviving the rationing and price freezes imposed during World War II. The War Price and Rationing Board not only rationed the basic commodities

Carlyn Berghoff, the fourth generation family owner, rescued the iconic restaurant after it was temporarily closed in 2005.

people could buy but also froze restaurant prices so they could not gouge their customers. Then operated by Herman's sons, the restaurant lived with the severely reduced prices until the war ended.

The restaurant was being run by the fourth generation, with the CEO, bar manager, restaurant manager, and other key management all family members, when in 2005 Herman and Jan Berghoff announced they were closing the restaurant, causing a tremendous outcry in Chicago. The plan was to lease the building to their granddaughter, Carlyn, who was going to run her catering business from the historic kitchen. But less than a year later she

managed to reopen to the cheers of longtime fans, and hopefully will keep the grand old lady of Windy City restaurants viable for another few decades. Her taking over is ironic, as up until 1968 the Berghoff bar was strictly all male, that practice only changing that year when a delegation of women from the NOW organization walked into the bar and demanded to be served.

As with many centenarian eateries, quite a few of the waitstaff have been here for years, but unlike many of the other restaurants, the Berghoff operated under the old German tradition of coins for the waiters. At the beginning of each shift, they would purchase metal coins from the restaurant and would use those coins to buy the food and beverages from the "house." The customers then paid the waiters in cash, and when the checks were audited they were supposed to balance, the waiters keeping any excess as their tips. This practice ended in 1980 when the Berghoff began accepting credit cards and using computers.

The kitchens are unlike those of many century-old restaurants, too. Because of the way the building sits, the kitchens are wide and very shallow, so to provide enough space for the hundreds of meals they prepare each day for the restaurant and for their catering, they are divided among four floors. The main kitchen, where most of the daily orders are cooked and served, is on the ground floor; the second floor is the bakery, pastry area, and catering kitchen; the third floor is for storage and several huge walk-in coolers and a large freezer; and the top (fourth) floor is the prep kitchen, with its huge cauldrons, fryers, ovens, and two large grills. With only one elevator, which is usually filled with incoming supplies, the stairs get quite a workout by both the chefs and waiters. Carlyn confesses that she doesn't need to belong to a gym, as one day here is equal to four to five solid hours on a stair climber.

The Berghoff's menu reflects its German heritage, with German sausages (bratwurst, knockwurst, and

Thüringen), Wiener Schnitzel, Jagerschnitzel, Schweins Filet, Rahm Schnitzel, Sauerbraten, Red Cabbage, Spaetzel, German Potato Salad, and Potato Pancakes. But it also includes beef steaks, lamb, salmon, cod, mahi mahi, beef medallions, chicken, burgers, mac and cheese, mashed potatoes, Caesar salad, and other more standard American fare.

The Berghoff sells an average of twelve thousand orders of sauerbraten a year. As you bite into the slices of beef you can close your eyes and imagine you're in Germany. The beef is tender, the sauce piquant yet tinged with sweetness, and the portion quite substantial. All that is missing is an oompah band in lederhosen. It is aptly complemented by a chilled Berghoff (when in Rome . . .) River Red Ale. Save room for a serving of their warm Apple Strudel, the flaky pastry bathed in caramel sauce and very generously sprinkled with confectioners' sugar. As with the rest of the meal . . . Wunderbar!

Sauerbraten

~ SERVES 6 TO 8 ~

5 to 6 pounds eye of round roast

MARINADE

4 cups cider vinegar

1 white or yellow onion, coarsely chopped

2 carrots, peeled and coarsely chopped

3 stalks celery, coarsely chopped

½ cup pickling spices

3 bay leaves

2 cups dry red wine

1 to 1½ cups sugar

2 beef bouillon cubes

2 tablespoons Worcestershire sauce

1 tablespoon Kitchen Bouquet
browning sauce

4 tablespoons unsalted butter

¼ cup all-purpose flour

Place the beef in a sealable plastic bag and pour the marinade ingredients over the beef to cover completely. Close the bag, enclose it in a second sealable plastic bag, and refrigerate for at least 3 days or up to 5 days, turning twice daily.

Preheat the oven to 350°F. Transfer the beef and the marinade to a Dutch oven. Cover and braise in the preheated oven, adding water as necessary to keep the meat moist, for 3 hours, or until fork-tender. Transfer to a platter, cover, and keep warm.

Add the wine, sugar, bouillon cubes, Worcestershire sauce, and Kitchen Bouquet to the Dutch oven. Bring to a simmer over medium heat and cook for 15 to 20 minutes.

Meanwhile, melt the butter in a small saucepan over low heat. Add the flour and stir until the resultant roux browns evenly, about 10 minutes. Gradually whisk the roux into the hot pan sauce, whisking until smooth. Bring to a boil, lower the heat, and simmer for 15 to 20 minutes, until thickened and smooth. Strain and add water to thin, if needed.

Slice the meat and serve family style on a warmed platter. Pour some of the warm sauce over the meat and serve the remainder on the side.

As for Herman's dream of selling his German-style beers, Falstaff bought the brewery in 1954, then the Huber Company took over brewing Herman's beers in 1960 and purchased the brand in 1995. So when you enjoy a Berghoff Boc, Prairie Lager, Sundown Dark, Genuine Dark, Hazelnut Winterfest, Hefewizen, Honey Maibock, take time to appreciate all the history that's behind the brew in front of you. Herman would appreciate that.

The Log Inn
HAUBSTADT, IN ~ EST. 1825

When Kathy Holzmayer's grandfather Peter Rettig bought the Log Inn in 1947, he was the fifteenth in a long line of owners but had no clue as to the treasure that was hidden in the small building he'd just purchased. It wasn't until 1963, when he was having the place remodeled, that he discovered a complete log cabin walled over inside the restaurant. It took two years to completely uncover the cabin, which had originally functioned as a stagecoach stop, restaurant, and trading post. It was in such good shape that nothing had to be repaired or replaced—and the building was 130 years old!

The cabin was an important place on the road between Evansville and Vincennes for people to get a bite to eat, stretch their legs, and buy provisions. After the stagecoaches stopped running, the road was paved over and became the Dixie Bee Highway, the main route from Chicago to Florida during the era of Model T's.

Perhaps the most famous log cabin guest was young Abraham Lincoln, who dined here while on a campaign tour on behalf of Henry Clay, the Whig Party candidate for president. On that same trip, he also visited his mother's grave near his boyhood home in Lincoln City, Indiana, about thirty miles east, where he had lived in a small log cabin with his family from age seven to twenty-one. That home is now in a National Park and is right across the highway from Lincoln State Park.

With the discovery of the hidden cabin inside their restaurant, the Rettigs realized what a historic gem they had and began using the "Lincoln room" as their main dining room. More renovation discovered beautiful poplar wood walls hidden under wallpaper in the barroom next door, and that was removed as well. Since pioneer construction involved logs with chinking between them, there are some gaps where you can look into the log cabin from the wall that adjoins the tavern.

The Log Inn was extremely popular with local folks, including dozens of construction crews and laborers who were working seven miles away building the Wabash & Erie Canal (1832 to 1849). On payday, the workers would flock here to drink

The Log Inn in 1869 served stagecoaches traveling in southern Indiana.

whiskey, often starting bar brawls that resulted in their being thrown out into the street to finish their rough-and-tumble knife fights.

As with many public places in the "free states" of the East and Midwest, slaves were sheltered here, ironically in the basement room directly under the Lincoln dining room. They escaped their owners in the Deep South until they were taken under the wing of many families along the various routes along the Underground Railroad.

In 1895, the inn added a popular dance hall upstairs, but the owners had to shore up the floor to keep it from falling into the bar below due to the heavy-booted stompin' and lively terpsichorean activities.

Through expansion, the oldest restaurant in the state has become one of the largest restaurants as well. The addition of three spacious dining rooms allows them to seat over five hundred people at one time. Service is generally family style, and as with many restaurants of this type the portions are huge. Piping-hot bowls of mashed or German fried potatoes, a basket of golden brown fried chicken, a tasty white gravy, green beans or corn, coleslaw or red cabbage, and heavenly freshly baked yeast-scented dinner rolls are standard. If you like fried chicken livers, I would highly suggest you order these as a side dish—but only if there are two to four in your party. The portion is massive.

Log Inn Chicken Livers

SERVES 4 AS AN APPETIZER,
1 AS A MAIN COURSE

1 cup cold whole milk

1 cup chicken livers, cleaned, sinews removed

1 cup all-purpose flour

1 tablespoon salt

1 teaspoon freshly ground black pepper

1 teaspoon garlic powder

1 teaspoon dried parsley

Vegetable oil, for frying

Pour the milk into a medium bowl, add the chicken livers, and stir to coat. In a large bowl, combine the flour and seasonings and stir well. Add the livers and turn until well coated.

In a large cast-iron skillet, heat 2 to 3 inches of the oil to 350°F on a deep-fat thermometer and cook the livers for 6 minutes, turning frequently. Using a slotted spoon, transfer to paper towels to drain briefly, then serve at once.

The chicken dinners are legendary around these parts. The cooks fry the poultry pieces in a long row of eighteen deep fryers, with each cook working his way along the assembly line of fried delights, turning the pieces over to make sure they're perfectly cooked on all sides. The smell is intoxicating.

The restaurant and the kitchen are both operated by members of the Elpers family, who bought the restaurant thirteen years ago. On any given day, Grandma Rita serves salads, Granddad Gene cuts potatoes, daughter Kathy handles orders and hands off finished plates to the waitstaff, son Daryl breads and fries the chicken and fish; and daughter Trish turns huge ham steaks on the grill. When asked if she was the restaurant manager, Kathy laughed. "No, we all manage the place. Mom and Dad work every day and every night, and they're seventy-two and seventy-six years old respectively."

This is down-home Grandma's-house (actually, she is in the kitchen most days) fare, high in calories and higher in flavor. It's food you'd eat every day, except for that nagging cardiologist or spouse. But even they like fried chicken. The pieces are lightly breaded and crispy golden brown outside, tender and moist inside. The side dishes are good if not fancy. The service is enthusiastic, pleasant, and relatively fast. And the ambiance (they call it "atmosphere" here), in a restaurant where Mr. Lincoln dined, is priceless.

Breitbach's Country Dining
BALLTOWN, IA ~ EST. 1852

In 1852, President Millard Fillmore issued a federal permit for the construction of a stagecoach stop in the tiny town of Balltown, Iowa. Ten years later, Jacob Breitbach, one of the original employees, bought the tavern, and it's been in his family for over 150 years. Three generations later, Mike and Cindy Breitbach run the popular restaurant, where everything is made from scratch. There are no frozen bags of prepared soup, no bottles of commercial salad dressings, and most especially, no pies come into the restaurant from outside bakeries. It's all done right in their kitchen.

It hasn't been an easy fifteen-decade run. On the day before Christmas, 2007, owner Mike, three of his sons, and his cousin were having breakfast at the restaurant prior to Mike preparing for a funeral dinner that afternoon. When he went into the kitchen, Mike smelled gas and hurriedly phoned the furnace repairman, but seconds later a huge explosion blew him through the kitchen door and knocked one of his sons to the floor. The other men fled into the street.

Mike shut off the vents and, as smoke began seeping through the walls, turned off the outside gas line and started removing important items from the restaurant—an antique clock, family portraits, a Victorian candy counter, antique rifles and shotguns, historic beer steins, and anything else he could grab. Then the fire broke through the walls and

Mike had to leave and watch as the building burned to the ground.

Insurance didn't cover the total destruction, but Mike and his family decided to rebuild, with help from the community and local farmers, including members of a local Amish commune. Dozens of local volunteers offered lumber, carpentry, handmade chairs, and help in framing and building a new restaurant. Cash also poured in, including money from a couple who celebrated their sixtieth anniversary by asking their kids for money to give to the

The family-run country restaurant has survived despite devastating fires, which twice destroyed the restaurant.

Breitbachs. While the building was under way, the restaurant continued serving folks in a small wine shed and beer garden beside the restaurant, offering coffee, sandwiches, and Cindy's pastries.

Miraculously, Breitbach's Country Dining reopened ten months later on Father's Day to a packed house filled with locals, tourists, and a tour bus of supporters. Everyone celebrated. Then, a mere four months later, Mike was awakened at 4 a.m. to learn that his restaurant was on fire again, and this time there was no opportunity to rescue anything. Antiques, photographs, furniture—everything went up in flames. The family was devastated. "Not again," Mike stammered as he arrived in the pre-dawn light to see his dream in ashes, "I can't go through this again."

saws, and the same farmers and Amish church members came to their aid again. More money came in through the mail, townspeople donated their own antiques to display in the new dining rooms and bar, and local women cooked up meals for the workers.

The cause of the 2008 fire was never determined, but the restaurant lives on, now protected by a state-of-the-art sprinkler system, and the Breitbachs refuse to look back. "It's not whether you get knocked down, it's how you get up and start over," Mike says. "The fire only destroyed a building, but the family, the history of Breitbach's, and the legacy we'll leave to our children lives on."

Four months before the restaurant was to reopen, Mike and Cindy flew with a small retinue to New York City to accept a James Beard America's Classic award for their culinary excellence and preservation of American cooking. In the cruelest of ironies, he'd first gotten word of the award the very morning of the second fire as he was walking through the ashes of his beloved restaurant.

But after much soul-searching and many long discussions with their family, the scene repeated itself as Mike and Cindy again decided to rebuild their legacy. More volunteers offered their services, waiters and waitresses rolled up their sleeves and took up hammers and

Cindy Breitbach's Raspberry Pie

∾ MAKES 1 (9-INCH) PIE ∾

4 cups fresh or thawed frozen raspberries

½ cup fresh or thawed frozen blackberries

1½ cups sugar, plus more for sprinkling

2 heaping tablespoons cornstarch

Pastry for 1 double-crust 9-inch pie

Vanilla ice cream, for serving (optional)

Preheat the oven to 350°F. In a large bowl, mix the raspberries, blackberries, the 1½ cups sugar, and the cornstarch together. Line a 9-inch pie plate with one pie pastry and add the berry mixture. Trim the overhang to ½ inch. Top with the second pastry, trim to ¾ inch, and fold under the bottom crust. Flute the edges. Cut slits in the top crust and sprinkle with sugar.

Bake for 1 hour, or until the crust is golden and the filling is bubbling. Let cool slightly and serve warm, with ice cream, if desired.

As Mike says, "What's past is passed," and the restaurant today is bigger, brighter, and some say even busier than ever before. Cindy's kitchen has vastly increased in size, the rooms are decorated with delightful antiques and memorabilia, (including clippings of news articles about the two fires), and things are going well for Breitbach's.

The menu features an extensive buffet at lunchtime, with a huge variety of fresh salads, vegetables, and entrees, and their dinner menu is impressive in both variety and originality, offering up everything from dinner-plate-sized ham steaks to frog's legs to catfish and pike, Iowa's iconic pork chops, deep-fried cheese curds and cauliflower, and of course Cindy's legendary fried chicken. Her style of "homemade goodness and homespun hospitality" has won legions of fans, and she produces some of the best fried chicken, ham steaks, soups, and, most important, pies on the planet. And if you didn't know it, you'd never guess from Mike's smile or Cindy's beaming face that they'd gone through a double tragedy.

"I guess we're kind of like the phoenix who rose from the ashes," Mike says. "But we've done it twice."

Hays House
Council Grove, KS ~ Est. 1847

Seth Hays, the great-grandson of Daniel Boone and a cousin to Kit Carson, moved to Council Grove in 1847 and built a log-cabin store on a wagon-train stop on the Santa Fe Trail. The original deed was signed by Abraham Lincoln. Hays soon began trading, selling goods to the local Kaw (Kansa) Indian tribe, and providing hearty meals and overnight accommodations for the drivers, families, cowpokes, and hungry travelers who were headed west on the dusty trail.

Ten years later, Hays built another structure. The two-story building had a peaked roof until 1889, when a nearby fire sent embers across the street, causing two walls and the roof of the store to burn. The building was reconstructed with a flat roof, and the walls were extended. The charred beams were left in place, and still support the roof today. The locals tell the story about how much of the town was burning, but the townsfolk formed a bucket brigade to save the tavern first.

From its early days, the tavern was uncharacteristically located on the second floor, where it still is located. When they rebuilt, they added ten guest rooms, which were in use until the 1940s. The present-day ladies' room sports the original claw-foot bathtub from those hotel days.

From its opening until the fire, the store had many uses. The U.S. government rented a room to hold court, and used another room as a post office. The tavern, of course, was the center of activity

Seth M. Hays, a great grandson of Daniel Boone, the first white settler in Council Grove in 1847, opened a trading post and a place where people could be served food.

in town, and occasionally they held "bawdy theatricals." On Saturday nights, the bottles of rye, whiskey, and rum were covered over so that church services could take place the following day. The store apparently did well, situated as it was in a key spot on the Santa Fe Trail, and it's reported that during one four-day buying spree, the Hays and the Cobb store across the street sold $15,000 worth of goods to the local tribes. That was pretty big money in those days!

The old cellar, used to store root vegetables and meat (the meat hooks still hang from the ceiling beams), had a floor installed when they remodeled and now is used as a sixth dining room and the gathering spot for the local Rotary Club. The original bar was moved down there as well. The cool, stone-walled cellar has been used for private wedding receptions, as have the three dining rooms

Five-year-old Sierra Wilkerson, daughter of the owners at the time, sits in the rustic, timbered dining room.

upstairs. The walls of the Seth Room have been laid bare to show the hand-split cottonwood lathe that was under the plaster for many years.

As with many of our Western taverns, saloons, and inns, the usual cast of characters—Kit Carson, Jesse James, Frederick Remington, and General George Armstrong Custer—are said to have visited here multiple times. You have to wonder when they had time to blaze trails, rob stages, make rifles, or chase Native Americans around while they were traveling, staying in inns, and chowing down on saloon food. Wonder if they got frequent-wagon miles?

The cuisine at Hays House could be labeled Old West country-style comfort food. Specialties include one of the best hot roast beef sandwiches I've ever had, the ubiquitous skillet-fried chicken, prime rib, rib-eye and strip steaks, thick slices of bone-in ham, center-cut pork chops, chicken-fried steak, beef brisket, and a chili that will warm both your belly and the cockles of your heart.

The pork chops are quite good, and the gravy on the mashed potatoes is a ten for its thick, rich flavor and creaminess. The onion straws are tasty and not greasy, and you get a generous serving. A bit of advice: Whatever you order, please, please save room for dessert. Chef Wilkerson and his wife, Sherry, own the Hays House Bakery two blocks away, and man oh man can Sherry bake an incredible pie. In a town too small to have displays of baked goods, Sherry will make

Fresh Strawberry Pie

∽ MAKES 1 (9-INCH) PIE ∽

1 cup granulated sugar

3 tablespoons cornstarch

6 tablespoons strawberry gelatin powder

1 cup water

10 cups sliced fresh strawberries

1 (9-inch) pie shell, baked and cooled

1 cup heavy cream (optional)

1 tablespoon confectioners' sugar (optional)

In a small saucepan, combine the granulated sugar, cornstarch, and gelatin. Stir in the water until blended. Place over medium heat and bring to a low boil; cook for 3 minutes, stirring, until the mixture is clear. Remove from the heat and let cool to room temperature.

In a large bowl, combine the cooled sugar mixture and the strawberries. Stir gently to blend. Pour into the pie shell and refrigerate for at least 1 hour or up to 3 hours.

In a deep bowl, beat the cream and confectioners' sugar together until stiff peaks form. Top the pie with the whipped cream, if desired, and cut into wedges to serve.

Chef Doug Wilkerson stands in front of a portrait of Chief Washunga of the Kaw (Kansa) tribe. Many portraits are scattered around the restaurant.

just about any pie to order, including peach, strawberry, blueberry, gooseberry, banana and coconut cream, chocolate, raspberry, rhubarb, lemon, and so on. The crust is superb, buttery and flaky. The fresh strawberry pie boasts several pints of fruit kissed with a light, sweet glaze and topped off with whipped cream. When you order your meal, ask what pies are available. You will seldom find a better pie anywhere, and they go fast.

With a meal like that under your belt, you could easily jump in a wagon and head down the trail toward Santa Fe. But I wonder, did they have doggie bags in those days?

∽ Hays House Fact ∽

A major fire on December 16, 2011, destroyed the kitchen and caused smoke and soot damage to the dining rooms, forcing the Hays House to close, but they scraped off the soot and rebuilt the kitchen and reopened in May 2012. This was the second major fire they had survived.

Old Stone Inn
SIMPSONVILLE, KY ~ EST. 1817

In 1817, Fleming Rogers took coarse limestone slabs from a quarry on his farm and constructed the only restaurant in this collection of centenarians that was built using slave labor, the Old Stone Inn. The building has survived unscathed for 194 years, and it has passed through more than a dozen owners over the last hundred of those years.

In its early days, it was a residence, then a stagecoach stop on the Midland Trail between Louisville and Shelbyville, Kentucky, and in the 1800s a tavern and inn, the latter three permutations all serving food to travelers who came by on horseback or in wagons and carriages. Visitors included former President Andrew Jackson, who stayed here while he was commuting from the Hermitage to Washington.

In 1922, the building was given the name Ye Olde Stone Inn when it was turned into a tearoom, then later it became a restaurant under the same owners and was added to the National Register of Historic Buildings in 1976. The side buildings were added in the 1970s to accommodate the crowds that began to come by for the legendary dinners.

Shelly Thompson purchased the restaurant in 2008. "This has been a dream of mine since I was fifteen or sixteen," Shelly says. "I've been in the restaurant business off and on for the last decade. It's a very big passion of mine. The opportunity that the Purnells [the building's former owners] have given me is just unbelievable. And for it to be this place—I can't even put it into words, it's just amazing."

Many of the doorways in the Inn are askew due to the age of the building and the settling that has occurred in 195 years.

The historic stone structure has walls that are two feet thick, wide plank hardwood floors, and today, four fireplaces. The original building had eight, but through several reconstructions the interior changed. The front of the building once had a separate door to the right of the main double-door entrance. This second door led directly into the former tavern in the 1830s. Records are unclear as to how long it remained in service, but it was eventually replaced by a window, which added symmetry to the facade.

Although the building looks small from the front, it is actually quite large. Shelly converted some of the upstairs rooms into small private dining rooms, and with the addition of three small rooms on the main level and a large dining area in one of the adjunct buildings, the restaurant seats 175, with the outdoor patio seating an additional seventy-five. There is also a bar and a separate lounge for pre- and postprandials such as the popular Stone Fence: twelve-year-old Glen Livet Scotch, club soda, and a dash of bitters.

The menu promises "Kentucky Cuisine," which is a blend of Southern and regional fare (fried green tomatoes, fried frog legs, shrimp and grits, tasso sauce, country ham, hot brown, fried chicken livers, and fried chicken), with comfort foods like burgers, Caesar salad, pork chops, steaks, French fries, and pastas. Chef Jerrett Berry also creates an incredibly delicious Chicken Fried Bacon: strips of bacon dipped in batter, fried, then served with sausage gravy.

I tried one piece of the six presented to me, marveled at the taste, then passed the plate to another table, where it was quickly emptied.

I also recommend the Bourbon Barrel Pork Chop, an exceedingly tender and moist fourteen-ounce bone-in chop accompanied with bourbon sauce, sausage-biscuit bread pudding, and asparagus.

I spent a warm summer evening on their lovely patio, enjoying a magical light show provided by a wandering and gregarious bunch of fireflies, and a small glass of locally distilled bourbon—this is, after all, bourbon country—all the while relishing a delightful meal at a historic inn, and only briefly wishing I'd taken another piece of that deep-fried bacon.

Bourbon Barrel Pork Chops

∽ SERVES 4 ∾

4 cups water

2 to 3 tablespoons beef base

3 tablespoons olive oil

5 apples, peeled, cored, and diced

2 shallots, chopped

2 tablespoons unsalted butter

1 tablespoon bacon grease

2 tablespoons all-purpose flour

½ cup Kentucky bourbon

1 tablespoon chopped fresh thyme

2 bay leaves

1 teaspoon salt

½ teaspoon freshly ground black pepper

4 (8- to 10-ounce) pork chops

In a stockpot, combine the water and beef base; stir to blend. Set aside. In a large skillet, heat the olive oil over medium-high heat and sauté the apples and shallots just until the apples soften. Set aside and keep warm.

In another skillet, melt the butter over medium heat and add the bacon grease. Stir in the flour and cook, stirring constantly, to make a medium brown roux. Do not burn. Measure out ½ cup and discard the rest.

Remove the apples and shallots from their pan and add the bourbon to the pan. Stir to scrape up the browned bits from the bottom of the pan, then add to the water and beef base. Add the apples and shallots, then the roux, thyme, bay leaves, salt, and pepper. Bring to a simmer and cook, stirring frequently, until thickened.

Preheat the oven to 350°F. Heat a large, heavy grill pan over high heat. Brush both sides of the chops with oil and season with salt and pepper. Cook in the hot grill pan for 4 minutes on each side. Transfer the pan to the oven and roast for 15 minutes.

Serve the pork chops with mashed potatoes or fresh-cooked vegetables and drizzle with the bourbon sauce.

The Old Talbott Tavern

BARDSTOWN, KY ~ EST. 1779

Of all the restaurants profiled in this book, the Talbott has had the most names. Today, it's the Old Talbott Tavern, but in the past it's been known as the Hynes House, the Bardstown Hotel, Chapman's House, the Shady Bower Hotel, the Newman House, the Talbott Hotel, the Old Stone Tavern, and the Talbott Tavern. One of America's oldest taverns, and reputed to be the "oldest western stagecoach stop" in the country, the tavern has never closed since its opening in 1779. Well, it did shut its doors in 1998 as the result of a fire, but it reopened the following year.

The tavern was originally built one year before the town of Salem (later Bardstown) was settled and began life as the Hynes Hotel. At that time, it was located at the end of the stagecoach road that led travelers from the east into Kentucky. It offered

spartan accommodations, simple meals, and thirst-quenching whiskeys and other liquors.

Like many of the historic inns and taverns in the South, it hosted the likes of Daniel Boone, Andrew Jackson, Henry Clay, William Henry Harrison, Abraham Lincoln, and Generals George Rogers Clark (a top military officer in the American Revolutionary War and father of William Clark, the co-leader of the Lewis and Clark expedition) and George S. Patton. Songwriter Stephen Foster (who penned "My Old Kentucky Home" and dozens of other songs of that era), author Washington Irving, and artist John James Audubon also took refreshment there. Jesse James once took too much refreshment and in a drunken stupor tried to shoot imaginary butterflies inside the hotel, leaving bullet holes in murals painted by exiled King Louis Philippe of France, who had painted

"Hot Brown" is a popular dish in Kentucky that features ham, turkey, bacon, breadcrumbs, pimentos or tomatoes, and cheese.

them on the walls when he lodged at the hotel. Unfortunately, the 1998 fire all but destroyed the murals and they have not been restored.

Today, the tavern functions as both a restaurant and a five-room bed-and-breakfast, with rooms named after famous folk (including Lincoln, Boone, Irving, and Patton). In the old days, there were only two rooms, one for gents and one for ladies. Apparently, some of its early residents and guests took a liking to the place and show up every now and then, or at least visages of them appear or their voices are heard in empty rooms and hallways. Six of second owner George Talbott's children died in the tavern, and Alan Brown, author of *Stories from the Haunted South*, has dubbed the Talbott as the "thirteenth most haunted inn in the country."

There are two dining rooms—one of which is the original tavern—and a small bar at the back of the building. It's a popular stop for people on the Kentucky Bourbon Trail tour of the seven bourbon distilleries in the area. Ninety-five percent of all U.S. bourbon comes from Kentucky, and Bardstown

Old Hot Brown

∽ SERVES 4 TO 8 ∽

MORNAY SAUCE

2½ tablespoons unsalted butter

3 tablespoons all-purpose flour

2 cups milk, warmed

¼ teaspoon salt

Pinch of ground white pepper

¾ cup (3 ounces) shredded mild Cheddar cheese

8 slices bread, toasted

8 slices ham

8 slices turkey, white or dark meat

8 (½-inch-thick) slices beefsteak or
other large tomato (see Note)

16 slices cooked bacon,
as crisp as you like

Preheat the oven to 375°F.

For the sauce: In a heavy, medium saucepan, melt the butter over medium heat. Add the flour and cook, stirring constantly, until the roux is golden brown. Gradually whisk in the milk and cook, whisking frequently, until thickened. Add the salt and pepper, then gradually stir in the cheese until melted. Set aside and keep warm.

Place the toast in one layer in the bottom of a large baking dish. Top each piece of toast with a slice of ham and turkey, then pour ¼ cup Mornay sauce over each one. Top each with a slice of tomato and bake until browned on the edges. Serve with 2 slices of bacon on top of each portion.

NOTE: To be even more authentic, use sliced pimientos in place of the tomatoes. Place the chicken pieces in a large serving bowl and pour the broth and dumplings over the chicken. Garnish with the parsley and serve immediately.

has christened itself "the Bourbon Capital of the World," a fact we don't dispute seeing that Maker's Mark, Jim Beam, Heaven Hill, Woodford Reserve, Wild Turkey, and Four Roses are all bottled nearby.

The Talbott bar, of course, serves all of these local potables, but the real culinary claim to fame hereabouts is another locally inspired offering: Hot Brown. Simply described, the dish is an open-faced hot turkey and ham sandwich smothered in cheese sauce and topped with bacon and tomato (or pimientos). It was invented in the early 1920s by the chef at the Brown Hotel in Louisville for customers attending supper dances at the hotel. Most Kentucky restaurants to this day offer up some form of Hot Brown.

The chefs here do themselves and this historic dish proud. Other menu favorites include the fried chicken (it takes forty-five minutes to cook from scratch—but it's worth every minute), fried green tomatoes in a beer batter, country-fried ham with red-eye gravy, and Chicken Phillipe (a boneless breast braised in Burgundy).

Sitting in the original tavern with its thick walls and huge beams, you quickly come to understand how it has survived for more than two centuries as you dine in front of a fireplace that was once used to cook all the meals served here. The food is hearty and satisfying, and the historic atmosphere is irreplaceable.

Acme Oyster House
NEW ORLEANS, LA ~ EST. 1910

In 1910, things were hopping in the French Quarter, and a new restaurant opened on Royal Street specializing in raw oysters at very low prices. The Acme Café lasted fourteen years before the building, which also housed the Acme Saloon, burned to the ground. The following year, the café reopened as the Acme Oyster House just around the corner on Iberville Street, where it sits proudly today.

Not a lot is known about the several decades that followed, other than the place survived Prohibition not only because of its extremely cheap and abundant raw oysters but also due to a bit of chicanery that somehow brought beer and alcohol into the restaurant through a back cellar door. At the time, very few restaurants bothered to cook oysters, since customers preferred the shellfish raw anyway,

on the half-shell with a shot of hot sauce or in a shot glass.

The restaurant puttered along during the fifties and sixties even though attempts to integrate the city schools drove a fair number of whites and educated black families from the central neighborhoods to the suburbs. Hurricane Camille tore through the city in 1969, but the Oyster House was spared and continued to do business, though suffering an economic downturn along with the rest of the city.

By the early 1980s, the restaurant was hurting and things were looking grim. They closed at 4 p.m. and had only one waitress, which prompted the Acme to post a "Waitress Available Sometimes" sign, warning customers not to expect great service. The sign still elicits laughter today, hanging front and center in the main dining area.

New Orleans native Mike Rodrigue brought the place back to life when he purchased it in 1985. He tried to keep much of the ambiance the same, employing the restaurant's red and white tablecloths, lots of bright neon signs, and, of course, serving what many consider the best oysters in town. Even Hurricane Katrina didn't stop the flow of bivalves coming into the restaurant, as Mike had such long-standing contracts with local oystermen that he got first choice of their wares when other restaurants went oysterless.

In addition to a very popular raw oyster bar in the dining room, the Acme has made a special effort to promote grilled oysters, with many customers ordering "half and half" and getting either a half or full dozen each of "fresh, iced" and "char-grilled" oysters. I tried the hot and cold combo, and much preferred the grilled in their tangy buttery sauce—that is, until I slurped down several icy cold, salty raw ones. Both were at the top of their game.

The interior of the Acme is bathed in an eerie yet playful red and blue tint because of the plethora of neon signs plastering the walls. One of the most popular signs, one of the only ones not lit by neon, is the Wall of Fame, which lists members of the 15 Dozen Club. You guessed it, these are folks who have downed fifteen dozen oysters at one sitting, including Man vs. Food host Adam Richman. But they are all pikers compared to the three superstars listed who have consumed 32, 34, and 42 dozen! The Acme also hosts a World Oyster Championship during the French Quarter Festival, a contest sanctioned by the International Federation of Competitive Oysters. The world record is held by Sonia "Black Widow" Thomas, who ate 46 dozen oysters (that's 552 shellfish) in ten minutes—almost an oyster a second.

Over the years, the Acme has also made a name for itself serving other shellfish and seafood dishes. If oysters or shrimp aren't your thing, you can select from a wide variety of its locally and nationally acclaimed po'boys: catfish, crawfish tail, ham, turkey, sausage, marinated chicken, or hamburger. The Acme's most famous meal on a roll is the 10 Napkin Roast Beef. This chuck roast sandwich earned its name because of the amount of juice it drips all over everything. Messy, sure, but you won't go away hungry. Their Fried Peace Maker Po-boy is a humongous roll overflowing with fried oysters, fried shrimp, lettuce, pickles, and tomato, smeared with a Tabasco-infused mayonnaise. You can hardly get your mouth around it. The crisp breading on the seafood is a nice counter to the tender insides.

They also serve various fried fish, gumbos, rice and beans, and other staples of the region and have received rave reviews for their fried soft-shell crab, either as an entree plate or yet another variety of po'boy. The golden-battered crabs look delicious, and tend to elicit moans and groans from those who order them.

Left: The chef prepares fried soft-shell crab. Above: Acme's signature shrimp and oyster Po'Boy.

Char-Grilled Oysters

∽ SERVES 5 TO 6 AS AN APPETIZER ∽

CHAR-GRILLED BUTTER

2 pounds unsalted butter

¼ cup freshly squeezed lemon juice

2 tablespoons Worcestershire sauce

2 bunches green onions, finely chopped,
   including green parts

20 cloves garlic, minced

2 teaspoons red pepper flakes

3 tablespoons minced fresh thyme

3 tablespoons minced fresh oregano

2 tablespoons Creole seasoning

3 ounces (about ⅓ cup) sauvignon blanc wine

3 to 4 dozen oysters of choice on the half shell

½ cup grated pecorino Romano cheese (Do not
   substitute another cheese.)

French bread and lemon wedges, for serving

For the butter: Mix all the ingredients in a large bowl
and blend with a whisk until thoroughly mixed. Keep at
room temperature to use.

Prepare a hot fire in a charcoal grill, or preheat a gas grill
to high. Place the oysters on the grill and heat until the
oysters release their liquor. Using tongs, tip each shell to
empty the liquor from the shell.

Put a heaping tablespoonful of the char-grilled butter on
top of each oyster. Cook until the rim of the shells turn
light brown. Sprinkle with the cheese and cook for 30
seconds. Transfer the oysters to plates, top with a little
more char-grilled butter, and serve at once, with French
bread and lemon wedges.

This recipe makes much more char-grilled butter than you
need, but the remainder can be stored in the refrigerator for
up to 1 week, and it's great on any other type of seafood.

Today, the Acme is one of the most respected
and popular seafood restaurants in the Quarter,
and it definitely has more than one waitress. In
fact, half a dozen are in a constant flow, as the
tables fill up promptly at 11:30 and remain that
way the rest of the day. Acme has expanded to
add restaurants in the nearby suburbs of Metairie
and Covington, as well as in Sandestin and Baton
Rouge. But the French Quarter restaurant is the
shining star in the Acme universe, winning seven
major awards for its seafood, oysters, and po'boys.

Unlike many of the city's older restaurants, the
Acme is not glitzy, fashionable, sophisticated, or
cultured, but it's just plain fun to visit. While you
can easily find a waitress now, she has to navigate
the dozens of packed tables, lines of waiting
customers, and the standing-room-only oyster bar
with your order. But be patient—it'll be worth it.

Antoine's
NEW ORLEANS, LA ~ EST. 1840

Antoine's has always been thought of as one of the restaurants that make the Big Easy one of the great dining cities of the world.

French immigrant chef Antoine Alciatore came to America in 1838 seeking his fortune like thousands of others, but after two years of living in New York City he moved to Louisiana, where he began working in the Hotel St. Charles kitchen. He soon rented a small building and opened Pension Alciatore, a small boardinghouse that included a restaurant. The twenty-seven-year-old spent the next five years building a reputation and, history tells us, a long list of satisfied customers.

At that time, Antoine brought his fiancée, Julie Freyss, whom he had met on the boat to America, to the Crescent City, where they were soon married

and began a partnership that lasted sixty-three years. The pension had become more restaurant than boardinghouse, and in 1898 they moved it to St. Louis Street, where it sits today. The couple developed the menu and further enhanced the pension's reputation as a fine restaurant. Sadly, in 1874 Antoine grew ill and returned to France alone, wanting to be buried on his native soil and not wanting his wife and family to see him deteriorate. He died a year later.

Julie brought her son, Jules, into the kitchen as an apprentice, teaching him techniques and recipes. When he was seventeen, she sent him to France to work in some of its best kitchens. After four years he came home, but Julie wanted him to get his initial restaurant experience elsewhere,

Antoine's, who brought Oysters Rockefeller and Baked Alaska to life, is one of New Orleans's finest restaurants.

so he worked as a chef at a private club until 1887, when his mother brought him back to take over the restaurant.

Under Jules's stewardship, Antoine's blossomed and firmly established a reputation as one of the finest restaurants in the city. Jules also is responsible for developing some of Antoine's most famous dishes—dishes that were copied by fine restaurants all over the world. You may have heard of many of them: eggs Sardou and pompano en papillote, and the most famous by far, oysters Rockefeller.

The dish was named after John D. Rockefeller but not intended to honor him. Jules thought that the green color of the dish was similar to "greenbacks" (dollars), and its ingredients were very rich. Since the Rockefeller name had been associated with the pinnacle of wealth, Jules used his name for his oyster dish. He first developed the recipe using snails (escargots), but they were in short supply in New Orleans, so he went looking for a local substitute and discovered that oysters suited the dish perfectly. He was one of the first chefs in America to cook oysters, since up until that time they were almost always consumed raw.

Since Jules swore his family to secrecy on his deathbed, to this day the exact recipe for this dish has never been revealed, and the only place you can enjoy true oysters Rockefeller is at Antoine's. Most attempts at duplicating the dish or recipe incorrectly use spinach as one of the main ingredients. Roy F. Guste, Jr., the fifth-generation owner, hints: "I will tell you only that the sauce is basically a purée of a number of green vegetables other than spinach." To date, Antoine's has served over 6 million orders of Oysters Rockefeller.

The restaurant itself is virtually a historical museum of New Orleans, Mardi Gras, and the Alciatore family. The fifteen dining rooms, some of them private, contain memorabilia, costumes, historic photographs and menus, antique kitchen tools, recipes and cookbooks, over two thousand autographs of distinguished visitors, and various family items and are a visual treasure trove of the history of the oldest family-run restaurant in America. By contrast, the main dining room is almost bare of decoration other than mirrors on the walls.

The menu, which has changed very little in the last fifty years, has been described as "Classic French Creole" and has always been published in French (English was added a few years ago). I sampled huitres en coquille à la Rockefeller, pommes de terre soufflés, filet de truite aux écrevisses cardinal, and omelette Alaska Antoine. Translation: Oysters Rockefeller, Puffed Double-Fried Potatoes, Trout with Crawfish, and Baked Alaska. Be advised though, that to order that artistic dessert they request twenty-four hours' notice.

Antoine's is also noted for its huge wine collection, stored in the most unusual wine cellar. It's about seven feet wide and 165 feet long, running along the back of the building, and contains over thirty-five thousand bottles, including an 1834 vintage, and a brandy that was bottled in 1811.

A splendid ending to a dinner at Antoine's is their signature Baked Alaska, frozen ice cream inside a baked cake and meringue shell.

Some interesting tidbits about Antoine's: Busboys must apprentice for ten years before they can become waiters. The Dungeon dining room functioned as a prison during the Spanish occupation of New Orleans. The private library contains over four hundred historic cookbooks, including several that are over two hundred years old and one that was written in 1659.

Antoine's finally published its own cookbook, with recipes for many of their classic Creole signature dishes, much to the delight of its fans and customers. But, true to form, author Roy Guste, Jr., left out the recipe for Oysters Rockefeller. You'll just have to go to Antoine's in person to try them.

Filet de Truite aux Écrevisses Cardinal
(FRIED TROUT WITH CRAWFISH TAILS IN A WHITE WINE SAUCE)

∽ SERVES 4 ∽

CRAYFISH CARDINAL

2 tablespoons unsalted butter, plus 1½ tablespoons

1½ tablespoons all-purpose flour

¼ cup minced fresh flat-leaf parsley

½ cup finely chopped green onion, including light green parts

½ cup finely chopped white onion

3 cloves garlic, minced

Pinch of dried thyme

Pinch of dried basil

2 tablespoons tomato paste

1 pound crayfish tails, steamed

6 to 8 tablespoons dry white wine

1 cup half-and-half

Salt and freshly ground white pepper

4 (7- to 9-ounce) speckled trout (brook trout) fillets, skin removed

Salt and freshly ground white pepper

Vegetable oil, for frying

Minced fresh flat-leaf parsley, for garnish

For the crayfish sauce: In a small saucepan, melt the 1½ tablespoons butter over medium-low heat. Stir in the flour and cook, stirring constantly, for 3 minutes; do not brown. Set the roux aside.

In a medium saucepan, melt the 2 tablespoons butter over medium heat and sauté the parsley, green onion, white onion, and garlic until the onion is translucent, about 3 minutes. Stir in the thyme, basil, and tomato paste, then add the crayfish. Cook for 2 to 3 minutes. Add the white wine and cook for 2 minutes. Stir in the roux and half-and-half. Simmer until lightly thickened. Add salt and pepper to taste. Set aside and keep warm.

Rub the fillets on both sides with salt and white pepper. Heat a large, heavy skillet over medium heat and film with oil. Add the fillets and cook for 3 to 6 minutes, then turn and cook another 3 to 5 minutes on the second side, or until the flesh is opaque throughout.

Place a fillet in the center of each warmed plate and top with the crayfish sauce. Garnish with parsley and serve at once.

Commander's Palace
NEW ORLEANS, LA ~ EST. 1880

The location of this New Orleans icon, far from the bustling and traffic-jammed French Quarter, is a large part of its charm. It sits on a corner in the upscale and historic Garden District, a residential neighborhood of Greek Revival homes, distinguished families, and more wrought-iron fences than just about anywhere on earth.

It also happens to be across the street from Lafayette Cemetery No. 1, the Big Easy's most famous graveyard, which is populated by many blue-blooded former residents. The proximity has prompted many a ghost tale of silverware being moved, mysterious footsteps in empty rooms, and lights being turned on and off by unseen hands in the restaurant. It's claimed that spirits on the second floor have helped themselves to unattended glasses of wine or liquor (spirits, if you will) on a few occasions.

The menu at Commander's Palace was never French like those of so many other restaurants in New Orleans. It was instead a delightful mix of Southern, Creole, and Cajun. The ground-floor restaurant was well known for the quality of its food, and also for its upscale ambiance. It was a local favorite for fancy Sunday brunches after church and for family celebrations, and by 1900 was attracting gourmets from all over the world. The upstairs was popular as well. These rooms were set aside for prostitution and gambling and were frequented by wealthy gentlemen, riverboat captains, and "sporting gentlemen" from the Garden District who took advantage of a private setting for clandestine meetings with working girls or mistresses.

The restaurant was sold in 1944 and continued to build its reputation as one of the best restaurants in New Orleans. In 1974, the Brennan family, who own a dozen bistros, steakhouses, and cafe's in the city, purchased Commander's Palace and completely refurbished the ninety-six-year-old building, opening up rooms, installing glass walls, commissioning paintings, redecorating every room, and completely redesigning and updating the kitchen.

Through the years, the Palace has remained one of the most highly regarded restaurants in a city chock a block with great eating places, specializing in what some call haute Creole cuisine, a blend of Cajun, Creole, and American cooking styles and recipes, some passed down from its early days and the rest developed by chefs like Paul Prudhomme and Emeril Lagasse, both of whom later became legends of American cooking. Chef Tory McPhail, who champions a "from dirt to plate within one hundred miles" philosophy, will undoubtedly one day have the same name recognition as his predecessors.

Chef Tory McPhail prepares his wondrous Foie Gras appetizer.

A favorite room is the second-floor Garden Room, one wall of which is made up of floor-to-ceiling windows overlooking a patio shaded by historic oak trees (some of which were severely damaged by Hurricane Katrina). It's the largest and most popular room at the Palace, especially for spring and summer brunches, and is often the first room of the three large dining rooms to fill up. Other dining rooms include the open-air Patio Room on the ground floor, the main dining room with its chandeliers, and several smaller private dining rooms on the second floor. A small brass band often wanders through the tables, playing New Orleans jazz.

One of the most visually stunning dishes I have ever seen is Foie Gras 2 Ways, an artistic plate containing both seared and poached Hudson Valley foie gras with spring berry beignets, pecan brittle, and blackberry jam, served alongside a demitasse of chicory coffee, with foie gras–infused whipped cream. The range of textures and the mix of tart, sweet, savory, and bitter flavors was amazing, making it truly a complex and creative appetizer.

The Black Skillet Seared Wild Fish is a large, crusty fillet accompanied with a hearty selection of spring vegetables, topped with char-grilled Meyer lemons, fresh herbs, and a brown butter vinaigrette. It was perfectly cooked, with a slight crunch outside and a moist tender inside. The blackened seasonings nicely accented the mild fish and the piquant butter sauce.

And then there is dessert. Their signature dessert is Creole Bread Pudding Soufflé, with warm whiskey cream. But it's so difficult to choose between that and a huge portion of strawberry shortcake with fresh whipped cream, and vanilla bean ice cream with a honey tuile, Chantilly cream, pecans, and praline syrup. Or how about the most creative crème brûlée I've ever seen, with scorched local sugarcane and a confectioners' sugar "fleur-de-lis"?

The kitchen is as immaculate as the dining rooms. Often, the "back of the house" at even some of the better restaurants is less than spic and span, but the Commander's Palace kitchen is so clean you could eat there. In fact, they have a chef's table right on the edge of the action, so you can watch soufflés being baked, fish being sautéed, garlic bread being dipped, salads being constructed, and soups simmering. I highly recommend asking the host or hostess if the chef's table is available when you call for a reservation. It will be one of the most fascinating lunches, brunches, or dinners you'll ever enjoy.

No matter where you sit, what you order, or whether you visit the Palace for lunch, brunch, or dinners you will come away with memories of gracious, efficient, and cheerful service and impeccably prepared food that you will talk about for years.

Bread Pudding Soufflé with Whiskey Sauce

∽ SERVES 6 ∽

BREAD PUDDING

¾ cup sugar

1 teaspoon ground cinnamon

Pinch of ground nutmeg

3 large eggs

1 cup heavy cream

1 teaspoon vanilla extract

5 cups 1-inch cubed French bread
(see Note)

⅓ cup raisins

WHISKEY SAUCE

1 cup heavy cream

½ tablespoon cornstarch

1 tablespoon water

3 tablespoons sugar

¼ cup bourbon

MERINGUE

9 large egg whites

¼ teaspoon cream of tartar

¾ cup sugar

For the bread pudding: Preheat the oven to 350°F and butter an 8-inch square baking pan. Combine the sugar, cinnamon, and nutmeg in a large bowl and stir to blend. Add the eggs and whisk until smooth, then whisk in the cream. Add the vanilla, then the bread cubes. Set aside to let the bread soak up the custard for 15 to 20 minutes, until all the liquid is absorbed.

Spread the raisins in the prepared pan and pour in the bread mixture. Bake for 25 to 30 minutes, until the pudding is golden brown and a toothpick inserted in the center comes out clean. Let cool to room temperature.

For the whiskey sauce: Place the cream in a small saucepan and bring to a boil over medium heat. In a small bowl, whisk the cornstarch and water together and whisk into the cream. Bring to a boil, taking care not to burn the mixture at the bottom. Whisk just until thickened. Remove from the heat. Stir in the sugar and bourbon. Let cool to room temperature.

To make the meringue: Preheat the oven to 350°F and butter six 6-ounce ramekins. In a clean large bowl with a clean whisk or beaters, beat the egg whites and cream of tartar until foamy. Gradually beat in the sugar and continue beating until stiff, glossy peaks form. Do not overbeat.

In a large bowl, break half the bread pudding into pieces using your hands or a spoon. Gently fold in one-quarter of the meringue. Divide this mixture among the prepared ramekins.

Place the remaining bread pudding in the bowl, break into pieces, and carefully fold in the rest of the meringue. Top the soufflés with this lighter mixture, leaving a 1½-inch gap at the top. Using a teaspoon, smooth and shape each soufflé into a dome rising above the ramekin rim. Immediately bake for 20 minutes, or until golden brown. Serve immediately. Using a spoon, poke a hole in the top of each soufflé at the table, and pour some of the whiskey sauce into the soufflé.

NOTE: New Orleans French bread is very light and tender. If bread is used that is too dense, it will soak up all the custard and the recipe won't work. You can substitute brioche, challah, or sweet Hawaiian bread.

Galatoire's
NEW ORLEANS, LA ~ EST. 1905

Waiters (from left) Charles Grimaldi, Imre Szalai, and Dorris Sylvester have welcomed guests to
Galatoire's for a combined 99 years.

For over a century, people in all walks of life, from senators to traveling salesmen, have stood in line in front of 209 Bourbon Street without reservations. Literally. There were no reservations at Galatoire's. Everyone was seated on a first-come, first-serve basis. And when the dining room was full, people stood in line and waited, sometimes for more than an hour, for the chance to experience one of America's finest restaurants. Not accepting reservations is not the norm at four-star restaurants, but Galatoire's clung to this tradition for more than ten decades until 2011, when they finally began accepting reservations—for the second floor only. To anyone who has dined there, that's like consigning you to eat with a busload of tourists in upper Siberia. The downstairs main floor, where all the action is and probably always will

be, is still seated on a first-come, first-served basis.

People don't mind waiting, because Galatoire's has captivated locals and visitors alike with its classic dishes, calm ambiance, and consistently great meals. As one regular customer told *Saveur* magazine, "It's another world, a place where you can go and know that things will never change." Those words would delight the restaurant's founder, Jean Galatoire, who brought gracious dining to the Crescent City from his small village of Pau, France. His philosophy was "copious portions of excellent food, very potent and generous cocktails, and great service."

Gourmet magazine named Galatoire's the number-one restaurant in New Orleans and one of the top twenty-five in America, joining the *New York Times, Los Angeles Times, USA Today,*

Food & Wine, *Zagat Survey*, *Condé Nast Traveler*, and *Bon Appétit*, all of whom have cited this eatery for excellence. In 2005, it received the James Beard Award for Outstanding Restaurant of the Year.

The restaurant purposefully has nothing hanging on the walls except mirrors. "We want people to see everyone enjoying themselves. We also don't have piped-in music; we want our customers to hear conversations, laughter, and people having a great time," says COO Melvin Rodrigue. "Five generations of customers have dined here, knowing that when they ask for a special dish they've ordered on twenty-three previous visits that it will taste just the same every time, so we don't change our classics."

Their mantra, "Indulge in Tradition," is a promise made to everyone who dines here. And a big part of Galatoire's tradition centers on their loyal and popular staff. The average waiter has been here for fifteen years, and fully one-half of them have served more than twenty-five years. "Because of that longevity, we encourage customers to ask for a favorite waiter, and they do," Melvin says. "Many of our staff have a long list of people who

not only ask for them but make sure to schedule their visits on days when they are working."

Lunch, especially on Friday, the day everyone wants to eat here, can stretch from morning to dinnertime. Only at Galatoire's do four to five hours seem to pass more quickly than a riverboat. Promptly at 11:30 a.m., Melvin opens the doors to the dining room, and regulars are ushered to their favorite tables, where many don't even ask for a menu, relying on "their" waiter for advice on what to order.

Following in their forksteps, I asked Imre, a dashing waiter who's been here for thirty-five years, what I should have, and he said that the classic Trout Meunière Amandine looked particularly fetching that day and suggested I add a basket of their signature Soufflé Potatoes with Hollandaise Sauce. He reappeared bearing my lunch quicker than that riverboat could blow its whistle three times. And after tasting one crisp souffléd potato and one forkful of golden fillet, I was happy that Jean Galatoire's insistence on "copious portions of excellent food" had survived intact for more than a century. The fillet, which fills the plate, is tender, perfectly cooked, and wears a gentle and sweet mantel of buttery sauce sprinkled with toasted sliced almonds. The potatoes, which look like a basket of ballooned potato chips, are crunchy, dusted with a light touch of salt, and are super when dipped in the hollandaise.

Executive chef Brian Landry, who came to New Orleans after a short stint at Galatoire's Bistro in Baton Rouge, has worked in the restaurant business in New Orleans since he was fifteen. Now he oversees five line cooks and two prep cooks per shift in the main kitchen, and four cooks and one prep cook in the second-floor kitchen. When asked about the potential for boredom in re-creating one-hundred-year-old recipes, he is philosophical. "My job is to give the customers the quality dishes they want. We love them having favorites. And we have so many private events

Many clubs and organizations, often in costume, begin Mardi Gras celebrations with lunches here. Below right: A basket of their iconic "soufflé potatoes."

Jean Galatoire came from France to open what many call one of the best restaurants in America.

Trout Meunière Amandine

❧ SERVES 6 ❧

MEUNIÈRE BUTTER

2 cups (4 sticks) salted butter

1 tablespoon freshly squeezed lemon juice

1 tablespoon red wine vinegar

3 cups (12 ounces) sliced almonds

2 large eggs

2 cups whole milk

6 (7- to 8-ounce) speckled trout (brook trout) or redfish fillets

Salt and freshly ground black pepper

2 cups all-purpose flour

1 gallon vegetable oil

3 lemons, cut into wedges

Preheat the oven to 350°F.

For the meunière butter: In a medium saucepan, melt the salted butter over medium heat, whisking constantly, for 8 to 10 minutes, until the sediment in the butter turns dark brown and the liquid is a deep golden color. Remove from the heat and gradually whisk in the lemon juice and vinegar. The sauce will froth until the acids are evaporated. When the frothing subsides, set the sauce aside and keep warm.

Spread the almonds in a rimmed baking sheet and toast them in the oven, stirring every 5 minutes for 10 to 15 minutes, until they are a light golden brown. Remove from the oven and set aside.

In a shallow bowl, make an egg wash by whisking the eggs and milk together. Season the trout fillets with salt and pepper and dust with flour. Submerge the floured trout in the egg wash. Using a slotted spatula, gently remove the fillets from the egg wash and allow the excess to drip off. Coat the fillets in the flour again, then gently shake off the excess flour.

In a Dutch oven or deep fryer, heat the oil to 350°F on a deep-fat thermometer, or test the readiness of the oil by sprinkling a pinch of flour over it; the flour will brown instantly when the oil has reached the correct temperature. Add the trout and fry for 4 to 5 minutes, or until golden brown.

Top each fried trout fillet with toasted almonds and the warm meunière butter. Garnish with the lemon wedges and serve at once.

that I get to try lots of new dishes and recipes at those."

As I was leaving I noticed that, true to form, two large tables, whose occupants had been seated the same time as I was five hours earlier, were still enjoying some of those potent potables and copious portions as we were nearing the dinner hour. I guess they took the "Indulge in Tradition" mantra quite seriously.

Tujague's
NEW ORLEANS, LA ~ EST. 1856

In 155 years, Tujague's (pronounced two-jacks) has never missed serving a meal. When the restaurant was occupied by Northern troops during the Civil War, it kept dishing up lunch, and when Hurricane Katrina wrecked much of the city the kitchen kept busy pumping out food for locals and the few brave tourists who ventured into the French Quarter.

As the Big Easy's second-oldest restaurant (Antoine's is the oldest), Tujague's is indeed one of the grande dames of American restaurants and has never forgotten its heritage, still serving several dishes that were originated in the mid-1850s by founders Guillaume and Marie Tujague.

Guillaume came to New Orleans from France to open a butcher shop, but after three years moved across the street from the French Market to open a restaurant. He served hearty breakfasts and a seven-course lunch to a ragtag bunch of dockworkers, market laborers, merchants, and sailors from the nearby waterfront. Two of the most popular dishes were the cold shrimp covered with rémoulade sauce and a tender boiled brisket with a tomato-horseradish sauce. Both are still on the six-course table d'hôte menu Tujague's serves today.

In the 1860s, Guillaume's main competition was Begue's, but that competition ended after both owners died and the two restaurants merged forces. Tujague's moved three doors down to replace Begue's at the corner of Decatur and Madison, where the restaurant

From left: Waiter Hugo Cabrera, Chef Rhett Byrd, and waiter Enio Raquel display the very, very, very garlicky Chicken Bonne Femme on the balcony of the restaurant.

stands today. Part of its charm is the saloon next door, with a soaring mirror imported from Paris in 1913 and a historic standing cypress bar Guillaume brought when he opened the restaurant. Steven Latter, who bought the restaurant in 1982, has carefully restored the restaurant and covered the walls with clippings, photographs, and other memorabilia to celebrate its history.

The saloon, rated one of the Quarter's best, is manned by one of the most charming icons of bartenderdom you'll ever meet; Paul Gustings. Paul, in his starched white shirt, dark vest, and bright scarlet bow tie, looks as if he was sent to the bar by central casting, but he's been serving Sazeracs and Hurricanes for the past seventeen years. He loves to share stories of famous guests and the century-and-a-half history of the bar with comments such as, "It's amazing to note that during Prohibition we couldn't serve liquor, but somehow managed to employ three bartenders."

The main dining room on the ground floor is small—three tables wide and five tables long—but there's another one at the back of the restaurant, and one large and two very small dining rooms on the second floor that are usually set aside for special parties and events. Also on that floor is a delightful wide balcony overlooking the historic French Market and bustling Decatur Street, a favorite spot for after-dinner drinks on warm summer evenings. The eclectically decorated main-floor dining rooms, and part of the bar itself, are adorned with shelves displaying five thousand miniature liquor and liqueur bottles, one of the largest collections in the country.

Tujague's is one of the only restaurants in the French Quarter to present a table d'hôte (fixed-price) menu. There are four choices for the entree, which change daily. There is

Bartender Paul Gustings has seen it all after 17 years behind the bar, and has many a tall tale to share about the history of Tujague's and the French Quarter.

Chicken Bonne Femme

∾ SERVES 4 TO 6 ∾

Vegetable oil, for deep-frying

1 (3- to 4-pound) chicken, cut into 8 pieces

3 tablespoons salt

3 tablespoons freshly ground black pepper

3 tablespoons garlic powder

3 large baking potatoes, unpeeled, thinly sliced

1 pound garlic, peeled and minced

2 bunches fresh flat-leaf parsley, stemmed and minced

In a large cast-iron skillet or pot, heat 2 inches of oil to 325°F on a deep-fat thermometer. Rub the chicken with the salt, pepper, and garlic powder. In 2 batches, fry the chicken pieces, skin side down, for 10 minutes, then turn and fry on the second side until golden brown. Using tongs, transfer the chicken to paper towels to drain. Set aside and keep warm. Add the potatoes to the hot oil and cook until crisp and lightly browned. Using a wire-mesh skimmer, transfer to paper towels to drain.

In a large bowl, combine the chicken and fried potatoes. Mix the fresh garlic and parsley together and sprinkle over the chicken. Stir gently to combine. Immediately serve on a large platter with plenty of napkins (and perhaps a handful of breath mints).

always filet mignon, plus two seafood and one non-seafood selections. The evening I was there, they were offering New Orleans–style barbecued shrimp, blackened redfish, and roasted pork loin with pecan rice along with the filet. The other courses were shrimp rémoulade, corn and crab soup (the soup of the day), beef brisket in Creole sauce, and pecan pie for dessert.

One dish you don't see on the menu, but which locals order with abandon, is the Chicken Bonne Femme, a golden pile of fried chicken and fried potatoes spinkled with garlic and parsley. It is the strongest garlic dish I've ever experienced and is definitely for garlic-lovers only.

The dishes here have been described as "nineteenth-century blue plate specials," and it's true that the offerings are simple, without any culinary frills. This unpretentious place could best be described as a New Orleans neighborhood restaurant. Folks have been coming here for decades because it has good food and a pleasant atmosphere, with all the charm of one of the oldest restaurants in the historic French Quarter.

Pleasant Point Inn
CENTER LOVELL, ME ~ EST. 1911

The history of Pleasant Point Inn has all the adventure and intrigue of a James Fenimore Cooper novel. The inn began when John and Sarah Farrington moved to the small town of Center Lovell in 1888 and turned the home they had purchased into the Lakeview Hotel. It was described as having a wide veranda on three sides, a barn behind it, "good stone steps," and accommodations for twenty guests, who could hike, swim, fish, and canoe in nearby Kezar Lake and were also taken on hayrides by John. Some days, he would fill the wagon with guests, pack in lunches, and head off for an all-day adventure.

The lake, one of the state's most revered, was named after the first white man known to inhabit the pinewoods there, George Ebenezer

Kezar. He became a local legend in the mid-1700s when he shot a large black bear in the head with his rifle, then went up to cut its throat with a small penknife to bleed it out. But the bear wasn't dead, merely stunned by the lead ball, and rose up, attacking him. According to legend, George grabbed the bear's tongue with one hand and kept stabbing the animal until it bled to death. He lost the arm that he had stuck in the bear's mouth, but he survived.

In 1911, John and Peggy's son, William, who had grown up in the Lakeview and helped his parents with various chores around the hotel, bought a farm on the shore of the lake and, with his father's help, built the Farrington Hotel. The Lakeview had turned into a boardinghouse, so he continued in the family business with his new establishment.

William named the hotel after his great-grandfather John, who had his own interesting life story. At ten, he had been kidnapped by members of the Passamaquoddy Indian tribe and grew up in their village. He managed to escape his captors several years later when the tribe made its annual pilgrimage to Quebec to trade. Young John ran away and approached some English soldiers, telling them his story, and was ransomed from the tribe by a merchant who paid $80 (a fortune at that time) to free him. He spent the next eight months in his service until he'd worked off his debt, then came back to Maine to live in the woods near the lake.

When William built the new hotel on the lakefront, he also began building a tent and cabin colony, which became a very popular and inexpensive place for tourists who were beginning to discover the area. The main hotel

The Pleasant Point Inn began life as the Farrington Hotel, then as the Lakeview Hotel and once had 23 bedrooms, which could house 90 people; today they offer 8 rooms and 2 large family suites.

included twenty-three sleeping rooms, and the hotel promised in early literature to "give the same service to tents as rooms in the hotel." Every year for the next five years, William added a new cabin until the resort could house ninety guests. In summer, guests arrived by train and were picked up in Fryeburg by William in his horse and buggy. In winter, they were brought to the hotel by horse-drawn sleigh.

After a number of owners kept the place running smoothly, time, brutal winter storms, and a hundred years of vacationing families began taking a toll. The inn was completely renovated and modernized. In the Main Lodge, there are now eight luxurious rooms and two large suites. On the first floor there's a relaxing lounge area that includes a fireplace, comfy couches, and large windows that afford a breathtaking view of the lake and the Presidential Mountain Range. While the inn no longer owns the cottages on its property, it does act as a leasing agent.

The large dining room overlooks the wide expanse of lawn that leads down to six hundred feet of private beach—a favorite spot for parties and wedding receptions. As with many resorts, the menus are seasonal and change according to what is available from local farms. When I visited, chef Marck Kurnick suggested Mediterranean Filet Mignon, an ample steak surrounded by artichoke hearts, kalamata olives, sun-dried tomatoes, crumbled feta cheese, and a Madeira wine reduction sauce. Out of the bevy of fresh fruit pies, I chose Pleasant Point's scrumptious Maine wild blueberry pie.

After dinner, the wide front porch and private screened-in gazebo are perfect places to just sit, enjoy the lake view, read a book, or play a game of checkers or backgammon. You can also take advantage of the canoes for early-morning paddles across the usually tranquil lake or romantic sojourns on warm and moonlight nights. If you are lucky, you might get to hear one of nature's most haunting sounds: the plaintive call of the northern loon. I did, and the chills are still running up my spine.

Mediterranean Filet Mignon

∽ SERVES 4 ∽

4 (6-ounce) center-cut filet mignon steaks

2 cups (10 ounces) crumbled feta cheese

3 to 4 oil-packed sun-dried tomatoes, drained and finely chopped

¼ to ⅓ cup kalamata olives, pitted and chopped, plus 6 pitted and halved olives, for garnish

1 tablespoon dried oregano

¼ cup extra-virgin olive oil, plus more for rubbing

Kosher salt and freshly ground mixed peppercorns

2 heaping tablespoons minced shallots

1½ cups Madeira or port wine

1 cup veal or beef demi-glace

6 to 8 whole canned tomatoes, coarsely chopped

12 thawed frozen or canned artichoke hearts

4 sprigs fresh oregano or minced fresh flat-leaf parsley, for garnish

Preheat the oven to 450°F. With a sharp paring knife, cut a slit in the side of each steak just large enough to insert a finger. Being careful to not pierce through an opposite side, hollow out each steak to make a pocket for stuffing.

In a medium bowl, combine the feta, sun-dried tomatoes, olives, and oregano. Stir gently to blend. Using a teaspoon, stuff each filet with as much of the feta mixture as it will hold without splitting (3 to 4 teaspoons). Rub each stuffed filet with olive oil and season with salt and pepper. Cover and refrigerate for at least 1 hour or up to overnight.

In a large nonreactive skillet (don't use a nonstick pan), heat the ¼ cup olive oil over medium-high heat until shimmering. Add the filets and cook for about 3 minutes on each side. Using tongs, transfer the filets to a roasting pan, reserving the skillet, and roast for 6 to 7 minutes for medium-rare. Remove from the oven and set aside; keep warm.

While the filets are roasting, start the sauce: Heat the oil remaining in the reserved skillet over medium heat and sauté the shallots for 3 minutes, or until translucent. Stir in the Madiera and stir to scrape up the browned bits from the bottom of the pan. Add the demi-glace and cook until reduced by half. Gently stir in the tomatoes and artichoke hearts. Bring the sauce to a simmer and remove from the heat. Taste and adjust the seasoning.

Place a filet in the center of each plate and ladle the sauce over and around it. Arrange a few artichoke quarters or halves and tomato pieces around each filet. Garnish each plate with 3 olive halves and a sprig of oregano or a sprinkle of parsley.

The Casselman Inn
GRANTSVILLE, MD ~ EST. 1842

The Casselman Inn began in 1842 as Drover's Inn, a resting spot for stagecoach passengers and for drovers who drove cattle, sheep, geese and even turkeys to the big-city markets in the east. The inn's large pens and corrals, good hot meals, and real beds made it the most popular lodging on the National Trail, the road first traversed by Native Americans, then later by British General Braddock for a march and battle at Ft. Duquesne.

From 1818, the road carried hundreds of thousands of pioneers and settlers in stagecoaches and covered wagons. An 1879 article in *Harper's Monthly* described the wagons as "so numerous that the leaders of one team had their noses in the trough at the end of the next wagon ahead. There would be thirty six-horse teams, one hundred Kentucky mules, and one thousand hogs and as many fat cattle on the trails or in fields alongside the highway."

Grantsville (pop. 615) was right on the National Trail, which became Highway 40. Today, it skirts the town by following I-68, though the original trail still runs through town as Alt. U.S. 40. The road bisects the grand forested peaks and valleys of the Appalachian Mountains. This upper northwest corner of the state is often referred to as the heart of Maryland's last frontier, for the surrounding hills are wild and rugged. There once was coal mining there, but that petered out. Mining was followed by lumbering, but that slowed to a crawl along with the economic fortunes of the area. But the Casselman Inn still serves the community, as the majority of their restaurant guests are locals.

Their Friday-night and Saturday-morning buffets are affordable and extremely popular. Bill Maust, who has lived and worked at the inn for forty-four years, says that on those two days they feed from six hundred to seven hundred people a day. In the summer months, tourists stop as well, especially since it's the only restaurant in town, but most of the regulars live within ten miles.

Over its 150-plus-year history, the hostelry has undergone many changes, starting with the addition of a larger kitchen in 1903, and a dining room, antiques shop, and bakery in 1973. The bakery provides all the pastries, breads, rolls, cakes, pies, and coffee cakes for the restaurant and sells to customers either from its lobby display or the basement bakery.

The inn has a large two-room suite and two other rooms available, plus a separate forty-unit motel. The floors and much of the woodwork in the inn were hand-hewn from local timbers, and even the bricks were hand-formed and baked on the property. The restaurant itself comprises the original small dining room in the oldest part of the inn, and the substantially larger dining room that was added in 1973. The popular Friday-night and Saturday-morning buffet dinners are served there.

If you want to order from the menu, you can choose the same entrees that are part of the buffet, along with bakery bread, a garden salad, and two side dishes. But the buffet is all-you-can eat and includes a dessert buffet (both for dinner and breakfast). The meals and serving style are not four- or five-star gourmet, but this is the kind of comfort food your grandmother served (if she was a good cook): fried chicken, beef stew, grilled ham, breaded fish fillets, roast beef, and meat loaf, which share the steam table with green beans, succotash, mashed potatoes, home fries, and baked beans.

Both dining rooms were filled for all of the meals I enjoyed there, and a line of hungry folks waited in the lobby next to the display of freshly baked goods.

The exterior of the Inn has changed very little since its early days. Here, a photo of the Inn and guests from the early 1900s.

Pumpkin Bread

∽ MAKES 2 LOAVES ∽

4 cups pumpkin puree

6 cups sugar

8 large eggs

2 teaspoons ground nutmeg

2 teaspoons ground cloves

1 tablespoon ground cinnamon

1 tablespoon salt

1 tablespoon plus
  1 teaspoon
  baking soda

1 cup hot water

2 cups canola oil

7 cups all-purpose flour

2 cups chopped or
  crushed walnuts

Unsalted butter,
  for serving

Preheat the oven to 350°F. Butter two 9 by 5-inch loaf pans.

In a large bowl, combine all the ingredients except the butter for serving and stir to blend well. Pour the batter into the prepared pans and tap them on the counter to remove any air bubbles.

Bake for 45 minutes, or until a knife inserted in the center of a loaf comes out clean. Remove from the oven, let cool for 5 minutes, then unmold. Cut into slices and serve warm, with lots of unsalted butter.

During a lull in the buffet line, I filled my plate with sliced ham, green beans, and succotash, and added a garden salad and several slices of their still-warm-from-the-bakery bread. And although a stranger, I was made to feel most welcome in the crowded dining room, filled with families. It was as if I'd eaten there for years.

I left the Casselman Inn with a full tummy and a warm feeling, somewhat enhanced, I believe, by the freshly baked loaf of raisin bread I purchased as I paid my bill at the register. Clever folks these. And darn good bread.

Bakers (from left): Heather Brova, Marcia Brenneman, and Christi Orendorf make all the restaurant's breads, pies, cakes, cookies, and other baked goods in the downstairs bakery.

"The Boys" (from left front, clockwise): Ralph "Reb" Beagle, Ed Miller, Jim Yoder, Jim Walker, and Jim Wengerd, have all gathered here for breakfast every day for 40 years, always sitting at the same table.

Middleton Tavern
ANNAPOLIS, MD ~ EST. 1750

In 1750, Horatio Middleton bought a home in Annapolis, Maryland, from Elizabeth Bennett. It was described in early papers as "a three-story brick structure, with a simple, balanced appearance that gives an impression of order and stability, true to the Georgian style." Its appearance is still the same, and it's still in use more than 270 years later.

Horatio was a ferry operator and under the laws of the day had to provide lodging for his customers. His ferry took folks from Annapolis to Baltimore in the north, and from Rock Hall to the eastern shore, thus saving many hours of travel for people wanting to cross Chesapeake Bay. After he purchased Elizabeth's home, he turned the ground floor into a popular tavern and the upper floor into an "Inn for Seafaring Men." He also gussied up the place with a beautiful garden that stretched several hundred yards down to the waterfront.

After he died, his wife, Anne, and then his son, Samuel, continued to run both the tavern and the ferry, as well as a shipbuilding and overseas trading company. During the Revolutionary War, innkeeper George Mann hosted notables such as Benjamin Franklin, Thomas Jefferson, and George Washington, who tarried a while at the tavern and stayed overnight before leaving on the ferry.

Taverns in those days were much more than just eating, drinking, and sleeping places. While sipping rum or Cognac or a local brew by the fireplace, men would catch up on news of the outside world, air political viewpoints, discuss their families, and share good times.

George Washington is reported to have lost a fair amount of money playing whist (sort of an early version of bridge) here with the boys.

When the Continental Congress met at the Maryland State House down the street, many of those enlightened, well-educated gentlemen took their meals and a few mulled wines or grogs (rum and water) here as well. The provisions must have stood them well, as the Ratification of the Treaty of Paris, which ended the Revolutionary War, was signed in the State House, and the convention that planned the Federal Constitutional Convention in Philadelphia was held here. If you passed tenth-grade U.S. history, you know that that gathering elected George Washington as the Convention president (a precursor to his next public office) and penned some paperwork you might have heard of: the Constitution of the United States of America.

Another historical nugget was mined here as well. It involves James Monroe, the gent holding the flag for General Washington in the famous painting of him crossing the Delaware in a small boat. After Monroe was elected president, it is said that he returned to the Middleton, arriving by, you guessed it, the Middleton ferry. When he arrived in Annapolis to celebrate with friends, he was warmly greeted by the mayor, John Randal, who at the time owned the tavern. A round of drinks for everyone!

After a succession of three more owners who operated the place under different names, the tavern rests today in the able hands of Jerry Hardesty, who completely restored the building inside and out and brought back the original Middleton Tavern name. Hardesty also opened the popular oyster bar and added a new dining room upstairs to accommodate the huge weekend crowds and some private parties.

In homage to the eighteenth-century fishing community into which the Middleton was launched, fish and shellfish are prominent among the appetizers and entrees, but there are ample pastas and meats as alternatives. Customer favorites include Clams Casino and Oysters Rockefeller, Lobster Ravioli, Smoked Chesapeake Bluefish, a ubiquitous but uncommonly large (18-ounce) Crab Cake, Pan-Seared Grouper with mango-lime butter, and Broiled Rockfish.

Having heard an adjoining table waxing poetic about the rockfish, Maryland's state fish, I followed an order of crab balls—delicious miniature versions of their humongous crab cake—with the seared striped bass. The substantial fillet is tenderly laid atop a bed of young salad greens in the center of a fish-shaped platter and covered with a hefty portion of sautéed lump crabmeat and mushrooms. It tastes even better than it looks.

The eighteenth-century Georgian building contains "little bits of history" on its walls, such as Civil War muskets, old Naval Academy uniforms, nautical-themed pictures, and classic Maryland landscape paintings. In winter, customers can sit by a fire in one of four different rooms, while in summer, those who prefer to dine alfresco line up to eat in the covered open-air front patio. Part of the tavern's year-round popularity is due to the opportunity to eat in a 250-year-old building.

And if you see a gentleman dressed in seaman's attire from the 1700s staring out to sea, pay no mind. He's not an actor. He's one of three apparitions that restaurant staff and sober customers have seen and reported over the years, perhaps one of those seafaring men who once stayed in Horatio's Inn, waiting for their ship to come in.

Pan-Seared Rockfish

∾ SERVES 2 ∾

Flour, for dusting

1 (1½-pound) rockfish fillet

6 tablespoons unsalted butter

3 cups mixed baby salad greens

¼ cup sautéed stemmed and sliced shiitake mushrooms

2 teaspoons balsamic vinegar, whisked with 4 teaspoons olive oil

2 ounces lump crabmeat, picked over for shell

⅓ cup sautéed mixed vegetables, such as carrots, green beans, onion, zucchini

¾ cup cooked rice pilaf

Chopped tomatoes, for garnish

Flat-leaf parsley sprigs or minced parsley, for garnish

Lemon wedges, for serving

Preheat the oven to 325°F. Lightly flour the rockfish. In a large ovenproof skillet, melt the butter over medium heat. Add the fish and sauté until golden brown, 2 to 3 minutes on each side. Transfer the pan to the oven and roast for 2 to 3 minutes, until opaque throughout. Remove from the oven and keep warm.

Place the salad greens and half of the shiitake mushrooms in the center of a platter and drizzle with the balsamic vinaigrette. Place the rockfish fillet on top of the salad. Top with the crabmeat and the remaining mushrooms. Place the vegetable medley and rice pilaf on the platter. Garnish with the tomatoes and parsley, and serve at once with the lemon wedges.

The Bell in Hand Tavern
BOSTON, MA ~ EST. 1795

It's 1780, and two men walk casually down Boston's Pi Alley, talking animatedly as they arrive at the Bell in Hand Tavern. They enter the door under a large carved wooden hand holding a town crier's bell. This place, after all, belongs to Jimmy Wilson, Boston's last town crier, who spent his career walking around town shouting out the news of the day and ringing his bell, then built the bar after he retired.

The air is thick inside from the clay-pipe smokers and the fire used to cook the simple food Jimmy offers. The men step onto the sawdust floor and shuffle their way in the dim light, looking for empty chairs or perhaps one of the tavern's low wooden benches. As they pass the small four by two-foot oak bar, they order two mugs of ale. They grab the two battered pewter mugs from the scarred wooden countertop and settle into two chairs.

Deciding that they are also hungry, one of the duo walks to the bar and catches the attention of a short, balding bearded man chopping meat on a well-used board. "What have we tonight, sir cook?" he asks. "We're quite short this day," comes a murmured reply, "but we have some good mutton, and one or two of the potato and leek pies." "Pray sir, let me have a plate of mutton for myself, and a pie for my companion," our gent asks.

Thick hunks of meat, swimming in fat and sitting alongside a potato occupy one of the pewter plates, and a huge crusty-brown steaming pie, covered in lumpy gravy, is slipped onto the other. Both men are hungry and tear into their simple suppers, sipping the ale and enjoying the spreading warmth of the small fireplace. The flickering light of a half-dozen candlelit lanterns throw curtains of light around the small room as they finish their meal and begin a game of checkers on a small table.

The other three tavern rooms are filled with tables, chairs, and loud conversation. The walls are festooned with lithographs, etchings, medallions, chromos, woodcuts, and elaborate engravings, barely visible through the wood and tobacco smoke. But where our friends sit musing over each checker, the tavern is quiet, with only muted conversations. Everyone is smoking long clay pipes, downing mugs of ale, or snoozing in the warmth and the dim light. It's a safe bet that no one will become unruly, loud, or belligerent, because Jimmy has forbidden "ardent liquor," having witnessed violent bar fights and drunken arguments that erupted on his town crier rounds. The only "ale" served here is the mildly alcoholic Smith's Philadelphia Cream Ale on tap.

There is a spirit of camaraderie. No drunken loafer tries to cadge a drink; instead, the men are offered more mugs in friendship and good cheer, and when the bell rings at nine o'clock the place quietly empties, after the snoozers have been pushed awake, the checkers game decided, and the mugs stacked on the bar for the morrow's customers.

It's 2012, two college students jump into their car and snake their way through crowded streets for a night in the city at the Bell in Hand. Since its move to Union Street, right around the corner from Faneuil Hall, the oldest tavern in America has become one of the city's most popular historic eateries during the day, and one of the hottest and most crowded dance clubs at night. After 9 p.m.,

Bell in Hand Crab Cakes

∽ MAKES 6 TO 8 CRAB CAKES ∽

1 tablespoon olive oil

½ cup finely chopped onion

¼ cup finely chopped red bell pepper

¼ cup finely chopped yellow bell pepper

3 tablespoons minced fresh flat-leaf parsley

1 teaspoon minced garlic

1 pound lump crabmeat, picked over for shell

½ to ¾ cup fresh bread crumbs

2 tablespoons mayonnaise

1 tablespoon Dijon mustard

1 teaspoon Old Bay Seasoning

½ teaspoon Tabasco sauce

1 large egg yolk, beaten

Kosher salt and freshly ground black pepper

2 tablespoons unsalted butter

Chipotle mayonnaise, for serving

Lemon wedges, for serving

In a large sauté pan, heat the olive oil over medium-low heat and sauté the onion, bell peppers, parsley, and garlic until the vegetables are tender, about 15 minutes. Remove from the heat and let cool to temperature.

In a large bowl, combine the crabmeat, bread crumbs, mayonnaise, mustard, Old Bay Seasoning, Tabasco sauce, and egg yolk. Toss gently to mix. Season with salt and pepper. Add the cooled vegetable mixture and toss to mix well.

Shape into 6 to 8 two-inch-thick patties about 3 inches in diameter. Cover and refrigerate for at least 1 hour or up to overnight.

In a large sauté pan, melt the butter over medium heat until the bubbles subside. In batches, add the crab cakes and fry until golden brown, 3 to 5 minutes on each side. Transfer to a low oven to keep warm until all are fried. Serve hot, with chipotle mayonnaise and lemon wedges.

it is usually jammed from wall to wall with lots of college kids as well as a twenty-one to thirty-something mixed singles crowd.

The Bell promises "Something for Everyone" and lives up to that reputation. A relatively high cover charge provides access to five bars, each unique in décor, and two floors of entertainment, offering karaoke contests, live music from solo artists and local groups on the ground floor, and hip DJ's and hip-hop dancing upstairs. Some nights, there are trivia contests for prizes. Plasma TVs are plastered on every wall of the bar, and from the glassed-in restaurant, you can watch the world go by in the daytime, and at night the world can watch you.

The Bell in Hand now features fifteen beers on tap and lists nineteen brands of bottled beers, and the bartenders are glad to pour about any liquor or mixed drink you could order. One of our duo orders a Boston Ice Tea (not the kind that comes from tea bags), the other a Sam Adams Brick Red.

Deciding not to begin what they hoped would be a long and successful evening hungry, they head to the dining room for a bite to eat. Usually, they order nachos, or fried calamari, or a burger, but tonight they select Buffalo Chicken Wings (with "blew" cheese dressing) and fried Mozzarella Sticks as appetizers, and, for the main course, one chooses the Popcorn Shrimp Po'Boy and the other the Marinated Steak Tips with French Fries. After their meal, they head upstairs to check out the action and a new DJ, then downstairs to the dance floor until closing at 2 a.m., when they reluctantly shuffle out the door, too hammered to drive, and take a cab back to their apartment.

History, they say, has a habit of repeating itself. A different world, different times, and different ways of enjoying a delightful bar, meetinghouse, and restaurant. I guess it just depends on for whom the "Bell" tolls.

Durgin-Park
BOSTON, MA ~ EST. 1827

The Durgin-Park restaurant menu says: "Your grandfather—and perhaps your great-grandfather—dined with us too!" Well not in my case, but my father did, as did my mother, my twin brother, and I during a trip to Boston in the late 1950s. I clearly remember my Mom exclaiming that the baked beans were the best she'd ever had, and she was a pretty darn good cook. For years, whenever she served baked beans at home she would say, "They're good, but they're not like the beans in Boston."

When Peter Faneuil erected a large two-story market house near the Boston harbor in 1742, one of his first tenants was a small unnamed eating place that served the market merchants and the crews of the ships anchored in the harbor. In 1827, John Durgin, a merchant, and Eldredge Park, a livery stable owner, bought the restaurant, named it Durgin-Park, and began what has become one of the biggest tourist draws in the city. Several years later, they brought in a third partner, John Chandler, a young dry-goods merchant. When Durgin and Eldredge died a short time later, Chandler honored their memory by keeping the restaurant name.

Under John Chandler's stewardship, the restaurant thrived due to the generous size of the servings, the quality and variety of the food served, and the reasonable tariffs. Chandler was once quoted as saying that he thought the best

The original restaurant included a cigar stand, and men freely smoked stogies in the dining rooms. Not today.

advertising for a restaurant was to put plenty of food on the table, and that he did! He owned D-P for sixty-three years, eventually bringing his son and later his grandson Jerry into the business.

In 1945, after his grandson was killed in World War II, the elder Chandler sold the restaurant to James Hallet, a former butcher and a loyal customer. Hallet helped to build and then cement Durgin-Park's reputation as one of the best restaurants in America. He began his days in the pre-dawn hours, going to the market to buy produce for the day, and usually stayed at the restaurant through dinner except on the nights he couldn't find a seat in the jammed eatery, which has never taken a single reservation.

Regular customers at one time included Teddy Roosevelt and his sons, Franklin Roosevelt and his sons, Calvin Coolidge, and radio and movie names Lillian and Dorothy

The secret to their legendary baked beans: long slow cooking, frequent basting, tender loving care, and individual bean pots.

Gish, Arthur Godfrey, Helen Hayes, Jack Benny, and Fred Allen. The women who waited tables, some of them for thirty-five to forty years, knew their customers so well that they'd just start bringing plates to the table when people sat down.

Between the red-and-white and mid-hall dining rooms more than five hundred people at a time can sit down to enjoy a sumptuous bowl of award-winning clam chowder, a bone-in prime rib the size of an aircraft carrier, the legendary bean pots of baked beans that have been cooked for six hours, and Durgin-Park's most popular and world-famed dish for dessert: Indian pudding. Long before Durgin, Park, and Chandler ran the restaurant, the recipe for this pudding was being taken to sea by clipper ship captains who were restaurant patrons. It was made by chefs in ships' galleys from Valparaiso to Hong Kong. The secret of its excellence lies in its slow and careful cooking.

The restaurant goes through an amazing fifty gallons of beans and sixty gallons of Indian pudding batter in an average week. And although people aren't eating as much beef these days as they did in the sixties, seventies, and eighties, they still manage to sell more than a ton of prime rib steaks in that same seven-day period.

The delicious prime rib is a whopping thirty-two ounces. The beans are slow-cooked with salt pork, molasses, mustard, and onion, and the bubbling bean pots are attended to by the chief bean man and his minions, who continually open the ovens to add small amounts of water to make sure the beans stay perfectly hydrated over the long cooking time. "You can't let the pot just sit in the oven," explains head chef Albert Savage. "You've got to add water as necessary to keep the beans moist. And you can't be impatient and add too much water at a time and flood the beans."

Baked Indian Pudding

∽ SERVES 2 TO 4 ∽

1 cup yellow cornmeal

½ cup dark molasses

¼ cup sugar

¼ cup lard or unsalted butter

¼ teaspoon salt

¼ teaspoon baking soda

2 large eggs, beaten

6 cups milk, heated

Preheat the oven to 225°F. Butter a stone crock or a heavy ovenproof casserole.

In a large, heavy saucepan, combine all the ingredients except the milk. Stir in 3 cups of the hot milk and cook over medium-high heat until it bubbles. Stir in the remaining 3 cups hot milk. Pour into the prepared pan and bake for 5 to 7 hours, or until set.

The second-floor kitchen is small and narrow by modern standards—not a place for a claustrophobic chef. So the waitstaff doesn't have to climb up to the kitchen with every order, the finished plates are delivered by two dumbwaiters.

General manager Seana Kelley, daughter of the previous owners, likes her job as commanding general in the battle to get customers their meals quickly, direct new arrivals to open tables, and coordinate everything that happens in the restaurant, exclaiming, "I love it! I love being a part of a place with character and tradition, a place people love to come to, and to come back to." She continues, "I love that I, and we, are keeping alive an old-fashioned restaurant that has charm, is part of the soul of Boston, and that so many people love. I think that's sooooooo cool!"

Agreed.

A floor-to-ceiling poster featuring a photo of some of the kitchen staff of the 1950s graces the ground floor entry hallway.

Longfellow's Wayside Inn
SUDBURY, MA ~ EST. 1716

This is the story of an inn whose name and, many say, character, were dramatically changed forever by a book of poems — sort of a colonial *Canterbury Tales* — that profiles a group of characters at a mythical wayside inn.

From 1716 until 1861, this "hous of entertainment," as it was known then, was located on the Boston Post Road, one of America's original roads for mail delivery. David Howe had expanded his own home to lodge and feed the many weary and hungry travelers bouncing by on stagecoaches traveling from New York to Boston. His son, Ezekiel, who led a minuteman militia group at the Battle of Concord, took over in 1830.

The tavern passed from son to son to son until it was bequeathed to relatives, the last son being unmarried. But they decided to close the inn to overnight guests, turning it into a boardinghouse for itinerate farmers, and renting out parts of the tavern for special parties and dances. After many years, because of their neglect, the building began to deteriorate and was no longer a popular stopping spot.

In 1862, Henry Wadsworth Longfellow and his publisher, James Fields, visited Howe's Tavern, which the poet later used as a template for the sad one that was "falling to decay," in what became a famous book of poems, *Tales of a Wayside Inn*. For years, people came from near and far to see the tumbledown structure, intrigued with the picture of it painted in the iconic poem. When visitors began

Bartender Marvin pours a Coow Woow, America's first cocktail.

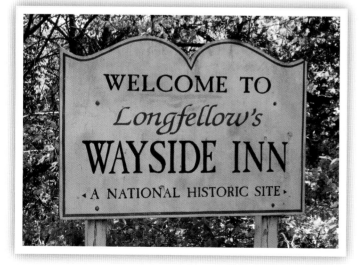

referring to the property as the inn in Longfellow's poem and local stores began selling souvenirs bearing the acquired name, the die was cast.

In 1896, a wealthy antiques and wool merchant, Edward Rivers Lemon, bought the tavern, renamed it Longfellow's Wayside Inn, and announced his intent to make it a haven for "literary pilgrims." In his drive to attract poets, writers, and artists, he formed the Paint and Clay Club, and they began to meet regularly at the inn. He also created a formal English country garden that attracted artists who came to paint the garden and the surrounding rural landscape.

Henry Ford was the next to take up the preservation of the inn, purchasing it and three thousand acres of surrounding land and beginning the job of turning the inn into a living museum of American history. Under Ford's private ownership, the inn continued to operate as a hotel and restaurant. His stature brought the inn to international significance, and with that came prominent visitors such as Calvin Coolidge and Charles Lindbergh.

Beloved additions to the inn's landscape made by Henry Ford include the Martha-Mary Chapel (1941), a popular wedding venue, and the Grist Mill (1929), which was a full-time Pepperidge Farm production facility from 1952 to 1967 and is the last fully operational mill in the Northeast. The mill today grinds the organically grown corn and wheat used in the bakery and sold in the gift shop. While you can still stay overnight, you'd better call ahead. The accommodations at the inn capture the flavor of colonial lodging, and there are only ten small rooms.

Eating at the inn, however, is a different matter. There are four dining rooms, which can seat a total of 280 at one time. Ask to be seated in the Old Kitchen, the room with the most colonial atmosphere. The main dining room, created in 1924, is a pleasant place to dine as well, and holds many more people.

The only restaurant in America with its own working gristmill, the Inn grinds much of its own flours.

You might want to begin the meal with either a historic Coow Woow, claimed to be America's first mixed drink (rum and ginger brandy), or a Stone Wall, a favorite Revolutionary War drink (gin and applejack). Favorite appetizers include Butternut Squash Ravioli, and Native Scallops wrapped in smoked bacon and served with a honey-mustard sauce. The Lobster Casserole, with a cracker stuffing, is a decadent entree, filling and beautiful. But if you don't care for the crustacean, give a shout to the Roast Half Duckling in a maple brandy and dried-cranberry sauce. Their traditional Baked Indian Pudding with vanilla ice cream is the favorite dessert, but their Deep Dish Apple Pie is a close second.

After dinner, you can tour several of their "museum rooms," which are set up as if you had just landed back in the 1800s, and include printed information about the history of the inn, the people who owned it and visited in its heyday, and what happened in the region during the formative years of this country.

The first part of Longfellow's *Tales of a Wayside Inn* deals with the decay of the mythical inn as well as providing vivid descriptions of its occupants. But even in this drab recounting, there is a stanza that could well be used to describe the Wayside Inn as it stands today:

*"Around the fireside at their ease
There sat a group of friends, entranced
With the delicious melodies
Who from the far-off noisy town
Had to the Wayside Inn come down,
To rest beneath its old oak-trees."*

Wayside Inn Lobster Casserole

~ SERVES 6 ~

3 tablespoons olive oil

½ onion, finely chopped

2 stalks celery, leaves removed and finely chopped

3 tablespoons dry sherry

2 teaspoons sweet paprika

2 tablespoons chopped fresh flat-leaf parsley

¾ cup (3 ounces) grated Parmesan cheese

Pinch of freshly ground white pepper

6 to 8 ounces cooked lobster meat, chopped

3 cups dried bread crumbs, mixed with
   3 cups crumbled Ritz crackers

½ cup melted clarified butter

Preheat the oven to 350°F. Butter an 8-cup casserole dish. In a medium skillet, heat the oil over medium heat and sauté the onion and celery until tender, about 5 minutes. Transfer to a large bowl and add the sherry, paprika, parsley, Parmesan cheese, white pepper, and lobster. Stir to blend.

Place the mixture in the prepared dish. Cover with the crumbs and pour the clarified butter over the crumbs. Bake until browned, 10 to 15 minutes.

Coow Woow

~ SERVES 2 ~

4 ounces light rum

1 ounce ginger brandy

Pour the rum and ginger brandy over crushed ice, stir, and strain into 2 cocktail glasses.

Upstairs above the dining rooms are rooms decorated to look like the Inn in its early days. There are also ten small guest rooms, all furnished with period antiques.

Omni Parker House

BOSTON, MA ~ EST. 1855

Harvey D. Parker, a twenty-year-old farm boy, arrived in Boston on a schooner from Maine in 1825. He had less than a dollar in his pocket and needed a job. He got one, taking care of a local gentleman's horse, and as strange as it sounds that was the beginning of a career in hospitality that lasted fifty-nine years and, along the way, created a legend.

The groom position turned into a stint as a coachman for a wealthy woman, and when Harvey trotted the horse-drawn carriage into the city he usually ate his noonday meal at a dark cellar café named the Court Square. After saving his salary and tips, he bought the café seven years later (for $432) and promptly changed its name to Parker's Restaurant.

Parker's quickly gained a reputation among the businessmen, lawyers, and newspapermen who worked nearby for excellent food and great service. Harvey did so well that in 1847 he added a partner, and in 1854 he bought, then razed, a decrepit old boardinghouse to build an ornate five-story stone and brick hotel, faced in white marble in the style of the Italian parliament house.

The first and second floors had beautiful arched windows, the foyer was marble, and the thick carpets and fashionable horsehair couches gave the place an elegant air. With his practiced eye for excellence, Harvey then astounded local hoteliers by importing chef M. Sanzian from Paris and paying him the mind-boggling (for that time and that profession) annual salary of $5,000. The going rate for Boston cooks then was a measly $416—a year! But Harvey wanted the best.

Among the French chef's techniques was using a revolving spit to cook beef and whole fowl over hot coals. But he forever engraved his name in the culinary hall of fame with the creation of Boston cream pie and Parker House rolls—both of which have been imitated, copied, and served around the world for decades. But nothing tastes as good as the originals, enjoyed in the place where they were born.

The hotel's baker, Toui Tran, makes a dozen large and one hundred small Boston cream pies a day. But the signature desserts began with the chef Sanzian. "Back in the mid-1800s, the only way people enjoyed chocolate was as a hot beverage or in puddings. But the chef thought he'd try to use it differently and had his bakers drizzle melted chocolate over a sponge cake that was filled with vanilla cream. And instantly a sensation dessert was born," chef Tran explained. I watched in fascination as she breezed through cake after cake, never hesitating a moment, as smooth in her movements as a ballerina. Surprisingly, both Ho Chi Minh and Malcolm X worked at Parker House in their youth, Ho as a baker and Malcolm Little (his real name) as a busboy. The famous Saturday Club, a group of literary giants that at different times included Longfellow, Ralph Waldo Emerson, Nathaniel Hawthorne, Daniel Webster, Charles Dickens, John Greenleaf Whittier, and Oliver Wendell Holmes, once met here. The Kennedy family is also connected to the hotel. At six years of age, JFK made his first speech here on his grandfather's birthday. Later, he would announce his candidacy for U.S. Congress in the Press Room, propose to Jacqueline Bouvier at table No. 40, and celebrate his bachelor party in the Press Room. The list of other famous folks who have stayed here takes up two full pages of fine print in the hotel brochure. You name the famous actor, author, philosopher, politician, sports personality, or person of repute and some of ill repute and odds are they've slept or dined here.

The elegant dining room has oak-paneled walls, crystal chandeliers, a luxurious carpet, and

President Kennedy and then Vice President Johnson are among the thousands of famous people who have dined at the Parker House over its long storied history. With them is former Boston Mayor John Hynes (next to Johnson) and Frank Kelly.

Service staff polishes glassware by table No. 40—famous as the spot where John F. Kennedy proposed to Jacqueline Lee Bouvier. She said yes!

immaculate table settings that make the room a romantic backdrop. Throw in the tuxedoed waitstaff, who are attentive without being intrusive; superb cuisine; and an extensive wine list, and Parker's Restaurant is one of the finest in the nation.

The Baked Boston Scrod (it's said the word was invented here) in Lemon Beurre Blanc is delicious. A crunchy breading shelters the moist, tender, and mild white fish inside. No wonder this has been a popular dish here since 1906. Even if you don't like fish, you'll probably scrape up every crumb. But the two dishes most diners look forward to most are the rolls and the cream pie. The mini pies arrive at the table decorated with drizzles of chocolate and bookended by two substantial dollops of fresh whipped cream. Each evaporates in just four bites.

While staying here, I had a rare opportunity to observe chef Tran making the famous rolls. She takes large mounds of dough and puts them into an ancient press that forms a large circle of thirty-six rolls. Then she brushes on a generous coat of vegetable oil and hand-folds almost three hundred rolls in about fifteen minutes. On an average day, she makes over one thousand. The huge trays are placed on a large sheet pan to rise before being baked to a perfect golden brown. The baked rolls are set on a marble table where the chef's fellow countryman, Ho, worked during his stint here. Then she tenderly brushes each steaming hot roll with butter. Giving me a dimpled smile, Tran gently asked, "Would you like to sample one?" "Yes, please," I whimpered, having been tortured for an hour inhaling the scent of fresh, yeasty, buttery pastries baking just feet away. A buttered Parker House roll, two minutes out of the oven, baked in the original kitchen where they were first made, was placed in my hand, where it lasted about .02 seconds.

Parker House Boston Cream Pie

∽ SERVES 6 TO 8 ∽

PASTRY CREAM

1 tablespoon unsalted butter

2 cups whole milk

2 cups light cream or half-and-half

½ cup sugar

3½ tablespoons cornstarch

6 large eggs

1 teaspoon dark rum

CHOCOLATE FONDANT ICING

2 cups sugar

⅛ teaspoon cream of tartar

1 cup water

CAKE

7 large eggs

1 cup sugar

1 cup cake flour

2 teaspoons unsalted butter, melted

3 ounces semisweet chocolate, chopped

½ cup sliced almonds

For the pastry cream: In a medium saucepan, combine the butter, milk, and light cream. Bring to a simmer over medium-high heat.

In a medium bowl, whisk together the sugar and cornstarch. Add the eggs and beat until the mixture forms a slowly dissolving ribbon on the surface of the batter when the whisk is lifted, about 5 minutes. Whisk into the hot milk mixture and bring to a boil, whisking constantly (to prevent the eggs from scrambling) until the mixture has thickened, about 1 minute. Transfer to a bowl and cover with plastic wrap pressed directly onto the surface (to keep a skin from forming). Let cool, then refrigerate for at least 2 hours until chilled. Whisk in the rum.

To start the chocolate fondant icing: Wipe a baking sheet or marble slab with a damp cloth.

In a heavy, medium saucepan, combine the sugar, cream of tartar, and water and bring to a boil over medium heat, stirring to dissolve the sugar. Cover and let boil for 3 minutes. Uncover and dip a pastry brush in cold water to wash down the sides of the pot. Boil until the syrup reaches the soft-ball stage (238°F), about 5 minutes. Remove from the heat and pour onto the damp baking sheet. Let cool until lukewarm, about 10 minutes.

Using a metal spatula, spread the sugar mixture out and repeatedly turn it over on itself until it starts to thicken and whiten. (It may be easier to knead the mixture with your hands.) Continue kneading the sugar mixture until it is very stiff. Scrape it off the sheet, place in an airtight container, and refrigerate for several hours.

For the cake: Preheat the oven to 350°F. Lightly grease a 10-inch spring-form pan. Separate the eggs, putting the whites in one large bowl and the yolks in another. Add ½ cup sugar to each bowl. Beat the egg whites until they form stiff, glossy peaks. Beat the egg yolks until they are thick and pale yellow in color, about 5 minutes. Gently fold the beaten whites into the yolk mixture. Gradually fold in the flour and then fold in the melted butter. Pour the batter into the prepared pan and bake for 18 to 20 minutes, or until a cake tester comes out clean when inserted into the center of the cake. Let cool.

To finish the chocolate fondant icing: Heat ¾ cup of the fondant and the chocolate in the top of a double boiler over simmering water until the chocolate is melted and the mixture is warm. Stir to a spreading consistency, adding a little water as necessary.

Using a long, serrated knife, slice the cake into 2 layers. Reserve 1 cup of the pastry cream. Spread the remaining pastry cream over the bottom layer. Place the second layer of cake over the pastry cream and spread the reserved pastry cream around the sides of the cake. Using an offset icing spatula, spread the chocolate icing over the top (work rapidly, since the icing sets very quickly) and press the almonds around the sides.

Serve immediately at room temperature, or refrigerate for up to 2 days and bring to room temperature before serving. (When refrigerated, the fudge-like icing becomes quite stiff.)

NOTE: This recipe makes 4 cups of custard filling—a fine amount if you're going to cut the cake into three layers. If you plan to cut the cake into two layers (as Parker House does), you might prefer to make a half portion of the pastry cream.

The Publick House
STURBRIDGE, MA ~ EST. 1771

Okay, here's what we're doing now: We're going to eat dessert first! I don't want to wait to share probably the best blueberry pie my wife and I, and about two hundred people a week (in summer), have had the privilege and pleasure of enjoying.

I know this violates some unwritten rule—history first, description second, review of an entree or side dish third, and then dessert—but not this time. I will leave the recipe to the end, but if you don't try it, I promise you will be missing a phenomenal treat you will more than likely want to make your own family's heirloom recipe.

On the first bite, a creamy texture lulls you into a blissful state. And then—blam! a whole

blueberry explodes in your mouth in a cascade of flavor, and then another. Fresh blueberries in a baked pie? No way. Yes, way! The restaurant's bakery had specially made two pies for us. It was out of season for blueberries, but somehow general manager Michael Glick secured enough fresh ones for their baker to work her wonders for us. I have to confess that after we ate one piece each, we felt guilty and wanted to give them back the second pie so someone else could enjoy its wonders. But they insisted we take it with us.

We did, however, present our waitress with the rest of the pie that we'd tasted. She had gasped when a box arrived at our table and we had opened it to reveal the locally treasured seasonal

cream pie inside. "You've got a blueberry cream pie!" she said in a reverent, envious tone. So, though we took the second pie with us per the baker's orders, we gave the waitress the rest of the sampled pie. It was as if we had given her a diamond necklace, or offered to clean her house for a year, or told her she'd be having dinner with Sean Connery. We felt vindicated.

The Publick House (a common name and spelling for combination inns and taverns during Colonial times) began its life in 1771 in the center of two main roads. In one direction the road ran from Boston to New York, in the other from Providence to Springfield. It was used by the Native Americans who first brought corn to the Pilgrims at Plymouth Rock. As a transportation hub of its time, Sturbridge figured into the Revolutionary War when an embargo prevented goods being shipped by sea from New York to Boston. So goods were transported by six-horse team wagons overland.

With an important tavern and inn in its midst, the town became a cultural center, and innkeeper and founder Colonel Ebenezer Crafts and his wife, Mehitabel, forever endeared themselves to Sturbridge by planting several large elms and maples that still stand tall on the grounds of the inn.

The Publick is not a large place, having but seventeen rooms, each one different and each charmingly decorated with period antiques. The hallways are long and canted and narrow. The floors are also tilted a bit, the stairway leading to the second floor is steep, and the doors and ceilings are low, so that guests staying here truly are transported back to Colonial days.

I was most intrigued by the "library," a private dining/meeting room, especially when I tried to remove a book from the floor-to-ceiling, wall-to-wall bookshelves. It wouldn't budge. I later learned when the inn was being remodeled and the owners wanted space for

tables and chairs, they reduced the depth of the shelves to about 4 inches. Then they had a collection of old books cut in half, leaving the spine and about 3 inches of the books, which were glued to the wall behind the shortened shelves.

The Publick's dining room menu proclaims that "every day is Thanksgiving Day" to remind folks a roast turkey dinner is served every day of the year, but a diverse selection of dishes is offered as well. Two standout appetizers are the Lobster Mac and Cheese, and Turkey Meatball Sliders. Two substantial and delicious entrees are the New England Baked Scrod and good old Yankee Pot Roast.

1950s staff in front of the Publick House.

I will only say this one more time. If you go there in the summer, try the Blueberry Cream Pie! Call ahead to reserve one. If you go there in fall or winter or spring, make plans to come back in the summer for the pie.

The Publick House Blueberry Cream Pie

∽ MAKES 2 (9-INCH) PIES ∽

½ tablespoon unflavored gelatin

2 tablespoons water, plus 2¼ cups

9 pints fresh blueberries

2 cups sugar

1 teaspoon salt

¾ cup all-purpose flour

2 (9-inch) baked pie shells

Whipped cream, for topping

In a small cup, sprinkle the gelatin over the 2 tablespoons water, stir, and set aside for 5 minutes.

Place half of the blueberries in a large saucepan, add 1½ cups of the water and the sugar and bring to a boil over medium-high heat. Combine the remaining ¾ cup water, the salt, and flour in a small bowl and whisk until smooth. Whisk into the boiling blueberries and cook until thickened, about 5 minutes. Remove from the heat.

Melt the gelatin in the microwave until all the granules have dissolved. Stir into the blueberry mixture and let cool to room temperature.

Add the remaining blueberries, reserving a handful for garnish, and pour the filling into the pie shells.

Refrigerate for at least 1 hour. Top the pies with whipped cream and garnish with a few of the reserved blueberries.

The Red Lion Inn
STOCKBRIDGE, MA ~ EST. 1773

In early 1773, Anna and Silas Bingham established a general store in the Berkshire Valley, which soon evolved into a stagecoach stop, and later an inn, which was operated by Silas Pepoon. The store and inn were built on land formerly owned by a Mahican chief.

Anna ran the inn with a firm hand and a strong sense of business. At that time, the inn consisted of eight rooms with the usual low ceilings, massive beams, and thick support posts, and had a large open fireplace that welcomed guests. The barroom was on the main floor, with rooms above it, and above that was a large hall. Unlike the luxurious inn today, it was poorly lit and time-stained, with unpainted woodwork and dingy plastering, and was filled with the "commonest of folk."

Over the next decades, the building became the J. Hick's Inn, then the Stockbridge Inn. The sign above the building showed a red lion, and like similar taverns, the Red Lion became the center of community life. People not only boarded and ate there but spent substantial hours in front of the fireplace catching up on local news, sharing farming tips, and discussing politics and the problems with British taxation of the colonies. The Boston Tea Party was just months away.

In 1807, Anna, then a widow, sold the Inn for $10,000, a fortune in those days, especially for an eight-room tavern. In 1848, the inn's owners added a substantial number of rooms, enough to accommodate over one hundred visitors. Successive owners collected and displayed antique pewter, furniture, and crockery, and greatly improved the quality of the meals and the food service. Franklin stoves were added to most of the guest rooms, and a large cold room was added to protect food from the heat and humidity of summer. Another wing and a new dining room were added as well.

But like many of its fellow centenarians, the Red Lion burned to the ground after a fire in 1896. However, thanks to town folks, who rushed to the rescue during the fire, many of the antiques, the crockery, fine china, and photographs were saved. A mere eight months later, the new Red Lion Inn opened. A huge front porch was added, as were two parlors and a new detached brick kitchen. The new inn had eighty bedrooms and twenty-two fireplaces, and the bathrooms had hot water and were illuminated by built-in gas lighting. The problem was, there were only two of these bathrooms, and guests had to have a porter carry up tin bathtubs if they wanted to bathe in their rooms.

Today, the inn offers 109 rooms, three dining rooms, two bars, and outside seating on a shaded back porch, and each room has its own tub or shower. Progress! There's also Simon, the lobby cat, who greets, gets petted by, approves of (hopefully), and then ignores everyone who comes to the inn, which even sells Simon postcards for feline fanciers.

The entire place conveys a Norman Rockwell charm. Wide porches with white rattan rocking chairs and settees, Victorian wallpaper, chandeliers, warm fireplaces, teapots, and antique crockery are everywhere, with displays of ceramic dolls in the hallways and antique photographs and paintings on every wall. It's appropriate to mention Mr. Rockwell, as he for many years had his studio next door to the inn, and he contributed the figures to the artistic drawing of the inn on its paper place mats. There are prints of many of his more famous works in just about every room, and the Norman Rockwell Museum, dedicated to America's "common man" artist, is nearby.

Today, the Red Lion menu is world class, and the dining rooms and bar tables are always filled. The mac and cheese on the lunch menu is a delicious mix of local Cheddar, bacon, and cream, topped with onion straws. If you stay for dinner, and you should, you can't go wrong with their signature Turkey Dinner (any time of the year) or the Vanilla-Cured Pheasant, which sits on a bed of saffron risotto (in the fall). And dessert? In two years of sampling incredible desserts at some of the finest restaurants in America, I can honestly say that the Red Lion Chef Brian Alberg's Warm Brown Sugar Cake with Coffee Ice Cream and Warm Caramel Sauce is one of the top five desserts I had the pleasure to enjoy. No kidding.

The delightful Widow Bingham's Tavern has everything but the kitchen sink mounted on the ceiling.

I could go on ad infinitum about the service, warm hospitality, genuine feeling of being in someone's home instead of an inn, and the wonderful treasures I discovered during my visit. But I'd rather let you discover them for yourself. If Simon approves, that is!

Red Lion Inn Warm Brown Sugar Cakes

~ MAKES 6 ~

CARAMEL

¾ cup firmly packed
   light brown sugar

2 tablespoons unsalted
   butter, softened

¼ cup heavy cream

CAKES

¾ cup (1½ sticks) unsalted
   butter, at room temperature

½ cup sugar

¼ cup firmly packed
   light brown sugar

½ teaspoon vanilla extract

3 large eggs

⅔ cup hazelnut flour (see Note)

1 cup all-purpose flour

½ teaspoon salt

1 teaspoon baking powder

Ice cream, for serving

For the caramel: Combine all of the ingredients in a medium-sized saucepan. Bring the mixture to a boil over high heat, then promptly remove from the heat. Transfer the caramel to a heat resistant bowl and place it in the freezer to cool.

Preheat the oven to 350°F. Grease a 2½ inch muffin pan.

For the cakes: In a large bowl, cream together the butter, sugar, brown sugar, and vanilla. Add the eggs and beat until incorporated.

Add the hazelnut flour, all-purpose flour, salt, and baking powder and mix to a cake batter consistency. Divide the batter evenly among the muffin cups and bake for 10 minutes until a crust forms. Remove the pans from the oven and place 1 tablespoon of caramel into the center of each cake. Bake an additional 20 minutes. Remove and let cool slightly before serving with a drizzle of the remaining caramel sauce and your favorite ice cream.

NOTE: Hazelnut flour is available online (see the Bob's Red Mill website), but you can also make your own. For 1 cup of flour, you will need about ⅓ pound of hazelnuts. Spread them on a rimmed baking sheet and toast in a preheated 350°F oven for 12 to 15 minutes, or until golden and fragrant. Wrap them in a clean kitchen towel and let cool for about 5 minutes, then rub them together inside the towel to remove the skins. Grind in a food processor to make a fine meal.

Simon, the hotel cat, is so popular with guests that he has his own postcard.

Union Oyster House
BOSTON, MA ~ EST. 1826

The Union Oyster House restaurant is the oldest continuously operated restaurant and the oldest continuously operated oyster bar in the United States. In fact, it's so old that it had a history even before it had a history.

Located along Boston's Freedom Trail, a 2½ mile walking path that links sixteen historic sites including Faneuil Hall, the Old North Church, and the Bunker Hill monument, the restaurant is a welcome spot for those who hike the historic pathway to grab lunch or an early dinner. No one really knows how old the building is; it was built before such records were kept. Some surmise that it was constructed in 1704, others aver that it was built in 1716, while yet others believe it was put up between 1713 and 1716. But no one really knows.

What is known is that it was opened as a restaurant in the early 1800s, and that before that the building housed a silk and dress goods importer; was used (the second floor, anyway) by Isaiah Thomas, the father of modern American publishing, as the home of *The Massachusetts Spy*, the oldest newspaper in the country; and later was headquarters of the paymaster for the Continental Army. Just imagine General Washington and his troops standing in line here to get their "war wages."

A most surprising fact is that the Oyster House used to be on the Boston waterfront. In those days, long before the city was expanded by landfill, the harbor came up to the back door, making it easier for workers to unload those silk dainties, satin dresses, and other women's fashions imported from Paris and Europe. Today, it's a half-mile away from the wharf, on the other side of busy U.S. Highway 93.

The Pine Room on the second floor is where Louis Philippe (royally known as the Duc de

orator and U.S. Senator from Massachusetts (1827–1841), who had a prodigious love of oysters. He would regularly stand at the oyster bar discoursing on various topics while he downed three to four dozen oysters, at the same time sipping several large tumblers of brandy and water. Current customers crowd around the same bar for their own oysters today. The restaurant was finally given the Union Oyster House moniker in 1916.

Ben Franklin (actually actor Dick Elliott) shares some Colonial humor with guests at the oyster bar.

In 1870, the Oyster House became the first U.S. restaurant to offer toothpicks. An enterprising inventor, one Charles Forster, who it's said could have sold a side of beef to a vegetarian, brought toothpicks to America after discovering them on a trip to Brazil. He collaborated with a Boston inventor to come up with a toothpick-making machine, but had trouble getting them used by restaurants.

Chartres—and later as the Citizen King of France, 1830–1848) taught ballroom dancing and French to local ladies while he was in exile. The dimly lit low-ceilinged room is also home to the tall-backed private wooden booth No. 18, where President Kennedy liked to read newspapers and eat lobster. The booth was dedicated in his memory in 1977.

Its life as a restaurant began as the Atwood & Bacon Oyster House in 1826, the year the historic semicircular oyster bar, the most iconic and famous feature of the place, was installed. It was frequented by Daniel Webster, the famed

So, clever Charles hired a bunch of Harvard men, dressed them up, and sent them to the Oyster House for dinner, where he paid for their meals. Their job was to ask for toothpicks after dinner, and when told the restaurant didn't have them to complain loudly, promising never to eat there again. Charles visited several days later with boxes of toothpicks for sale, and eventually the restaurant and some local stores began ordering them. Soon other we-want-them-

Oyster shuckers from the 1920s.
Right: Anton Christen has worked at the Oyster House for 13 years as both a shucker and a chef.

too restaurant owners began providing toothpicks, spreading the after-dinner dental aids across Boston and the East Coast, and, as they say, the rest is history.

It is also alleged that the Oyster House hired Boston's first waitress, Rose Carey, who began working here in the 1920s and efficiently served her tables for more than sixty years. Another employee, Jim "Pop" Farren, shucked oysters here for sixty-five years, and fellow oysterman Tommy Butt retired after his eightieth birthday, having spent fifty-two years at the restaurant.

Like many other centenarian restaurants, the OH has been frequented by dozens of notables and celebrities, including Paul Newman, Steven Spielberg, Luciano Pavarotti, Robin Williams, Ted Kennedy, Billy Crystal, Jay Leno, Sammy Sosa, Larry Bird, Ted Koppel,

Rose Carey

Dan Rather, Meryl Streep, Robert Redford, Al Pacino, three U.S. Presidents (Carter, Clinton, and G. W. Bush), Ozzie Osborn, Alanis Morrisette, and Wayne Newton. To commemorate many of those visits, a large painting by Stan Korzen of several dozen of the notables hangs in the main bar.

It is said that one evening when Pavarotti was dining here, there was a birthday party at the next table and the opera star surprised them with a special operatic version of "Happy Birthday." Stories shared with me by general manager Jim Malinn, who himself has worked here for thirty-two years, about visits by Sir Laurence Olivier and Carol Burnett among others reinforce the feeling of warmth many have felt while dining here. Today, the restaurant is owned and run by Joseph A. Milano, Jr., and his sister Mary Ann, who expanded it in 1982 and again in 1995 so that it now can serve more than one thousand meals a day during the week and twice that on weekends. Mary Ann keeps her own library of pictures, clippings, and articles about the restaurant. Several staff avow that the Milanos are great stewards and good businesspeople who put their money back into the restaurant and take great care of their workers.

The menu concentrates on shellfish and seafood. Steaks are also available, but lobster, oysters, and Boston clam chowder rule the roost. Every year, shuckers at the bar open over 360,000 oysters, servers dish out at least fifteen thousand gallons of clam chowder, and chefs broil or boil more than thirty-three thousand lobsters.

I pretended I was Daniel Webster standing at the bar and downed a half-dozen oysters, fresh with the salty tang of the sea, washing them down with a cold, crisp local brew instead of the senator's brandy and water. Then I enjoyed

ATWOOD & BACON.

ESTABLISHED 1826.

OYSTERS.		SCALLOPS. (in Season.)	
VIRGINIA:		Fried,	35
Stewed,	15	Stewed,	30
" large,	20		
Roast,	15		
" Fancy	20	Crackers and Milk,	15
NARRAGANSETT:		Bread and Milk,	15
Raw, plate,	15	Dry Toast,	10
Half-Shell, doz.	15	Buttered Toast,	10
" half-doz.	10	Milk Toast,	15
Stewed,	25	Boiled Eggs, (3)	20
" bench-opened,	30	Fried Eggs, 3)	20
Roast,	25	Dropped Eggs, (3)	20
" bench-opened,	30	Eggs on Toast,	20
Fried, crumbs or batter,	25	Bread and Butter,	5
" bench-opened,	35	Extra Crackers,	5
Roast in shell,	35		
CAPES:		Apple Pie,	5
Half-shell, doz.	20	Mince "	5
" half-doz.	10	Lemon "	5
Stewed,	35	Squash "	5
Roast,	35	Custard"	5
Fried,	40		
Roast in shell,	40		
CLAMS.		Tea,	5
IPSWICH:		Coffee,	5
Stewed,	15	Milk,	5
Steamed,	25	Ginger Ale, (Pureoxia)	5
Fried, crumbs or batter	25	Sarsaparilla,	5
Chowder,	15		
LITTLE NECKS:			
Dozen,	20		
Half-Dozen,	10		
Stewed,	40		
Fried,	45		
Quahaugs, Stewed,	25		
" Fried,	35		

PLEASE PAY THE WAITER.

The Oyster House in 1932.

a cup of thick, rich clam chowder before diving into a huge bowl of the signature Sautéed Lobster Scampi, a whole disjointed lobster sautéed in garlic butter and white wine, served on a bed of perfectly al dente linguine and festooned with fresh basil. The lobster didn't stand a chance.

Lucius Beebe, famed food writer of the *New York Herald Tribune*, perhaps penned up the best description of the Union Oyster House in a 1931 review: "The Union Oyster House has been a cathedral, or more properly speaking a chapel, of seafood, its high altar the oyster bar, its acolytes and priests the white-coated experts who render available its Cotuits and Little Necks, its worshippers the patrons whose mouths water and whose nostrils quiver at the salt odor of lobster broiling on a coal fire in its kitchens."

Sautéed Lobster Scampi

∽ SERVES 4 ∽

4 (1¼-pound) live New England lobsters, or 1 pound cooked lobster meat

6 tablespoons unsalted butter

1 tablespoon minced garlic

1 tablespoon minced fresh basil, plus sprigs for garnish

1 teaspoon minced fresh chives

2 cups chopped canned or fresh plum (Roma) tomatoes

¼ cup dry white wine

1 pound hot cooked linguine, for serving

In a large pot of boiling water, cook the lobsters for 10 minutes or until slightly undercooked. Drain, let cool, and remove the meat from the shell. Cut the meat into large chunks. Set aside.

In a large sauté pan, melt 4 tablespoons of the butter over medium heat. Add the garlic and sauté until fragrant, about 1 minute. Add the basil, chives, tomatoes, and white wine and sauté for 3 to 4 minutes. Swirl in the remaining 2 tablespoons of butter.

When the butter is completely incorporated, add the lobster and cook until the lobster is warmed through. Serve at once over hot linguine, garnished with basil sprigs.

The Warren Tavern

CHARLESTOWN, MA ~ EST. 1780

The oldest tavern among Boston's many historic bars and taverns, and some say the most famous watering hole in America, the Warren Tavern was the first building erected after the British burned the town during the Battle of Bunker Hill in 1775. It was built by Captain Eliphelet Newell, who played an important role in the Boston Tea Party, and who named his "publick house" after General (Dr.) Joseph Warren, whom he fought beside at the Battle of Bunker Hill. The general was mortally wounded near the end of the battle when the Brits pushed up nearby Breeds Hill.

You may not have heard of this patriot, but he had a direct hand in many aspects of the American Revolution and, with his friends Paul Revere, Samuel Adams, and John Hancock, led Boston's resistance to Britain's rule with both action and strong words. He not only sent Mr. Revere galloping through the streets to warn of the movement of British troops from the sea but he volunteered to be part of the militia that raided the redcoats as they moved toward Boston.

The tavern was constructed in the Federal style, and the low beamed ceiling, lace-covered windows, and large fireplace make you feel as if you are stepping back into Colonial history. The beams are in fact older than the building itself, as they were salvaged from old boats that were destroyed by the British at the nearby Charlestown Navy Yard.

The Warren was Paul Revere's favorite watering place, and, as a Grand Master in the Masons, like Dr. Warren, he presided over Masonic Lodge meetings later held here.

George Washington visited on more than one occasion, and when he died, a procession of mourners came there for a funeral oration in the former president's honor. The Reverend Jedidiah Morse, who gave the oration, was the father of Samuel F. B. Morse, the inventor of the telegraph.

There are no battle swords, battle maps, flintlock rifles, or historic parchment scrolls hidden behind glass display cases here. But you are walking on the same floor trod by Warren, Revere, Washington, and many of their contemporaries through history.

There are three eating areas. The original tavern room has the requisite bevy of flat-screen plasma TV's, some high tables and tall stools, a beautiful brass tap, and brass foot and hand rails. Then there's Kate's Room, a tiny enclave that seats about sixteen, just inside the door. Last, there's the large dining room at the back of the building, with its shuttered windows, hand-hewn beams, historic photos on the walls, and a large fireplace, all adding to the charm of the space.

The menu has an abundance of finger foods but also lists some more unusual vittles, such as Philadelphia Cheese Steak Spring Rolls, Artichoke and Asparagus Crostini, and a Crab BLT. Dinner entrees include such ubiquitous pub grub as fish and chips, fried calamari, and half-pound burgers.

The exterior of the Tavern has changed little over the years as this picture from the early 1950s shows.

Or you can be more adventurous and order Seafood Fra Diablo (shrimp, scallops, mussels, and calamari in a marinara sauce), Thai Chicken Stir-Fry, or a tavern favorite, Shepherd's Pie.

Word has gotten around about the Corned Beef Dinner, probably the most traditional meal anyone can enjoy at any pub or tavern in Boston. It consists of a generous helping of tender corned beef, cabbage, new potatoes, turnips, and carrots, best washed down with a very chilled Sam Adams Boston Lager.

The Tavern has the same floors once trod on by George Washington and Paul Revere, among other Colonial notables.

Dr. Joseph Warren, a hero who fell in action at the Battle of Bunker Hill.

Afterward, let yourself be lured in by the siren call of the Raspberry Crumb Pie, described thusly on the menu: "Shortbread pie shell and fresh raspberries with an oatmeal and granola topping, served with vanilla ice cream." Splendiferous! It may not have been on the menu for the past two centuries, but it darn well should be for the next two.

While reading about the history of the tavern, I was touched by a comment made by a Vivian D. of Los Angeles on the Yelp restaurant-review website: "Such places are rare in this world, dear friend. And only the wise will treasure them."

Corned Beef and Cabbage

∽ SERVES 6 TO 8 ∽

1 (5-pound) gray corned beef (see Note)

1 pound baby carrots

8 ounces turnips, peeled and diced

1 pound small red potatoes, halved (peeled or unpeeled)

8 ounces boiling onions, peeled

1 (1- to 2-pound) cabbage, cored and cut into wedges

Assorted prepared mustards, for serving

Preheat the oven to 300°F. Place the corned beef in a Dutch oven and add water to the pan to cover the meat. Cover and bake for 2 to 2½ hours. If the level of the liquid goes down, add more water.

Add the carrots, turnips, potatoes, and boiling onions, cover, and cook for 1 more hour, or until the corned beef is fork-tender. Add the cabbage, cover, and cook until tender, 7 to 9 minutes. Remove from the oven.

Using a slotted spoon, transfer the vegetables to a platter. Transfer the brisket to a carving board and cut into thin slices.

Serve the sliced meat on the platter, surrounded with the vegetables. Accompany with a variety of mustards.

NOTE: Gray corned beef is processed without saltpeter, so it will be gray instead of red, and a lot less salty.

∽ Warren Tavern Fact ∽

The Warren Tavern holds within its walls the spirit of this nation's history more than nearly any museum I have ever been to. There are no elaborate eighteenth-century paintings on the walls, no artifacts carefully preserved and guarded behind glass. There is only the same floor Paul Revere and George Washington walked upon. But there is a spirit within the wood, left here by giants. I declare the Warren Tavern should be thought of by the citizens of this nation as not only a fantastic tavern but more importantly as one of America's truly great historic sites. ~ David McBride, American Public House Review

White Horse Inn
METAMORA, MI ~ EST. 1850

The year was 1850. The safety pin had just been invented, Levi Strauss had just made his first blue jeans, and California was the newest state. And in Metamora, Michigan, a Civil War veteran and former New York state innkeeper named Lorenzo Hoard purchased a tiny store in the small town. Over the years, he turned it into a boardinghouse, a restaurant, a stagecoach stop, and a general store. Early overnighters were charged fifty cents for a small bed and dinner for themselves and feed and stabling for their horses.

Under Lorenzo's guidance, the inn prospered. In these early years, he began using leftover bread to create the inn's signature Bread Pudding, a recipe that has survived to this day with only a few slight modifications. He also introduced fish and chips to the small menu, another dish that is still popular today.

After Lorenzo's death, his family continued to run the Inn until it was sold in 1906 to a partnership that introduced liquor to their customers. After a series of owners, Frank Peters acquired the inn during Prohibition and brought it financial success by instituting breakfast specials, including the French Toast they serve today. Peters also changed the name from the Hoard House to the White Horse Inn.

The inn today looks much as it has for more than one hundred years, with hand-hewn wooden ceiling beams throughout. "It's crooked, it tips,

Tavern owner Tim Wilkins.

the floors cant this way and that way, the ceiling dips in places, but we really believe the building is the key, the charm, and the focus," says innkeeper Tim Wilkins. The second floor, which once housed overnight guests, is now a tearoom and parlor named after Lorenzo's wife, Lucy, a popular place for Saturday and afternoon teas.

This is horse country, and throughout the inn are images of horses, foxhunts, foxes, and equestrian contests and exhibitions. On one wall hangs a stunning photograph by local photographer Peter Gilles taken during one of the local September foxhunts. If you're in the area on a Saturday morning in the fall, don't miss this stirring scene.

Michigan's oldest continuously running restaurant, the White Horse is popular with both locals and travelers. Owners Tim and Lisa Wilkins, who bought the inn in 2001, have retained many of the old traditions and recipes while updating the menu. "We try and run the place and do business the way old Lorenzo intended the inn to be operated," says Tim. Not a bad idea, since apparently his ghost makes regular appearances both in the bar and upstairs in the tearoom.

The food, which has been described as "old-fashioned country style cuisine," is served in

generous portions at reasonable prices. The White Horse is known for its Fox Hunt Salad with Gorgonzola cheese and a scrumptious poppy seed dressing, all-you-can eat Fish and Chips, a thick beef and vegetable soup, pierogies that melt in your mouth, and of course the famous French Toast and Bread Pudding.

Never having been a fan of pierogies, I was convinced by a charming waitress who

In September, a local landowner hosts a foxhunt and the riders, horses, and dogs gather in front of the White Horse before they head for the hunt. Photo© Peter Gilles, used with permission.

Historic White Horse Inn Bread Pudding with Rum Sauce

∼ SERVES 6 TO 8 ∼

BREAD PUDDING

1 loaf plain Texas toast
  or French bread

4 large eggs

2 large egg yolks

2 cups granulated sugar

4 cups heavy cream

1 teaspoon vanilla extract

½ teaspoon ground cinnamon

Pinch of ground nutmeg

½ cup (1 stick) unsalted butter

1 cup confectioners' sugar

RUM SAUCE

2 tablespoons dark rum

1 cup (2 sticks) unsalted butter,
  at room temperature

2 cups confectioners' sugar

1 cup heavy cream

For the bread pudding: Preheat the oven to 350°F. Cut the Texas toast into 1-inch cubes. If using French bread, cut the loaf into ¾-inch-thick slices, then into 1-inch cubes. In a large bowl, beat the eggs, egg yolks, and granulated sugar together until blended. Whisk in the cream, vanilla, cinnamon, and nutmeg. Set aside.

In a small saucepan, melt the butter over low heat and stir in the confectioners' sugar until blended.

Pour half of the butter mixture into a 9 by 9-inch baking pan. Add the bread cubes to the pan and pour the egg mixture over the bread to soak it evenly. Pour the remaining butter mixture over the bread. Bake until golden brown, 20 to 25 minutes. Remove from the oven.

While the pudding is baking, make the rum sauce. In a medium saucepan, combine all the ingredients and stir to blend. Bring to a low simmer over low heat and cook for 5 minutes to burn off the alcohol. Do not boil.

To serve, cut the warm pudding into squares and serve in shallow bowls with the rum sauce drizzled over the top.

said they were her favorite and I ought to give them a chance. They are delicious. The lightly browned and crisp-at-the-edges pastry is filled with a subtly sweet farmer cheese and set off with a handful of grilled sweet onions.

When you taste the Bread Pudding you will know why this dessert has stayed on the menu for 160 years. The bread is infused with the rich flavor of eggs and milk, lightly kissed with nutmeg and cinnamon, sweetened with just the right amount of brown sugar, and bathed in dark rum. Fresh Michigan strawberries add their tart sweetness to this filling dessert.

The Wilkinses continue to consult with Lorenzo and a few other resident spirits on how to run the inn. "Someone is watching this building, someone is taking care of it. These ghosts are here for a reason, and I'm not going to ignore them," Tim promises. So don't expect them to change the siding, replace the historic sign, revamp the menu, or make other radical changes. They plan on keeping the place just the way it is. With Lorenzo's permission, that is.

Win Schuler's
MARSHALL, MI ~ EST. 1909

Schuler's is not like any other restaurant in this book. I don't own stock, I haven't married into the family, and I don't hold the deed, yet Win Schuler's is an important part of my personal and family history. It was where my family went for special occasions. We took out-of-town guests there, and I took my first prom date there for dinner.

One reason it was our favorite place was the treatment we received from everyone, and most especially from Win Schuler himself. Win was a consummate restaurateur who made everyone welcome, and who took great pride in remembering every customer's name.

My twin brother and I were dazzled when he greeted our parents. "Good evening, Dorothy

and Arnold," he would say, "and I'm delighted you brought Rick and Bob." Wow! Win Schuler remembered our names! We felt like kings. But that's the way Win treated everyone at this historic restaurant in the center of Michigan, about halfway between Chicago and Detroit.

Win's father, Albert Schuler, Sr., was a cigar-maker and peace officer who bought a small hotel in 1924, named it the Schuler Hotel, and successfully managed both the hotel and its small restaurant. Ten years later, Win joined the family business and took over managing the restaurant while his father ran the hotel.

Walking into the Centennial Room, Schuler's main dining room, is like a trip to jolly old England. It looks like a tavern in the Cotswolds with its moody interior, dark wood wainscoting, historic murals, and famous quotes inscribed in gold old English script on the ceiling beams.

In the early days, the restaurant was popular and a lot smaller, so that there were almost always long lines waiting to dine. When finally seated, people were served free appetizers: a crock of Bar Scheeze, a spreadable tangy cheese, plus a generous portion of meatballs in barbecue sauce and a fresh loaf of warm bread. This bighearted practice changed the restaurant forever; in fact, my mother would move heaven and earth to eat at Schuler's just because of the appetizers. The practice continues today, and though the portions are a bit smaller, the Bar Scheeze is as good as ever, and the meatballs in their smoky sauce bring back memories.

On my last visit, I relived my high school English class reading the literary quotes engraved on the beams until the reverie was broken by the arrival of a huge slice of perfectly medium-rare prime rib served on a large platter, garnished simply with a tiny sprig of rosemary. It was delicious and huge, and unlike in my teen years, I had to have half of it put into a doggie bag to take home.

Win's son Hans and grandson Larry are running the award-winning restaurant today, providing the same quality food, tradition, and warm hospitality. "We've never lost our focus on our guests," says fourth-generation-owner Larry Schuler. "Certainly we've evolved and changed with the times, but we've never given up on Win's idea that quality, and reinvesting in our own restaurant and in our community will bring the most long-lasting and best results that we could possibly ask for. As Win used to say, 'It's not how much, but how well.' We think this is our legacy and the most important part of Win Schuler's."

As a loyal customer for so many years, I would humbly suggest that the scrumptious

Chef Phil Schuknecht with Schuler's signature prime ribs of beef from the oven.

Bar Scheeze, savory meatballs, and world-class prime rib also have a bit to do with their longevity. I'll be back, and I'll bet you a crock of Bar Scheeze it will be soon.

Win Schuler checks out a fresh roll from their in-house bakery (1954).

Win Schuler's Heritage Cheese Spread

(AKA BAR SCHEEZE)

∼ SERVES 8 TO 12 ∼

1 cup (4 ounces) shredded sharp Cheddar cheese

1 cup canned garbanzo beans (chickpeas), drained and rinsed

8 ounces cream cheese, at room temperature

⅔ cup sour cream

4 tablespoons (½ stick) unsalted butter, at room temperature

1 tablespoon distilled white vinegar

2 teaspoons salt

1 tablespoon sugar

1 tablespoon sweet paprika

½ cup mayonnaise

¼ cup buttermilk

2 tablespoons prepared horseradish

Dash of brown ale

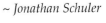

In a food processor, grind the Cheddar cheese.

Add the garbanzo beans and puree. Transfer the mixture to a stand mixer with a paddle attachment.

Add the cream cheese, sour cream, and butter and beat until smooth. Add all the remaining ingredients and beat until the cheese is blended and spreadable. Serve in a bowl or crock with bread and/or crackers.

"No matter how good a restaurant is, it has to change with the times, while still maintaining what has drawn them there to begin with. People want to have an anchor. They want to feel comfortable where they are."
~ Jonathan Schuler

Zehnder's

FRANKENMUTH, MI ~ EST. 1856

In 2010, Zehnder's restaurant in the Bavarian-inspired town of Frankenmuth, Michigan, served more meals than any other independent restaurant in the country—a total of almost 1 million. Those meals consisted of 900,000 pounds of chicken, 640 tons of cabbage, 180,000 pounds of mashed potatoes, 130,000 pounds of mixed vegetables, 40 tons of squash, 17,800 pounds of coffee, 26,000 gallons of ice cream, and over 1 million bakery items prepared in their own bakery. As America's largest family restaurant, Zehnder's nine dining rooms can seat more than fifteen hundred people at a time. They have served over 30 million guests in their 150 years, and they employ a staff of 750. Additionally, Zehnder's owns a 146-room hotel

with its own restaurant, indoor water park, arcade, championship golf course, gift shop, and cafeteria-style café for guests who want fast service.

To say this restaurant is successful is the height of understatement, especially considering its humble beginning in 1927 when William and Emilie Zehnder sold their nearby eighty-acre farm and scraped together an $8,000 down payment to take over the existing Exchange Hotel. The hotel was built in 1856 to house and feed travelers, farmers, and the legions of lumberjacks who worked the fields and forests around Frankenmuth, which had been settled by Bavarian settlers ten years earlier. One of the most popular dishes served at the hotel was a fried chicken dinner, a practice that the future owners took to heart, thereby preserving a tradition and building a restaurant dynasty unlike any in the country.

The Bavarian look of the town didn't begin until William Zehnder organized a Bavarian Festival in 1958 to make up for lost tourism when the main highway bypassed the town. He redesigned the restaurant and began an architectural tradition that lives on today, formally protected by local building codes and ordinances guarding the town's Germanic character.

With its German heritage, Frankenmuth has a strong tradition of beer making, and during Prohibition (1920–1933), the restaurant served beer in teapots to special customers who asked for "tea." This backfired when a tea-drinking official from the Treasury Department (who enforced the Volstead Act) ordered his favorite beverage, but found his

Right: Mama Zehnder cooks up batches of fried chicken on the stove in the 1920s.
Below: Zehnder's famed fried chicken lunch for four.

teapot full of a certain other "brew." The federal government came down hard, and William, Sr., and Emilie Zehnder received one of the largest fines ever levied for violating the Volstead Act. The Zehnders were fined $5,000 but agreed to chop up the restaurant's hand-carved oak bar to reduce the fine by $1,200.

Through hard work and innovative marketing, the family came through Prohibition and the Depression, though there were times when they thought they would have to close their doors. Al Zehnder, current chairman and CEO, shares how bad it was: "On one day during the Depression, receipts show that we made only seven cents that day when a customer bought a cigar and smoked it in the bar." In 1936, the restaurant installed a brand-new neon sign out in front, a sign that remains today and is reputed to be one of the longest continually used neon signs in the United States.

The large two-story kitchen churns out thousands of meals a day, including one monumental twenty-four-hour period in 1986 when they served a staggering 5,916 guests. Most days, however, they cater to two thousand to twenty-five hundred people, a number many restaurants would be happy to serve

in a week or a month. The cooks go through as many as a thousand chickens a day, precooking them overnight, then cutting them into pieces that are then breaded and fried in huge batches. While at Zehnder's, you must try their signature All-You-Can-Eat Chicken Dinner. It is a feast fit for an army: Twelve pieces of chicken, toast rounds with pâté and vegetable spread, creamy cabbage salad, large-curd cottage cheese, a veggie of your choice, buttered egg noodles topped with bread crumbs, mashed potatoes, stuffing, cranberry relish, fruit preserves, a bowl of chicken gravy, sliced fruit bread, and cups of chicken noodle soup. It's all-you-can-eat, and anything you run out of is speedily replaced.

Though the main dining room is almost always completely full, you'll wait no more than a few minutes for your food, and the waiter will no doubt be as attentive as if you were at a tiny café. The chicken is perfectly crisp and not the slightest bit greasy outside, and tender and moist inside. Lest you think they only serve chicken, other offerings include Beef Tenderloin Medallions with Morels, Veal Schnitzel, Bavarian Sausage, Broiled Whitefish (a local favorite), Breaded Yellow Perch (another favorite local fish), and a twelve-ounce Wiltshire Cured Pork Chop. All come with the same legion of side dishes that the chicken dinner offers.

The sheer variety of breads, rolls, pastries, cookies, donuts, cakes, pies, cupcakes, and other baked foods fresh from the bakery is amazing. In an average year they produce: 70,000 loaves of their fruit bread, 57,000 hand-rolled butter horns, 52,000 loaves of French bread, 30,000 hand-decorated sugar cookies, 20,000 loaves of Backofen round bread, 10,000 specialty Christmas and holiday cookies, 10,000 specialty cakes, 6,000 Z-King donuts (each the size of 3 regular donuts), and 6,000 fruit and cream pies. Oh, and a special treat called the Croissant Donut. You have to ask for one, as they make just a few each day, and I highly suggest you do. The tasty sweet croissant "donuts" are deep-fried and covered with a glaze that virtually melts in your mouth. It is perhaps the best donut I've ever had, and I've tried zillions of the yeasty wonders. Completely sated from my meal at Zehnder's, I waddled up the stairs. I had thought earlier of an afternoon of golf, but after that meal and those croissants, I knew the only driving I'd be doing was to their nearby hotel, though I thought maybe I would try the water park later. That is, if I could still fit in one of their giant float-tubes.

Zehnder's Creamy Cabbage Salad

✑ SERVES 4 TO 6 ✑

DRESSING
½ cup sour cream
½ cup half-and-half
1½ cups mayonnaise (not Miracle Whip)
⅞ cup (7 ounces) distilled white vinegar
1½ cups sugar
½ tablespoon Zehnder's Chicken Seasoning (see Note)

1 head green cabbage, cored and cut into fine shreds
¼ cup shredded red cabbage
¼ cup shredded carrot
¼ cup finely diced onion
¼ cup finely diced green bell pepper

For the dressing: In a medium bowl, combine all the ingredients and stir until the sugar is dissolved. Cover and refrigerate for 2 to 3 hours.

Place the shredded and diced vegetables in a large bowl and add half of the dressing. Toss to coat. Gradually add just enough of the remaining dressing to coat the salad well, but not enough to make it soggy.

NOTE: *The cabbage salad is Zehnder's most requested recipe. It has been part of the family-style chicken dinner since day 1. They call it "cabbage salad" rather than coleslaw because the cabbage is cut into long fine shreds rather than being chopped. You can purchase Zehnder's Chicken Seasoning in the gift shop and online.*

Al Zehnder, Chairman and CEO, and the restaurant's historic sign which was installed in 1936 and is believed to be one of the oldest working neon signs in America.

Gluek's Restaurant & Bar
MINNEAPOLIS, MN ~ EST. 1857

Everyone who has had the good fortune to eat walleye, please raise your hands. I see there aren't many hands in the air. Not surprising, because unless you live in one of the states along the Great Lakes or near other frigid bodies of water in North America, you probably haven't had walleye. Too bad, as it is delicious.

The walleye is a white fish found in the deep cold lakes of the northern United States and Canada. Its mild, sweet flesh has few bones and a meaty texture like that of salmon. In their native habitat, walleye have been known to live for up to twenty years.

The reason for this ichthyology lesson? One of our century-old restaurants is one of the few restaurants I know of to feature this delicious native fish on its menu.

Gluek's (pronounced Glick's) Restaurant & Bar, in the heart of downtown Minneapolis, began as a brewery in 1857. As the city grew so did the brewery, at one time producing five varieties of beer. They moved into their new building in 1902, the same building they occupy today, though they had to completely rebuild after a massive fire in 1989. Today, the place has the same Bavarian charm that it had in its earlier years. The restaurant is reminiscent of the beer halls of Munich—essentially one very large barroom, with stools at the bar, tall tables with backed stools in the center, and tables with benches and chairs at the back. The walls are decorated with historic pictures of the original brewery and of the restaurant through the years, and there are more than a half dozen framed photographs of various celebrations when

with locals but with tourists who give it a try, often at the prompting of either a local friend or a member of the waitstaff. You can order beer-battered Walleye Fingers or Walleye Croquettes in butter sauce as a starter, sautéed Citrus Walleye Pike Fillets for an entree, and their Famous Walleye Sandwich, either deep-fried or grilled, for lunch.

A relative neophyte to walleye, I decided to sample three of the four specialties. The croquettes are delicious, especially bathed in the lemon butter sauce, and the fingers are tasty, dipped in tartar sauce or sprinkled with vinegar. But the grilled walleye sandwich was outstanding. The firm-fleshed fil-let is served in a bakery-fresh roll, layered with fresh lettuce, tomato, and heavy dabs of the piquant sweet dill-caper-tartar sauce, spritzed with a lemon wedge.

Chef Al Imbrome applies the finishing touches to a walleye sandwich.

Prohibition ended. One shows several dozen folks waiting outside the bar at midnight for the bar to open so they could quaff a few brews to celebrate. Another shows four men either pushing the first truckload of beer out of the brewery, or caught in the act of trying to grab a case or two. Only history knows.

Sadly, Gluek's three beers—Pilsner, Dark, and Red— are available only on tap at the restaurant these days, as the Cold Spring brewery, which took over brewing their beers in 1990, phased out mass production of the brand in 2010. But this is a bar in beer-drinkin' Minneapolis, and believe me they have enough varieties of beers to satisfy anyone. As of this writing, they have forty-four varieties, seventeen of which are on tap.

But back to the fishing hole. Walleye has been on the menu for decades and is popular not only

The bar is always packed at night, but on nights the Twins play games two blocks away, it becomes a madhouse, awash with the sounds of raucous

The original Gluek's Brewery opened in 1857; the restaurant today that evolved from the brewery offers 44 varieties of beer, but sadly today, the brewery is closed.

celebrating when the home team wins, and resonating with the sounds of "how loud can we play this music" tunes from various local bands blaring from the wall speakers. At lunch, though, the only sound is the clinking of glasses and the excited oohs and aahs from fellow walleye virgins as they enjoy their first delighted bites of Minnesota's official state fish.

You can put down your hands now. Class is over.

Walleye Croquettes

∽ SERVES 2 ∽

1 walleye fillet (about 8 ounces)

1 teaspoon Cajun seasoning

2 tablespoons olive oil

2 tablespoons finely diced
   red bell pepper

2 tablespoons finely diced
   green bell pepper

1 teaspoon minced garlic

½ cup heavy cream

3 tablespoons cream cheese

¼ cup grated Provolone cheese

2 tablespoons grated
   Parmesan cheese

¼ cup finely diced green onion,
   including green parts

2 tablespoons unsalted butter

2 tablespoons all-purpose flour,
   plus more for rolling

Vegetable oil for deep-frying

1 large egg, beaten with ¼ cup milk

1 cup Italian bread crumbs

Dill-Caper Tartar Sauce, for serving
   (recipe follows)

Lemon wedges, for serving

Dust the fillet with the Cajun seasoning. In a medium skillet, heat 1 tablespoon of the olive oil over medium heat and sauté the fish until opaque throughout, 2 to 3 minutes on each side. Transfer to a plate and set aside.

In a medium saucepan, heat the remaining olive oil over low heat and sauté the bell peppers until tender. Add the garlic and sauté for 2 to 3 minutes (do not brown). Add the cream, cream cheese, Provolone, Parmesan, and green onion and bring to a simmer, then crumble the walleye and add to the mixture. Remove from the heat and set aside.

In a small saucepan, melt the butter over medium-low heat and stir in the 2 tablespoons flour. Cook, stirring constantly, until the mixture is a medium brown color and becomes very thick. Add to the pan with the fish and stir to blend. Let cool completely.

Scoop the fish mixture into golf-ball-sized balls, then roll in flour to coat evenly. Place on a baking sheet lined with parchment paper and freeze until firm, at least 2 hours. In a Dutch oven or deep fryer, bring 3 inches of oil to 375°F on a deep-fat thermometer. Dip the frozen balls into the egg-milk mixture to coat evenly, and then into the bread crumbs. Cook in batches until golden brown, 3 to 4 minutes. Using a wire-mesh skimmer, transfer to paper towels to drain. Serve at once with the tartar sauce and lemon wedges.

Dill-Caper Tartar Sauce

∽ MAKES ABOUT 1¼ CUPS ∽

1 cup mayonnaise

1 tablespoon dill or
   sweet pickle relish

Juice and grated zest of ½ lemon

1 tablespoon capers, drained

1½ teaspoons dried dill

½ teaspoon sugar

¼ teaspoon freshly ground white pepper

¼ teaspoon onion powder

In a medium bowl, combine all the ingredients and stir to blend. Use now, or cover and refrigerate for up to a week.

Savoy Grill
KANSAS CITY, MO ~ EST. 1903

In the late 1800s, Kansas City, like many American cities, experienced a building boom, and brothers John and Charles Arbuckle of the Arbuckle Coffee Company decided the city needed a luxury hotel and then set out to build one.

The hotel immediately attracted political bigwigs, stage personalities, and the wealthy cattlemen and grain merchants who had money to burn because of the success of the KC cattle yards and the demand for Western beef from East Coast restaurants. As elegant as any hotel in Chicago or New York or Boston, the Savoy Hotel featured imported marble and tile, carved woodwork, gleaming brass fixtures, a rooftop garden, and a large ballroom. The stained-glass windows and a magnificent skylight beamed a rainbow of vivid color into the Victorian lobby.

By 1903, the Arbuckles had added a new west wing, installing the Savoy Grill dining room. Famed artist Edward Holslag painted expansive murals above the oak paneling depicting wagon trains heading west on the Santa Fe Trail from Kansas City's Westport Landing. The high-beamed ceiling, distinctive lanterns made from old gaslights, and an enormous carved oak bar that dated back to the McKinley presidency all contributed to what was essentially an all-boys' club; women weren't admitted until 1907. The waiters then, as they do now, sported crisp starched and pressed white jackets, bow ties, and numbered silver pins. Often you didn't ask for John or Henry, you asked for number two or number thirty-one.

Celebrities such as Teddy Roosevelt, William Howard Taft, actresses Marie Dressler and Sarah

Bernhardt, comedian W. C. Fields, political comedian Will Rogers, and oilman John D. Rockefeller stayed in the luxurious suites and dined in the formal dining room. Kansas City strip and T-bone steaks were all the rage, as was a new culinary treat, prairie chicken, a kind of grouse. The Savoy also somehow managed to get in live lobsters, an unheard-of treat in the middle of the country.

In 1919, local businessman Harry Truman opened a haberdashery store on West Twelfth Street and often walked to the Savoy for lunch. He came so often that when he became president, the Savoy put a brass plaque on the wall of his favorite booth. Presidents Harding, McKinley, Gerald Ford, and Ronald Reagan also dined here and were usually seated in the presidential booth.

As were other big-city restaurants of its kind, the Savoy was badly affected by both the Depression and the movement of families out of the citys to suburban neighborhoods. In 1960, when the hotel and dining room was failing badly, twenty-seven-year-old restaurateur Don Lee purchased the Grill. Five years later, he also bought the hotel, which was then experiencing about 30 percent occupancy. Lee believed the area would come back with new

Magician Harry Houdini was once tricked into answering a phone in an outside phone booth, which an employee then locked. The fire department had to be called to get him out. Below left: Owner Don Lee rolls up his sleeves in the kitchen.

businesses. By 1970, his faith was rewarded when the hotel was added to the National Register of Historic Places, and after seeing his success at resuscitating the Savoy, investors gradually began developing other buildings in the area, bringing more people back downtown.

Lee kept renovating the hotel, turning the old rooms into luxurious Victorian-era bed-and-breakfast suites, adding antiques, upgrading the bathrooms, widening the halls, and promoting the history of the hotel and Grill. Hollywood took notice and filmed segments of two movies here:

Mr. and Mrs. Bridge, starring Paul Newman and Joanne Woodward, and *Cross of Fire*, starring John Heard.

The Grill could be described as a sophisticated steak and seafood house. For a restaurant in cattle country, it has a surprising amount of seafood entrees (thirty-three on the dinner menu), and it is known regionally as the best place for lobster. But it is no slouch in the steak department; choices include Chateaubriand, Strip, Sirloin, Steak au Poivre, T-Bone, Top Sirloin, and Prime Rib. The beef for the 4H Strip Sirloin is supplied by 4H Club members, who raise the animals to help pay for college.

I was torn between their signature KC Strip and the Steak au Poivre, but opted for a steak without culinary distractions or fancy side dishes. They have those aplenty but I wanted steak, salad, and a spud. The only distractions then were the historic murals, huge wooden columns, and white table linens that tempted me to imagine sitting next to John D. or W. C. in the city's premier restaurant.

Personable and very hands-on owner Don Lee can often be found helping in the kitchen, but at dinner he dons a Kelly green sport coat and heads to the dining room to greet guests, many of whom he knows on a first-name basis. "I love this place," Don confesses. "It's sort of a historic monument, and the restaurant has always been first class. Time marches on for all of us. I've been at the front door every Saturday night for forty-nine years." If I had to guess, I would guess that Don Lee is the reason the Grill has been successful for that half-century, as he is pretty first class himself.

Steak au Poivre

∾ SERVES 2 ∾

3 tablespoons freshly cracked black pepper

2 (6- to 8-ounce) strip steaks

2 tablespoons unsalted butter

1½ tablespoons chopped shallots

½ cup dry red wine

2 tablespoons brandy

1½ cups homemade brown sauce (sauce á l'espagnole) or HP Brown Sauce (see Note)

1 teaspoon olive oil

Pour the pepper into a shallow dish and roll each steak in the pepper, pressing down to make sure some adheres to both sides.

Preheat the oven to 200°F. In a large skillet, melt the butter over medium heat until it begins to turn brown. Add the steaks and sear for 2 minutes on each side. Transfer the steaks to a plate, cover with aluminum foil, and place in the oven for 5 to 6 minutes to keep warm.

Add the shallots, wine, and brandy to the skillet the steaks were cooked in and simmer for 1 minute, then add the brown sauce and simmer for 1 to 1½ minutes. Set aside.

Heat a clean large skillet over high heat. Add the olive oil and swirl the pan to distribute it evenly. Add the steaks and pour on the sauce. Take the skillet to the table, serving the steaks right from the hot pan. Serve the sauce alongside.

NOTE: HP Brown Sauce is available in some gourmet foods stores and online.

Grand Union Hotel
FORT BENTON, MT ~ EST. 1882

To say the Grand Union Hotel has overcome a rocky past would be the height of understatement. After facing one local disaster and downturn after another, the Grand Union has returned to "grand" status despite problems that would have destroyed most other hotels.

The hotel was built on the banks of the Missouri River at the peak of the steamboat era by William H. Todd, and was designed to provide weary travelers with a comfortable place to stay and enjoy exceptional meals after disembarking from the steamboats and before they joined the waiting wagon trains heading to the frontier. At that time, Fort Benton was a rapidly growing community and the transportation hub of Montana Territory. Because of the harsh winters, Todd had the three-story hotel built with bricks, a half-million of them.

The fleet of steamers plying the Missouri brought in just about everything they needed to build and furnish the massive hotel. All of the construction and the interior furnishings cost a staggering $200,000, which was big, big money in 1882. Building the same hotel today would cost more than $3,750,000! The hotel was "something else," says current co-owner Cheryl Gagnon. "It had a popular saloon (off limits to unescorted ladies), a luxurious dining room, a women's parlor with a separate staircase (so women would avoid the dirty old

men in the saloon or playing poker in the gaming room) where the ladies would wait for a gentleman to escort them into the dining room. For calls to nature, both sexes headed to a two-story-high sixteen-hole outhouse."

A newspaper commemorating the hotel's 125th birthday shared the menu for the 1882 Christmas dinner: canapé of Russian caviar, orange oyster cocktail, mock turtle soup, consommé White House, fried fillet of sole, mushrooms à la français, haunch of elk, asparagus au beurre, mashed potatoes, lobster à la Newburg, stuffed

The former ladies lounge has been turned into a guest suite.

young Montana turkey, bread dressing, roast suckling pig with baked apple, saddle of venison, Yorkshire pudding, sweet corn on the cob, New Century punch, loin of beef, hot mince pie, pumpkin pie, steamed English pudding with brandy sauce, apple pie à la mode, and Christmas ice cream with cake.

Sadly, beginning the very next year, fate and progress were not kind to the hotel and its seventeen successive proprietors. When the railroads came to town (both the Utah Northern and the Canadian Pacific), the steamers stopped running. The population of Fort Benton plunged. Two years after the grand (some said ostentatious) opening, the hotel was sold in a sheriff's sale to a local bank. New owners faced bad crop years, World War I, Prohibition, the Depression, and World War II. The hotel fell apart and became infested with insect and animal vermin—a situation not conducive to attracting guests. So the hotel kept changing hands and, in 1995, went to a contractor who was given the deed when the owners were unable to pay him for work he'd done.

That's when Jim and Cheryl Gagnon, both native Montanans, discovered the hotel. While visiting Jim's dad, they noticed the intriguing old hotel for sale, took a peek, and the next day toured with a realtor. After months of research, they bought it and began a multimillion-dollar restoration program that returned it to almost-new. The dining room, guest rooms, and lobby are now as crisp and new as they must have been in 1882. Antiques are everywhere, the carpets are new, the wood is refinished, and the plumbing and wiring are updated. The restored rooms are comfortable, quiet, and peaceful. And it has what the original hotel lacked: en suite bathrooms and spacious closets.

Chef Scott Meyers has elevated the hotel's cuisine to world-class levels. Emphasizing local farm-to-table and seasonal ingredients, his menu is impressive for its variety and creativity. His buffalo steak on a bed of spring vegetables is astounding, considering the hotel is in a tiny town in the middle of rural Montana. His other dishes are equally sophisticated and perfectly presented. They include Moulard Duck Rillettes with red onion jam, crostini, and micro thyme; Baby Spinach Salad with Strawberries, Goat Cheese, and Balsamic Vinaigrette; Twin Hills Roast Pork with Lime and Chipotle, served with spring vegetables, red quinoa grains, and huckleberry and cabernet sauce.

It's plain to see that with the the passion and tender care of the new owners and the expenditure of thousands of hours of sweat and toil, not to mention millions of dollars, the Grand Union is grand once more.

Grand Union Buffalo Rib Eye with Spring Vegetables

∾ SERVES 1 ∾

ZINFANDEL-TRUFFLE SAUCE

1 tablespoon oil

Buffalo meat scraps (fat trimmed from the steak)

1 small carrot, peeled and diced

1 stalk celery, diced

½ medium yellow onion, diced

1 bay leaf

5 peppercorns

1½ cups zinfandel wine

½ cup veal or rich chicken broth

2 sprigs fresh thyme

Kosher salt

3 cups water

¼ cup kamut berries (see Note)

1 (10-ounce) buffalo rib-eye steak, trimmed of excess fat

½ teaspoon kosher salt

½ teaspoon freshly ground black pepper

2 tablespoons olive oil

3 tablespoons unsalted butter

5 sprigs fresh thyme

2 sprigs fresh rosemary

5 small morel mushrooms

5 wild ramps (see Note)

4 baby squash, preferably with blossoms

6 fiddleheads (see Note)

3 whole cloves black garlic, plus 1 minced black garlic clove (see Note)

1 shallot, minced

½ cup chicken broth

1 teaspoon minced fresh chives

3 to 4 chive blossoms

Pinches of Maldon salt, for garnish (see Note)

For the sauce: In a small saucepan, heat the oil over medium-high heat and sauté the buffalo scraps until browned. Using a slotted spoon, transfer the scraps to a plate. Add the carrot, celery, onion, bay leaf, and peppercorns. Cover the pan with a piece of aluminum foil, then the lid of the pan. Reduce the heat to low and cook for 5 minutes. Add the wine and cook until reduced by three-quarters. Add the broth and cook to reduce by half. Add the thyme, remove from the heat, and let steep for 3 minutes. Strain through a fine-mesh sieve and season with kosher salt to taste. Set aside and keep warm.

In a medium saucepan, bring the water to a boil. Add the kamut berries, reduce the heat to a simmer, and cook until tender, 45 minutes or so. Add more water if necessary to keep the berries from burning. Drain and spread the berries on a rimmed baking sheet to cool.

Season the steak with salt and pepper on both sides. Heat a large cast-iron skillet over high heat. Add 1 tablespoon of the oil to the pan and cook the steak for 5 minutes on one side. Turn the steak over and cook for 2 minutes, then add 1 tablespoon of the butter, 2 sprigs of the thyme, and 1 sprig of the rosemary. Turn the heat off and baste the steak with the butter for 1 minute. Using tongs, transfer the steak to a wire rack on a plate; tent with aluminum foil.

In a medium skillet, melt 1 more tablespoon of the butter with the remaining 1 tablespoon olive oil over medium-low heat. Add the morels, ramps, squash, and fiddleheads and sauté for 2 minutes. Add the whole black garlic cloves and half of the minced shallot and cook for another minute. Add ¼ cup of the chicken broth, the 3 remaining sprigs of thyme, and the remaining sprig of rosemary; cook for 2 minutes. Taste and adjust the seasoning.

To finish the kamut berries, bring the remaining ¼ cup chicken broth to a simmer in a small saucepan. Add the shallot, the minced garlic, the remaining 1 tablespoon butter, and the kamut. Toss until heated through.

Spoon the kamut onto a warmed serving plate and garnish with the chives. Spoon the vegetables around the kamut. Place the buffalo steak on top of the berries (either in slices or whole). Drizzle the Zinfandel-Truffle Sauce over the plate. Sprinkle with the chive flowers and pinches of Maldon salt. Serve at once.

NOTE: Kamut is an ancient relative of wheat available in many natural foods stores. The berries, or whole grains, are large and chewy when cooked. Wild ramps, also known as wild leeks, come into season early in the spring and are available at many farmers' markets. Black garlic is a sweet and savory Korean specialty created through a month-long fermentation process; it is available online and can also be made at home. Fiddleheads are the young fronds of the ostrich fern, available in spring at farmers' markets and specialty grocers. Maldon salt is a flaky sea salt produced in Maldon, England, and found at specialty foods stores.

M&M Cigar Store
BUTTE, MT ~ EST. 1890

The M & M Cigar Store daytime staff, from left: Kacie Rayboulb, Crystal Albrecht, Brian McLeod, Shana Fortune, Jerry Isaacson, and Wendy Hoar.

Miners from China, England, Ireland, Finland, Italy, Mexico, Sweden, South America, Canada, and just about every state of the union turned small, sleepy Butte, Montana, into a boomtown in the 1870s, at one point swelling the small city's population to a whopping 100,000 people.

It started with discovery of gold in 1860, increased in tempo when silver was discovered in 1870, and grew to a fever pitch when the largest deposit of copper the world had ever seen was unearthed in 1881. During that period, one-third of all the copper used in the United States came from mines here.

Even after a massive fire that destroyed the entire central business district in 1879, Butte was the most prosperous town in the country. During World War I, every single bullet manufactured in the U.S. used Montana copper. And the metal was just what the new electrical age required. By the mid-1880s, the mines here were yielding almost two thousand tons of copper and silver ore every day, well over a million dollars every month. Its citizens boasted that they lived on the "richest hill on earth."

With the miners and the money came a second boom—of taverns, saloons, and bars where the miners could spend their dollars, eat and drink, and make whoopee in the twenty-four-hour-a-day red-light district. Thus, in 1890, Sam Martin and William F. Mosby decided to open a saloon and restaurant. Shortly thereafter, they built a bowling alley in the basement, and, more important for many, opened a gambling hall on the second floor. It was an entertainment megacenter of the day, an unabashed all-day, all-night drinking establishment.

Faced with competition from more than two hundred other saloons and bars, the owners of the M & M Cigar Store decided that providing good, hearty, and filling meals would set M & M above the others, and it quickly became known for the quality of its vittles, as well as the generous pours of whiskey and the wide variety of cigars it stocked.

Prohibition, in a state where you could drink and drive until 2005, was almost totally ignored. Sure, the "cigar stores" sold cigars, but these were enjoyed along with shots of whiskey and rye, literally buckets of beer (called "growlers"), and a favorite drink of the time: the Shawn O'Farrell, a shot of whiskey with a beer chaser. When Carrie A.

The M & M Cigar Store in 1939 when it actually sold cigars and whiskey, now legally, in addition to food.

Nation, the Prohibition-loving leader of the Women's Christian Temperance Union, came to Butte she found a less-than-welcoming reception. Many of the bars in town displayed a sign that said "All Nations Welcomed But Carrie." Her last foray was in Butte, where she assaulted May Maloy, a popular madam and the owner of a brothel, dance hall, and café, with the intention of destroying some erotic paintings and Maloy's liquor supply. But May, a strong woman herself, stopped Carrie in her tracks and drove her out of town. It was the only recorded failure of more than thirty-five of Carrie's barroom attacks across the country.

In 1949, writer Jack Kerouac visited Butte and, after spending a Sunday night at the M & M, wrote,

"It was Sunday night, I had hoped the saloons would stay open long enough for me to see them. They never even closed. In a great old-time saloon I had a giant beer. On the wall was a big electric signboard flashing gambling numbers . . . . What characters in there: old prospectors, gamblers, whores, miners, Indians, cowboys, tobacco-chewing businessmen! Groups of sullen Indians drank rotgut in the john. Hundreds of men played cards in an atmosphere of smoke and spittoons. It was the end of my quest for an ideal bar . . ."

M & M closed briefly for one year (2009–2010), much to the anguish and chagrin of many loyal customers. But new owner Sam Jankovich reopened the iconic bar and restaurant on St. Patrick's Day, 2010, and promised that as with Martin and Mosby (who threw away the keys the day they opened the place), "the place will never be closed. Even for a minute." The reopened bar and restaurant sports a freshly scrubbed interior, fresh paint, new and larger windows, exposed brick walls, bright signage, and large period photographs of downtown Butte in its glory days. The menu, as always, features burgers, fries, pork chops and steaks, Polish sausage, ravioli, breaded chicken and omelets, as well as cold sandwiches and other typical diner foods, all in large portions. The Whatzit is a popular bacon and cheese hamburger served on toasted Texas toast. Brian, the cook, points out that "our beef is always fresh, never frozen." The large portion of French fries is piping hot, sprinkled with vinegar and a dash or two of salt.

The Garbage Omelet, a mass of ham, bacon, sausage, onions, peppers, tomatoes, and mushrooms, served with a plateful of crisp hash browns and toast, would feed two to three normal people or perhaps one hungry miner.

The Art Deco façade has been freshened, and the now-repaired historic neon sign is flashing out a welcome to "all nations." The M & M Cigar Store is open for business again—24/7.

Garbage Omelet

∾ SERVES 1 OR 2 ∾

4 large eggs

2 tablespoons unsalted butter or clarified butter

½ cup cooked ground sausage

½ cup crumbled cooked bacon

½ cup cubed cooked ham

¼ cup chopped yellow onion

¼ cup sliced mushrooms

¼ cup chopped tomatoes

¼ cup diced green bell pepper

4 slices Cheddar, pepper Jack, Swiss, or American cheese

Hash browns and brown gravy, for serving

In a large bowl, whisk the eggs until they are a pale yellow, then whisk another 2 minutes to incorporate air into the liquid.

In a heavy, medium sauté pan, melt the butter over medium-low heat. When the butter in the pan is hot enough to make a drop of water hiss, pour in the eggs. Don't stir! Let the eggs cook for up to 1 minute, or until the bottom starts to set. With a heat-resistant rubber spatula, gently push one edge of the beaten eggs into the center of the pan, while tilting the pan to allow the still liquid egg to flow in underneath. Repeat with the other edges until there's no liquid left. Your eggs should now resemble a bright yellow pancake that should easily slide around on the nonstick surface. If it sticks at all, loosen it with your spatula.

Gently flip the egg pancake over, using your spatula to ease it over if necessary. Cook for another few seconds, or until there is no uncooked egg left. Add the sausage, bacon, ham, vegetables, and cheese to one-half of the egg pancake. With your spatula, lift one edge of the egg and fold it across and over, so that the edges line up. Cook for another minute or so, but don't overcook or allow the egg to turn brown.

Gently transfer the finished omelet to a plate. Serve with hash browns and brown gravy.

Glur's Tavern
COLUMBUS, NE ~ EST. 1876

In 1882, officials of the small town of Columbus, Nebraska, asked a local man to help prepare for the town's upcoming Fourth of July celebration. So the man gathered a few cowboy and rancher friends, rounded up some horses, some local Native Americans, a couple of wagons, and put on what many agreed was a great Western-themed show. The success of the holiday show gave him an idea, and he decided to take the show on the road to national and then worldwide acclaim.

You might have heard the gentleman's name: William Cody, or as he's more widely known, Buffalo Bill. And thus was born Buffalo Bill's Wild West (they did not use the word "Show" in the early days). The live theatrical troupe not only performed across the United States but also put on shows in France, Italy, Belgium, and the United Kingdom.

Cody secured his nickname when he and another buffalo hunter (Bill Comstock), who was also using the name Buffalo Bill, competed in a contest to see who could kill the most buffalo in one day. Cody shot sixty-nine and Comstock bagged forty-eight, so William "Buffalo Bill" Cody got to keep the legendary honorific.

Because of Columbus's proximity to Omaha and the availability of a well-developed fairground, Cody decided to rehearse the show there. Cody's best friend and one of the star performers of the show, former Pawnee Scouts leader Major Frank North, also lived in town. In May 1883, the entire production company—seven railcars filled with animals, equipment, and more than seventy staff—arrived to prepare for their first national tour. Days were spent rehearsing and training the horses and developing the script that the troupe would end up performing around the world for three decades.

After a few weeks, North became seriously ill and died. Several days later, many of the cast of cowboys, in their chaps with holsters strapped on, and Indians in their full feather and paint costumes attended the funeral with Colonel Cody and afterward headed to Bucher's Tavern (as Glur's was known then) to celebrate Major North with a few drinks.

Being a showman and the PR genius of his day, Buffalo Bill footed the entire tab by placing a $1,000 bill on the bar to the absolute shock of owner William Bucher. The word of this spread around town, and everyone who heard about it came to

Buffalo Bill Cody and his troupe of cowboys and Indian performers once held a celebration for one of their own at Bucher's Tavern (Glur's predecessor) after the funeral.

Buffalo Bill Baked Beans

∾ SERVES 6 TO 8 ∾

1 pound bacon, cooked and crumbled

1 pound hamburger, browned

1 cup diced onion

¾ cup ketchup

½ cup firmly packed brown sugar

3 tablespoons yellow (ballpark) mustard

1 tablespoon cider vinegar

1 (15-ounce) can black beans, rinsed and drained

1 (15-ounce) can chili beans, rinsed and drained

1 (15-ounce) can kidney beans, rinsed and drained

1 (15-ounce) can pork and beans

Garlic toast, for serving (optional)

In a deep pot, combine all of the ingredients except the garlic toast and cook over medium-high heat until the liquid is bubbling. You can also cook the beans in a slow cooker, covered, on low heat for 4 to 5 hours. Serve with garlic toast or alongside burgers or hot dogs.

Tom and Carrie Trofholz used to be loyal customers, but are now the tavern's owners.

the tavern to see the first, and last, $1,000 bill they would ever see. A copy of the bill, a newspaper article describing the incident, and an original Wild West poster is on display in Glur's today.

Swiss immigrant Joseph Bucher founded Glur's in 1876; his brother Louis took over fourteen years later. He worked for Bucher's for eleven years before purchasing the tavern, which he then operated for fifty-five years, when sons Louis and Conrad took over, surviving Prohibition by turning the building into a "soft drink parlor." Unlike many such places, they actually sold only soft drinks.

Todd Trofholz, a regular customer before he moved to Omaha, purchased the bar in 1992. "The community has been very supportive, and since we took over we've made dozens of new friends and met a lot of great people," he says. "Because of their love of the place, people who have moved away stop by when they visit town, just to see if the old place is still here."

Throughout Glur's history, food has always been secondary in the minds of patrons, but they do serve food. Their "kitchen" is a tiny 2 by 3-foot grill and a tiny deep fryer at the back of the bar. They have assorted sandwiches and hot dogs, and sometimes soup, beans, or other offerings, but the burger is king. And of course their circular fries, which have been named "Best Fries in Columbus" for several years: round slices of whole potato, skin left on, deep-fried and sprinkled with seasoned salt.

The interior looks much as it probably did during the Wild West days (minus the myriad signs, pennants, and balloons), with creaky floors, tilted walls, worn wooden support beams, and a low ceiling. The tables are over one hundred years old, the walls are lined with historic pictures and posters, and there are several mounted deer heads. Take away the neon lights, wide-screen TVs, and advertising and you could be standing there with Buffalo Bill himself, enjoying a refreshing brew or shot. But for heaven's sake, don't try to pay with a $1,000 bill. They might not have change.

The Martin Hotel
WINNEMUCCA, NV ~ EST. 1898

The Martin Hotel is stuck in the middle of Nevada nothingness, 150 miles from the nearest big city (Reno) to the west and 350 miles to the biggest city (Salt Lake City) to the east. In 1986, *Life* magazine reported that driving there was an adventure in staying awake and called this section of Highway 80 "the loneliest highway in America," though Winnemucca, Nevada, population 8,283, was a small beacon of civilization in the desert.

It hasn't all been sleepiness, though. Butch Cassidy's gang (and maybe Butch himself) robbed a bank here on September 13, 1900. And Winnemucca, in a state that legalizes prostitution, has a popular red-light district on a small cul-de-sac one block from the center of town, advertised with neon lights. Most important to foodies everywhere, the small city is a haven for Basque food, with four Basque restaurants serving hearty meals family style on long community tables.

Winnemucca, named for a famous Paiute Indian chief, was settled in the late 1800s in the center of the most direct route across the Great Basin for the wagons heading to California. The town sprang out of the wilderness as a place to buy water and feed for the animals, fill the water barrels, and replenish the food supplies for the hardy pioneers.

With the coming of the Southern Pacific Railroad, the town boomed, well, actually it banged, and a passel of boardinghouses and small hotels opened in response. It is rumored that the hotel functioned as a bordello in the 1880s, and then sometime around 1898, Alfonso Pasquale opened the Roman Tavern and Restaurant in the building. Over the years, the ownership changed several times until it became the Martin Hotel in 1913.

Somewhere around this time, Basque sheepherders arrived from Spain and France to take over the flocks, most arriving with nothing but their packs and a loyal dog or two, hence the introduction of the traditional Basque style of dining. There weren't enough tables for everyone, so the small local dining rooms were filled with long communal tables where big bowls of food were distributed family style.

Basque restaurants are still around in the sheep country of Idaho, Arizona, California, and Nevada, where they are found in small towns like Winnemucca, Gardnerville, Elko, Los Banos, San Juan Bautista, and Tacna. Sheep were wintered in the mountains and valleys where the snows didn't fall, and were brought to town in the spring. Shepherds, hungry from their long trek, dug into huge plates of beef and lamb, homemade soups, salads, beans, spaghetti, bread, red wine, and Picon Punch.

From the outside, the Martin looks like a latter-day Western saloon, with iron hitching posts; a second-floor veranda shading the entryway; American, Basque, and Nevada state flags out front; and a garland of Christmas lights circling the entrance. (The hitching posts, by the way, still get occasional use by local cowpokes and shepherds.) Inside, you're likely to be seated with strangers at one of the long communal tables. Both the bar area and the larger two-sectioned dining room are sparsely decorated, with a few paintings and drawings by local artists hanging on the wood-paneled or historic pressed-tin walls.

Each diner chooses his or her own entree from a surprisingly sophisticated and extensive menu that includes Black Angus rib eye (14, 16, or 18 ounces), daily lamb selections, huge pork chops, Solomo (boneless pork simmered in garlic and pimientos), sweetbreads, beef tongue, salmon or cod steaks, fried prawns, pasta, chicken-fried steak, liver and onions, and chicken Marsala. The lamb shank is exceedingly tender, and loaded with garlic. When slightly nudged with a fork, the meat literally falls off the bone. The lamb is moist and full of flavor. The shank is accompanied with a florescent green mint jelly. The fries are remarkably good, but you can also choose garlic mashed potatoes— if your lamb wasn't garlicky enough.

First courses and side dishes consist of large bowls of homemade chicken noodle or garlic soup, green salad topped with smoky Basque beans, tarragon-spiced carrots, buttered skillet corn, freshly baked bread, and hand-cut locally grown French fries or garlic mashed potatoes, all created in a kitchen cooking area smaller than the restaurant's longest table (which seats twelve). The dessert of choice is a very rich bread pudding mantled in whipped cream.

Lamb Shanks with Garlic

∾ SERVES 8 TO 10 ∾

10 lamb shanks

2 teaspoons kosher salt

1 teaspoon freshly ground black pepper

1 tablespoon garlic powder

2 tablespoons minced fresh rosemary leaves

1 tablespoon minced fresh thyme leaves

1 cup minced garlic

1 (750-ml) bottle Pisano Merlot Tannat Cisplatino red wine (see Note)

3 quarts water

½ cup chicken base

Preheat the oven to 350°F. Add the shanks to an oiled Dutch oven and sprinkle them with the salt, pepper, garlic powder, rosemary, and thyme. Spread the minced garlic over the shanks. Cover and roast for 1 hour, turning the meat frequently to brown both sides. Pour the wine, water, and chicken base into the pan around, not over the lamb. Reduce the oven temperature to 300°F. Cover the pan and braise for 2 hours, or until the meat is falling from the bone. Serve with some of the sauce poured over the shanks.

NOTE: If you don't like garlic, avoid, shun, steer clear of, evade, pass on this recipe. If you do plan on making it, have a bottle of mouthwash and a tin of breath mints nearby. Breathing on anyone after eating this is a felony in nine states and Puerto Rico.

Martin Hotel owner John Arant says that this dish must be made with Pisano wine from Uruguay: "There is no substituting other wines in this recipe; we've tried it and they don't work." You can purchase Pisano online, or just use a good merlot or cabernet and don't tell John.

Red wine is included with dinner, but you must try the Picon Punch, a Basque tradition and a Martin Hotel favorite. The Picon, a delicious cocktail with a subtle orange flavor that isn't so much bittersweet as nicely balanced between bitter and sweet, originated with the shepherds in the Old West. It consists of Amer Picon—a French liqueur made with burnt orange peel and herbs—grenadine and club soda, poured over lots of ice cubes, with a float of brandy on top and a twist of lemon floating in the glass. *Topa!* (Basque for "cheers.")

A review from a visitor on Tripadvisor.com sums up the Martin Hotel with this comment: "Huge amounts of terrific food. Unusual dishes. Fun atmosphere. The side dishes alone are more than a full meal. It was extremely busy but the wait was minimal. The service was fast, very friendly, and we all had a wonderful time."

Not too shabby for a place in the middle of Nevada nothingness.

The Hanover Inn
HANOVER, NH ~ EST. 1780

Dartmouth College, in the Royal Province of New Hampshire, was founded in 1769 via a charter granted by King George III as an institution "for the education and instruction of Youth of the Indian Tribes in this Land . . . and also of English Youth and any others." It is the nation's ninth-oldest college.

Daniel Webster (class of 1801), a famous orator, U.S. senator, member of the House of Representatives, and the nation's secretary of state for three presidents, came to the college's rescue in a famous case he argued before the U.S. Supreme Court. The state of New Hampshire was attempting to take control of the privately chartered college, and the landmark decision in Dartmouth's favor settled the nature of public versus private charters and resulted in the rise of American business corporations.

Thirteen years after assuming his role as college steward, General Ebenezer Brewster decided to turn his home into a tavern, apparently with less than hearty approval from the college administration. It became so successful that his son, Amos, had the tavern moved to another site while his father was away on an extended trip. He tripled the size of the building, turning it into the Dartmouth Hotel.

In 1815, a new building was built back on the site of Ebenezer's original home/tavern, and the name was changed to the Wheelock Hotel after the college's founder, Eleazer Wheelock. Since then, the hotel has undergone dozens of expansions, changes, and reconstructions, which have added rooms, an outdoor dining terrace, and much landscaping. Renamed the Hanover Inn in 1903, the inn today has ninety-three guest rooms, two restaurants, meeting facilities, and a busy catering service. As the only accommodation on the Dartmouth campus, the rooms and dining rooms are usually filled with students, alumni, faculty, students' families, and visitors with business at the college across the street.

The Daniel Webster Dining Room, with an imposing oil portrait of the Dartmouth alumnus, is the largest and most active and is open for breakfast and lunch. Zins, a wine bistro, which is open for Sunday brunch and dinner, features a large selection of wines and received an Award of Excellence from the *Wine Spectator*, is also popular for cocktails and bar snacks. The terrace, which serves Sunday brunch and dinner, is across the

Lobby lamp with an engraving of the historic Dartmouth Baker Tower.

street from the famous Baker Tower and allows diners a great view of the busy lawn where many of the college's fifty-eight hundred undergrads and graduate students pass by. The iconic tower was designed after Independence Hall in Philadelphia, and its bells chime out a lively tune on the hour, and on special occasions the college anthem or other Dartmouth tunes.

The dinner menus are top of the line, featuring entrees such as Duet of Seared Diver Scallops and Scallop Cannelloni, Garlic-Roasted Vermont Guinea Hen, and Maple-and-Mint-Rubbed Rack of Lamb. Lunch selections include Flash-Fried Panko-Crusted Cod, Mozzarella-Basil-Roasted

The Daniel Webster dining room.

Red Pepper and Caramelized Onion Panini, Artichoke and Opal Basil-Filled Fresh Tortellini, and—my favorite—Ginger-and-Soy-Laced Pork Belly Sliders.

The meaty, fork-tender, stick-to-your-ribs Red Wine-Braised Beef Short Ribs is four-star comfort food, served with sautéed spinach and truly great Parmesan gnocchi. Chinese five-spice powder takes the short ribs over the top. The scallops are great, and the scallop cannelloni is fantastic. The tender scallops and large pasta are swaddled in wild mushrooms, chardonnay-chive cream, shaved truffles, and a few magic drops of truffle oil.

The Hanover's kitchen is making a big push to "go green," recycling as much as possible, using locally sourced produce, and emphasizing sustainable fish and shellfish on their menu. Considering that the Dartmouth mascot is "Big Green," a name inspired by the school colors and the large open lawn that Hanover's tavern overlooks, this is a perfect fit.

The Hanover's lobby looks more like a comfortable living room than a hotel.

Boneless Beef Short Ribs with Parmesan Gnocchi

∽ SERVES 6 ∽

1 tablespoon olive oil

4 pounds boneless short ribs

2 stalks celery, chopped

1 large carrot, chopped

1 white onion, chopped

8 cloves garlic, minced

3 cups dry red wine

½ tablespoon five-spice powder

Salt and freshly ground black pepper

8 cups veal broth or beef broth

PARMESAN GNOCCHI

2 cups water

1 cup (2 sticks) unsalted butter

1 tablespoon salt

2 cups all-purpose flour

1 cup grated Parmesan cheese

7 large eggs

PARMESAN CREAM SAUCE

2 tablespoons cornstarch

½ cup water

2 cups heavy cream

½ cup grated
  Parmesan cheese

Salt and freshly ground white
  pepper to taste

6 green onions,
  including green parts

In a Dutch oven, heat the olive oil over medium-high heat and brown the short ribs on all sides. Add the celery, carrot, onion, and garlic and sauté until the vegetables are lightly browned. Add the red wine and stir to scrape up the browned bits from the bottom of the pan. Add the five-spice powder and salt and pepper. Cook until the liquid is reduced by half. Add the veal broth, reduce the heat to low, cover, and cook for 2 hours. Uncover and cook 2 more hours, or until the sauce is thickened and the short ribs are very tender.

About 30 minutes before the short ribs are done, make the gnocchi. In a large saucepan, combine the water, butter, and salt. Bring to a boil over medium heat. Add the flour and stir until blended. Transfer the mixture to a stand mixer fitted with the paddle attachment. Add the Parmesan cheese and mix for 30 seconds. With the motor running, add the eggs one at a time. Transfer the mixture to a pastry bag fitted with a large, plain tip. In several batches, pipe small pieces of the mixture into a large pot of salted boiling water and cook for 1 minute. Using a wire-mesh skimmer, transfer each batch to a colander to drain, then to a deep plate. Cover and keep warm while making the sauce.

For the Parmesan cream sauce: Just before serving, whisk the cornstarch and water together in a small bowl. In a small saucepan, bring the cream to a boil over medium heat. Gradually whisk in the cornstarch mixture and cook, whisking, until thickened. Remove from the heat. Whisk in the Parmesan cheese until melted. Season with salt and white pepper to taste. Set aside and keep warm.

In an oiled grill pan over high heat, or under a preheated broiler, grill the green onions, turning as needed, until lightly charred.

To serve, divide the short ribs among 6 plates and top with some of the pan sauce. Serve the gnocchi alongside, topped with the cream sauce. Garnish each plate with a grilled green onion and serve at once.

The Stockton Inn
STOCKTON, NJ ~ EST. 1796

There's a small hotel,
with a wishing well,
I wish that we were there, together.
~ Richard Rogers and Lorenz Hart

If you're under forty, you may never have heard this song. But if you're a baby boomer, you more than likely have listened to Frank Sinatra, Ray Bolger, Jo Stafford, Ella Fitzgerald, or Della Reese sing this wistful melody. The song was intended for the movie *Jumbo* and was cut at the last minute. But if you saw either *On Your Toes* (1937) or *Pal Joey* (1957), you certainly heard about the romantic hotel and its wishing well "somewhere."

Well, "somewhere" is in southern New Jersey, in the small town of Stockton. The hotel is actually the Stockton Inn, which has been entrancing folks

since 1910. But the inn has been around a lot longer. It was built as a private residence in 1710 and, at the suggestion of the local Lenni Lanape Indians, who warned of frequent flooding in the valley, was solidly constructed of local quarry stone. Three hundred years later, the original exterior has barely been touched by several major fires and floods.

In 1776, Howell's Ferry, now the town of Stockton, had its ferryboat pressed into service to facilitate the crossing of the Delaware by General George Washington and his troops when they recaptured Trenton over Christmas and thus turned the tide of the Revolutionary War. Twenty years later, Daniel Howell received a tavern license and opened the Farmer's Bar in the tavern. But with the construction of the Delaware and Raritan

Owner Fred Strackhouse loves to barbecue on Thursday "Grill Night."

canals nearby, there was a need for a place for travelers to stay. So in 1832, new owner Asher Johnson turned the place into a hotel to house and feed the canal workers, many of them Irish immigrants. In 1850, it was enlarged and the road was moved to run from the Centre Bridge to the hotel's front door.

Two owners later, the hotel was sold at auction to Elizabeth Colligan and her husband, Joe, who was a bartender there at the time. Three generations of their family continued to operate the inn, simply called Colligan's, for the next seventy years. Charlie, one of their sons, had a brief career running the iconic Stage Door Deli in New York City before he returned to help manage the inn. During that time, they added the garden patio, the famous wishing well, and a waterfall.

When Prohibition was in force, the Colligans set up several stills in the gardens behind the inn and, using hard cider, distilled what many considered the best applejack in the state. At the same time, they had dozens of phone lines installed, not for use by their guests, but for the four or five bookmakers hidden in an upstairs office.

In 1922, Joe Colligan brought in a local artist R.A.D. Miller to paint murals in several of the dining rooms. Miller went on to great fame for his landscapes, still lifes, and portraits. He in turn brought in Kurt Wiese, a friend and the illustrator of the original *Bambi* book, to paint one of the walls.

It was in 1933 that Lorenz Hart and Richard Rogers visited the inn. In the midst of writing a song for the movie *Jumbo*, they were entranced by the wishing well in the garden and composed the famous song about a small hotel.

When Bruno Richard Hauptman was tried for the kidnapping and murder of the Lindbergh baby in Flemington, New Jersey, ten miles away, many of the reporters covering the trial, including Damon Runyon, stayed at the inn in 1935. It had the advantage of being a peaceful place with great food and an active bar, and it was perfect for reporters because for some strange reason it had an inordinate number of phone lines, so they could telephone their newspapers with trial results.

In the 1940s glitterati from the entertainment, literary, and political world flocked to the quiet Stockton Inn for some R & R.

During the forties, the hotel became a favorite weekend spot for some Algonquin round table members, including F. Scott Fitzgerald, Dorothy Parker, Robert Benchley, Runyon, and S. J. Perelman. Other writers, along with actors and artists of all kinds, flocked to the quiet south Jersey inn for getaway weekends. Bandleader Paul Whiteman, who lived near the inn, is reported to have ridden his horse there for his frequent nighttime visits. He was quoted as saying that he rode a horse because he knew he'd drink too much—and the horse knew the way home.

Today, the inn is full of surprises that begin when you walk into the dining rooms, once the living quarters of the Howell and Stockton families. The walls are covered with R.A.D. Miller's colorful murals, and each of the three main dining rooms has a fireplace. Proceeding through the hallway to the Glass Dining Room, the inn's original patio, you can't fail to notice the silver dollars, dating from the mid- to late-1800s, embedded in the flagstone floor; a whimsical touch from the Colligan's.

Outside is a delightful trilevel covered and heated patio, with terraced gardens, two waterfalls, and a resident hippopotamus lazily circling in a large fish pond. Say what! A hippo in southern Jersey? Relax, it's plastic, a harmless gag that delights old and young alike as it calmly floats by in the current from the waterfall.

On the top level, where several nights a week musical groups perform, owner Fred Strackhouse loves to barbecue on Thursday nights. "Grill Nights" are popular, and the night I was there he cooked over one hundred pounds of steak, shrimp, scallops, and lobster for what he considered a modest crowd. Not only is it fun to watch him at the grill (I have a special fondness for such activities), but the smell of the charcoal-grilled steaks, chops, and seafood entices folks who had just stopped by for a drink to settle in for dinner. If you can't get there on a Thursday, do not despair. Chef Abe Berisha, an

Albanian who grew up in Italy and learned to cook there, will dazzle you with appetizers such as Calamari Fritti or House-Made Stuffed Mozzarella, and entrees such as Pork Osso Buco, Gaszpacho Basil Pesto Penne, or Lobster Tail Stuffed with Crab.

Their House Salad is not only delicious but one of the most colorful gatherings of greens, fruits, nuts, and blue cheese ever to wear a cloak of chef Berisha's own honey-mustard dressing. And don't miss the Pan-Seared Duck Breast, nesting on a thick wedge of cranberry polenta and generously ladled with a cranberry-port reduction sauce.

While at the Stockton Inn, I couldn't resist the chance to sample the Rack of Lamb, ten

Pan-Seared Duck Breast with Cranberry Polenta and Cranberry-Port Reduction Sauce

∽ SERVES 4 ∽

CRANBERRY-PORT REDUCTION

1 cup fresh cranberries

1 cup port wine

1 teaspoon coarsely chopped orange zest

2 tablespoons orange juice

POLENTA

3 cups water

1 cup polenta

½ cup dried cranberries

2 Muscovy duck full breasts (about 1 pound)

Salt and freshly ground black pepper

Fresh mint sprigs or other herbs, for garnish

For the cranberry-port reduction: In a small saucepan, combine all the ingredients and cook over medium-low heat until reduced by half. Set aside.

For the polenta: In a medium pot, bring the water to a boil over high heat and reduce the heat to a simmer. Gradually whisk in the polenta in a fine stream. Add the dried cranberries and cook, stirring constantly, until the polenta has thickened enough to come away from the sides of the pan and a spoon inserted in the center remains upright, 20 to 50 minutes. Pour the polenta onto a wooden cutting board, spread to about 1 inch high if necessary, and let cool for 10 to 15 minutes. Cut into 1 by 2½-inch slices. Set aside and keep warm.

Using a sharp knife, score the fat of the duck breasts in a crisscross pattern. Season the duck with salt and pepper. Heat a large ovenproof skillet over medium heat. Place the duck breasts, fat side down, in the skillet and cook to render the fat for about 6 minutes. Spoon off and reserve the rendered duck fat for another use. Turn the duck breasts over and sear for 1 minute. Turn the fat side down again and place the skillet in the oven to roast for 7 to 9 minutes, until medium-rare. Transfer the duck breasts to a carving board and let rest for 5 minutes, then thinly slice.

To serve, divide the sliced polenta among the plates and top with some of the cranberry-port reduction over it. Top with slices of duck breast and garnish with mint sprigs.

medium-rare lamb chops in a crunchy-tangy mustard-herb crust, served over mashed potatoes and accompanied with a rosemary and white bean ragout. A few tender young asparagus spears stacked like, well, spears, guard one flank of the rack. Even if I had ordered this as my only entree I would have been hard-pressed to finish it.

One last anecdote, in honor of Peggy Marsh, a woman who stayed at the inn for a short time in the mid-thirties after

Owners Janet and Fred Strackhouse with decorative carving representing the Inn's famous wishing well.

visiting a friend in nearby Bucks County, Pennsylvania. According to local legend, she wrote several chapters of a novel while sitting in the dining room in front of the fireplace. The book became quite a hit. But you may not have recognized her married name. Peggy was what her friends and husband called her, but she is better known by the name she used on the cover of the book and in the movie credits. Meet Margaret Mitchell—author of *Gone With the Wind*.

Ye Olde Centerton Inn
CENTERTON, NJ ~ EST. 1706

Like most Colonial taverns of the early 1700s, Ye Olde Centerton Inn (while it was still young) was a pretty rough place. The drink of choice was rum, and it was served hot. To make it hot, the innkeepers heated a poker in the fire, then plunged it into a tankard of rum until the poker stopped sizzling. The Centerton was a meetingplace where folks drank, ate a bit, drank, argued a bit, drank, wenched a bit, drank, and sometimes plotted revolution or a way to abuse a tax collector. It was allegedly built in 1706 during Queen Anne's War, one of many early conflicts between England and France. The spoils for the winner were New England and the rest of the country. The Centerton was on the main road from Philadelphia, the villages in lower New Jersey, and the royal ports of Salem and Greenwich, and was used early on as a customs inventory station.

When the Revolution began, the inn became a repository for ammunition and black powder, food, clothing, and other strategic goods that were smuggled through British lines to supply the Colonial army. In fact, when General Washington and his troops were fighting their way through Valley Forge and Trenton, he dispatched General "Mad" Anthony Wayne to the Centerton Inn to forage for food for the starving army. During the same period, the French general, the Marquis de Lafayette, is said to have planned war strategy while visiting here, often with a lovely and mysterious woman friend.

A colorful (read: bloody) legend involves some British Queen's Rangers, regular soldiers, who had just expended all their shot fighting a local battle and stopped by the inn and began commandeering anything metal to melt down for shot. Supposedly, four of them were hacked to death with scythes and hay forks and their bodies buried in the basement. Occasionally, their ghosts have been reported walking around the outside of the Inn, supposedly looking for their heads.

In the late 1700s, the inn was used for Methodist and Episcopal church meetings on the Sabbath. In the early 1800s, it was a polling place in the presidential contest between John Quincy Adams and Andrew Jackson, which Adams won. It was used again in 1828 when they had a presidential rematch where Jackson and the incumbent vice-president John C. Calhoun teamed up and were elected. The inn made it through Prohibition by selling ice cream over the bar. During World War II, German prisoners were interned nearby in barracks in a state park, and an unknown prisoner created an oil painting of the inn that hangs today over the historic fireplace.

A painting of the Inn over the historic fireplace was done by an unknown German prisoner-of-war who was interned at a state park World War II POW camp located near the Inn. Below: Employees in costume in the 1950s.

Co-owner chef Joanne Goode whips up a cheese sauce for pasta.

Following a baker's dozen of owners, the inn has come into the hands of two unlikely but perfectly suited proprietors. Joanne Goode was a successful chef working at Jean Georges at Trump International; her husband, Brian, was a successful chef at the Russian Tea Room. In their spare time, they worked together at Bette Midler's New Leaf Café. But they were looking for a place of their own when they chanced on an Internet ad for an eighteenth-century inn in Salem County, New Jersey.

In 2003, they purchased the inn and have set about to bring the restaurant's menu up to the standards of midtown Manhattan while retaining a country-Colonial style. They kept the existing staff of servers, many of whom had worked for the previous owner. As Brian points out, "In New York, many of the servers are just waiting for the next casting call, but here they love their jobs and aren't looking to leave."

No detail escapes their attempts to maintain the historic atmosphere of the inn. The dining rooms are filled with treasures of the past, and

Crab Imperial

∾ SERVES 4 TO 6 AS AN ENTREE ∾

2 tablespoons finely chopped green bell pepper

1 tablespoon finely chopped red bell pepper

1 tablespoon finely chopped Spanish onion

2 large eggs, beaten

2 cups (16 ounces) mayonnaise

2 teaspoons Old Bay Seasoning

2 teaspoons Worcestershire sauce

Dash of Tabasco sauce

2 pounds lump crabmeat, picked over for shell

1 cup fresh bread crumbs

1 tablespoon sweet paprika

Preheat the oven to 400°F. Butter 4 ramekins or porcelain scallop shells.

In a blender, combine the bell peppers, onion, eggs, mayonnaise, Old Bay, Worcestershire, and Tabasco. Pulse until coarsely blended (there should be small pieces of pepper and onion left). Empty into a medium bowl and gently stir in the crabmeat to blend.

Pour into buttered ramekins or porcelain scallop shells, cover with bread crumbs, sprinkle with paprika, and bake under a broiler until browned and bubbly, 5 to 8 minutes. Serve with chilled white wine.

NOTE: To make Crab Imperial Sauce, reduce the amount of crabmeat to 1 pound and omit the bread crumbs and paprika. Use as a sauce for seafod or steaks. Makes enough for 8 servings.

they've continued the decades-old tradition of serving roasted peanuts on the tables. The menu is decidedly American, with some small touches of Italian. Steak, veal, pork, and chicken dishes are offered, as are several pasta entrees. The signature dish is New York Strip Steak, covered, and I mean covered, with Crab Imperial: lump crabmeat in a luscious sauce of garlic, white wine, mayonnaise, and seasonings. In a double portion, the crab dish is also served as an entree in a huge scallop shell ramekin, topped with buttered bread crumbs and broiled until golden and bubbly. If you love garlic, begin the meal with the Centerton Salad, a combination of iceberg and romaine lettuces, with shredded carrots, a delicious blend of secret spices, fresh garlic, and a blend of four cheeses.

On weekends, the crowds are large, but the six dining rooms easily accommodate the hungry Philadelphians, New Yorkers, and New Jerseyites who travel to this tiny town for elegant meals in an authentic eighteenth-century inn lovingly preserved by two New York chefs. Headless ghosts and all, they have a pretty good thing going here.

La Fonda

SANTA FE, NM ~ EST. 1822

La Fonda on the Plaza, in Santa Fe, New Mexico, sits on one of the oldest hotel sites in the United States. Journals of the pioneers who traveled to the end of the Santa Fe Trail in the earliest days of the country mention an inn, or fonda, here in 1822, but official historical rec-ords describe overnight accommodations in this location as one of the first businesses opened in 1607, the same year Santa Fe was founded by the Spaniards.

In the early days, the Exchange Hotel, as it was known then, was a popular resting and dining spot for trappers, traders, mountain men, gold miners, merchants, soldiers, politicians, and other weary and hungry travelers. In 1833, even before New Mexico became a U.S. Territory, Americans William and Mary Donoho purchased the inn. A few

incidents during their stewardship remind us that this truly was the "Wild West."

In 1862, an enraged cowboy who started shooting folks in the lobby, to get even for a friend who had been killed (he didn't say by who), was captured and hanged that night in the hotel's backyard by a lynch mob. Six years later, the Chief Justice of the Territorial Supreme Court was killed in a duel in the same lobby, but the man who shot him was found not guilty. On Saturday nights, it was not uncommon to see cockfights in the coral out back.

By 1920, the Exchange had fallen into such disrepair that the owners decided it would be cheaper, and faster, to demolish the old building and build a new hotel, so they held a Liberty Bond rally. Every time a $100 bond was sold, a World War I tank would go crashing into the walls.

The Atchison, Topeka and Santa Fe Railroad then bought the property and began building La Fonda hotel, with a six-story bell tower and two new wings, tripling the size of the hotel from 46 to 156 rooms. The interior had wrought-iron railings, tin light fixtures, wooden beams and corbels, and hand-painted furniture in the rooms. When completed, La Fonda became one of the famed Harvey Houses, a chain of eighty-four fine hotels that featured great restaurants and iconic "Harvey Girl" waitresses in their pinafores and starched aprons.

In the late sixties, having once more deteriorated, the hotel was sold to the Ballen family, who still retain ownership. The courtyard was roofed over; the kitchen was greatly enlarged; more rooms, a ballroom, and a spa and fitness center were added; and La Plazuela restaurant was remodeled to bring back the dining glory of the Harvey House years. Today, the dazzling dining room is open for breakfast, lunch, and dinner. In the center of the room is the water fountain that was once the center of the courtyard, and the room features hand-carved furnishings, intricate wood detailing, flagstone flooring, and hand-forged railings. The room is stunning in the morning, lively at lunch, and romantic in the evening.

Of special note are the historic hand-painted glass panels on the walls. They were painted by Ernest Martinez, a resident artist here for fifty-six years. He is responsible as well for the painted beams

Chef Lane Warner tests out a new dish as Octavio Uvalcabo, Bernardino Jaquez, Josh Ortiz (PM sous chef), and Jimmy Garcia oversee.

and columns, furniture, large murals, and small paintings throughout the hotel. Even the concrete columns in the three-story parking garage bear his scenes of flowers, birds, and animals.

Executive chef Lane Warner, a CIA graduate and an avid hunter and fisherman, uses locally sourced ingredients and promotes the culinary heritage of New Mexico. His award-winning versions of traditional dishes are some of the most innovative west of the Mississippi, including Mango Gazpacho, a bright chilled soup tinged with cucumber, roasted peppers, mango, and lime, with green grapes floating on the surface. Other popular items are roasted poblano rellenos filled with corn, leeks, and wild mushrooms, grilled cheese-stuffed prawns wrapped in bacon, and a popular pork tenderloin that is rubbed with spices and char-grilled with a papaya vinaigrette. The Mexican chocolate cake with streusel topping, served warm and finished with a scoop of roasted banana ice cream, is the perfect end to your meal.

One of the breakfast dishes that has been served at La Fonda for decades is Rellenos de la Fonda. Two large green chiles are filled with Mexican cheeses, lightly battered and panfried, then topped with chile sauce and served with black beans and pork posole.

Spectacular sunrises and sunsets are a regular feature of life in Santa Fe, and La Fonda offers a rooftop café so guests can view them in all their glory.

In his very early days, a young man by the name of William Henry McCarty, Jr., took a job at La Fonda washing dishes. He was said to be friendly and personable, and although of diminutive stature, and some thought, frail, he was more than willing to help with any chore assigned him. Later in life he was given a nickname that he was very proud of—Billy the Kid.

To continue the irony, the night after Sheriff Pat Garrett shot and killed the Kid, he reportedly checked into the Exchange and enjoyed an overnight stay. As they say, this really was the Wild West.

In the 1920s, La Fonda became one of the iconic Harvey Houses of the West. Here two "Harvey Girls" wait outside the old entrance.

The whimsical windows in La Plazuela are decorated with paintings by artist Ernest Martinez.

Chiles Rellenos de la Fonda

Hatch or poblano chiles

2 cups (8 ounces) shredded Chihuahua cheese

2 cups (8 ounces) shredded Asedero cheese

½ cup half-and-half

BEER BATTER

1½ cups all-purpose flour

1 tablespoon baking powder

½ tablespoon sugar

½ tablespoon salt

1 teaspoon freshly ground white pepper

1 teaspoon sweet paprika

1 large egg

12 ounces beer

Peanut or canola oil, for frying

RED CHILE SAUCE

3 tablespoons peanut or canola oil

3 tablespoons flour

4 cups water

6 tablespoons (3 ounces) Chimayó chile powder

¾ teaspoon minced garlic

½ teaspoon dried oregano

½ teaspoon garlic powder

½ teaspoon onion powder

½ teaspoon ground cumin

¾ teaspoon salt

Shredded Chihuahua cheese, for garnish

Black beans, for serving

Preheat the broiler and place the chiles under the broiler about 2 inches from the heat source. Turn as needed to blacken the chiles on both sides. Transfer the chiles to a paper bag, close the bag, and let cool for about 15 minutes. Rub off the burned skin with your fingers. Cut a slit in the side of each chile and remove the seeds and veins, leaving the top of the chiles intact.

In a large bowl, combine the cheeses and half-and-half and stir to blend. Using a tablespoon, stuff each chile with the cheese mixture until plump. Set the chiles aside.

For the beer batter: In a large bowl, combine the dry ingredients and stir with a whisk to blend. In a small bowl, whisk the egg and beer together until smooth, then stir into the dry ingredients to make a smooth batter.

Dip each stuffed chile in the beer batter to lightly coat. In a large, heavy sauté pan or Dutch oven, heat ¾ inch of the oil until shimmering and fry the chiles in batches, turning them as necessary, until golden. Using tongs, transfer to paper towels to drain. Keep warm in a low oven while frying the remaining chiles.

For the red chile sauce: In a small saucepan, make a roux by whisking the oil and flour together over medium-low heat until the roux turns golden brown; do not burn. In a medium saucepan, combine all the remaining ingredients and bring to a boil. Whisk in the roux and cook, whisking frequently, until thickened. Taste and adjust the seasoning.

To serve, place 2 stuffed chiles on each of 4 warmed plates. Top with about 1 cup of sauce and sprinkle with more shredded cheese. Serve at once, accompanied with black beans.

Barbetta

NEW YORK, NY ~ EST. 1906

From the outside, Barbetta looks like a typical New York brownstone, but once inside you would swear you had been transported to Versailles. A cascading crystal chandelier, which (speaking of palaces) once graced a palazzo owned by Italy's royal family, is suspended above tables covered with white tablecloths and antique chairs with beautiful tapestry upholstery. Tables are topped with pots of flowers, antique gilt sconces decorate the walls, and Venetian silk shades frame the windows. Barbetta is one of the most stunning and opulent dining rooms in the country.

In its early days, the place was not quite as impressive. When Sebastiano Maioglio, a twenty-six-year-old from Turin, Italy, opened the first Italian restaurant featuring Piemontese-style food in New York City, it was large and bare. It was said that the only antiques were the waiters. It had an inexpensive menu featuring foods that were new to New York, including porcini mushrooms, risotto, and polenta, and Maioglio installed the city's first espresso machine in a restaurant.

In 1925, Sebastiano bought four town houses in the center of the theater district from the wealthy Astor family, and turned two of them into the new Barbetta. Actors, opera singers, and fans of both flocked to the unassuming, cheerful restaurant.

When he became ill, Sebastiano was preparing to sell the business when his only daughter, Laura, stepped in. "I asked him, how could you dispose of something that's been in the family for fifty-five years," she says. "He was helpless before my determination. Essentially, I confiscated the restaurant. Sadly, he was unable to see the changes I made."

The restaurant was shuttered for a year while Laura, whose husband won a Nobel Prize for medicine in 1999, worked her magic, gathering museum-grade antiques, importing that massive chandelier, and bringing in restorers and woodworkers to spruce up the dining rooms and parlors. When she spotted a quintessential dining room chair in a Turin museum, she had a master craftsman make 180 perfect replicas. Wanting a garden setting, in the heart of Manhattan no less, she created a delightful back patio dining area and brought in lacy white wrought-iron chairs and tables, added a baroque fountain, and planted oleanders, wisteria, jasmine, and gardenias.

Then she turned her attention to the old kitchen, spending over a million dollars to completely refurbish it in stainless steel and white marble. Finally, after being exasperated for years by the limited wine cellar, she began importing Italian wines that no one had ever seen in the United States. Today, their impressive wine list contains over seventeen hundred different labels. In 1977, Barbetta won first prize from the Italian government for the most outstanding Italian wine list in America. Additionally, for fourteen straight years they have received a Best of Award of Excellence from *Wine Spectator* magazine.

Barbetta introduced another Italian import to Big Apple diners when it began importing white truffles the year it reopened. It is perhaps the only restaurant on the continent that has its own truffle dogs searching the forests of Piemonte. So if you

are visiting between October and late December, you must order one of the dishes that feature these pungently flavored delicacies. Their Fonduta con Tartufi (Truffle Fondue) is said to be sublime.

That word can also be applied to the incredible dishes that come out of chef Abdul Sebti's world-class kitchen. He turns scallops into a work of art—five large Maine diver scallops are capped with a julienned crust of Yukon Gold potatoes and bathed in an intense fresh tomato reduction. In the center of the plate, the crunchy white stalks and dark green slightly bitter leaves of a baby bok choy contrasts with the buttery soft scallops and tart-sweet tomato sauce. The Risotto al Cambozola, made with olive oil instead of butter and deliciously flavored with a cheese that combines a French triple-cream and Gorgonzola, is also amazing, and the Roast Rack of Venison is perfectly cooked and served resting on a scrumptious baked apple, accompanied with a delightful pear and potato croquette.

Maine Diver Scallops in Potato Crust with Fresh Tomato Sauce

∽ SERVES 6 ∽

6 baby bok choys

FRESH TOMATO SAUCE

2 tablespoons extra-virgin olive oil

5 ripe plum tomatoes, halved and seeded

2 shallots, coarsely chopped

1 clove garlic, coarsely chopped

1 teaspoon tomato paste

1 cup dry white wine

3 cups water

Salt and freshly ground black pepper to taste

3 leaves fresh basil, thinly sliced

3 Yukon Gold potatoes, peeled, thinly sliced, and julienned

30 large Maine diver sea scallops, cleaned

Salt and freshly ground black pepper

2 large eggs

2 cups all-purpose flour, for coating

2 tablespoons olive oil

Freshly ground white pepper

Cook the baby bok choys in a large saucepan of salted boiling water for 3 minutes. Drain in a colander.

For the tomato sauce: In a medium saucepan, heat the olive oil over medium heat and sauté the tomatoes, shallots, and garlic. Add the tomato paste, wine, and water. Simmer until the tomatoes are tender. Remove from the heat and let cool. Transfer to a blender and puree for 1 to 3 minutes, or until smooth. Strain through a fine-mesh sieve into a bowl. Add salt and pepper to taste. Stir in the basil and set aside.

Rinse the julienned potatoes in cold water. Drain and transfer to paper towels. Squeeze until dry. Season the scallops with salt and black pepper. With half of the julienned potatoes, make 30 mounds the same size as the scallops on a rimmed baking sheet.

In a shallow bowl, whisk the eggs until blended. Place the flour in a second shallow bowl. Dip the scallops in the flour and then in the eggs, and place one on each mound of potatoes on the baking sheet. Cover the top of each scallop with some of the remaining potatoes.

In a large skillet, heat 2 tablespoons olive oil over medium heat. Sauté the scallops until golden brown on both sides. Season with white pepper. Using a slotted metal spatula, transfer to paper towels to drain.

In a small saucepan, reheat the tomato sauce. To serve, pool some sauce on each of 6 dinner plates. Place a baby bok choy in the center of each plate and surround it with 5 scallops. Serve at once.

Their dessert carts—yes, there are two—are legendary and offer more than twenty compelling indulgences, including Mousse of Orange Bittersweet Chocolate, Seckel Pears Baked in Red Wine, and Lemon and Pistachio Tart.

Barbetta is one of the finest restaurants in America. And if they ever add the category, I would be first in line to cast my ballot and nominate Laura Maioglio to receive the world's first Nobel Prize for Restaurateurs.

Chef Abdul Sebti creates culinary works of art in the kitchen.

The Tavern at the Beekman Arms
RHINEBECK, NY ~ EST. 1766

In the early 1700s, the small settlement of Ryn Beck was carved out of a forest first inhabited by the Sepasco Indian tribe. Willem Traphagen, the son of Dutch immigrants, was a wheelwright and blacksmith who turned his home in Ryn Beck into a small travelers' inn and tavern. In 1766, his son Arent moved the newly christened Traphagen Tavern to the town crossroads, where the King's Highway intersected the Sepasco Trail. Three years later, the tavern was sold to Everadus Bogardus, thus becoming the Bogardus Tavern. I see a pattern here.

But I will let the rest of the owners go unmentioned. You see, the tavern has had twenty-eight landlords, by far the most of any of our centenarians. The average ownership lasted only 2 to 2½ years, but two longer stints stand out. William Jacques owned the tavern for thirty years,

and Charles La Forge, Jr., ran the ship for forty-four years before he sold it to the present owner George Banta in 2002.

During the Bogardus Tavern period, the Revolutionary War was taking place, and tiny Rhinebeck was right in the center of the conflict. The Fourth Regiment of the Continental Army drilled on the lawn, and when the State Capitol across the river in Kingston was burned by the British, quite a few of the residents took shelter at the tavern. Other folks involved in the uprising stayed there as well, including George Washington, Alexander Hamilton, Benedict Arnold, and Aaron Burr. It was during an argument at the tavern that Vice President Burr and former Secretary of the Treasury Hamilton challenged each other to a duel. After Hamilton fired into the air over Burr's

Two men pass the front of the Beekman in the winter of 1917. Photo courtesy of the Rhinebeck Historical Society.

ballroom was the scene of lodge meetings, teas, public auctions, and Sunday services held by traveling preachers. When Benjamin Harrison was running for president, he and his VP assembled in the taproom, where they learned they had been nominated. A young politician who ran for governor twice, winning both elections, as well as winning both of his runs for the White House, ended all four of his campaigns talking to crowds from the front porch. And after each election, Franklin Delano Roosevelt was a frequent and enthusiastic visitor.

head, a common practice in such duels, Burr shot Hamilton in the abdomen, killing him. The ultimate bar fight, it seems.

In later years, the Bogardus became the Rhinebeck Hotel; then in 1933 was named for the original land holder, Judge Henry Beekman. It assumed roles as the town hall, a theater, post office, and a newspaper office, while the

The present tavern living room or entrance hall, the large room behind it, and part of the kitchen were part of the original Beekman Arms. The fireplace in the kitchen has been removed, but the other two historic fireplaces remain. A lot of the historic inn has been updated and modernized. Although well built to withstand Indian attacks, which never came, repairs and additions have brought the dining rooms, kitchen, and taproom up to today's standards. But the broad plank floors and sturdy oaken beams have virtually been untouched.

The menu offers a wide selection of steaks, lamb, chicken, seafood, and pasta dishes. Some are Colonial in heritage, but most are the typical fare of upscale city restaurants. The butternut squash soup was a standout, thick and buttery, as was the Camembert in Phyllo Dough. The Coffee-Braised Beef Short Ribs and the Stuffed Shrimp were divine. But the treat of the evening was the Seared Long Island Duck Breast. The tender duck meat, wrapped in a golden brown blanket of crispy skin, is served on top of a delicious mound of sage polenta, accompanied with a tart-sweet golden raisin and apple chutney.

You can enjoy your duck in the tavern in the middle of the Parlor of Dutchess County, so named because of its shady streets, village hospitality, gracious homes, and grand estates, and easily imagine a quieter time when horses and buggies bearing fine gentlemen and ladies pulled up to the "Beek." One famous couple was quoted in 1970 as saying, "It's a gentle, quiet and hospitable place. We love it as our personal getaway. One can be oneself here forgetting the outside world for a while." Both Elizabeth Taylor and Sir Richard Burton lived stormy lives, and it seems needed some quiet time in a small, quiet village.

Roasted Long Island Duck

∾ SERVES 2 ∾

1 Long Island duck full breast

Salt and freshly ground black pepper

2 yellow onions, quartered

1 stalk celery, diced

3 large carrots, peeled and diced

8 juniper berries

1 bay leaf

4 cardamom pods

Preheat the oven to 350°F. Season the duck with salt and pepper and place in a large roasting pan, skin side up. Arrange the vegetables, herbs, and spices around it. Roast, uncovered, for 1½ hours, or until tender and golden brown.

Transfer the duck to a wire rack set over a rimmed baking sheet. Tent with aluminum foil and let rest for 12 minutes. Carve and serve with side dishes of your choice.

Bridge Café
NEW YORK, NY ~ EST. 1794

Built in 1794 as a "grocery and wine and porter bottler," the wooden building that is today's Bridge Café was later leased to a series of boardinghouse and saloon operators. At that time, the East River came right up to the building's foundation on Water Street. Later, landfill and the Brooklyn Bridge would add substantial land to this part of Lower Manhattan.

An article in the *New York Times* states: "The 1794 date is significant because from that date the building has been 'the site of a food and/or drinking establishment' and is the oldest business in New York City." And because Henry Williams bought the establishment and began serving liquor in 1847, it established its future claim as the oldest continuously running bar in the city.

In fact, Williams rented out the back room to another owner who opened the Empire House, a second porter house. Not wanting to let any space go unused, all or part of the second and third floors were later rented out for another kind of entertainment. This caused the porter house to be indicted by the district attorney in 1879 as a "disorderly house," or, in modern terms, a brothel. Historical records show that Water Street in those days was a string of saloons and brothels. During Prohibition, the saloon was run as a restaurant that sold "cider," but a local bootlegger did a fine business quietly supplying them with beer.

As do many historic saloons, the Bridge has a legacy of ghost stories—tales of footsteps on the second floor, the smell of cheap lavender perfume from a ghostly lady of the night, and shadows that mysteriously move across empty rooms. The current owners bought the building in 1979 and began upgrading the old place while taking care to preserve the 1920s interior. The dining room is small but accommodates fifty to sixty people, and the walls are paneled in wood, painted a hollandaise yellow, and decorated with paintings, photographs, and old posters, all showing the Bridge Café. Several framed engraved certificates, including the 1890 saloon license, are also displayed.

The original pressed-tin ceiling has been preserved and painted white to lighten the dining room. The deep-set casement windows also add some light, despite the onramp to the Brooklyn Bridge throwing the building into shadow much of the day. The building, as one may expect, has its share of tilts and warps, but considering its age is in remarkable condition. In the evening, dim lights and the glow from the two red neon "Bridge Café" signs cast a romantic glow around the place.

Decidedly not a tourist trap, despite the tourist-haven South Street Seaport Village nearby, the restaurant is usually occupied by couples, businesspeople from Wall Street, and a few scattered in-the-know New Yorkers. Regular customers treasure this quiet, unassuming café with its interesting menu and a bar that has perhaps the city's greatest collection of whiskeys, bourbons, and Scotches. The menu is small, but every dish is a nine or ten. The cuisine is described as "American regional with global influences," and features such choices as Aged Provolone, Sage, and Panko Crusted Chicken; Buffalo Steak with Lingonberry Sauce; Scallops on Risotto, and the plate-filling Grilled Prime Bone-in Rib Eye with caramelized onion and cheddar pudding. The platings are simple, the servings generous.

The rib eye is fork-tender, nicely seasoned and perfect by itself. But a dab of their house-made

tangy and slightly smoky steak sauce makes it even better. The pudding is a perfect side to the steak, with sweet onions and sharp Cheddar adding depth of flavor. The legendary Softshell Crab Cakes are said to be the preferred lunch of former New York Mayor Ed Koch, a regular customer, and a favorite of Vice President Joe Biden, but they are only available seasonally (in spring).

With a congenial staff, a comfortable and quiet atmosphere, and food that rivals any of the big-name restaurants uptown, this is a special place. Usually patronized by locals and an occasional lucky "drop by" visitor, it hasn't been discovered by tourists yet. Shhhh, don't tell anyone; this could be our secret.

Grilled Petite Lamb Chops with Chimichurri and Sweet Potato Flans

~ SERVES 6 ~

SPICE RUB

2 tablespoons dried oregano

2 tablespoons dried basil

2 tablespoons dried parsley

1 tablespoon dried thyme

1 tablespoon smoked paprika

1 teaspoon red pepper flakes

SWEET POTATO FLANS

2 pounds sweet potatoes,
    peeled and cubed

1⅔ cups heavy cream

1⅔ cups milk

5 large eggs

1 large egg yolk

Kosher salt and freshly ground black pepper

CHIMICHURRI SAUCE

1 bunch fresh flat-leaf parsley,
    stemmed and minced

3 tablespoons minced garlic

3 tablespoons freshly squeezed lemon juice

1 teaspoon red pepper flakes

1 teaspoon salt

½ teaspoon freshly ground black pepper

1 cup extra-virgin olive oil

24 baby American lamb chops,
    from frenched racks

Salt and freshly ground black pepper

Extra-virgin olive oil, for brushing

For the spice rub: Combine all the ingredients in a glass jar and stir to mix. Set aside.

For the flans: Preheat the oven to 275°F and butter 6 muffin cups.

In a large saucepan, combine the sweet potatoes, cream, and milk. Bring to a boil over medium-high heat, then reduce the heat to a simmer. Cook until the sweet potatoes are fork-tender. In batches, transfer the mixture to a blender and puree until smooth. Empty into a fine-mesh sieve set over a bowl to strain, pushing the solids through with the back of a large spoon. Let cool.

In a small bowl, whisk the eggs and egg yolk until blended. Stir into the sweet potato mixture until smooth. Season with salt and pepper. Pour into the prepared muffin cups, filling them almost full. Cover the tin with aluminum foil and place in a large pan. Add water to the pan to come halfway up the side of the muffin tin.

Bake until the flans are firm and a tester inserted in the center comes out clean. Let cool in the tin on a wire rack. Place a small baking sheet over the muffin tin and invert to unmold the flans. Cover and set aside.

For the sauce: In a small bowl, combine all the ingredients, stir well, cover, and set aside.

Season the lamb chops on both sides with salt and pepper and then rub the spice rub on both sides of each chop. Prepare a medium fire in a charcoal grill, preheat a gas grill to medium, or heat a large grill pan over medium-high heat. Lightly brush the chops on both sides with olive oil and grill for about 4 minutes on the first side and 2 to 3 minutes on the other side for medium-rare.

To serve, place a flan in the center of each serving plate and lean 3 or 4 chops against the flan, meat side down. Put several spoonfuls of chimichurri on the plate around each chop and serve at once.

Delmonico's Restaurant
NEW YORK, NY ~ EST. 1830

Delmonico's Restaurant in New York City is the first dining establishment in America to be referred to by its French name, "restaurant."

Before Swiss brothers Giovanni and Pietro Delmonico opened their Restaurant Français in 1830, people ate meals outside their homes at hotels, taverns, and inns. They were all served the same meal—whatever the innkeeper or cook wanted to serve that day—they could eat only at set times, and they were charged a flat all-inclusive rate for the meal. Delmonico's revolutionized American dining by offering their customers a "bill of fare," following the style of restaurants in Paris, where each person could choose his or her own combination of dishes, each priced separately.

At first, the public was skeptical, but local merchants who frequented the restaurant loved

it. The revolutionary dining style was soon imitated by other restaurants in the city, and then nationwide. The modest café and the brothers Delmonico had forever changed American dining habits.

In 1835, a devastating fire in lower New York burned much of the neighborhood and the restaurant to the ground. But John and Peter Delmonico (who had since Americanized their names) converted the bottom floors of a lodging house they had purchased a year earlier into a restaurant and began rebuilding near the original location on the corner of Beaver and William streets.

The new restaurant was opened in 1837 and was the most incredible restaurant in America at the time. It was 3½ stories high, with three

floors of dining rooms, pillars at the entrance that were brought over from Pompeii, a cellar that contained over fifteen thousand bottles of French wine, and expensive décor. It was a huge source of pride to New Yorkers and welcomed people from around the world.

Over the next twenty-five years, the Delmonico name was attached to a hotel, a second lodging house, and three more restaurants, all of which were described as huge, opulent, and serving the best meals in the city. It was in the Fifth Avenue and Twenty-sixth Street restaurant, opened in 1876, that an American culinary legend was born.

Charles Delmonico had a sea captain friend who regularly sailed from Cuba to New York bringing in fruit, some of which found its way to Delmonico's kitchens. Captain Ben Wenberg, an acknowledged gourmet, came to the restaurant and prepared a lobster dish that he had learned on his travels. Charles loved it and had chef Charles Ranhofer, at that time the most respected chef in America, begin serving it, with his own touches of course, and Lobster Wenberg became the most popular dish on the menu.

∾ Delmonico's Facts ∾

- The first eating place called by the French name "restaurant"
- The first eating place where guests sat at their own tables
- The first printed menu
- The first tablecloths
- The first restaurant to let women congregate as a group
- The first restaurant to offer private dining rooms
- Invented Lobster Newburg, first called Lobster Wenberg
- Invented Baked Alaska, Eggs Benedict (although the Waldorf Astoria claims this too), Delmonico Potatoes, and Delmonico Steak

Delmonico's is one of several U.S. restaurants who claim to have invented Baked Alaska. Here it is served as an individual portion.

A short time later, Wenberg and Delmonico had a falling out, and Ranhofer was ordered to stop serving the dish. But it was so popular that Delmonico was forced to return it to the menu, cleverly transposing two letters and thus changing the name to Lobster Newburg, a name familiar with diners today.

Another culinary chapter of history was written in 1867, when chef Ranhofer changed the name of Omelette à la Norvégienne, a popular Delmonico's dessert, to Baked Alaska, honoring the purchase of the territory. Even today it's their most frequently requested dessert and has been imitated countless times by restaurants all over America. They serve a staggering forty to fifty of these pastry, meringue, and ice cream delights a day.

And then there's Steak Delmonico, yet another culinary innovation crafted by the famed chef, who established the restaurant's claim to excellence and innovation during more than three decades in the kitchen. First presented as Bifteck de Contrefilet Delmonico au Beurre

et aux Fines Herbes Cuites, the dish soon became known simply as Steak Delmonico, and is without a doubt the dish most ordered in the restaurant.

"We go through 550 to six hundred 20-ounce boneless rib-eye steaks a week," says executive chef William Oliva. (They also offer a three-pound bone-in version.) "In the old days, the chefs didn't specify what steak they served; instead, they promised 'the best steak available that day,' but through the years the rib eye has evolved as the Delmonico steak," he continues. "It's said you can't claim you've been to Delmonico's until you've enjoyed one of these."

So, based on that challenge, and a crazed affection for rib eye, I sat down and enjoyed this signature steak. It is perfect, juicy, tender, and sizzling to the last bite. Of course, the chef then put a plate of Lobster Newburg in front of me, suggesting I taste that too. The "taste" turned into cleaning the plate of the tender chunks

Chefs in the kitchen in 1902. Copyright © Museum of the City of New York, used with permission.

Mark Twain's 70th birthday party at Delmonico's in 1905. Copyright © Museum of the City of New York, used with permission.

of tail meat and shelled claws drenched in a brandy-cream sauce. Then, laughing, he threw down the gauntlet (actually, the Baked Alaska) and dared me to walk away after taking just a spoonful. Twenty spoonfuls later, the lightly browned meringue, ice cream, and cake masterpiece had vanished.

I also took lunch in the Grill, one of their five dining rooms, but most folks sit in the main dining room for lunch or dinner. One of the most romantic and elegant dining rooms in the country, with gilded ceilings, mahogany-paneled walls, large oil paintings of diners at Delmonico's in the 1930s, damask-upholstered chairs, frosted and etched windows, lovely chandeliers, and lush carpeting, it looks exactly like what you would expect at America's first fine-dining restaurant.

Over the years, literally thousands of celebrities, politicians, authors, actors, musicians, athletes, and captains of business and industry have dined here, appreciating the quiet and elegant atmosphere, the impeccable service, the superb wines and superlative food. "Del's" was a favorite haunt of stripper Gypsy Rose Lee, and the preferred restaurant of Mark Twain, Charles Dickens, and William Makepeace Thackeray. Samuel F. B. Morse sent the first transatlantic cable from one of its ballrooms.

The restaurant today has no affiliation with the original Delmonico family, having passed through five or six owners since they left the business. It has been run by the Ocinomled Partnership since 1999. Thankfully, the tradition of using only the best, freshest, and highest-quality ingredients and paying intense attention to detail and customer satisfaction is unchanged from the days when Giovanni and Pietro began their American quest with a small homespun café a half-block away. The fairytale that changed their names, their lives, American dining, and the history of restaurants lives on.

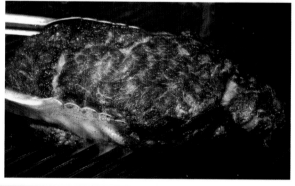

Lobster Newburg

2 (1-pound) live
New England lobsters

3 tablespoons unsalted butter

½ cup diced carrots

½ cup diced yellow onion

½ cup diced celery

2 tablespoons tomato paste

¼ cup plus 1 tablespoon brandy

3 cups heavy cream

Coarse salt and freshly
ground white pepper

2 shallots, minced

Cayenne pepper

Freshly ground nutmeg

1 large egg yolk,
at room temperature

1 tablespoon freshly
squeezed lemon juice

1 ounce American sturgeon
caviar (optional)

Place a lobster on a cutting board. Using a sharp chef's knife held vertically, plunge the point into the lobster's head about 1 inch behind the eyes. Push the knife completely in to touch the cutting board, then move it forward to cut the entire head in half. This is the quickest and easiest (and most humane) way to kill a lobster. Pull the claws from the body. Prepare an ice-water bath in a bowl large enough to hold all the lobster parts and set it aside.

Place the claws and bodies in the top half of a steamer over boiling water. Cover and steam the lobsters for 4 minutes. Remove the bodies and continue steaming the claws for an additional 3 minutes. Immerse both the bodies and claws in the ice-water bath as soon as you remove them from the steamer to stop the cooking. Crack the shells on the bodies and claws and carefully remove the meat, keeping it in pieces as large as possible. Separately reserve the meat and the shells.

Preheat the oven to 350°F. Place the lobster shells in a roasting pan to roast, turning occasionally, for about 12 minutes, or until nicely colored and fragrant. Remove from the oven and set aside.

In a large saucepan, melt 2 tablespoons of the butter over medium heat. Add the carrots, onion, and celery and sauté for about 4 minutes, or just until the vegetables begin to soften without taking on any color. Add the tomato paste and sauté for about 1 minute, or until well incorporated. Stir in the reserved lobster shells, followed by the ¼ cup brandy. Cook for about 3 minutes, stirring to deglaze the pan, then immediately lower the heat to a gentle simmer. Add the cream, season with salt and pepper, and cook gently for about 1½ hours, or until very thick and well seasoned.

Remove the sauce from the heat and pour it through a fine-mesh sieve into a clean container, pressing on the solids with the back of a large spoon to extract all of the flavor. Discard the solids and set the sauce aside.

In a medium sauté pan, melt the remaining 1 tablespoon butter over medium-low heat. Add the shallots and season to taste with cayenne and nutmeg. Cook, stirring constantly, for about 2 minutes, or until the seasonings have colored and are fragrant. Add the reserved lobster meat and sauté for 1 minute. Add the remaining 1 tablespoon brandy, stirring to deglaze the pan. Add the reserved cream sauce, raise the heat, and bring to a gentle simmer.

Place the egg yolk in a small bowl. Remove the pan from the heat and, using a slotted spoon, transfer an equal portion of the lobster meat to each of 4 shallow soup bowls. Whisk a bit of the hot sauce into the egg yolk to temper it, and then whisk the egg mixture into the sauce. Add the lemon juice. Taste and adjust the seasoning. Pour the sauce over the lobster in each bowl. If using, spoon an equal portion of the caviar into the center of each bowl. Serve immediately.

Ferrara
NEW YORK, NY ~ EST. 1892

In the late 1800s, the last years of the Gay Nineties, New Yorkers loved their opera and theater but had nowhere to go after the performances. Up stepped Enrico Scoppa and Antonio Ferrara, who opened an espresso café called Caffè A. Ferrara that featured pastries from the Old Country. It was a place for people to sit, discuss the opera or theater they'd just enjoyed, and possibly play a popular card game called skopa. It was a huge success.

In 1903, the great tenor Enrico Caruso was appearing in *Rigoletto* at the Metropolitan Opera and after his performance was said to have stopped by Ferrara for espresso. While there, he sampled some of the desserts they offered and was hooked by the Italian pastries, which reminded him of home. Caruso became a regular and enthusiastic customer.

In 1930, after World War I, Antonio's nephew, Pietro (Peter) Lepore, wanted to come to America but didn't have enough money to buy passage on a ship. He cleverly disguised himself as a clown and walked onboard a departing passenger liner with a circus troupe. When he got to New York, he jumped ship.

Peter began working for his uncle at the café and two years later married Enrico's daughter. When his father-in-law died, Peter bought out his interest and began running the business. It was his idea to ship boxes of their torrone, a traditional nougat candy, to Italian-American soldiers on the front lines. Since the candy is dairy-free, there was no trouble shipping it that distance. Thus began Ferrara's successful mail-order division, which is now going strong online. You can have just about

everything they sell in the store shipped to you, including frozen pastries, cakes, and cheesecakes.

The family lived in apartments over the bakery, and just about everyone, including grandpa, mom and dad, and all the kids worked here at one time. Ernest, the fifth-generation owner, speaks reverently of his predecessors: "There was a real work ethic here. We were and are all about family tradition, and in this family that includes discipline. If you wanted to work here, even though you were family, you had to step up."

When Ernest was younger and working in the bakery, he recalls there were some bakers who had been there for sixty years. Head baker Franco Amati has forty-two years of service, and several of the other bakery staff have thirty-plus. And these aren't even family members, though they are considered family by Ernest.

Spending a day in the bakery with Ernest is not the way to watch your diet. As we moved around the large room, every time I even glanced at something, Ernest offered it to me: "Try this," he would say, or "Eat one of these!" or "Which of these do you like better?" On more than a few occasions, I had to stop to eat a Pignoli cookie, a piece of Chocolate Truffle Cake, a Lobster Tail (not the New England crustacean but rather a puff pastry filled with Bavarian cream), a Rainbow Cookie, and both a plain and a chocolate giant cannoli that were thrust into my hands.

When my tour entered the main café, I stopped and took a couple of photos of the gelato freezer, and ten seconds later I was handed a huge dish bulging with three flavors of Italian ice cream. "We make our own gelato," Ernest proudly said, "I wanted you to try some of my favorite flavors." Mercifully, Ernest received an important phone call and left the room. I had been terrified of walking past the display cases with their incredible variety of tarts, cakes, cookies, cannoli, éclairs, cream puffs, biscuits, and candied nuts. As it was, when I left he presented me with a box filled with two layers of exquisite pastries. You should have seen the look on people's faces as I walked down Mulberry Street handing out all those pastries. Well, almost all. I did keep a couple.

In addition to their baked and frozen goodies, Ferrara has a wonderful selection of coffees, espressos, cappuccinos, and lattes, including a half-dozen or so enhanced with various liqueurs. After all, they began as an espresso café.

When asked what he thought brought about their longevity and success, Ernest didn't hesitate for a second. "It's because we say 'I love you' through our pastries." We love you too Ferrara, especially your cannoli, your Lobster Tails, your Pignoli cookies, and most especially, your Pasticciotto Ricotta (their heaven-sent "Mini Italian Cheesecake" tart).

Two fans of great pastries: Enrico Caruso (above), and Ferrara owner Ernest Lapore (right).

Cannoli

∾ MAKES ABOUT 24 PIECES ∾

SHELLS

3 cups sifted all-purpose flour

3 tablespoons melted unsalted butter

1 tablespoon granulated sugar

Pinch of salt

About ¾ cup dry red wine (see Note)

1 large egg yolk, lightly beaten

Canola oil, for deep-frying

FILLING

3 pounds whole-milk ricotta cheese, drained in a cheesecloth-lined colander for 8 hours or overnight

¾ cup confectioners' sugar

¼ cup crème de cacao or other sweet liqueur

3 tablespoons grated bittersweet chocolate

2 tablespoons minced candied orange peel

½ cup chopped pistachio nuts, for garnish

For the shells: In a medium bowl, combine the flour, butter, granulated sugar, and salt. Gradually stir in enough wine to make a stiff but manageable dough. On a floured board, knead the dough for about 15 minutes, or until smooth and soft. Add a bit more flour if necessary to prevent sticking. Roll into a ball, cover, and refrigerate for 1 hour. Divide the dough in half and roll into paper-thin sheets on a lightly floured board. Cut into 4-inch squares. Place a cannoli tube (see Notes) from corner to corner, diagonally across the square. Fold the opposite corners together around the tube. Brush the corners with the beaten egg yolk to seal and press together.

In a Dutch oven or deep fryer, heat 3 inches of oil to 390°F on a deep-fat thermometer. Using tongs, add the cannoli, 2 or 3 at a time to the oil and fry, turning if necessary, until a deep, golden brown. Using tongs, transfer to paper towels to drain. Let cool to the touch. Remove the tubes, being careful not to break the shells. Set aside and let cool completely. If not using now, store in an airtight container in a cool place for several weeks.

For the filling: Using an electric mixer, beat the ricotta on high speed for 2 minutes. Add the confectioners' sugar and liqueur and continue beating for 5 minutes, or until smooth. Stir in the chocolate and candied orange peel. If not using now, cover and refrigerate for up to 3 days.

Just before serving, stuff the filling into the shells using a teaspoon, allowing the filling to come slightly outside the end of each shell. Dip the ends of each shell in the pistachios.

NOTE: This Italian pastry is unusual in that it uses red wine in the dough to give it color. Stuffed with a creamy ricotta mixture and surrounded with a crisp, golden shell, it is a treat both in texture and in taste. It is delicious served with a piping-hot cup of espresso. Cannoli tubes can be bought at kitchen-supply stores, or you may use clean, unpainted wooden dowels 1 inch in diameter and 6 inches long.

Fraunces Tavern
NEW YORK, NY ~ EST. 1762

In 1671, New York Mayor Stephanus van Cortlandt built a large yellow-brick house that was one of the best homes in the city at the time. He passed the place to his son-in-law, and then when he died in 1762, his heirs sold the property to Samuel Fraunces, who converted the home into the popular Queen's Head tavern. Samuel then opened a wax museum in a local mansion, but with the Revolution approaching he returned to the Queen's Head and changed the name to Fraunces Tavern.

There is an unsolved controversy about the racial identity of Samuel, who was nicknamed "Black Sam," was born in Jamaica, and was listed as "mulatto" at the time of his baptism, but as "white" on census rolls. The issue is still a passionate topic of discussion to this very day.

In August 1774, in order to quell the growing resentment of the American patriots, the British warship *Asia* fired hundreds of cannonballs from its thirty-two guns into the city, sending one through the roof of the tavern. Samuel and many fellow New Yorkers had already fled to safer cities nearby, but by 1776, the British had captured the city, and Samuel had been captured by the British in New Jersey. He was brought back to the tavern to cook for a British colonel, who had allegedly enjoyed several meals there before the hostilities began.

With the available buildings on land overflowing with prisoners, the British anchored old ships in the bay to serve as prisons. More than eleven thousand of the prisoners died, which is more than all the deaths in battle during the war, but Samuel is credited with secretly spying for Washington and for using his influence with the British colonel and other officers to persuade them to allow him to feed the prisoners, saving thousands from starvation.

The British army left New York City on November 25, 1783. That afternoon, there was a grand parade, with George Washington leading the American army through the city. A large dinner party and turtle feast was held at Fraunces Tavern that night, and fireworks lit up the sky.

Having dined previously with General Washington at The Old '76 House in Tappan, New York (page 247), and cooking a meal for him there, Samuel and the general maintained a friendship that lasted for years. After Washington was elected president (the nation's capital at that time was New York City), he hired Samuel as steward and chief cook for his household. Four years later, Samuel opened the Golden Tun Tavern in the city, a place popular with Washington and other U.S. and foreign dignitaries. Samuel died at seventy-two, claiming that the government still owed him money for housing and feeding soldiers during the war.

The tavern building was threatened with demolition by its owners in 1900, but a number of

organizations, especially the Sons and Daughters of the American Revolution, convinced New York leaders to designate the building and grounds as a park. The building was given to the Sons of the Revolution in 1904 in exchange for a long-term lease with owner Robert Norden, and underwent a "conjectural reconstruction," which means that some of the original walls remain, but that the style of the extensive rebuilding was based on conjecture.

The tavern meandered on its way for the next ten decades, surviving two wars, the Depression, Prohibition, and a bomb in 1975 that killed four people and wounded more than fifty, including Robert Norden, the owner at that time. His son Robert, Jr., who worked for his father at the restaurant, was uninjured.

After a dispute with the landlords, to whom Norden's family had given the building in exchange for a long-term lease, lease-renewal negotiations fell through and Norden packed up everything he could and retired. The place suffered from neglect and was dying a slow death until the Ireland-based Porterhouse Group took over. They closed it briefly in 2010, making additional changes and updates while attempting to preserve the heritage of the tavern.

Historic image of the Long Room, where George Washington was honored with a dinner, now part of the Fraunces Tavern Museum operated by the D.A.R. Photo courtesy of Fraunces Tavern Museum, New York City.

Pan-Seared Salmon

2 cups whole milk

2 medium parsnips,
  peeled and chopped

2 teaspoons olive oil

½ cup shiitake mushrooms

½ cup oyster mushrooms

½ cup cremini mushrooms

2 tablespoons chopped shallots

3 tablespoons chopped garlic

½ cup white wine

½ cup sherry wine

1 tablespoon sherry vinegar

1 tablespoon lemon juice

2 tablespoons unsalted butter

½ cup water

1 tablespoon chopped
  fresh parsley

1 tablespoon chopped
  fresh chives

1½ teaspoons chopped
  fresh tarragon

½ teaspoon salt

¼ teaspoon freshly ground
  black pepper

3 tablespoons soy oil

2 cups lightly packed spinach

2 (6-ounce) salmon fillets, skin on

Place the milk and parsnips in a pot and cook over medium-high heat until tender. Transfer the parsnips to a blender and puree, adding cooking milk as needed. Season with salt. Set aside and keep warm.

Heat 1 teaspoon of the olive oil in a large sauté pan over medium-high heat. Add the mushrooms and cook until dry. Add the shallots, 1 tablespoon of the garlic, and the white wine and sherry and cook until reduced by half, about 15 minutes. Add the sherry vinegar, lemon juice, butter, water, parsley, chives, and tarragon, and season with ½ teaspoon salt and the black pepper. Set aside and keep warm.

In a separate sauté pan, heat the soy oil over medium-high heat. Sauté the spinach and the remaining 2 tablespoons of garlic.

In another sauté pan, heat the remaining 1 teaspoon of olive oil over high heat. When the oil is hot, pan sear the salmon skin side down, about 3 minutes, then turn and sear the other side for 2 to 3 minutes.

Spread the parsnip puree on each of the serving plates. Form a ring with the sautéed spinach to hold the braised mushrooms, place the salmon on top, and serve at once.

They exposed the original ceiling and had tables made from some of the original floorboards that were no longer usable as flooring.

The menu features updated old favorites, such as Shepherd's Pie, Pork Chops, British Bangers, Haddock Chowder, Country Terrines, Roast Chicken, and Soda Bread. The Grilled Pork Chop and Belly with bacon-braised lentils and frisée, served with a hearty mustard sauce, certainly would have satisfied any Colonial gentleman. But while beets, green beans, and goat cheese might have been available to cooks in the early tavern, they probably never would have put them in one dish, as the restaurant serves today.

While it may make "Black Sam" turn over in his grave to know that a company based in the United Kingdom owns his precious Fraunces Tavern, he can take comfort in the fact that it has been saved to such an extent that it is said to be the oldest surviving building in Manhattan.

So, a toast to Samuel Fraunces, an unsung hero of the American Revolution, tavern keeper, husband, father, and, we almost forgot, the first White House chef.

Katz's Delicatessen
NEW YORK, NY ~ EST. 1888

Katz's Deli is perhaps the only famous restaurant in America made even more famous by a fake orgasm. Although known worldwide for its pastrami sandwiches and incredible hot dogs, the restaurant gained even wider recognition when Meg Ryan acted out a counterfeit orgasm for Billy Crystal in the film *When Harry Met Sally*. Startled diners react with shock, and Director Carl Reiner's mother, playing a customer, delivers one of the movie's most memorable lines: "I'll have what she's having."

Actually, many fans taking their first bite of the legendary pastrami, or the nearly-as-famous Reuben sandwich, agree that it could indeed cause an only slightly less enthusiastic reaction. Some have said, and I'm certainly not going to disagree, that Katz's smoked pastrami sandwich is the world's best. It's also said that if you've been to New York City and failed to visit America's oldest Jewish deli (first opened in 1888 by a Russian immigrant family), you've not really been to New York.

Katz's is located on Houston Street (pronounced HOWston) in New York's Lower East Side, for many years one of the poorer areas of the city. But despite its humble birth, it has become perhaps the most famous Jewish deli in the world. Begun when the area was teeming with thousands of new immigrants, Katz's was established as a vital and important part of the community. Friday-night dinner specials (knockwurst and beans) were a neighborhood tradition, the restaurant

WHERE HARRY
MET SALLY...
HOPE YOU HAVE
WHAT SHE HAD!

↓

ENJOY!

providing the flavors of the Old World many of the immigrants had left behind.

Today Katz's is run by Fred Austin, Alan Dell, and Alan's son Jake. When asked why he thinks they've survived for more than a century, Alan says: "It's the food, no debate. The quality of the food we serve here is unparalleled, unmatched in New York, and we think, the world. And of course the other aspect is nostalgia. You came here with your grandfather and grandmother, and you bring your own family here. You always remember your first visit, and want to re-create that moment."

Katz's is the only deli in town that still hand-carves meat for every order. When you enter, you are given a ticket, then you join one of the lines snaking through the crowded tables to place your order with one of the cutters. He or she will ask if you want your meat "lean or juicy"—juicy means it comes with some moist, flavorful fat attached. Your cutter then takes a fresh-from-the-oven beef brisket, smoked pastrami, or moist corned beef roast and with magical strokes carves up what seems enough meat to feed the whole line. Tradition has it that as they make the sandwich they put a slice or two of the meat on a small plate and offer it to you to taste.

The sandwiches are big. The pastrami is twelve ounces of smoky, dripping, tender, and flavorful meat on your choice of bread or roll, though if you order corned beef you will get it on Jewish rye, period. To do otherwise is considered a culinary sin. The sandwiches are a bit pricey, but one easily feeds two, or is enough to take half of it home for dinner or another lunch.

There are of course other foods you can sample: their hot dogs are great (rated the No. 1 in New York by *Gourmet* magazine); order them "burned" if you want extra-crispy skin. The knishes are loaded with a deliciously spiced potato and onion filling. Their dessert, noodle pudding (kugel), is rich, sweet, and custardy, with chunks of pineapple, mandarin oranges, and raisins. And

their tangy, crunchy pickles (whole sour, half sour, and tomatoes) are another Katz tradition.

In World War II, the sons of the restaurant's owners were serving overseas, and the restaurant started a tradition of sending salamis to them in Europe, which led to the "Send a Salami to Your Boy in the Army" campaign, which continues today. Over the years, they estimate that they have sent hundreds of thousands of salamis to troops overseas, including those serving in Iraq and Afghanistan.

Jake, twenty-three, is slated to take over the deli when his father hangs up his apron. He began working at the restaurant at age five, handing out tickets to people as they arrived, and continued to work here until college, when he decided against continuing in the family business. "I was headed to medical school," he says, "but then I looked closely at this place and my family's history here, and decided to come back. I guess you could say I was captured by the magic."

It's certainly not the fanciest place in town—there are no white tablecloths—and it isn't the quietest or the quickest place to get lunch, nor is it a place for an elegant or romantic dinner (despite Meg Ryan's experience), but it has been an important tradition over many years and is a bustling, noisy, authentically historic place to eat great food.

And for heaven's sake, when you go for the first time, order the pastrami!

Katz's Noodle Kugel

∾ SERVES 10 TO 12 ∾

KUGEL

1 pound wide egg noodles, cooked and drained

8 ounces farmer cheese, or cottage cheese drained
 in a cheesecloth-lined colander for 30 minutes

1 cup sour cream

4 large eggs, beaten

2 tablespoons vanilla extract

1 teaspoon ground cinnamon

½ cup sugar

½ cup golden raisins

½ cup canned mandarin orange slices, drained

½ cup canned crushed pineapple, drained

1 teaspoon ground cinnamon

1 teaspoon sugar

Whipped cream

For the kugel: Preheat the oven to 350°F. Butter a 9 by 13-inch
baking pan. In a large bowl, combine all the ingredients and
stir gently to mix. Transfer to the prepared pan.

In a small bowl, stir the cinnamon and sugar together. Sprinkle
this mixture over the pudding.

Bake until golden brown, about 1 hour. Let cool slightly
and cut into 3-inch squares. Serve each square topped with
a dollop of whipped cream.

∾ Katz's Food Facts ∾

- *10,000–12,000 pounds of pastrami per week*
- *6,000–8,000 pounds of corned beef per week*
- *750–800 pounds of sauerkraut per week*
- *5,000–7,000 hot dogs per week*
- *12,000–14,000 pickles per week*

Katz's owners: (from left) Fred Austin, Jake Dell, and his father Alan Dell.

Keens Steakhouse
NEW YORK, NY ~ EST. 1885

In my travels around the country, I've experienced great steaks at many steakhouses and restaurants. I've sampled prodigious Porterhouses, superb sirloins, fantastic filet mignons, and delicious Delmonico's. But in New York City, in the heart of the old Herald Square Theater District, I had a chance to taste one of the most incredible cuts of red meat I've ever eaten in a restaurant. And believe me, after touring forty-six states in researching this book, that's saying something. Keens Steakhouse (aka Chophouse) is a truly unique eating place for that and several other reasons.

First, the meat of our story. Literally. No other menu in America features a mutton chop like the one served here. The twenty-eight-ounce "chop" is cut from a saddle of lamb, and the wing-shaped chop includes two pieces of tenderloin, two of the eye, and two T-bones. And never mind what the menu says, real mutton was replaced by the milder-flavored and more tender lamb a number of years ago. Think of it. You are eating the three best cuts of lamb all in one rather large chunk. And the way it is simply roasted brings out the flavor, moistness, and tenderness of all three. Last year they served almost sixteen thousand orders (more than 11½ tons of lamb). And when the perfectly medium-rare chop is put before you and you gaze at the side flaps of meat, there is no doubt where the term "mutton chop" for long, full sideburns comes from. But dig in while it's hot.

Early in the twentieth century, the owners of what was then the Lambs Club restaurant/tavern began collecting long, thin-stemmed clay Colonial "churchwarden" pipes. Tradition dictated that after you smoked your pipe in the tavern you gave it to a "warden" to store for you, as they were so fragile they broke easily when transported. When you returned to the tavern, you asked for your pipe and the warden retrieved it. When the Lambs Club became Keens in 1885, Albert Keen continued the tradition. The membership of his Pipe Club grew to over ninety thousand men at its peak, including Teddy Roosevelt, Babe Ruth, Will Rogers, Bill Rose, Albert Einstein, George M. Cohan, J. P. Morgan, Stanford White, General Douglas MacArthur, and "Buffalo Bill" Cody.

Still, the pipes kept coming in—to date, there are fifty-two thousand of them. So Mr. Keen decided to display many of them on the ceilings of their four dining rooms, the pub room, and the barroom. Today there are tens of thousands of pipes hanging over the heads of everyone who dines there, and there are boxes and boxes more in a storage room.

Keens began life in what was then one of two of New York's most important theater districts. The restaurant and bar naturally became a popular haunt of the actors, conductors, and opera singers, some of whom came in the back door in full costume and makeup for a quick bite or a bracing beverage before or after their performances nearby. Sometimes they even showed up during intermission.

After more than one hundred years, the building was worn out and needed a major face-lift. What seemed at first to be a minor task ended up forcing the owners to replace floors, repair footings, dig a new sewer line, install new air conditioning and a new sprinkler system, remove six staircases, and install a new cement and metal staircase from the first to the sixth floor. All the clay pipes were taken down, new kitchen

Line cooks: (front row - left to right) Miguel Cocotl, Marcelino Hernandez, Luis Yaurincela. Back row: Rafael Cruz, Eduardo Barrios, and Jose Luis Villafana line up for the camera.

appliances were brought in, and more than five hundred items were removed from the walls and cleaned. The complete renovation took three years and cost more than $1.4 million dollars.

The restaurant is huge. There are four dining rooms, all decorated with memorabilia, historic photographs, and theater and circus posters. Each is furnished in old wood and old leather booths. In one there is a display honoring Abraham Lincoln, which includes the program he was holding when he was shot. The Roosevelt Room is adorned by a huge moose head, a gift from Teddy himself. The topmost room is named after actress Lillie Langtry, who sued Keens because it, like other steakhouses of that era, refused to allow women to eat there. The day she won the lawsuit, she showed up wearing a feather boa and ordered a mutton chop, and the rest is history.

We mustn't forget the potent potables that the bar is famed for as well. It stocks over 260 single-malt whiskies, one of the largest such collections in the United States, and whiskey buyer Tim McBride has a goal of expanding the whiskey list to three hundred.

Keens is a steakhouse that still calls itself a chophouse on its awning. It's most famous for a non-steak dish, and is a nonsmoking establishment festooned with more pipes than anywhere else in the world. And then there's the non-mutton mutton chop. But despite its contradictions, it's one of the best places for steaks and chops in the country.

1940 luncheon of the Sixth Ave. Association, complete with smoking pipes.

Keens Mutton Chop
(Lamb Double-Loin Chop)

∾ SERVES 2 ∾

Canola oil, for searing

1 (28-ounce) saddle-cut lamb chop

1 teaspoon kosher salt

Mint jelly, for serving (see Note)

Preheat the oven to 425°F. Brush a grill pan with oil and heat until almost smoking over medium-high heat. Sear the lamb chop on both sides until lightly browned, then transfer to the oven and roast for 30 minutes, turning several times, for medium-rare.

Remove from the oven and tent with aluminum foil. Let rest for 10 minutes. Sprinkle with salt and serve on a warmed plate with the mint jelly in a small bowl or ramekin.

NOTE: While this is served for one at the restaurant, it makes more sense to serve this massive portion of meat to two people.

Keens shared their mint jelly ingredients but wanted to keep the proportions of their historic recipe a secret. If you're a seasoned cook or jelly maker, perhaps you can experiment and come up with a pretty good imitation. Here are the ingredients: apple juice, sugar, 1 (1.75-ounce) package Sure-Jell, lemon juice, mint extract, and 1 bunch fresh mint, julienned.

The Old '76 House
TAPPAN, NY ~ EST. 1668

While it's debatable whether The Old '76 House (aka '76 House) is the oldest or second oldest restaurant in America, and there is some uncertainty that it is the only one that functioned as a prison, there is no doubt that it is one of only two that we know of (see La Fonda, page 211) that witnessed a hanging, virtually in its backyard.

In 1780, during the Revolutionary War, Benedict Arnold, then commander of West Point, was conspiring to help the British and enlisted the aid of Major John André in his plot to turn West Point over to them. It would have given the king's army a strategic position for cutting New England off from the other revolutionary states. Arnold was selling secret diagrams of West Point for

20,000 pounds. When André was caught in civilian clothes on September 23, 1780, he had papers disclosing the plot and was charged as a spy.

During the trial, André was incarcerated in what was then called the Mabie Tavern, today's The Old '76 House. He was tried by a military court across the street in the Dutch Church and found guilty on September 29. He was taken from his room at the tavern and marched up the hill behind it, where 1,550 soldiers and onlookers witnessed him being hanged.

André was buried at the foot of the gallows, but almost a hundred years later the Duke of York asked that his remains be brought back to England, where they were interred in Hero's

Kate Mohan
prepares a Caesar
salad in the historic
dining room.

Corner in Westminster Abbey. But somehow, one of his big toes was removed and put in a snuff box. Today, the pilfered phalange resides somewhere in Tappan (pronounced Tap-PAN) under the care of one of the local historical societies.

The Mabie Tavern was a favorite resting and dining spot, and during the war General Washington, Alexander Hamilton, and French General Lafayette took many of their meals there. The Orangetown Resolutions, precursors to the Declaration of Independence, were signed at the tavern on July 4, 1774.

The Old '76 House is smack dab in the middle of an eighty-five-acre downtown historic district in Tappan and is surrounded by other historic sites, including the oldest Dutch church in America, an idyllic village green, and quite a few turn-of-the-century Victorian homes.

In 1987, owner Robert Norden invested over a million dollars to preserve the building, bring it up to code, and ensure it another couple of centuries of serving the public. Workers hand-dug two-foot sections under the entire foundation, removing more than thirty tons of clay and replacing it with concrete. Authentic ceiling joists were located in a barn in Ontario, Canada, and original red pine flooring was secured from an Amish schoolhouse outside of Lancaster, Pennsylvania. Re-created Delft tile was hand-painted in Holland and shipped back to Tappan to be set in the taproom, and the original horsehair plaster was retouched in the four original rooms.

The atmosphere of a Colonial pub has been re-created with such authenticity that a guest walking into The Old '76 might expect to see

General Washington or Alexander Hamilton there, drinking a tankard of ale or smoking a long clay pipe. The typical clothing of a Colonial lady, a British officer, and an authentic Colonial military man is on display, as are historic drawings and memorabilia. Of particular interest are three drawings over the fireplace and above two crossed military sabers. On one side is a charcoal sketch of André (the spy); in the center is a depiction of his arrest; and on the other side is a hand-colored drawing of Benedict Arnold (the traitor) that is deliberately hung upside-down.

Today's menu is incredibly diverse. Appetizers include Alligator Empanadas (no kidding), Wild Boar Sausage, Escargots with Pine Nuts in Puff Pastry, and Filet Mignon Rosemary Skewers over caramelized Vidalia onions. Among the entrees are Veal Milanese over Arugula,

Undated photograph of the '76 House where Major John André was tried and sentenced to hang, which he did on a hill behind the restaurant.

Double-Cut Pork Chops, Seven-Fish Scampi (lobster, shrimp, scallops, clams, mussels, calamari, and salmon in a chardonnay sauce), Medallions of Red Deer, and a wonderful Salmon Terrine.

As you sit in the woody warmth of the more than three-hundred-year-old tavern, enjoying a warm fire, a cool drink, and the intriguing menu, it's sobering to think of the incredible history that has taken place within these walls. And we are lucky indeed that The Old '76 House has an innkeeper like Robert Norden, Jr., who treasures every inch of its heritage.

The spy General André and the traitor Benedict Arnold (upside down) displayed above the fireplace. Below: Period costumes.

Salmon Terrine

⌒ SERVES 2 ⌒

VIN BLANC SAUCE

½ cup dry white wine

4 cups fish velouté (see Note)

½ cup heavy cream, heated

2 tablespoons unsalted butter

Salt and freshly ground white pepper

Freshly squeezed lemon juice

1 tablespoon lobster base

SALMON TERRINE

3 tablespoons unsalted
butter, melted

½ cup fine fresh bread crumbs

1 tablespoon canola oil

8 ounces shrimp, shelled

8 ounces scallops, muscle removed

2 tablespoons minced garlic

½ cup fruity white wine

1 cup mayonnaise

1 teaspoon freshly ground
black pepper

1½ teaspoons Old Bay Seasoning

Juice of 1 lemon

8 ounces lump crabmeat,
picked over for shell

2 cups ½-inch-diced bread cubes

1 (2-pound) salmon fillet, skinned,
pinbones removed, and thinly
sliced on a diagonal

For the sauce: In a small nonreactive saucepan, cook the wine over medium heat until reduced by half. Add the velouté and simmer until thickened. Gradually whisk in the cream. Remove from the heat and swirl in the butter. Season to taste with salt, white pepper, and lemon juice. Strain through a sieve lined with cheesecloth. Stir in the lobster base until blended. Set aside and keep warm.

For the terrine: Preheat the oven to 400°F. Brush two 3- or 4-inch ramekins with some of the melted butter and dust with the bread crumbs. Reserve the remaining melted butter.

In a medium sauté pan, heat the oil over medium heat and sauté the shrimp and scallops until opaque. Using a slotted spoon, transfer to a rimmed baking sheet to cool. Add the garlic to the pan and cook until fragrant, about 1 minute, then add the white wine and stir to deglaze the pan. Cook to reduce the liquid by one-third. Remove from the heat and let cool completely.

In a small bowl, combine the mayonnaise, black pepper, Old Bay, and lemon juice. Stir in the white wine pan reduction.

Dice the shrimp and scallops and transfer to a medium bowl. Add the crabmeat and bread cubes. Stir in the mayonnaise mixture.

Line the sides and bottom of each prepared ramekin with thin slices of salmon. Fill with the stuffing mixture and lightly brush the tops with the reserved melted butter. Bake for 12 to 15 minutes, or until lightly browned.

To serve, loosen the terrines with a rubber spatula and unmold onto serving plates. Serve warm, with the warm sauce poured over.

NOTE: To make fish velouté, melt 3 tablespoons unsalted butter in a medium saucepan over medium-low heat and stir in 3 tablespoons flour. Cook and stir for 3 minutes; do not brown. Gradually whisk in 5 cups fish broth. Cook, stirring frequently, for about 20 minutes, or until lightly thickened and reduced to about 4 cups.

Old Homestead Steakhouse
NEW YORK, NY ~ EST. 1868

It was 1952 in New York City when the door opened and in walked Jackie Gleason, fresh from the set of *The Honeymooners* and still in his bus driver's uniform. The waiters knew what he wanted, so they first brought him Lobster Thermidor, followed closely by a Double-Cut Porterhouse steak. The Scotch on the rocks came before, during, and after.

One night in the mid 1960s, Frank Sinatra and his Rat Pack moved into the steakhouse dining room and proceeded to run up a huge tab for filet mignons, vintage Champagne, and other fine wines. Legend has it that Old Blue Eyes also enjoyed a few rounds of "gasoline" (his term for alcoholic beverages) in the form of Scotch and water. The

bill reportedly ran into several thousands—a huge amount in those days, when the average annual salary was just over eight grand.

"The Yankee Clipper," Joe DiMaggio, began his eighteen-month courtship of Marilyn Monroe at the back of the restaurant in 1952. The couple would sit at a table sharing private conversation and a steak or two. These are just some of the stories from the Old Homestead Steakhouse, a restaurant in the heart of New York's meatpacking district that has been serving legendary aged prime sirloin, Porterhouse, and filet mignon steaks for the past 144 years.

Back when it opened, the same year Ulysses S. Grant was elected president, it was a fancy place where well-off gents and ladies went to dine in style. The steakhouse survived World War I, the Depression, and Prohibition, though like every other restaurant of the time, they must have played a few tricks to get around the stringent liquor laws. In 1940, they hired Harry Sherry as a dishwasher, and the hard-working and thrifty young man started saving his paychecks. Eleven years later, with the help of some investor friends, he bought the place. It has remained in the Sherry family to this day. Harry's grandsons Greg and Marc direct all operations here, and at their Atlantic City, New Jersey, sister restaurant as well.

As a premier steakhouse in the Big Apple, the OH has entertained about every movie and TV star, star athlete, political notable, and President of the United States since Andrew Johnson, who came here to celebrate after surviving his impeachment by one vote. A star of the big and little screens itself, the restaurant has been featured in various episodes of *Law and Order*, *Seinfeld*, *The Sopranos*, and *Real Housewives of New Jersey*.

Their fame is not just because of the celebrities, or their acclaimed steaks, or the ambiance. There's also Annabelle, a full-sized fake bovine that is perched on the two-story Broadway-like marquee over the entrance. When the building underwent a multimillion-dollar makeover, Annabelle got some nips and tucks as well. The main dining room and three other smaller rooms upstairs (one of which looks out on Annabelle's hindquarters) can hold

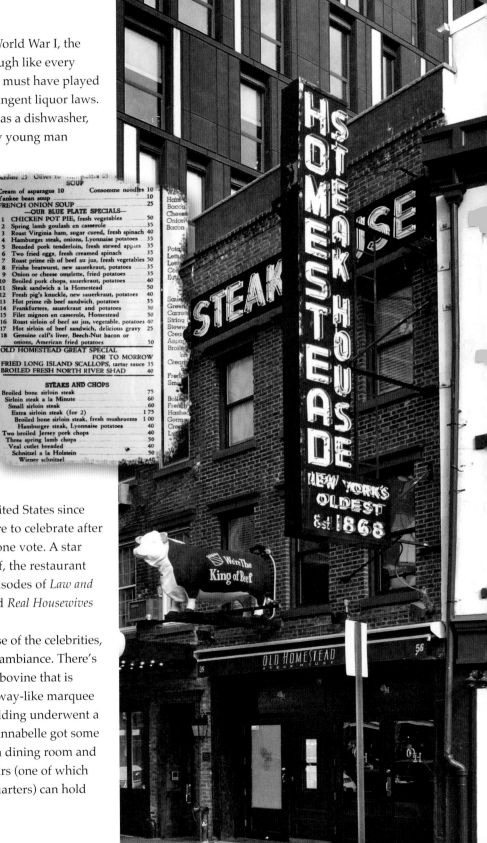

Toast Tower with Parmesan Cheese Sauce

∽ SERVES 2 TO 4 ∽

1 tablespoon unsalted butter

1 cup thinly sliced Spanish onions

1 tablespoon all-purpose flour

4¾ cups heavy cream

2½ cups (10 ounces) grated Parmigiano-Reggiano cheese

1 teaspoon salt

1 teaspoon freshly ground white pepper

3 to 4 (1-inch-thick) slices of white or sourdough bread.

In a medium skillet, melt the butter over medium heat and sauté the onions until translucent, about 3 minutes. Stir in the flour and cook, stirring, for 1 minute. Gradually whisk in the cream and bring to a boil. Cook, whisking constantly, until thickened.

Add the Parmesan cheese, salt, and white pepper, whisking until smooth. Remove from the heat. Puree using a hand blender. Strain through a fine-mesh sieve into a bowl. Set aside and keep warm.

Slice the bread into square logs and toast on a hot griddle or in a hot grill pan until lightly browned on all sides. Stack the logs like cordwood on a plate and pour the sauce around, but not over, the stack.

a total of 225 customers. But for me the real story here is the athleticism of the waiters. The kitchen is on the basement level of the restaurant, and there are fourteen stair steps up to the main floor of the restaurant. But then there are eighteen stair steps to the second-floor dining rooms, and another eighteen up to the third-floor rooms. Not much, you say? Try climbing fifty stairs twenty to thirty times a night, carrying a tray that can weigh ten to fifteen pounds!

In 1995, the restaurant, after a multiyear collaboration with health officials in Japan and the USDA, negotiated the lifting of a ban on importing Japanese Kobe beef. At that time, they were the only restaurant in the country serving this super-tender, super-flavorful beef. Ten years later, they created the most expensive hamburger in New York City, deemed the "most decadent burgers in the world" by the Travel Channel. I sampled one and found the twenty ounces of beef to be incredibly tender and flavorful. The rib eye is also top of the line, again tender and loaded with the flavor only Prime beef attains. And for an appetizer that draws gasps, try the tower of toast logs perched in a puddle of a sauce of Parmesan cheese, cream, and butter. Pure indulgence.

In 2010, the steakhouse served its one-millionth customer. Please don't tell old Annabelle, but many, many, many of her relatives made the ultimate sacrifice to achieve that number.

Pete's Tavern
NEW YORK, NY ~ EST. 1864

William Sydney Porter lived at 55 Irving Place in New York City from 1903 to 1907. Before that time, he had had a checkered career, first as a pharmacist, then as a draftsman, then as a bank teller and bookkeeper in Austin, Texas, then as a newspaper writer in Houston. While in an Ohio prison for embezzling from the Texas bank, he became a freelance magazine writer, then emerged from jail and moved to New York City, where he was hired as a columnist for the *New York World Sunday Magazine*. One of his most famous works was, some say, penned while sitting in a booth by a window at Healy's, a small dusty Gramercy Park tavern several blocks from his home, which he visited almost every day.

The tavern was purchased thirty years later by Pete Belle, who changed the name to Pete's

Tavern, the name it still carries seventy-eight years later. The writer? He changed his name too. Not many people have heard of William Sydney Porter, but everyone knows about O. Henry. And just about everyone has read the story he supposedly wrote in his notebook on a red and white checked tablecloth in the tavern: "A Gift of the Magi."

The building that housed Healy's and now Pete's was built in 1829 as the Portman Hotel. It is believed that liquor was sold there beginning in 1851, when it had evolved into a "grocery and grog" store. The store officially began its life as a drinking establishment in 1864, and thirty-five years later became Healy's.

When Prohibition reared its ugly head, the owners disguised the tavern as a flower shop

but continued selling alcohol. One can imagine buying a bouquet of roses with a bottle of whiskey hidden in the long stems, or perhaps a small bottle of rye buried in a potted geranium. Who knows, maybe the expression "getting potted," for someone who drank too much, came from here.

Pete's is now New York's oldest continuously operating tavern, having never closed since its unheralded opening in the mid-1860s. The pressed-tin ceiling is the same, many of the wooden booths are over a century old, the floor has held up remarkably, and the thirty-foot rosewood bar reinforces the old-time ambiance.

There are several pen-and-ink portraits of the inimitable Mr. Porter scattered around the bar and dining rooms, and a sign on the awning outside claims that Pete's is "the Tavern O. Henry Made Famous." Whether or not he wrote his magical magi tale here, he does mention a place named Kenealy's in his short story "The Lost Blend," and some of the descriptions of that fictional tavern sound like a tribute to his favorite drinking place.

The walls are decorated (or rather plastered) with photographs of celebrities from the sports, TV, and movie worlds who have visited Pete's. One is a simple black and white portrait, flanked by two small American flags and an early portrait of a barefoot and casual John F. Kennedy sitting with Jackie, who is looking up adoringly at her husband.

Pete's has often been featured on CNN, VH1, *Seinfeld*, *Law and Order*, *Sex and the City*, Fox Cable News, and the Food Network. And Hollywood has visited, bringing their cameras to record the historic setting in *Ragtime*, *Endless Love*, and *Across the Sea of Time*. Samuel Adams Brewery and Miller Beer have also recorded videos here for various TV commercials.

The menu, while leaning heavily toward Italian, has just about every bar food and steakhouse staple you could crave. More unexpected dishes include Baked Goat Cheese in Mixed Nut Crust Salad, Veal Meatballs, and Shrimp Parmigiana.

The Italian food is wonderful, as is the massive and inexpensive (not too often do you see those words used together) Roast Prime Rib: tender, juicy, perfectly cooked to order and served with Yorkshire pudding, a baked potato (or garlic mashed), and a veggie of your choice. Weighing in at fourteen to sixteen ounces, and hitting the cash register at $15.95, this is a bargain in any restaurant, but most especially in New York where other restaurants charge $30 to $45 for a similar cut of Prime beef.

Another culinary treasure is the Seared Five-Spice Duck, something you'd expect in a fine Hong Kong restaurant, not in a centenarian Gramercy Park tavern.

Because Pete's is off the tourist-beaten path, it's usually filled with locals and regular customers who dine here weekly. The bar fills up first, so if you want to dine here make an early reservation, fight your way through the crowds to the back two dining rooms, and enjoy the atmosphere of one of the most historic bars in New York City.

Like O. Henry's famous story, it's a classic.

Seared Five-Spice Duck Breast with Plum Wine Sauce
∾ SERVES 2 ∾

2 teaspoons five-spice powder

2 tablespoons minced fresh ginger

6 green onions, white part only, finely chopped

¾ cup Asian sesame oil

Salt and freshly ground black pepper

2 (10-ounce) boneless duck half breasts with skin

1 cup plum wine

2 cups duck broth or chicken broth

4 tablespoons (½ stick) unsalted butter

In a small bowl, combine the five-spice powder, ginger, green onions, sesame oil, salt, and pepper; stir to blend. Transfer to a sealable plastic bag, add the duck, and seal. Refrigerate for at least 6 hours or overnight, turning the bag several times.

Preheat the oven to 400°F. Heat a large nonreactive skillet over medium-high heat. Add the duck breasts, skin side down. Cook until seared on the bottom, then turn and sear on the other side. Transfer the duck to a large ovenproof skillet and roast for 10 minutes for medium-rare. Remove the duck from the oven, transfer to a carving board, and tent with aluminum foil for at least 5 minutes.

While the duck is resting, pour off the fat from the skillet and add the plum wine and duck broth. Cook over medium heat to reduce to 1 cup. Whisk in the butter. Season with salt and pepper to taste. Set aside and keep warm.

To serve, cut the duck into slices on the diagonal and serve on warmed plates, topped with the sauce.

Peter Luger Steakhouse
BROOKLYN, NY ~ EST. 1887

When even your competitors agree that your steaks are the best, you've done something right. I'm not saying they're going to take out ads or set up billboards heralding the quality of Luger's porterhouse steaks. But when asked "off the record," a pair of chefs at two other major U.S. steakhouses, one in New York and one in Dallas, told me that Luger's can't be beat.

Luger's first opened in 1887 as Carl Luger's Café—Billiards and Bowling Alley. Peter Luger was the owner and his nephew Carl was the chef, but according to critics, when Peter died the restaurant drifted downward. In 1950, Carl put the place up for auction, and the only bidder, Sol Forman, a customer of twenty-five years who owned a giftware factory across the street, bought

it for a low bid. Sol lived to the ripe old age of ninety-eight, during which time Luger's became the place to eat in New York, in Brooklyn, just across the East River from Manhattan.

Today, the restaurant is owned by a group, but it's run by Sol's daughter Marilyn and her sister Amy, and Jody Storch, Sol's granddaughter, who regularly walks through the testosterone-loaded Manhattan wholesale meat district selecting sides of (mostly) Midwest beef to bring to the restaurant for its super-secret dry-aging process—not a small job when you're serving up ten tons (that's twenty-thousand pounds) of beef a week.

The dry-aging process involves storing the bone-in loins of beef in a temperature-controlled room at a secret temperature for a secret amount of time. The result is simply great steaks.

With the hand selection, hand trimming, aging, and careful preparation, the steaks aren't cheap, and the restaurant accepts only cash, or their own credit cards. At last count, they had something like 85,000 cardholders.

The restaurant is an icon in a city of famous eating places, but unlike many of them it has a spartan décor, which tells you the owners and managers put their money into the food, not into wall sconces and imported crystal wineglasses. The main dining room is as bare bones as you can get, with

The present owners of Peter Luger: Marilyn, Jody, and Amy. Below is one week of table reservations written by hand, which they prefer over a computerized system.

wood floors, wood paneling, dark wood ceiling beams, and polished wood tables.

But people don't go to Luger's for décor. They go for thirty-two-ounce Porterhouse steaks. Of course, there are the almost-as-legendary side dishes: creamed spinach, German fried potatoes, grilled bacon, and a hefty tomato and onion salad with house-made dressing. And they do offer lamb chops, and salmon and pot roast and chicken, usually as daily specials. But I don't know why. This is steak country, or as one fan put it: "the cathedral of steak." Amen. The steaks are seared in an 800°F-plus broiler, then placed on a puddle of clarified butter on a serving plate, which is put into an oven to finish cooking. Then each steak is cut into slices before it is placed on a hot platter for serving. The 1¾-inch-thick Porterhouse is crunchy and dark on the outside, especially on the thin edge of fat they leave on the steak, and butter tender all the way to the bone inside. The only condiment offered, unless you're crass and ask for ketchup, is their own brand of rich brown steak sauce. And for anyone counting calories while they down the creamed spinach, fried potatoes, and two-pound steak, there's some good news—the sauce is fat-free!

Peter Luger German Fried Potatoes

∽ SERVES 6 TO 8 ∽

5 large Idaho potatoes

3 cups plus 2 tablespoons vegetable oil

1 large Spanish onion, diced

1 teaspoon kosher salt

1 teaspoon sweet paprika

6 tablespoons unsalted butter

¼ teaspoon freshly ground white pepper

Parsley sprigs, for garnish

Preheat the oven to 400°F. Butter an 8-cup baking dish.

Peel the potatoes and cut into ½-inch fries.

In a Dutch oven or deep fryer, heat the 3 cups oil to 375°F on a deep-fat thermometer and cook the potato strips, in batches if necessary to prevent crowding, until a light golden brown. Using a wire-mesh skimmer, transfer to paper towels to drain.

In a small skillet, heat the 2 tablespoons oil over medium heat and sauté the diced onion until golden brown. Season with ½ teaspoon of the salt and ½ teaspoon of the paprika and set aside. Transfer the cooked potatoes to a cutting board and cut into ¼-inch dice.

In a large, heavy skillet, melt the butter over medium heat and add the potatoes. Sauté for 2 to 3 minutes, then add the cooked onions, the remaining ½ teaspoon salt, and the white pepper. Stir to blend.

Transfer the mixture to the prepared dish, sprinkle with the remaining ½ teaspoon paprika, bake for 10 to 15 minutes, until lightly crisp on the top.

To serve, spoon the potatoes onto warmed plates and garnish with the parsley. Serve hot.

Above: Serving up one of America's best steaks.
Below: Heaven-scent grilled bacon.

Balsam Mountain Inn
BALSAM, NC ~ EST. 1855

In 1884, the Southern Railway completed a 110-mile line through the Great Smoky Mountains from Asheville to Murphy, thereby allowing people easy access to the towns scattered throughout the mountains. One of the places the tracks passed through was tiny Balsam station. At that time, the line was the second steepest line in America, and at thirty-five-hundred feet, the highest east of the Rocky Mountains.

It was at this high point in the Smoky Mountains that Joseph Kenney and Walter Christy, brothers-in-law from Georgia, decided to build the 107-room Balsam Mountain Hotel. Modeled after the famous Saratoga Inn of New York, it opened in 1908 and was solely reached by steam train.

Apparently, the builders framed in the first two floors of the hotel, and then went down to the bottom of the hill to view their handiwork from the train depot. From that viewpoint, the building appeared to have no roof and to their eyes was unimpressive. So, without permission from the owners, they took it on themselves to build a third floor. Then they added a mansard roof of embossed tin and several dormers.

Understandably, the owners weren't happy with all those extra rooms to heat and fill with furniture. This mountain has a history of six-foot-high snowfalls and storms with ninety-mile-an-hour winds, and the temperatures in the winter can hit twenty degrees below zero. In its first years, the only heat in the place was provided by fireplaces, quilts, and close personal contact. But when Western Carolina University was remodeling a dormitory, they offered the old radiators to the hotel, and they were retrofitted into the rooms and hallways.

Then there was the slight problem of getting water to that unwanted and unasked-for top floor. In the early days, all of the hotel's water came from a gravity-fed system built on a higher mountain across the valley. While the first and second floors had plenty of water, even gravity failed to get much, if any, up to the top floor. This was a problem the owners put up with for a few years, and then that floor was abandoned.

In the summer, the hotel is actually quite comfortable even though it still doesn't have air conditioning. The elevation produces temperatures that average ten degrees less than in the flatlands below, and the hotel was built to cool itself. The long covered porches, large windows, attic fans, wide hallways, and chimney-like stairways all promote airflow, and the rooms have fans to draw the cool outside air into the rooms.

Like many of the great resorts in the region, the hotel began falling apart over time, the ravages of weather, poor maintenance, and the reduced number of travelers all taking their toll. The building was virtually abandoned in the late 1980s. But when veteran innkeeper Merrily Teasley discovered the dilapidated hotel while hiking and saw its potential, she purchased it.

A veteran of restoring various crumbling buildings into successful inns, Merrily set about renovating the inn, turning one hundred bedrooms into fifty, giving each new room its own bathroom, and bringing in a modern water system so that all the rooms, even those on the third floor, got plenty of hot water. After recently taking back the Inn from some interim owners, Merrily says she wants visitors to "recapture the simplicity of life," and thus has not updated the Inn with television sets

and telephones. Instead, visitors can have messages taken by the front desk, or they can stand facing east on the far side of the parking lot, next to the big pine tree, with their cell phones.

Merrily says, "Surprisingly, families and their children find it actually quite easy to relax without the distraction of TV. They can hike, play checkers in the lounge, or go horseback riding, kayaking, or river rafting." Less athletic folks can explore the two-thousand-book library or watch the world go by from one of the two dozen locally made Troutman rockers on the two 100-foot-long covered porches.

HOTEL BALSAM
BALSAM, N. C.

In summer, you have your choice of eating breakfast or dinner in the bright Grand Ol' Dining Room. Lunch is served only on Sundays. Merrily says that she would rather have their guests "out and about, exploring the back roads and small mountain towns nearby."

The menu is somewhat limited, with only six entrees and a daily special. The food is good, filling comfort food: pork tenderloin, meat loaf, roast chicken, trout, and a vegetarian entree. The side dishes are probably the kind your mom made: collard greens, green beans, coleslaw, mac and cheese, scalloped potatoes, iceberg lettuce salad. When I visited, the Sunday special was one of the favorite Sunday supper meals of my youth: thick chunks of tender pot roast fighting for space with carrots, potatoes, onions, and a pool of succulent gravy. Three-and-a-half rolls' worth of gravy!

Sitting in "my" rocker after dinner, I watched the curtain of night draw slowly across the vibrant green hills, while swathes and swirls of mist curled up between the majestic mountain peaks, and just breathed. I guess I found my own way to capture life's simplicity. Thank you, Merrily.

Pecan Encrusted Catfish with Red Pepper Cream Sauce

∽ SERVES 4 TO 6 ∽

SAUCE

½ cup finely diced onion

½ cup roasted red peppers

1 tablespoon clarified butter

1 teaspoon garlic

¼ teaspoon freshly ground black pepper

1 tablespoon of Chablis

1 cup heavy cream

½ cup Parmesan cheese

BREADING

1 cup toasted fresh breadcrumbs

1 teaspoon curry powder

1 teaspoon tumeric

1 tablespoon paprika

1 tablespoon Paul Prudhomme's Blackened Steak Magic

½ cup crushed pecans

10 to 12 catfish fillets

1 tablespoon clarified butter

1 tablespoon fresh lemon juice

Salt and freshly ground black pepper

Preheat the oven to 350°F.

For the sauce: Sauté the onion and red pepper in the clarified butter, then add the garlic and black pepper. When the onion softens, add the Chablis and cook until reduced by half. Add the heavy cream and reduce by one half to two-thirds. Stir in the parmesan cheese and remove from the heat. The sauce will thicken as it cools

For the breading: Mix all the ingredients and set aside.

Spray or oil a baking pan or cast-iron skillet. Place the fillets in the pan. Mix the clarified butter with the lemon juice and brush over the fillets. Bake the fish for 4 minutes. Remove from the oven, sprinkle with the breading mixture, season with salt and pepper, then return to the oven and cook for another 4 minutes. Remove from the oven, add the sauce, and serve.

Old Salem Tavern
WINSTON-SALEM, NC ~ EST. 1816

Perhaps the only tavern in America that was built and operated by a church, the Salem Tavern, which was rebuilt when the original building burnt to the ground, is a delightful spot for lunch or dinner in historic Old Salem. The town of Salem and the original tavern were both built by a Moravian congregation on land purchased by Bishop Spangenberg in 1766. The religious group had been expelled from the colony of New York and moved on to Pennsylvania, where they founded the city of Bethlehem. They then moved into the Tarheel State and built the cities of Bethabara, Bethania, and then Salem.

The plan was for Salem to become a settlement congregation where the residents were expected to be church members in good standing. There was no civil government, as the church directed the economic and spiritual affairs of the residents. The tavern was to help the town develop as a trading center, offering food and lodging to visitors who would purchase goods and perhaps even employ local craftsmen. But even then, the tavern was built on the outskirts of town (one whole block from the town square) to avoid the influence of "strangers" on the citizenry.

The first tavern keepers were a married couple, chosen because of their strong character. They in turn hired a hostler to take care of customers' horses, and local women to do cooking and cleaning. It is also believed that a slave family was kept there to do manual labor.

Among the early guests was a Revolutionary War general who stayed here in May 1791. He was touring the Southern battlefields, studying the city's intricate waterworks system, and giving a speech to the townsfolk. Perhaps even then, George Washington had political aspirations. Unfortunately, there are no records of what he paid for his room at the tavern, what he ate, or whether he was a good tipper. We'll just have to guess. From the history books, we know he liked hoecakes, fish, garden vegetables, smoked ham, and ice cream. Other than the ice cream, those were pretty much the staples of every eating establishment of the era.

If you arrive in Old Salem these days and are not aware of local history, you might be startled to see women in eighteenth-century dresses and men wearing breeches, cravats, and tri-corner hats calmly walking down the cobblestone streets. Old Salem, where the tavern is located, is the historic district of Winston-Salem, and a living-history museum where eighteenth- and nineteenth-century Moravian culture is showcased on the streets, in the shops and museums, and of course in the Salem Tavern.

The wide plank floors, rustic wooden tables and chairs, a half-dozen welcoming hearths, and the cheerful servers in costume all welcome you to lunch or dinner in the 1700s. You can dine in any one of the half-dozen small dining rooms on three floors, or on the shaded back porch, or under a fragrant and colorful wisteria arbor at the back of the property. Many of the dishes on the menu are based on recipes of that era, and the tavern has received regional and national awards for its cuisine.

Lunch begins with baskets of yeasty rolls and pumpkin muffins, which are refilled for a ridiculously low price. Then it's on to bratwurst, sauerkraut stew, pot roast, salmon corn cakes, meat loaf, peanut chicken salad, or cornmeal-crusted catfish. The dinner menu offers a wide selection of salads (the grilled peach salad is especially good), baked crab dip, sweet potato fries, fried green tomatoes, and a dozen other first courses. The entrees include Pumpkin and Sunflower Seed Crusted Salmon, Cioppino, Porcini-Crusted Filet of Beef, Veal Schnitzel, Grilled Honey-Lime Tri-tip, and Buttermilk Fried Chicken Breast (with spiced peach gravy), and their most popular and most historic dish, Moravian Chicken Pie.

But there is one dessert that you must order: their Moravian Gingerbread, a toothy but nevertheless soft cake made with fresh ginger and grated orange zest, and topped with lemon ice cream. The recipe was passed down from Louisa Senseman, the daughter of one of Salem's first citizens, silversmith John Vogler. Warm from the oven, the thick brown cake sends out an aroma that will beguile your senses. I guarantee that you'll make it vanish in seconds. I did. Both the first and the second piece.

The Tavern as it looked in 1918; today the upper balcony has vanished.

Moravian Gingerbread

∾ MAKES 1 CAKE ∾

1¼ cups (2½ sticks) unsalted butter, at room temperature

2 cups sugar

3 large eggs

1 cup dark molasses (not bootstrap)

½ cup peeled and minced fresh ginger (see Note)

1 teaspoon ground cinnamon

½ teaspoon freshly grated nutmeg

Pinch of ground cloves

1 teaspoon baking soda

1 tablespoon cider vinegar

3½ cups sifted all-purpose flour (see Note)

1 cup whole milk

Whipped cream, or lemon or vanilla ice cream, for serving

Preheat the oven to 375°F. Butter and flour a 9 by 13-inch baking pan. Tap out the excess flour and set the pan aside.

In a large bowl, using an electric mixer on medium speed, cream the butter for 1 minute, or until fluffy, then gradually beat in the sugar. Add the eggs one at a time, beating well after each addition. Stir in the molasses, ginger, cinnamon, nutmeg, and cloves.

In a small bowl, combine the baking soda and vinegar. (The soda will foam when you add the vinegar. This is an old-fashioned way to leaven cakes and breads, used before there were reliable baking powders.) Stir this mixture into the butter mixture. Stir in the flour alternately with the milk in increments, beginning and ending with the flour and stirring after each addition only enough to combine.

Spread the batter evenly in the pan and bake on the center shelf for 45 to 50 minutes, until a cake tester inserted in the middle of the gingerbread comes out clean. Transfer the pan to a wire rack and let cool to room temperature before serving.

To serve, cut into squares and top with generous dollops of whipped cream, or scoops of lemon or vanilla ice cream.

NOTE: The secret to this recipe is the fresh ginger. It will not taste the same if you use any other form of ginger.

Sift the flour before you measure it, even if the bag says "pre-sifted."

The Buxton Inn
GRANVILLE, OH ~ EST. 1812

This book features many restaurants with special cuisines, unique décor, or distinctive historical relevance, and a few that have their very own ghostly presences. But the small Buxton Inn in Granville, Ohio, houses not just ghostly shadows, moving lights, or strange sounds but highly recognizable historic ghosts. Apparently, there are four ghosts who regularly appear in the hallways, kitchen, or bedrooms of the Inn. Three are former innkeepers; the fourth, an innkeeper's cat. The ghostly personages include one Orin Granger, who built the Inn in 1812 and appears sometimes as a man in blue who steals pies from the pantry. Major Horton Buxton, who operated the Inn between 1865 and 1905, is often seen sitting in a chair by the dining room fireplace. People warming their hands at the fire have actually seen his disembodied

hands next to theirs. Ethel "Bonnie" Bounell, the innkeeper from 1934 to 1960, is known as the "blue lady" and tends to visit rooms seven and nine, the latter being the room where she died. And Bonnie's cat, Major Buxton, has been felt in that room, landing on the bed of several guests in the middle of the night.

Reports of these ghostly visits are legend and have been described in dozens of magazine and newspaper articles and websites such as haunted-places-to-go.com and ghostsofohio.org. These are not unfriendly ghosts; there are no reports of any of the four phantoms doing anything other than visiting and asking guests if they slept well, except for the pie thief that is.

When Granger built the Inn in 1812, he included a ballroom, a stagecoach court, and a dining room. Current innkeeper Orville Orr relates how one of Granger's best friends was General William Henry Harrison (later elected ninth U.S. president): "After having perhaps one flagon of grog too much, he left a dinner party, walked outside, mounted his horse and then rode it into the lobby and up the stairs to a second-floor ballroom, where he announced that was where his horse would be lodged that night. They had to blindfold the horse and lead him down the stairway after he left."

Other historic notables who've stayed here include Presidents Lincoln and McKinley, John Philip Sousa, Harriet Beecher Stowe, Henry Ford, Van Johnson, Yo-Yo Ma, Hal Holbrook, and Cameron Diaz. In the following years, the Inn became known for its excellent cuisine and homey atmosphere, and as a home-away-from-home for many students from nearby Dennison University.

Audrey and Orville Orr bought the Inn in 1972 when they learned that it was about to be torn down and spent two years completely gutting the

Owners Audrey and Orville Orr in the kitchen.

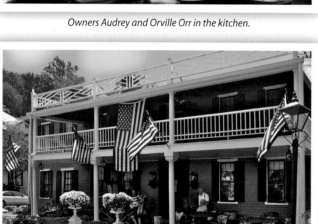

Buxton Inn Roast Duckling

∾ SERVES 4 ∾

1 (4½- to 5-pound) young duckling

1 large orange, halved

SAUCE

1 (14-ounce) can whole cranberry sauce

2 oranges, peeled, quartered, and seeded

2 unpeeled apples, cored and cut into chunks

¾ cup apple juice

¾ cup orange juice

Rice pilaf or steamed rice, for serving

Preheat the oven to 350°F. Remove the excess fat and giblets from the body and neck cavities of the duck. Place the duck, breast side up, on a roasting rack in a roasting pan. Squeeze the juice of the orange over the duck and place the orange in the body cavity.

Roast the duck for 1½ hours, or until golden brown. Spoon or drain off the fat in the pan and turn the duck over on the rack. Roast for another 1½ hours. Remove from the oven, leaving the oven on, and let cool slightly on a carving board.

While the duck is roasting, make the sauce: In a blender or food processor, combine all the ingredients and purée (you may have to do this in batches). Pour into a medium saucepan and bring to a simmer. Remove from the heat; cover and keep warm.

Cut the duck in half lengthwise and remove the spine and breastbone. Place on a rimmed baking sheet, skin side up, and return to the oven to crisp the skin for 10 to 15 minutes.

To serve, carve the duck into serving pieces and place on a bed of rice pilaf or steamed rice; ladle the cranberry-orange sauce over the top.

historic building and installing new plumbing, wiring, and other features to bring it up to code. After thirty-eight years of their stewardship, the Inn now has twenty-five guest suites in several adjoining houses, seven dining rooms, a historic and popular cellar bar, and a three-star rating from the AAA. In the old part of the Inn they rent only rooms seven and nine; the remaining ones are offices, with one set aside for a full-time resident certified hypnotherapist. Complete with flagstone walkways, picturesque fountains, porches, and floral gardens, the complex is unique in the Midwest.

Although they call their cuisine "down home," their menu reads more like "uptown sophisticated," with dishes like Southern Fried Brie with raspberry drizzle, Cream of Chicken Curry Soup with white grapes and almonds, Dried Cranberry and Toasted Almond Salad, Veal Oscar with Back-Fin Crabmeat, and Chesapeake Seafood Platter (shrimp, scallops, and whitefish in a crunchy-smooth pecan-cheese sauce). Just one slice of the slow-roasted crisp-skinned duck, glazed with a tart sauce, and you'll understand why they've kept it on the menu for many decades. The accompanying pilaf perfectly balances the rich duck. There is such a relaxed and calm feeling here that it's no wonder those ghosts don't want to leave. You may want to extend your stay as well.

The ghost of 1934 innkeeper Ethel "Bonnie" Bounell has been seen walking the hallways in a blue gown, earning her the nickname "The Blue Ghost."

The Golden Lamb
LEBANON, OH ~ EST. 1803

Two days before Christmas in 1803, Jonas Seaman appeared before the Warren County Court to secure a license "to keep a house of Public Entertainment" in the building he occupied in Lebanon, Ohio. The license was issued for a four-dollar fee, and Seaman walked down Lebanon's wide main street to his new log house to tell his wife, Martha, and children that they were the new owners of the Golden Lamb tavern.

Martha was a good cook, set a good table, and made up comfortable beds in clean rooms, and the Lamb soon became known as a fine place to stop for meals or to rest after a long day of travel. In 1805, a courthouse was built across the street, making the Golden Lamb more popular than ever for lawyers, politicians, and local gentry. Guests were served deer, bear, raccoon, wild duck, wild turkey, boiled potatoes, hot corn bread, and old-fashioned apple butter. At first, everyone sat at a common table set with pewter flagons and wooden dishes, but as more and more guests flocked to the tavern, the Lamb became the pride of the city with six tables, each lavishly set with individual knives and forks (no more sharing cutlery), glassware, and ceramic plates.

At the turn of the nineteenth century, the rising cost of living forced Jonas to first mortgage the tavern, and finally in 1809 to hold a public sale to meet his debts. Ichabod Corwin, one of the founders of the city itself, bought the building and built a fine brick hotel to replace the old log tavern, calling it The Ohio and Pennsylvania Hotel at the Sign of The Golden Lamb.

As they are both very bad, and the water is worse, I ask for brandy; but it is a temperance hotel, and spirits were not to be had for love or money."

After a series of owners each failed to make a go of the hotel, Isaac Stubbs, who owned the land, took over the building, named it the Lebanon Hotel, and he and his heirs owned it until 1914. But with the coming of the railroad and the decline of stagecoach travel, old roadside taverns like the Golden Lamb were isolated and the highways neglected. For more than half a century, this was just another hotel in a small town, serving fewer and fewer guests until 1926, when Robert H. Jones took over and transformed the old place into the great attraction and marvelous restaurant it is today and rechristened it the Golden Lamb.

Painting of Charles Dickens's visit in 1842 by artist William Fay.

Early in 1820, Pennsylvanians Henry Share and his wife, Mary, became the proprietors of the hotel and operated it successfully until Henry passed away in 1830; then Mary managed it alone for seven years. In addition to its role feeding and housing travelers, the tavern had by this time become a house of public entertainment, with plays, magic and animal acts, freak shows, musical concerts, and even operas performed on its stage.

In April 1842, Charles Dickens, the most famous author in the world, arrived in a plush stagecoach and "took dinner" at the Golden Lamb, which was then called the Bradley House. He alighted from the top of the stagecoach immediately after its arrival and demanded a drink, but was informed that the Bradley was a temperance hotel. He wrote an acerbic comment about the incident: "We dine soon after with the boarders in the house, and have nothing to drink but tea and coffee.

Each of the inn's twenty-two rooms is named for a famous person, many of whom stayed in the hotel in its early days, including twelve U.S. presidents, Harriet Beecher Stowe, Mark Twain, thirsty Mr. Dickens, De Witt Clinton, James Whitcomb Riley, and Ulysses S. Grant. With four upstairs private dining rooms, four ground-floor dining rooms, and a tavern, the Golden Lamb can hold half the population of the town at any one time.

Sauerkraut Meatballs

∾ SERVES 6 TO 8 AS AN APPETIZER ∾

1 tablespoon canola oil, plus more for frying

1 pound ground pork

1 yellow onion, sliced

12 ounces chopped ham

5 ounces chopped corned beef

1½ cups all-purpose flour

8 ounces sauerkraut, drained

1 teaspoon dry mustard

¼ teaspoon dried thyme

1 large egg, beaten with 1 cup milk

1½ to 2 cups fresh bread crumbs

Cocktail sauce, sweet hot mustard, or barbecue sauce, for dipping

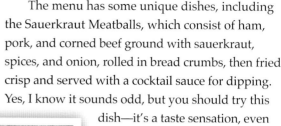

In a heavy, medium saucepan, heat the 1 tablespoon oil over medium heat and sauté the pork until nicely browned. Add the onion, ham, and corned beef and sauté until the onion is tender, about 5 minutes. Stir in 1 cup of the flour until blended. Stir in the sauerkraut, mustard, and thyme.

In a food processor, grind the mixture until smooth, then shape into 1-inch-diameter meatballs. Roll the meatballs in the remaining ½ cup flour, then dip into the egg-milk mixture. Finally, roll the meatballs in the bread crumbs and set aside.

In a Dutch oven or deep fryer, heat 1½ to 2 inches oil to 350°F on a deep-fat thermometer and fry 5 to 6 meatballs at a time until golden brown. Using a slotted spoon, transfer to paper towels to drain.

Serve hot, with cocktail sauce, sweet hot mustard, or barbecue sauce for dipping.

The menu has some unique dishes, including the Sauerkraut Meatballs, which consist of ham, pork, and corned beef ground with sauerkraut, spices, and onion, rolled in bread crumbs, then fried crisp and served with a cocktail sauce for dipping. Yes, I know it sounds odd, but you should try this dish—it's a taste sensation, even for those who don't particularly care for sauerkraut.

The salad has a fantastic celery seed dressing and is excellent as well. The roast turkey with onion-sage dressing, mashed potatoes, and a healthy ramekin of fresh cranberry sauce is generous and satisfying. And Sister Lizzie's Shaker Sugar Pie, sitting in a pond of caramel sauce, with a mound of whipped cream crowning the golden brown filling and tender crust, is another smash hit.

Martha and Jonas would be popping their buttons with pride to know that the log cabin tavern they purchased more than two centuries ago has carried on the gentle, gracious hospitality they worked so hard to provide. Martha would probably agree that the chefs here set a pretty good table themselves.

Cattlemen's Steakhouse
OKLAHOMA CITY, OK ~ EST. 1910

In 1910, two major U.S. meat packers began construction of huge packing houses in the stockyards just outside downtown Oklahoma City, thus creating an industrial community that also included a bank, several hotels, saddleries, Western clothing stores, cattle-trade suppliers, and a steakhouse. Today, Stockyard City, or "Packing Town," as locals call the area, is the world's largest livestock trading center and market.

In the early 1900s, cattle were driven to Oklahoma City in a virtually unending stream to satisfy the growing hunger for beef in the major cities of the East. Soon after those packing houses were built, Cattlemen's Steakhouse, the oldest continuously operating restaurant in Oklahoma City, was opened for the hungry cowboys, ranchers, cattle haulers, and meat buyers.

But over the years the restaurant has gathered a huge and loyal following among locals and tourists as well for its great steaks, as well as its more unusual dishes such as lamb fries, steak soup, and calf brains and eggs.

In 1926, H. V. "Homer" Paul took over and guided the restaurant through Prohibition, serving home-brewed "liquid delights" to what the restaurant today calls "a colorful clientele." Hank Frey, who loved to gamble, took over in the early forties. But in a smoke-filled Biltmore Hotel room when he was hemorrhaging money in a craps game, in desperation he put up the deed to the Cattlemen's in a bet with local rancher Gene Wade, who countered by wagering his life savings. The bet: Wade wouldn't roll a "hard six" (two 3's) on one roll.

Wade celebrated his win by having a "33" branding iron made, which is on display in the dining room alongside drawings of famous cowboy heroes. Wade was also responsible for expanding the restaurant beyond the small café on the north side of the building, adding the slightly more upscale South Dining Room and the Hereford Room.

Dick Stubbs, who assumed ownership when the restaurant was already eighty years old, wants to do nothing to change what has been a successful formula for more than one hundred years. After all, selling nine thousand steaks a week is nothing to scoff at. Plus, Cattlemen's has a loyal following of fans, many, such as former president George W. Bush, who claim their steaks are the best they've ever had. In honor of the president's hearty appreciation, Cattlemen's named their signature twenty-ounce T-bone the "Presidential Choice." It is cut from a bone-in USDA Prime or Choice corn-fed short loin, which is run through a

Pencil drawings of famous "Western" heroes by artist Jack L. Wells. From top left clockwise: Gabby Hayes, Gene Autry, Henry Fonda, and John Wayne.

needling machine to tenderize and break down the connective tissues. Then it is vacuum packed in its own juices to wet-age for thirty-four days, so the natural enzymes in the meat continue to tenderize the tissue and add flavor. After aging, the loin is cut into twenty-ounce T-bones (consisting of filet and strip sides). Their steaks are never frozen.

The steaks are brought to room temperature, generously sprinkled with a special steak seasoning, and then seared on a 650°F to 700°F charcoal grill. Just before the steaks are served, the cooks add a ladle or two of natural au jus to make sure every bite is super moist. They say it's so tender you can cut it with a butter knife, and lo and behold it is. The outside of the seared meat is slightly salty (love that seasoning). The glowing pink interior is juicy, carries a light smoky flavor from the charcoal grill, and stays hot from the first bite to the last. The softball-size fresh rolls can be dipped into the juices, forming a moat around the rapidly disappearing steak. The side salad topped with their house dressing has garlicky-cheesy flavor with a slight tang of vinegar and pepper that is the perfect complement to the greens, onions, and tomatoes.

More adventurous diners try the lamb (or prairie) fries: breaded and fried slices of lamb

In the early days, the dining room consisted of stools and a counter and a Wild West décor.

testicles. Slightly chewy, and with a mild flavor, they are probably more of a macho appetizer that many people (guys) order in mixed groups to surprise the women they are dining with.

Of the three dining areas, the original coffee shop café looks as it did one hundred years ago in the historic photographs on the walls, with small two-person booths and counter stools. The larger dining room also features booths, with a mural of a cattle drive on the back wall. In the glass-enclosed Hereford Room, a concession to smokers, Gene himself is shown driving cattle in a large color transparency that covers the back wall.

You almost expect Roy Rogers or Gene Autry or Ransom Stoddard (Jimmy Stewart's character in *The Man Who Shot Liberty Valance*) to saunter in, spurs clicking on the wood floors, hang his hat on the wall, and order up some prairie fries and the biggest steak they have. Because if there is a restaurant that exudes the adventure of long cattle drives and the best of the Old West, it's nestled here in the Oklahoma Stockyards.

So tie up your horse and come in and get some rib-stickin' vittles.

Cattlemen's Seasoned Salt

∾ MAKES ABOUT 2 CUPS ∾

½ cup salt

½ cup Lawry's seasoned salt

½ cup freshly ground black pepper

½ cup garlic salt

2 tablespoons onion salt

In a small bowl, combine all the ingredients and stir to blend. Sprinkle on steaks before cooking, and add a light pinch before serving. Store in an airtight container in a cool, dark place.

Cattlemen's Peppercorn Sauce

∾ MAKES ABOUT 4 CUPS ∾

4 tablespoons unsalted butter

3 tablespoons all-purpose flour

4 cups beef broth (made from beef base)

¼ cup crème fraîche

¼ cup brandy

1½ tablespoons cracked black pepper

In a heavy, medium saucepan, melt the butter over medium heat and stir in the flour. Cook, stirring constantly, for 3 to 4 minutes, or until the roux is medium brown.

Gradually whisk in the beef broth, then whisk in the crème fraîche. Add the brandy and pepper. Simmer for 2 to 3 minutes, but do not boil; the sauce will thicken slightly.

Dan & Louis Oyster Bar
PORTLAND, OR ~ EST. 1907

Louis Meinert shucked his first oyster when he was only five years old and growing up in Oysterville, Washington. Little did he know then that his life and the next five generations of his family's would revolve around those tasty shellfish.

As an adult, Louis continued his bivalve focus, first as a cook at Lemp's Oyster Parlor in Portland, Oregon, then as a driver for the Oysterville Oyster Company, then selling the shellfish to both wholesale and retail customers from a tiny store in downtown Portland. Louis began his restaurant business by serving customers oyster cocktails, and then, around 1917, on a frigid and damp morning, not an unusual thing in that part of the Pacific Northwest, he decided to make a hot stew of oysters, milk, butter, and spices. He cooked the

soup in a double boiler and began serving it to some of his customers. The buttery and salty stew became a huge hit.

In fact, the word spread so fast, and so many folks came in for his bowls of oyster stew, that he was forced to move his office out of the small building, replacing his desk and files with two tables and eight chairs. Louis began serving two-course meals. "Our stew is mighty nice, but so is my oyster loaf and oyster pie," he once told a local newspaperman. "But for me, I like 'em raw. The best way of all is to eat 'em alive."

Word of his delicious stews, freshly shucked oysters on the half shell, and his tangy oyster cocktails, loaves, and pies spread like wildfire, and before long he had to add five more tables and twenty more chairs. In 1927, Louis renamed the place Louis' Oyster Bar, and in seeking a less expensive

Oyster Bar founder Louis C. Wachsmuth (right) loads oysters on a plane in 1933 for an overnight flight from Portland to San Francisco.

source of the tasty bivalves bought rights to some oyster beds on the coast to begin raising his own oysters to sell both wholesale and retail. It was around this time that he began adding steins and decorative plates to the nautical-themed dining room.

Louis's oldest son Dan, the general manager at the time, worked side by side with his father, so much so that a local newspaperman began calling the place Dan & Louis Oyster Bar. When Dan died suddenly at the age of twenty-seven, the family officially changed the name to just that.

In the 1930s, Louis and his two remaining sons began making daily shipments of fresh oysters from their oyster beds all over the Pacific Northwest, even flying the critters from nearby Swan Island to San Francisco in a single propeller biplane on overnight flights to the Bay Area. In 1940, they built yet another dining room and a second kitchen, as they were selling a staggering twenty-five thousand sacks of oysters a year.

Today, the restaurant is owned by Louis's grandsons Louis and Douglas, and managed by Doug's son Keoni. It is flourishing on a busy corner in downtown Portland, having grown into a restaurant that seats over two hundred people. It still features oysters—raw, fried, baked, and broiled—but also offers a wide variety of fresh seafood for those who aren't big bivalve fans.

As I was talking to Keoni about the success of the restaurant, a customer called us over to his table. "I haven't been here in thirty-plus years since the seventies, when I was chasing the Grateful Dead around the West Coast, but I was bound and determined not to leave here until I came back and had a big bowl of oyster stew. It tastes just the same today as it did three decades ago. You can't come here without trying it," he said.

I took his suggestion and sat down to a large pewter bowl filled to the brim with creamy soup with several large oysters floating serenely in a pool of sunshine-yellow butter. The first bite will take

Above: The original Oysterville Oyster Company. Below: Oyster shucker Kyle Rathert opens up a batch of Willapa Bay, Washington, oysters.

you to the seaside of Oregon, the fresh salty taste of superb oysters and milk so rich that you may be tempted to accuse them of substituting cream in the recipe. But it is just milk, reduced to a thick consistency by slow cooking and flavored with a barely discernible hint of seasoned salt and fresh black pepper. The oysters themselves are decadently abundant, tender, flavorful, and cooked perfectly, the outside nice and firm, the edges just beginning to curl, the inside tender and juicy, the way oyster lovers enjoy them the most.

I asked Doug the secret of the restaurant's success over the years. "Customer loyalty, the comfort level they feel here, and their love of tradition and history are what keeps them coming in the door," he said. Keoni echoes, "We try and keep up our traditional dishes while still adding things to bring in a new customer base. But our main concern is our repeat customers, some of whom have come back after ten to fifteen years and tell us they are delighted we haven't changed very much at all."

You bet they haven't. The bowl of oyster stew is a perfect example. The only change they've made to their signature dish in one hundred years? They now use a little less salt.

Dan & Louis Oyster Bar Oyster Stew

∞ SERVES 4 TO 6 ∞

8 cups whole milk

1 teaspoon salt

½ teaspoon Morton Season-All salt,
  plus more for serving

½ teaspoon freshly ground black pepper

3 to 4 tablespoons unsalted butter

1 pound oysters, shucked, or 1 pint shucked oysters

Oyster crackers and bread rolls, for serving

Tabasco sauce, for serving (optional)

In a double boiler, cook the milk over simmering water for 30 minutes. Add the salt, the ½ teaspoon seasoned salt, and the pepper. Add 3 to 4 tablespoons of the butter and stir vigorously until the butter is completely melted and incorporated into the liquid.

Add the oysters and stir gently. When most of the oysters have floated to the surface and the edges of the oysters are curled, spoon out the oysters and portion into serving bowls.

Ladle the hot milk mixture into the bowls over the oysters. Add 3 to 4 tablespoons of butter per bowl and serve very hot. Accompany with oyster crackers, a good-quality bread roll, and some Season-All on the side. Those who like a spicier dish can add a dash or two of Tabasco sauce.

Huber's Cafe
PORTLAND, OR ~ EST. 1879

Portland's oldest bar, Huber's, began life as the Bureau Saloon in 1879 and for the first eight years was under the tutelage of W. H. Lightner. In a stroke of either genius or luck, he hired bartender Frank Huber a few years later, and the young man so impressed W. H. that they became partners after three years. Huber became the sole proprietor a year later, operating it until 1912.

During his ownership, the bar changed its name to Huber's, moved to a better downtown location, and became one of Portland's most popular drinking and gathering spots. The year after he bought the place, Frank Huber hired Jim Louie, an immigrant from China, as chef. Following Frank's death a year later, "Uncle Jim" took over the restaurant. Pictures of the jovial chef in his jaunty chef's cap, posing with a roasted

turkey, are scattered around the restaurant. To increase the bar business, Uncle Jim started offering free turkey sandwiches, cut from a whole roasted bird, to anyone who bought a drink. Thus began Huber's lifelong association with roasted turkeys.

When Prohibition removed the paying part of this practice, Louie began offering traditional turkey dinners as well as steaks, seafood, duck, and salads, in addition to the iconic sandwiches. But now you had to pay for your meals, albeit at very low prices, and the drinks became tea, coffee, or sodas. At least that's what they said. Some savvy patrons could come in the back door and get a special cup of "coffee." The coffee: rye whiskey, sweet vermouth, and bitters, known in other times as a Manhattan.

The restaurant has continued in the Louie family for three generations; James, David, and Lucille Louie took over in 1991. James worked for awhile as a line cook, and David also cooked but not with the same fervor, opting more for management, menu planning, and bookkeeping duties. They co-manage the restaurant, taking turns greeting guests, seeing to their needs, and overseeing their heritage restaurant and popular bar.

The restaurant today has a split personality. The front dining room is a casual, quiet room where guests enjoy their turkey dinners, hot turkey sandwiches, and non-poultry entrees. The barroom takes you back to the early 1900s as you enter through an arched doorway into the mahogany paneled room with its huge vaulted skylight, original tile floor, and massive wooden bar. The lighting is enhanced during the day by amber, orange, and yellow glass panels that mix with the light from distinctive period chandeliers, giving the historic room a warm glow. This room is always crowded with guests who have headed down the hallway past the open kitchen or have

The Gothic arched doorways, vaulted skylight, and massive wooden bar in Huber's popular 1910 Room.

entered by that famous back door to eat and enjoy cocktails in a historic setting.

In the early seventies, the bar and restaurant experienced a substantial drop in business, and in an attempt to bring customers back James "reinvented" a drink he'd seen made in another restaurant, coming up with his own version of Spanish Coffee. And that, as they say, has made all the difference. Slowly at first, then in increasing numbers, people began to order Spanish Coffee, some because they loved the rich taste of the hot drink: Bacardi 151 rum, Bols Triple Sec, Kahlúa, coffee, and whipped cream with a touch of nutmeg. But many order it for the sheer pleasure of watching the waiters make it tableside. First, they light one match from a book of matches with one hand (no mean feat; try it yourself); next, they ignite several ounces of 151 rum in a stemmed cocktail glass, and then, while holding the glass at arm's length below the waist with one hand, pour a thin stream of

Owners James and David Louie with portrait of bartender-then-owner Frank Huber.

Kahlúa from the other hand held high above their head. And somehow, they never spill a drop.

Some nights, fifty to sixty of these drinks are served, often to applause. Waiter Terry Barton, considered by many to be the master pourer, and who has been making the drink for twenty-one years, figures that in an average year he alone pours more than fifteen thousand Spanish Coffees, and

"Uncle Jim" Louie, an immigrant from China, was hired as a cook in 1911 and became the owner a year later.

Waiter Terry Barton has worked here for 21 years and figures he's poured over 315,000 Spanish Coffee's for appreciative guests.

over his tenure here has poured over 315,000 of the flaming drinks. Even though the restaurant and bar are relatively small, Huber's is the largest user of Kahlúa in the United States by an independent restaurant.

Huber's calls their cuisine Classic American, and turkey is still a huge part of the menu, with seven featured entrees ranging from the traditional roast turkey dinner with all the trimmings to turkey potpie and turkey legs; hot turkey, Reuben, smoked turkey, and club sandwiches; turkey and Brie melt; turkey Tetrazzini, piccata, Marsala, and Florentine; turkey crepes; turkey soup; and turkey enchiladas. If you like fresh turkey, this is the place for you.

The traditional turkey dinner is almost as good as Grandma's, and the turkey Marsala, the turkey club, turkey Piccata, and the hot turkey sandwich with mashed potatoes, rich mushroom gravy, and homemade cranberry sauce will make you wonder why in America turkey is only a two-holiday dish. Huber's also serves up steaks, baked ham, and a wide variety of seafood and desserts. But everyone comes here for turkey or the Spanish Coffee. So, if you make the trip to Portland, come in by the back door. You may not get a "coffee cup" Manhattan, but you can enjoy their famous flaming coffee. After all, it's not every day you can order a drink that literally saved Portland's oldest bar from fading away.

Turkey Piccata
∞ SERVES 2 ∾

4 (6-ounce) turkey breast cutlets

1 cup panko (Japanese bread crumbs)

¼ cup extra-virgin olive oil

½ tablespoon minced garlic

½ tablespoon minced shallot

2 tablespoons capers, drained

¼ cup freshly squeezed lemon juice

¼ cup dry white wine (preferably Chablis)

½ cup heavy cream

½ cup (1 stick) unsalted butter

½ teaspoon salt

½ teaspoon freshly ground black pepper

Pasta or rice pilaf, for serving

Pound the turkey cutlets flat with a meat mallet or a heavy skillet, then dredge each cutlet in the panko.

In a large nonstick skillet, heat the olive oil over medium-high heat until a drop of water sizzles when dropped in the skillet. Fry the breaded cutlets, in batches if necessary, until both sides are golden brown. Using a slotted metal spatula, transfer the cutlets to a pan, cover, and keep warm.

Spoon off all but 1 or 2 tablespoons of oil from the skillet, reduce the heat to medium, and sauté the garlic and shallot until just beginning to color; add the capers, lemon juice, and white wine and cook, stirring frequently, until the liquid is reduced by half.

Add the cream to the skillet, decrease the heat to low, and cook, stirring frequently, until the liquid is reduced by half. Add the butter, swirl to incorporate, and season with salt and pepper. Immediately pour the sauce over the fried turkey cutlets. Serve with pasta or rice pilaf.

Jake's Famous Crawfish
PORTLAND, OR ~ EST. 1892

Like many centenarian restaurants, Jake's began life as a bar. Actually, the bar was shipped to the West Coast around Cape Horn in 1880. In 1892, people began standing at it when Mueller & Meyer's saloon/restaurant opened in what years later became downtown Portland. It served all the popular libations of the time and offered sandwiches, soups, and other simple food to accompany the liquor.

In 1908, the restaurant moved to its present location. It survived Prohibition by becoming a soft-drink parlor, then, in 1920, Jacob "Jake" Freiman came aboard along with partner J. Rometsch, and the duo began the legacy of featuring fresh seafood. They went so far as to help hand-dig several ponds under the bar to hold live crawfish, making Jake's the only West

Coast restaurant that served fresh crawfish. On the restaurant's 35th birthday it was renamed Jake's Famous Crawfish in his honor. By the way, these were Pacific Northwest crawfish, caught in local streams and rivers, not their more well-known Louisiana cousins. But they were so popular Jake's sent them all over the country by rail in iced five-gallon tins. One well-known customer was beer magnate August Busch who not only imported them but served them at parties in Portland that he hosted on his private rail car.

Some remnants of the old saloon linger in the bar today. Over the bar hangs an original oil painting of Alice, Jake's girlfriend. Legend has it that in 1925 she wanted to surprise him with a nude portrait of herself, a fashion of the times, and commissioned a local artist to create his artistic birthday present. When the painting was finished and she and the artist presented it to him, Jake exploded in rage, apparently incensed that someone else had seen his girlfriend sans clothes. He allegedly got a pistol and began firing as the terrified artist headed for the hills; Jake missed him but put a bullet hole in the painting. It remains there today as a reminder of how not to surprise your man.

The second carryover is the tiled drain on the floor right in front of the bar, testimony to a not-unheard-of practice at the time (some bars had troughs for the purpose) of men not bothering to go to the restroom when they needed to urinate. Ah, the Old West.

In the late twenties and early thirties, the restaurant was one of the most popular on the West Coast, attracting tourists, touring entertainers, and locals eager to experience the extensive seafood menu. Many locals went to dances held at some nearby hotels, then, early in the morning, came to Jake's for a late dinner or early breakfast. It is said that on some nights more than one thousand customers jammed the restaurant. In the late sixties and early seventies, Jake's seemed to be on its last legs, as people moved to other restaurants that sprang up in the area, called Stumptown, in those years. It was called that because in a frantic growth spurt hundreds of trees were cut down to make room for new construction, and it was quite some time before they had the manpower to remove the stumps.

In 1972, Bill McCormick and Doug Schmick purchased the building for $55,000 and began the task of saving the restaurant. They researched various cookbooks, including *Joy of Cooking*, consulted with chefs, and decided to emphasize the restaurant's culinary focus on fresh seafood. People began to come back, and soon getting a dinner reservation here became difficult. Thus Jake's was brought back to life, and the national restaurant group of McCormick & Schmick was born.

Jake's ambiance is that of a typical saloon or tavern in the early 1900s: dark wood paneling, a maze of booths, period lighting, an extensive collection of historic oyster trays, nineteenth-century oil paintings and historic photographs on the walls. Crisp white tablecloths and napkins and formal place settings complete the picture of a quality restaurant of that era.

The booths and tables are usually filled, and most days a group of walk-ins stand between the bar and the main dining room waiting for the chance at a table. Those in the know have been reported to wait up to two hours for a chance to sit at Bogart's Table, where Humphrey Bogart and other actors dined while *Treasure of the Sierra Madre* was partially filmed nearby. The adjacent bar also has a number of tables and a long row of bar stools that are usually filled as well, especially during happy hour and dinner hours. Even with a capacity of over 325 customers, Jake's is routinely full, but no one seems to mind the difficulty in getting reservations or the long wait if you don't have one, and many show up anyway.

Like other long-lasting restaurants, Jake's has a lengthy list of employees who have several decades of service, including five of the waiters working on the day I was there, who had a total of 148 years among them. In their smart white dress shirts, black bow ties, pressed black trousers, and white jackets, they are the epitome of their craft. Weaving through the tables and booths, they operate like well-honed machines bringing bread, refilling water glasses, checking on coffee or drinks, delivering orders so efficiently that you barely know they have been to your table, and participating in good-humored repartee with their customers.

Jake's flies in thirty varieties of fresh fish, clams, and oysters from around North America every day. To get fresher fish, you would have to cook it on the back of a fishing boat. There are good reasons why they are considered one of the top ten seafood restaurants in the

nation. To name just a few selections and their origins: ahi tuna, Honolulu, Hawaii; Manila clams, razor clams, Kumamoto oysters, Goose Point oysters, mussels, and Dungeness crab, Washington state; Gigamoto oysters, Buckley

Jake's seasoned waiters and their years of service: (from left) James Stevenson (24), Susy Baker (30), John Castro (35), Paul Lillig (38), and Carol Clayton (25).

Bay oysters, and Atlantic salmon, Canada; chinook salmon, rockfish, true cod, petrale sole, and crawfish, Oregon; scallops, Nova Scotia; and trout, Idaho. Jake's also offers the most elaborate cold seafood platter I've seen anywhere. The towering and jam-packed platter contains Dungeness crab, oysters, crab legs, bay shrimp, jumbo prawns, lox, smoked trout, and crawfish.

On a recent visit, I enjoyed the crawfish étouffée. The crawfish were as fresh as any I've had in Louisiana, since they are trucked in every day from April to October from a lake in eastern Oregon. During those months, Jake's goes through twenty thousand pounds of the tasty small crustaceans.

In a crowning culinary touch, Jake's also provides a choice of desserts that just by themselves cement its reputation as one of the finest restaurants on the West Coast, including Banana Cream Pie with caramel sauce; Chocolate Bag (white chocolate mousse, raspberries, blueberries, and blackberries topped with whipped cream and served with raspberry coulis); and Upside-Down Walnut Apple Pie.

To sum up, here's a quote from general manager John Underhill: "One of the reasons for a restaurant's longevity and our own success is the idea that we don't chase trends. We are not a trend, we are a tradition. We fervently maintain our legacy of tradition in order to someday pass Jake's and its history on to the next generation."

Jake's bar in 1925. Note the tiled drain in front of the bar, reputed to be for the convenience of gents who needed to answer a "call to nature" but didn't want to leave the bar.

Crawfish Étouffée

∽ SERVES 4 ∾

ÉTOUFFÉE BASE

½ cup canola oil

¾ cup all-purpose flour

½ teaspoon salt

½ teaspoon freshly ground black pepper

½ teaspoon dried thyme

½ teaspoon sweet paprika

½ teaspoon dried basil

¼ teaspoon ground white pepper

½ teaspoon cayenne pepper

½ cup chopped celery

¾ cup chopped yellow onion

⅓ cup finely chopped green bell pepper

¼ cup finely chopped red bell pepper

3 cups water

1 tablespoons fish boullion powder

1 tablespoon olive oil

8 ounces boneless shredded or chopped chicken meat

8 ounces peeled rock shrimp

8 ounces crawfish tails

Steamed rice, for serving

In a heavy, medium saucepan, heat the oil over medium-high heat to just below the smoking point. Add the flour and stir constantly until the mixture turns a dark golden brown. Reduce the heat to low and add all the seasonings. Cook, stirring, for 10 minutes. Add the vegetables and cook for another 5 minutes. Add the water and fish bouillon, increase the heat to a simmer, and cook, stirring frequently, for 15 minutes, or until thickened and smooth. Set aside and keep warm.

In a medium sauté pan, heat the oil over medium-high heat and sauté the chicken for 4 to 5 minutes. Add the shrimp and sauté for about 2 minutes, or until the shrimp are pink on both sides, then add the crawfish tails and cook for 2 to 3 minutes to heat through. Stir in the étouffée base and simmer for 10 to 12 minutes, stirring frequently. Serve over steamed rice in shallow bowls.

Black Bass Hotel
LUMBERVILLE, PA ~ EST. 1740

Many inns in America proclaim "George Washington slept here." This is not one of them. In fact, the Black Bass Hotel might just be the only place in the country where future president George Washington, at that time the commander-in-chief of the Continental Army, was turned away when he knocked on the door one night.

It seems the innkeeper was a Tory, loyal to the British Crown and King George II, and told the future president he'd have to go elsewhere. It probably didn't help that, at the time, Washington was planning to attack the Hessian Troops camped out in Trenton, New Jersey, a few miles to the south.

Built in 1740, thirty-five years before the American Revolution, the tavern stood alongside

a gristmill, two stores, and a dozen houses, and served wayfarers, traders, sportsmen, and bargemen traveling up and down the Delaware River nearby. At various times in its early history, the building also functioned as a stagecoach stop and a post office, and as the Lumberville Hotel.

When workmen began to dig the Delaware Canal in 1830 many of the laborers stayed at the hotel, and some believe they caused the fire that severely damaged the building in 1833. Innkeeper Major Anthony Fry risked his life when he broke into the cellar and removed a quantity of gunpowder that the canal company had stored there. Because the building was built so solidly, the framework survived, and within a year a new

The main dining room provides guests with a delightful view overlooking the historic Delaware River and Canal.

LUMBERVILLE
LUMBERVILLE, F

brick tavern replaced the old wooden structure. It was then that the new owner, Ben Carver, changed the name to the Black Bass.

The Bass became a favorite with bargemen for the next one hundred years. They stopped at the tavern to take refreshment, and their favorite libation was a strong brew of hot ale, apple pulp, sugar, cinnamon, and cloves, served in steaming mugs.

In 1949, Herbert Ward, a collector of French provincial furniture and British royal family memorabilia, took over the hotel and ran it until 2004. Sadly, he paid more attention to his antiques than to the building, and the ravages of time and the damage done to the roads leading to the hotel by a series of floods all but destroyed the business.

Jack Thompson purchased the hotel at auction in 2008, and set out to completely renovate it with his daughter Laura's help. Everything from the building supports and foundation, kitchens, dining rooms, bars, and guest rooms were restored, and hundreds of antiques and original paintings, including Ward's royal family memorabilia, were cleaned.

One of the prize pieces saved was a priceless pewter bar that had been brought to Pennsylvania from the famous Maxim's restaurant in Paris.

It sits today in the tavern beside three walls of display cases displaying the royal family collection, perhaps the largest grouping of such memorabilia in the state, and perhaps in the country, outside of a museum.

Each suite is decorated with period furniture and antiques, and most have a view of the Delaware River Canal and the Lumberville–Raven Rock pedestrian footbridge adjacent to the hotel. Grover Cleveland loved to come here to fish while governor of New York, and the room where he always stayed is named in his honor. The original furniture he used has been restored.

The Black Bass has multiple dining options. You can enjoy breakfast, lunch, or dinner on the River Deck overlooking the water in the Canal Dining Room or the Canal Bar, or in the main dining room, which also has a view of the water, or in several smaller private dining rooms.

Executive chef John Barrett describes his cuisine as American with Creole and Mediterranean touches. Swordfish Saltimbocca, Classic Beef Wellington, Salmon Fillet in Red Thai Curry, Coffee Lacquered Duck, and Roasted Stuffed Pork Loin highlight the menu. Their signature dish, Maryland Meeting Street Crab, is one of the most popular. It is the perfect marriage of sherry and fresh crabmeat, complemented with Cheddar cheese and cream. Onion-cheese biscuits are placed temptingly on the table in front of guests, and as the famous potato chip ad says, you can't eat just one! They are baked right across the street in the Lumberville General Store, a bakery and small grocery shop owned by the hotel.

Pewter bar brought to Pennsylvania from famed Maxim's in Paris sits in the lower bar that displays an amazing collection of British royalty memorabilia.

Happy bakers make up a batch of onion-cheese biscuits in the kitchen of the hotel's General Store annex.

The Black Bass Hotel has served road and river travelers for more than 2½ centuries, and thanks to the Thompsons' stewardship and care, this living, breathing piece of the Colonial past is so steeped in legend that along with the fragrance of the gardens and the tantalizing smells coming from the kitchen, there is the unmistakable scent of history in every room.

George would have loved it.

Charleston Meeting Street Crab

~ SERVES 4 ~

1 pound lump crabmeat, picked over for shell

3 tablespoons dry sherry

¼ teaspoon salt

¼ teaspoon freshly ground black pepper

1 cup shredded sharp Cheddar cheese

1 cup heavy cream

Preheat the oven to 350°F. Butter a 6-cup casserole dish.

Place the crabmeat in the prepared dish and stir in the sherry. Season with the salt and pepper. Top evenly with the shredded cheese. Set aside.

In a small saucepan, cook the cream over medium heat until reduced to ⅔ cup. Add the reduced cream to the casserole.

Bake until bubbly and lightly browned, 10 to 15 minutes. Remove from the oven, let cool slightly, and serve.

Century Inn
SCENERY HILL, PA ~ EST. 1794

The National Road, also called the Cumberland Road, was the first east-west improved highway in the United States, and by 1818 had crossed the Allegheny Mountains and reached West Virginia (then a part of Virginia). Before it was built, settlers heading west followed a dirt road that sometimes resembled a wide path to make the difficult journey, stopping often at a series of stagecoach or wagon stops along the way. The stops were placed at twelve-mile intervals, the distance a horse could comfortably travel in a day, and provided food and water for both the travelers and their teams of horses or oxen.

In 1788, Stephen Hill built a small inn and tavern beside the road. The main building housed the tavern, with a small number of rooms on the second floor. The kitchen, or keeping room as they called it, with its huge open fireplace, was in a separate building behind the tavern in case of fire.

After the Revolutionary War, Congress found it had a huge debt looming overhead. Someone had to pay for the war. Sound familiar? So they decided, among other things, to levy a tax on the production of local goods and products to pay off the national debt. The local farmers and distillers claimed that the tax on their most profitable product, whiskey, was unfair, and many refused to pay.

When armed men surrounded and threatened the U.S. marshals who had arrived to serve writs on the distillers and five hundred armed men attacked the woeful tax inspector's home, things got rough. The state militia was called, and President Washington sent a delegation to negotiate with

The old kitchen and the fireplace where they cooked their meals looks much like it did two hundred years ago, but it is now a dining room.

The parlor and the original dining room are parts of the original building constructed in 1788, furnished with period antiques and reproductions.

the rebels. Thankfully, the insurrection dissolved before the arrival of the troops.

That rebellion took place in the area of the Century Inn, and the inn somehow acquired one of the tax rebel's Whiskey Rebellion flags, today displayed proudly on the wall of the tavern. It shows an eagle in flight with red and white bunting in its beak, a clutch of arrows in one claw, and thirteen stars in the background.

After the war, Washington himself, as well as Andrew Jackson, Thomas Jefferson (who loved the peanut soup), James Polk, General Santa Anna, the Marquis de Lafayette, and other famous personages patronized the inn. One famous "guest" was Chief Black Hawk, who was captured after the war for aiding the British, and was on his way to Washington when his captors tarried overnight at the Century Inn. There is conjecture that he probably wasn't allowed inside the inn, but was housed in the stable or even tied to a tree outside.

In 1945, at the end of World War II, Dr. Gordon Harrington and his wife, Mary Amanda, bought the Century but sold it a year later. When the Harringtons took over, there wasn't a stick of furniture in the inn, but they diligently went about collecting many of the antiques that grace its rooms today. Megan Harrington, daughter-in-law to the wartime owners, has been the innkeeper for the past thirty-seven years and has worked to add more authentic antiques and to renovate the inn while preserving the eighteenth-century charm of the five dining rooms, bar, hallways, and lovely grounds.

The separate old kitchen is one of the most delightful rooms I found in all of the centenarian establishments in this book. The wide-open hearth is festooned with various cooking implements of the period, and the nearby shelves and mantel are filled with period crockery, tea- and coffeepots, jugs and bowls, and antique serving plates and mugs.

No longer in use as a kitchen, the small room looks like the set of a Charles Dickens movie. When the fireplace is lit, usually only in the winter or for pesky photographers, the room quickly zooms to a temperature that turkeys enjoy on Thanksgiving Day. When it served as a kitchen, on a hot, humid western Pennsylvania day, it must have been scorching to cook there.

Fortunately, on warm days you can take lunch on the covered patio at the rear of the inn. Delightfully airy and bright, the room was as cool as a summer breeze and a most pleasant spot to dine while watching butterflies and hummingbirds investigate the gardens.

I asked to sample two of the chef's offerings, requesting dishes that reflected the history of the restaurant, area, and local produce. I expected tavern fare on pewter plates. Instead, I was served edible works of art.

The scallop dish looked like a vivid painting. They were perfectly medium-rare in the center, slightly crisp outside, and served on a bed of spaghetti squash flanked by crisp-tender asparagus spears. The beef tenderloin and portobello mushroom plate was equally artistic, with a thick medallion of very tender, medium-rare beef leaning on a large grilled mushroom, both floating on top of a rich beef and wine reduction and the creamiest of polentas. The Century Inn is surprisingly a restful stop on the old National Road that's no longer trafficked by buggies, horses, and teams of oxen dragging lumbering wagons. But somehow I'd prefer that traffic to the 10-wheel semis, plodding RV's, and cars crammed with tourists on today's Highway 40. Ah, progress, ain't it wonderful?

Sea Scallops with Spiced Spaghetti Squash and Asparagus Salad

∽ SERVES 2 TO 4 ∽

SPAGHETTI SQUASH

1 (1½-pound) spaghetti squash, halved lengthwise and seeded

Salt and white pepper, to taste

½ teaspoon fresh thyme

3 tablespoons unsalted butter, melted

Pinch of cinnamon

ASPARAGUS SALAD

1 bunch young asparagus

2 or 3 watermelon or other radish

1 small red onion

1 teaspoon lemon oil

1 teaspoon Champagne vinegar

1 tablespoon balsamic vinegar

1 tablespoon minced fresh cilantro

Salt and freshly ground black pepper

SCALLOPS

1 pound diver sea scallops

½ teaspoon sea salt

Several grinds of cracked black pepper

2 tablespoons extra-virgin olive oil

Preheat the oven to 375°F and line a baking sheet with parchment paper. Season the squash with salt and pepper and the thyme. Place the squash halves, cut side down, on the prepared pan and bake for about 40 minutes, or until tender. Let cool. Remove the squash in strands from its skin using a fork and put them in a bowl. Toss with salt and pepper to taste, and the cinnamon, if you like. Set aside and keep warm.

In a skillet of heavily salted boiling water, cook the asparagus until crisp-tender, 2 to 3 minutes. Drain and transfer to a bowl of ice water to stop the cooking. Drain again.

Cut the asparagus in half lengthwise. Cut the radishes and onion into paper-thin slices using a mandoline. In a medium bowl, combine the asparagus, radishes, and onion with the oil, vinegars, cilantro, and salt and pepper. Toss lightly to coat the vegetables. Set aside.

Pat the scallops dry with paper towels and season with salt and pepper. In a large sauté pan, heat the oil over medium-high heat until shimmering. Sear the scallops for 1 minute on each side, or until golden brown and opaque on the outside and still slightly translucent in the center.

Place ¼ cup of spaghetti squash strands on each plate and top with 2 to 3 scallops. Garnish with some of the marinated vegetables and serve at once.

City Tavern

PHILADELPHIA, PA ~ EST. 1773

They say that anything designed by a committee is doomed to fail. But in the City of Brotherly Love, the City Tavern, now more than two hundred years old, soundly disproves that cliché.

In the early days of Philadelphia, fifty-three prominent citizens gathered and commissioned the building of "a large and commodious tavern" worthy of the city's standing at that time as the most prosperous city in British North America (aka the Colonies). When completed a year later, the building was not only "commodious," with five floors, a kitchen, a barroom, two coffee rooms, two dining rooms, a grand ballroom, servants' quarters, and five guest rooms, but it became the center of political life in America. There was simply nothing its equal in the country.

A list of events that occurred here could form the basis for a history book detailing how the country was formed. Some examples:

1774: Paul Revere arrives to announce the British Parliament's closing of the port of Boston, causing two hundred to three hundred prominent Philadelphians to draft a letter of sympathy for him to take back to Boston.

1774: The tavern becomes the unofficial site of the first Continental Congress. Participants included George Washington, Thomas Jefferson, John Adams, Benjamin Harrison, Richard Henry Lee, and Peyton Randolph.

1776–1777: Continental and British troops alternated using the City Tavern to house prisoners of war and to hold military court-martials.

1777: America's first celebration of the Fourth of July is held here. George Washington and some aides-de-camp move into the tavern, making it the official headquarters of the Continental Army for a short period.

1789: The tavern prepares a banquet honoring George Washington, who stopped here on the way to his inauguration.

When the tavern first opened, the port was bustling and the famed city market was overflowing with the finest fruits and vegetables, great tubs of butter and wheels of cheese, and fish fresh from the sea. Massive roasts of beef, whole lambs and pigs, long strings of sausages, and a large variety of wild game were readily available.

The cooks at the tavern took advantage of this bounty and produced meals known both for their excellence and for their excesses. City Tavern was the place to lodge, eat, drink, socialize, argue political viewpoints, and catch up on the news from the other colonies and England. From its first day to the late winter of 1834, it was the most-happening place in the most important city in the country.

In 1834, a fire damaged the roof but the restaurant stayed open. Then, in 1854, it was destroyed by a second fire. The building and its history vanished from the American scene, the site at one point serving as a parking lot, until Congress created the Independence National Historical Park and the long task of rebuilding the tavern began. In 1948, the owners and the city began gathering old documents, period drawings and paintings, written accounts, and insurance surveys. It took twenty-eight years to rebuild the tavern exactly as it was during the Colonial period.

The City Tavern reopened in time for the bicentennial in 1976, after more than a century and a half of dormancy. Although technically the building is not one hundred years old, I am including it in this collection anyway, as its reconstruction was done with such care. Frankly, I would have done so anyway because of its importance in early American history, and although it wasn't serving customers for those years, it still has been open for over 116 years.

The architectural detail of the tavern is amazing, with rooms decorated in reproduction furniture and fabrics, the walls painted the exact color as those in the original tavern, and the staff dressed in custom-tailored eighteenth-century attire. Even the table settings add to the atmosphere. The brass candlesticks, (lead-free) pewter goblets, plates with a pattern based on a 1793 design, and hand-blown glassware all reflect the tableware of the late eighteenth century.

And then there is the most authentically Colonial menu in America. Chef Walter Staib is a purist when it comes to serving food and drink in a manner that reflects the tavern's long culinary history. Fresh produce is delivered two or three times

a day, and all the breads and baked goods are prepared in the basement bakery. There is no walk-in freezer. Instead meats, fish, and poultry arrive daily and are prepared as they were in the 1700s. Even their beers and shrubs (a popular Colonial beverage) are custom brewed by a local microbrewery. Chef Staib in his spare time hosts *A Taste of History*, a fascinating series on PBS where he explores the lives of the nation's

founders through the recipes they prepared and the dishes they served.

A short list of dishes from the extensive menu will give you the idea of chef Staib's interpretation of the foods of Colonial America.

For lunch: Mallard Stuffed Sausage, Giant Cornmeal Fried Oysters, West Indies Pepperpot Soup, Salmagundi (a classic eighteenth-century salad), Martha Washington's Turkey Pot Pie, Crab Cakes "Chesapeake Style."

Dinner appetizers and salads include Basil Shrimp, Black Forest Ham and Asparagus; Hearty Turkey Noodle Soup; Seafood Mélange (a salad of salmon, trout, shrimp, and crab with garden greens); and Romaine and Roquefort Salad. Entrees are where chef Staib reaches the pinnacle of his Colonial gourmet dishes. Braised Rabbit,

The Cincinnati room on the second floor is one of the most popular dining rooms.

Medallions of Venison, and Roasted Duckling are three favorites, but because of his German heritage, he adds Münchner Style Veal and Herb Sausage, Wiener Schnitzel, and an Apple-Wood Smoked Pork Chop with Sauerkraut.

The baked goods are some of the most genuinely historic foods on the menu, and three of the breads are baked daily in the basement bakery. The Sally Lunn (a sweet bread baked in a decorative round mold), Anadama loaves (made from cornmeal and molasses), and Thomas Jefferson's favorite Sweet Potato and Pecan Biscuits are all fantastic. But resist the temptation to clean out the basket placed in front of you, because there's lots of good eating ahead, and I won't even

mention the desserts. Whenever possible, chef Staib has used recipes discovered in his extensive research, updating them when necessary, but creating dishes you would have experienced sitting beside Ben Franklin or General Washington in the early days of the tavern.

One dish on the menu is delicious as well as a complete surprise. It's from a recipe Mr. Franklin sent to a friend in Philadelphia in 1770. The pan-seared spinach, vegetables, sautéed tomatoes, and linguine, though strikingly modern, is not the surprise. Ben's recipe instructed his pal on how to make the main ingredient: tofu. Just another historic and flavorful surprise served up by chef Staib from the kitchens of the City Tavern.

Pan-Seared Venison Medallions with Bourbon-Mushroom Sauce

∼ Serves 4 to 6 ∼

1½ pounds venison tenderloin, fat trimmed and silver skin removed

2 cups red Burgundy wine

3 shallots, chopped

2 cloves garlic, minced

Leaves from 1 sprig fresh rosemary

1 teaspoon rubbed dried sage

2 teaspoons unsalted butter

1 leek (white part only), well rinsed, cut into 2-inch lengths, and finely julienned

1½ cups sliced button mushrooms

½ cup bourbon

2 cups veal demi-glace

Salt and freshly ground black pepper

Herbed barley, for serving

Cut the venison into ¼-inch-thick medallions (about 3 ounces each). Place the medallions in a shallow dish and add the wine, shallots, garlic, rosemary, and sage. Cover with plastic wrap and marinate in the refrigerator for 8 hours or overnight.

Remove the venison from the marinade and discard the marinade. Pat the venison dry with paper towels.

In a large skillet, melt the butter over high heat, add the venison, and cook for 3 minutes on each side for medium-rare. Using tongs, transfer the medallions to a plate and keep warm.

Add the leek to the pan and sauté for about 2 minutes, or until tender. Add the mushrooms and sauté for about 3 minutes, until tender. Add the bourbon and stir to scrape up the browned bits on the bottom of the pan. Stir in the demi-glace, reduce the heat to medium, and simmer for 3 minutes. Season with salt and pepper to taste.

To serve, fan the venison on a bed of herbed barley and top with the mushroom mixture.

NOTE: This recipe is reprinted with permission from City Tavern: Recipes from the Birthplace of American Cuisine, *©2009 by Walter Staib.*

Fairfield Inn
FAIRFIELD, PA ~ EST. 1757

Gettysburg, Pennsylvania, July 4, 1863: The Confederate Army of Northern Virginia under General Robert E. Lee had just been soundly defeated during Pickett's Charge up Cemetery Ridge and was in full retreat. As they trudged out of the town, they were hit with a fierce rainstorm, slowed by muddy roads, and further hampered by the movement of up to ten thousand cattle and sheep crowding the road.

Three Confederate colonels, who had been injured, and scores of wounded soldiers made it the eight tortuous miles to the Fairfield Inn, which the army had taken over as a field hospital. A local doctor, who had an office in the inn, had treated wounded cavalry and soldiers there during three days of local fighting. On the fourth day forty

thousand exhausted and hungry rebel soldiers camped out on the wet grounds of the small inn, many too weak to move farther.

The innkeepers and helpful women from town fed as many of the troops as they could, providing huge pots of a thick ham and bean soup. For General Robert E. Lee, General J.E.B. Stuart, and some of the officers, they rounded up all their hens and made up plates of chicken and biscuits. When the rains stopped, most of the troops left, leaving behind those who were too injured to travel.

The inn was built in 1757 by Squire William Miller and his wife, Isabella. The land was from a large holding that had been deeded to a local family by Lord Baltimore in 1735. Squire Miller built not only the Fairfield Inn but also laid out the

A photo of the Inn from the late 1800s.

surrounding town of Fairfield, which was then in the state of Maryland. When the Mason-Dixon Line was redrawn in 1767, the inn "moved" to Pennsylvania.

In its pre-Civil War days, the Fairfield served first as a Colonial meetinghouse in the mid-1700s, and then in the early 1800s as a stagecoach stop and drovers' tavern until the Squire came on the scene.

During and after the Civil War, the inn was part of the Underground Railroad, a loose network of inns, taverns, churches, and individuals who aided the escape and resettlement of slaves. On the third floor is a hidden trap door that leads to a secret attic room where escaped slaves were hidden while in transit north.

In 2005, the owners discovered the original tavern license, dated 1786, proving that the Fairfield is one of the oldest continuously operating inns in America. Today, it's on one of the main roads tourists take to visit Gettysburg National Military Park.

Joan and Sal Chandon purchased the Fairfield in 2003, and have been occupied since with not only running the inn but in restoring and refurbishing the building to its historic peak. Each of the six rooms is named for historical persons who stayed in those rooms. Five are named for famous Civil War officers (the Three Colonels Suite being named for those injured who sought shelter here), and the remaining one honors Patrick Henry who, it seems, was a cousin of Isabella Williams, the wife of founder Squire Williams.

The dining rooms and tavern on the ground floor, like the sleeping rooms, are furnished in original antiques and closely reflect how the inn looked in the mid-to-late 1800s. The period fireplace treatments, moldings, Colonial-style curtains and sconces, and various military memorabilia add to the historic ambiance. Then there are the paintings of war scenes, various generals, Abraham Lincoln, and local cavalry battles scattered on the walls, in bookcases, and on shelves in every room.

While they have a well-rounded assortment of soups, salads, and appetizers, on my visit I began with the filling and flavorful 1863 ham and bean soup. The entrees include Seared Tuna, Crab Stuffed Basa (a catfish cousin), Rack of Lamb, Strip Steak, "Confederate" Crab Cakes, Filet Mignon, Prime Rib, and Oven Roasted Duck, but here again I went for history and had the signature Chicken and Biscuits. The biscuits are split open and topped with a rich creamed chicken stew, a historic version of comfort food.

Visiting the Gettysburg battlefield down the road, then exploring the inn and enjoying a truly historic meal, was one of the most moving experiences I had in writing this book. Every American should visit this part of Pennsylvania at least once.

Ham and Bean Soup

∽ MAKES ABOUT 1 GALLON ∽

1 large smoked ham hock

8 cups water

1 yellow onion

3 to 4 bay leaves

6 cups cooked Great Northern beans with broth

Place the ham hock in a large stockpot with the water. Bring to a boil, then add the onion and bay leaves. Reduce the heat to a simmer, cover, and cook for 1½ hours. Remove the ham hock and let cool.

Add the beans, including their broth, to the pot. Return the soup to a low simmer and cook for 30 to 45 minutes; do not boil. While the soup is simmering, pull the meat from the ham hocks and add to the soup. Serve hot, in deep bowls.

NOTE: Owner Sal Chandon notes, "Our traditional ham and bean soup has been served for many generations. The recipe is very basic, and the finished soup has a flavor reminiscent of the nineteenth century, especially when cooked over an open fire in one of the inn's nine fireplaces. Many recipes call for celery and carrots in ham and bean soup. You may certainly experiment with variations to your liking."

Kimberton Inn
KIMBERTON, PA ~ EST. 1796

The village of Kimberton came into being in the late eighteenth century, but it remained nameless until 1817. The first major building constructed was a tavern that George Chrisman named after himself, and which received its license in 1771.

It was followed by a large gristmill and Smiley's general store, and within a year Quaker teacher Emmor Kimber opened the French Creek Boarding School for Girls in a house on another corner. After discovering the need for a place for parents to stay while visiting their daughters, Kimber built the Boarding School Inn on the fourth corner. Essentially, the village grew up around these four buildings. At one time, Kimber owned all four, and the village was named after him in 1820. It is now a suburb of Phoenixville, Pennsylvania.

The school, which Emmor Kimber and his four daughters ran for sixty-one years, became a model for progressive education until it was closed in the mid-eighteenth century, when parents discovered that Kimber was running slaves through the village on the Underground Railroad.

The busy Kimber also had a hand in bringing the Reading Railroad to town. The arrival of regular train service changed Kimberton forever. New buildings sprang up, produce could easily be shipped to Philadelphia, and farm animals that were auctioned off at the hotel were then loaded into train cars and sent to the big city.

Not much is recorded about the inn in the early twentieth century. We do know it stayed open during the Depression and Prohibition, but we don't have any information about how it survived. Today, the boardinghouse and general store are private residences, the grain mill is the post office, and the inn, after multiple changes in name and ownership, is a popular restaurant. A delightful painting by artist John Peirce that hangs in the lobby depicts the intersection (practically the whole village) as it supposedly existed in 1834.

Jeff Effgen bought the inn in 1980 and has spent almost twenty years restoring and improving it. He calls it "stressing the authentic." There are three private dining areas and three public dining rooms. Each is decorated in period or reproduction furniture, with original oil paintings, candlelit tables, and cozy original wood-burning fireplaces. My favorites are the two French dining rooms (Upper and Lower), where it seems that someone in a powdered wig and breeches might arrive any second.

Each month, the Kimberton features a five-course wine dinner that showcases fine wines from around the world to accompany chef Jim Trainer's gourmet offerings. A peek at a recent wine dinner menu gives you an idea of the high level of cuisine offered in the century-old environs. The country origin of the wine for each course is given in parentheses after the name of the dish.

First course: Chilled Crab, Lobster, and Cucumber Salad on Toasted Brioche with Baby Celery (Germany). Second course: Sweet Corn and Red Pepper Crêpe with Seared Striped Bass Fillet (Argentina). Third course: Swiss Chard and Asiago

Below: Lobby painting by John Peirce depicts the Inn and the village surrounding it as it looked in 1834.

Calves Liver and Bacon

∽ SERVES 2 ∽

1 tablespoon olive oil

1 large Spanish onion, halved and cut into ¼-inch-thick slices

Salt

3 cups ruby port wine

10 ounces calves liver, sliced about ¼ inch thick

Freshly ground black pepper

Flour, for dredging

Canola oil, for frying

Mashed potatoes, for serving (optional)

6 slices applewood-smoked bacon, cooked and kept warm

1 tablespoon chopped green onion, including some green parts, for garnish

In a medium sauté pan, heat the olive oil over medium-low heat. Add the onion slices and cook, stirring often, for about 1 hour, or until deep golden brown and sweet. Season lightly with salt. Set aside and keep warm. To make ahead, cover and refrigerate for up to 3 days, then reheat just before serving.

In a small, heavy nonreactive saucepan, bring the ruby port to a simmer and cook until it is reduced to a light syrup, about ½ cup; do not let it brown. Remove from the heat and keep warm. To make ahead, cover and refrigerate for up to 3 days, then reheat just before serving.

Lightly season the sliced liver with salt and pepper and dredge it in flour. Shake off the excess flour.

Heat a large sauté pan over medium-high heat and add the canola oil. Add the dredged liver strips in a single layer, not crowding them, in the pan. Cook for 30 seconds to 1 minute until nicely browned. Turn and cook for 30 seconds to 1 minute on the second side. Using a slotted spoon, transfer to paper towels to drain.

To serve, place the potatoes, if desired, in the center of each warmed plate. Surround them with about ¼ cup warm port wine reduction. Top with the cooked liver, then about ¼ cup warm caramelized onions and 3 bacon slices. Sprinkle with the green onion and serve.

Cheese Ravioli with Pan-Roasted Guinea Hen and Cèpes (Italy). Fourth course: Roasted Colorado Leg of Lamb with Popcorn Lamb Sweetbreads and Pommes Maxine (USA). Fifth course: Frozen Spearmint Yogurt with Lemon Verbena Custard and Local Berries (Canada).

Their standard menu includes everything from lobster and crab cakes to lamb chops, seared yellowfin tuna, hazelnut chicken breast, and a salad entree they humbly call "Probably The Best Salad You'll Ever Have."

If you're in a Colonial mood, try something that has been on the menu for much of their history: Sautéed Calf's Liver. If you like liver, you will love their version, tender and perfectly cooked, slightly pink in the center, cut into slices and served on a bed of mashed potatoes with apple-wood-smoked bacon and drizzled with a port wine reduction.

The Kimberton is also famous for its desserts, which include Belgian Chocolate Ice Cream, Warm Blueberry Buckle, and Chocolate Praline Tart (with ice cream, of course).

From its very beginning, the inn has been much more than a place to get a good meal and satisfy one's thirst. It was then, and is still, the center of a small southeastern Pennsylvania community, a restful place that blends a bit of big-city sophistication with casual rural surroundings and has remained unspoiled by the trappings of the twenty-first century.

McCoole's at the Historic Red Lion Inn

QUAKERTOWN, PA ~ EST. 1750

One of the most famous features of this historic inn is a small section of the dining room floor. But before we get into that, let's talk about its role in the Revolutionary War, and the time it served as a resting place for the Liberty Bell. Yes, the genuine, yet-uncracked Liberty Bell.

Walter McCoole opened his small tavern in Quakertown, Pennsylvania, in 1750. The area was beginning to attract a lot of settlers, many of them Quakers. In 1876, a book about the history of Bucks County observed: "It was probably called Quakertown from the first, possibly as a slur upon the Friends who settled it; and very likely was first called 'the Quaker's town.' In this time Walter McCoole kept tavern at the cross-roads ... and built one of the first mills in the township."

During the Revolutionary War, the tavern became the center of a historic rebellion by Germanic Pennsylvanians against a tax imposed by the federal government to fund a possible, some said imminent, war with France. The taxes were based on real estate and slave ownership. Since there weren't a lot of slaves in the state, the burden fell on homeowners, with the taxed value based on the number and size of the windows in their homes.

When tax assessors were harassed, intimidated, and threatened with jail by local militia, the government responded by sending troops to capture and imprison the protestors. John Fries, the organizer, and several others were arrested, tried, found guilty of treason, and sentenced to hang.

The Red Lion in 1918.

The gallows happened to be across the street from the Tavern, where they had held organizational meetings. But two days before the execution, President John Adams pardoned them.

In 1810, the inn added two rooms and expanded the kitchen. In 1865, more rooms were added as the new railroad began bringing in potential customers to the area. Today's owner, Jan Hench, brought the Red Lion back to its former glory, even turning their old stables into McCoole's Arts and Events Place, with room for large meetings and gatherings.

The menu spans history and geography, with foods from Europe, Asia, the Mediterranean, the Deep South, the Eastern states, the Caribbean, and the Southwest. Of course, you can also order tavern fare such as burgers, finger foods, a wide variety of steaks, and pasta. They have twenty-five or so tap or bottled beers to wash it all down.

In a beefy mood, I ordered the Tournedos au Cognac, which are pan-seared in butter, slathered with demi-glace, and flamed with Cognac, then topped with a mountain of delicious hickory-smoked mushrooms. I had room for their Warm Bavarian Apple Torte, with fire-roasted apples and buttery pastry, made even more decadent with a large scoop of cinnamon-caramel ice cream.

While sitting in the dining room, I looked out the window and thought I spotted the Liberty Bell right across the street. It is a duplicate, put there to commemorate the real bell's visit in 1777. When it seemed as if the British would capture Philadelphia (which they did), the bell was moved to Allentown, Pennsylvania, and hidden—the fear being that the redcoats would melt it down for cannonballs to use against the Colonial army. On the way to its hiding place in an Allentown church, the famous bell briefly rested in Quakertown, right across the street from the Red Lion.

Replica of the Liberty Bell, which was hidden from the British across the street from the Inn.

And that famous floor? From 1939 to 1942, Erick Knight, an English-American author, sat in the dining room. When his wife's dog was killed by a car, he bought her a new puppy—which soon bonded with him and became his shadow for nine years. He began writing a book about her, typing notes while she happily slept beside his chair at home, or rode shotgun when he drove around town, did chores, or just wanted to get away from the typewriter. And when she was good, he took her to his favorite restaurant, the Red Lion Inn, and he bought her a raw steak which she gobbled right off the floor beside his favorite table. She must have been on her very best behavior many times, because she ate so many steaks there that the flooring began to deteriorate and it eventually had to be replaced for safety and sanitation reasons.

Inns, taverns, and restaurants all over the country brag that "George Washington slept here," or "Ernest Hemingway drank here," and so on. But the Red Lion

Lassie ate here! This section of flooring had to be replaced because of Lassie's love of steaks.

upstages them all. The book Erick wrote, was, and is, perhaps the most beloved canine yarn ever. And his four-legged pal became the role model for a dozen movies, a radio series on ABC and one on NBC, a dozen TV series, and sixty more books. Which makes McCoole's Red Lion Inn the only place in America that proudly proclaims: "Lassie Ate Here!"

Tournedos au Cognac

∽ SERVES 2 TO 4 ∽

¼ cup olive oil

1 (32-ounce) beef tenderloin, cut into 16 medallions

¾ cup Cognac or brandy

1½ cups hickory-smoked mushrooms (see Note)

2 cups beef or veal demi-glace (see Note)

2 parsley sprigs or minced fresh chives, for garnish

In a large skillet, heat the olive oil over medium-high heat and sauté the medallions, in batches if necessary, for 1 to 2 minutes on each side for medium-rare. Using tongs, transfer the medallions to a heated platter and set aside.

Reduce the heat to medium and add the Cognac to the pan, being careful with the resulting flame-up, and stir to scrape up the browned bits from the bottom of the pan. Cook to reduce the liquid to about ½ cup.

Add the mushrooms and demi-glace and bring to a boil. Reduce the heat to a simmer and cook for 5 minutes, stirring constantly.

Divide the medallions between two or four plates and spoon the mushroom mixture on top. Garnish with parsley or chives and serve at once.

NOTE: If you don't want to smoke your own mushrooms, you can substitute any unsmoked mushroom.

You can buy demi-glace in jars at specialty foods stores. The Red Lion makes its own.

White Horse Tavern
NEWPORT, RI ~ EST. 1673

Undoubtedly the oldest operating tavern in the United States, the White Horse has one of the most interesting histories of any of its centenarian brethren. In 1673, William Mayes, Sr., bought and transformed a two-room home into a large tavern that became a popular meeting place for the Rhode Island Colony's General Assembly and the Newport City Council. Sometimes it functioned as a city hall or as a place to conduct criminal court hearings.

After running the tavern for twenty-nine years, Mayes, Sr., passed ownership to his son William Mayes, Jr., who subsequently was granted a license to sell "all sorts of Strong Drink." But Junior was not exactly the type of tavern owner who would please the officials of the British Colony. In fact, he was a pirate. For 4½ years he had sailed the waters

of the Indian Ocean and the Red Sea as a privateer authorized to raid French ships. But his zeal took him beyond his warrant, and he attacked British ships as well, and it is said that he returned home with more than £300,000 of booty.

He was also a lucky pirate, as opposed to his fellow buccaneer Captain Kidd. When Kidd returned home, he was arrested, shipped to England, tried, and hanged. Mayes, a popular fellow with the local citizenry (perhaps partially because his father owned the biggest tavern in Newport) was sheltered and protected when the authorities came after him.

William, Jr., successfully operated the tavern for twenty-eight years and passed it on to his sister and her husband, Jonathan Nichols, who named it the White Horse Tavern. His son Walter took over upon Jonathan's death and operated the White Horse through the Revolution, at one point moving his family out because of the Hessian mercenaries the British had lodged there. After the war he returned, enlarged the tavern, and added the signature gambrel roof.

For the next fifty years or so the building became a rooming house and was sadly neglected. Happily, it was rescued by the Preservation Society of Newport and meticulously restored, opening again in 1957. One of the finest examples of Colonial Newport buildings, the tavern's clapboard walls, steep staircases, plain pediment doors, giant beams, and cavernous fireplaces are a testament to the simple grandeur of seventeenth-century American architecture. Paul Hogan, the tavern's present proprietor, is only the sixth owner in the tavern's entire 350-year history and promises to preserve the traditions, warm hospitality, great food, and "strong drink."

Its three private dining rooms upstairs and the main dining room and original barroom on the main floor are popular with locals and tourists alike. The second-floor Pub Room, the largest of the tavern's dining rooms, has a private bar, which was the original bar for the tavern. Owner Paul pointed to a series of wooden shutters that were attached to the ceiling but which could be lowered to close off the bar from the room. "Do you know what those are?" he asked. I hadn't a clue, so he explained, "During the first colonization of the Americas, the corner of a tavern or inn devoted to the sale of alcohol was separated from the rest of the room with a bar or series of bars. It's from this barrier that the word *bar* evolved. So tradition dictates that the barred shutters are locked down at night and, as shown here, are raised during the day."

The menu features modern twists on Colonial cuisine. Every year, they hold a special Fourth of July Founding Fathers Luncheon, which last year featured Pheasant Soup, Dandelion Greens Salad, Roasted Bluefish Fillet or Grilled Mutton Steak, and Indian Pudding or Martha Washington Fruit and Sherry Cake. Their everyday menu lists such dishes as Seasonal Sausage Tasting, or the decadent Lobster "Mac and Cheese," and then there's chef Rich Silvia's Lobster, Corn, and Poblano Bisque.

I had heard glowing comments about the tavern's Beef Wellington and was eager to taste their most historic and popular entree. The medium-rare filet is cloaked with truffled foie gras pâté and baked in puff pastry, then

"The bar" – the original wooden barrier that locked in the liquor at night and became the word used to describe a place where you drink alcohol and beer. Here, the bar is raised for the day.

Above: The original Pub Room on the second floor is part of the original structure built in 1652.
Below: Tavern artwork.

served in a pool of succulent Madeira-shallot-veal-demi-glace reduction sauce. It is flawless.

As I handed my credit card to the waiter he reminded me of a piece of history he'd shared with me as I asked him about the history of the tavern in a previous phone call. He had mentioned pirates, and I'd commented that yes, I knew about William Mayes, Jr., and his exploits.

"No, no, not that pirate," he said, laughing. "This place is responsible for some of the boldest acts of piracy that have ever been perpetrated—dastardly acts that began in the 1700s and continue today." Confused, I asked, "What kind of piracy?" "Well, back in 1708, the White Horse Tavern began allowing government officials to run up huge tabs, charging frequent and prodigious lunches to the public treasury."

Yes, gentle readers, the White Horse Tavern is responsible for promoting one of the most brazen acts of piracy ever . . . the "businessman's lunch."

∾ Tavern Ghosts ∾

The Tavern's famous, haunted tale goes that two travelers arrived there late one night in the 1720s. The next morning, one of the men was gone and the other man was dead, found lying by the fireplace in his room with no sign of struggle. The mystery was never solved, and so the tales of being able to see a ghost at the right-hand side of the fireplace continues to this day. Nearly every member of the tavern's staff will say they've had some kind of encounter, from reports of being tapped on the shoulder or hearing footsteps in otherwise empty rooms.

The ground floor dining room in 1939.

White Horse Tavern Beef Wellington

∾ SERVES 6 ∾

MADEIRA SAUCE

1 tablespoon grapeseed or canola oil

1 tablespoon minced shallot

¼ cup Madeira wine

1½ cups veal demi-glace

1 tablespoon minced canned black truffles

1 tablespoon truffle juice from canned truffles

Kosher salt and freshly ground black pepper

6 (5-ounce) Prime filet mignon steaks

Kosher salt and freshly ground black pepper

2 tablespoons grapeseed or canola oil

1½ sheets thawed frozen puff pastry

9 ounces truffled foie gras pâté

3 large egg yolks beaten with 2 tablespoons water

6 baby carrots

12 haricots verts or baby Blue Lake green beans

12 asparagus stalks

Mashed potatoes, for serving

For the sauce: In a small, heavy saucepan, heat the oil over medium heat and sauté the shallot until translucent, about 3 minutes. Add the Madeira and cook until reduced to a syrup-like consistency. Add the demi-glace and simmer until the sauce is thick enough to coat a spoon. Add the truffles and truffle juice and season to taste with salt and pepper. Remove from the heat; cover and keep warm.

Season the filets liberally on both sides with salt and pepper. In a large sauté pan, heat the oil over medium-high heat and sauté the filets on each side for 2 minutes for rare. Transfer the meat to a plate. Let cool, then cover and refrigerate for at least 2 hours.

Cut the whole piece of puff pastry into 6 even squares and spread out on a work surface. Add one-sixth of the pâté to the center of each square, then top each with a cooled filet. Pull all four corners of the pastry together at the top and seal them well. Brush the entire outside of the puff pastry with the egg yolk mixture to coat evenly.

Place the half piece of puff pastry on a work surface and cut out shapes to decorate the tops of the Wellingtons.

Preheat the oven to 450°F. Spray a baking sheet with cooking spray and arrange the Wellingtons on the prepared pan. Bake on the center rack of the oven for 20 minutes for medium-rare steaks. Remove from the oven and let rest for 3 to 4 minutes.

While the Wellingtons are baking, separately blanch the carrots, haricots verts, and asparagus in salted boiling water for 60 seconds, then transfer to an ice-water bath to stop the cooking. Drain and cut each vegetable in half lengthwise.

Spoon the sauce into the center of 6 dinner plates. Add a scoop of mashed potatoes to the left of the sauce on each plate. Add 2 halved carrots, green beans, and asparagus spears stacked together against the mashed potatoes, and place a Wellington leaning against the vegetables and mashed potatoes. Serve at once.

Wilcox Tavern
CHARLESTOWN, RI ~ EST. 1850

The land where the present-day Wilcox Tavern is located has an interesting history that began almost two hundred years before the historic inn was built. In 1655, a tribe of Manesses Indians from Block Island came to the mainland and attacked the Niantic Indians who lived there, taking an Indian princess as a hostage. When they demanded an extremely high ransom, the Niantics went to Thomas Stanton, a celebrated Indian interpreter, for help.

When Stanton negotiated the release of the princess, the tribe deeded a large section of their land to Stanton to show their gratitude. The new Stanton estate included land where the city of Charleston and the Wilcox Tavern are now located. In 1730, Stanton built his home on the Old Post

Road, where the Wilcox Tavern now stands. His son Joseph later became a general in the Revolutionary Army, was a member of the Colonial Congress, and was the first senator representing Rhode Island at the First Constitutional Congress. When he died, the property was divided and the Wilcox family took over part of the estate.

"Governor" Edward Wilcox (who actually was only a lieutenant governor) lived in the house for a number of years. In 1850, a member of his family turned the house into the Old Wilcox Tavern on the Old Post Road. He added a general store annex on the east end of the building and a front porch along the entire front. In a later transfiguration, the store was turned into a bunkhouse, and even later Joseph and Peggy

Szydlowski, the present owners, removed the porch in 1954, restoring the profile of the building to its original configuration.

A succession of owners over the years had fortunately left much of the historic building virtually untouched, and the tavern looks much as it did in its early years. The owners have added a wing, which now holds two dining rooms, and have modified and reconfigured the bunkhouse wing, where Benjamin Franklin once spent two nights, into the largest dining room in the tavern. The third floor was used during a short period of time as a smokehouse, a

is the crackle and snap of fires in the fireplaces in the winter months and the hum of friendly conversation year-round.

The restaurant has four distinctive dining rooms, one overlooking the garden, and a pleasant lounge. The cuisine is New England comfort food, focusing on seafood, though steak, prime rib, chicken, and lamb are available as well, as are a few international dishes.

Seafood starters include Shrimp Cocktail, a rich Lobster Bisque, Fried Pt. Judith Calamari, Stuffed Quahog Clams, Crab Cakes, and Steamed

Chef Jamie Grider plates up dinner.

chimney from below supplying wood smoke to cure the hundreds of hams hanging from the roof above. Now it's just a ham and smoke-scented attic.

The tavern's tranquil interior is filled with antiques and reproductions of the period. There is no piped-in music; the only sound you can hear

Mussels. Featured entrees include Seared "Bomster" Sea Scallops, Cedar Plank Roasted Salmon, Baked Cod with shrimp, and fish and chips in a local beer batter.

After experiencing Corn Fritters with maple syrup as an appetizer, and a divine roasted

butternut squash soup, I decided to try their Shellfish Paella. It is absolutely wonderful—the saffron rice tender and flavorful, the lobster, scallops, shrimp, clams and mussels perfect, the chorizo and leeks adding spicy elements to the dish, and the threads of saffron and turmeric turning the rice a golden hue.

As Ben Franklin once mused, perhaps after a bit of dinner and a tankard of ale at the Wilcox, "Beer is proof that God loves us and wants us to be happy. There cannot be good living where there is not good eating and drinking." That wise man would agree that the Wilcox Inn is a place where much good living is found.

Left: The Tavern's menu of New England comfort food includes a roasted butternut squash soup, which is world class, and comes with freshly baked (of course) yeasty rolls.

Below: The compact Rose Dining Room looks out over the rose garden and is the brightest, most cheerful room in the place, perfect for small parties.

Shellfish Paella

∾ SERVES 4 ∾

2 tablespoons olive oil

4 ounces Spanish chorizo sausage, sliced into "coins"

¼ cup diced yellow onion

¼ cup sliced leek, white part only, well rinsed and drained

1 tablespoon minced garlic

1½ teaspoons ground turmeric

1 tablespoon kosher salt

2 teaspoons freshly ground black pepper

1 cup dry white wine

1 (24-ounce) can diced tomatoes

2 cups chicken broth

1 cup clam broth

2 (1¼- to 1½-pound) New England lobsters, halved lengthwise

6 littleneck (countneck) clams, scrubbed

1 pound mussels, scrubbed and debearded if necessary

6 large white shrimp, shelled

8 ounces sea scallops

2 cups parboiled rice

1 tablespoon saffron threads

1 tablespoon chopped fresh flat-leaf parsley

FRIED LEEK

1 leek, white part only

Canola oil, for deep-frying

In a Dutch oven, heat the oil over medium heat. Add the chorizo sausage and onion. Sauté until the onion is translucent, about 3 minutes. Add the leek and cook until wilted. Add the garlic, turmeric, salt, and pepper. Sauté for 1 minute.

Add the white wine and cook until almost dry, 5 to 7 minutes. Add the tomatoes, chicken broth, and clam broth and bring to a boil. Add the lobsters, clams, mussels, shrimp, and scallops and stir. Add the rice and reduce the heat to a simmer. Stir in the saffron and parsley. Cover with a tight-fitting lid and simmer for about 18 minutes, or until most of the liquid is absorbed and the clams and mussels are open. Discard any clams and mussels that don't open.

For the fried leek: While the paella is cooking, slice the leek into thin rounds. In a small, heavy saucepan, heat 2 inches of canola oil to 365°F on a deep-fat thermometer and drop in the leek, cooking until golden brown. Using a wire-mesh skimmer, transfer to paper towels to drain. Transfer the paella to a serving bowl and sprinkle with the fried leek. Serve at once.

McCrady's

CHARLESTON, SC ~ EST. 1778

Many of the restaurants, inns, and taverns profiled in this book have retained dishes that were served in their early days. But McCrady's, which began as a tavern in 1778, has moved in the opposite direction. There is nothing on the menu today that was served in the late-eighteenth or even nineteenth century. Instead, the dishes are all authentically twenty-first century.

The food is wonderful, mixing exotic and rare ingredients, spices, and sauces with beef, lamb, duck, swordfish, scallops, and snapper. The only dishes on the current menu that even hint of tradition is the dessert cheese course, featuring three artisanal cheeses. You will not find chicken potpie, baked potatoes, shrimp cocktail, or T-bone steaks here. You may, however, discover dishes

like Pork Skin Noodles with a stew of Matsutakes, English Peas, Spicy Pepper Broth, and Poached Pullet Egg; Geoduck Clam with its own broth, Green Strawberries, Squid Ink, and Phytoplankton; Aged Wood Pigeon Baked in Salt and Hay with Beets, Guanciale, and White Chocolate; and Trio of Kathadin Lamb by Craig Rogers of Border Springs Farm, Virginia Salsify, Wild Mushrooms, Huckleberry, and Chamomile, all items you probably couldn't taste at your local 1-, 2-, 3-, or even 4-star eateries.

You see, Sean Brock, who was named James Beard Best Chef Southeast in 2010, has turned one of America's oldest restaurant kitchens into one of the most modern in the country. The cooks and chefs of its early years would be dazzled by the complexity and creativity of his food. Instead of cooking over a woodstove or on a fireplace hearth, Brock is among the generation of chefs who practice what has been called molecular gastronomy—cooking that involves immersion circulators, kitchen centrifuges, and sous-vide units, and which produces emulsions, foams, gelifications, and spherifications. Yum.

The Tavern's first owner and namesake, Edward McCrady, was a Charleston barber who fulfilled a life long ambition of opening a tavern that offered lodging and meals in addition to ale, porter, and hard cider. A leader in the local militia, he was arrested and imprisoned by the British during the American Revolution when Charleston was captured. When he was released, he built the Longroom, which was connected to the tavern by a two-story piazza. He hosted a dinner for President George Washington there in 1791.

Following Edward's death, the tavern changed hands a number of times, being converted into a coffeehouse, a warehouse, and a paper company, and then was abandoned. In the 1970s, the old structure was added to the National Register of Historic Places and new owners began plans to restore it. The two-story building is in Charleston's French Quarter, with the main entryway almost hidden in diminutive Unity Alley.

The Longroom was converted into a dining room, mahogany paneling and a Baccarat crystal chandelier were added, and the old horse stalls on the ground floor were converted into a small dining room and the present-day bar. The outside was restored to its former appearance, but the interior was completely changed and updated.

Where firewood, salt pork, potatoes, cooking oil, and flour were once stockpiled, the restaurant now stores carrageenan, gellan gum, methyl cellulose, and liquid nitrogen. The bar area now features large booths framed with brick archways. The dining room has exposed brick walls,

heart-pine floors, beamed ceilings, colorful original oil paintings, and fireplaces from the original tavern. The original upstairs Longroom is an elegant rose-hued venue for private gatherings. And finally, there's the Society Room, which leads to the chef's table.

Spending time with the chef in the kitchen is more akin to being invited to witness brain surgery in a high-tech operating room than being in the kitchen in one of the oldest eateries in America. The surroundings are a tribute to the most modern of ovens, warmers, grills, and fryers. But also there are those space-age circulators and the Cryovac machine, which seals foods into plastic to be cooked for hours in a water bath at a

Chef Sean Brock presides over a high-tech kitchen that is as pristine as a surgical suite and produces gastronomic wonders daily. Desserts are fantastic, including this chocolate mousse pie with nitrogen pearls, coffee ice cream, and artsy caramel swirls.

very low temperature. The area where Sean does his plating is spotless and brightly lit. He huddles over a series of plates with a long pair of medical tweezers, artfully placing tiny sprigs of arugula or a chiffonade of shiso in exactly the right place. Every plate is a masterpiece of design, as well as of taste.

The Charred Octopus with Gold Beets, Orange Puree, and Fennel was an intriguing mix of flavors and textures—sweet, bitter, tart, and slightly smoky. The Duo of Beets with Maria's Broccoli, Fried Farro, and Kimchee Purée was deliciously confusing in its simplicity (beets) and complexity (fried wheat grains and a Korean sauce). A world-class sculpture of Chocolate Mousse Pie with Nitrogen Pearls was finished with a scoop of coffee ice cream and artistic caramel swirls.

McCrady's is extremely popular, especially with the thirties and under crowd, and certainly this was the most technically and visually complex meal of all the 100 restaurants I visited. The food is above reproach in its blending of multiple tastes, textures, and visual effects, though it was perhaps a meal that old Ed McCrady might not have appreciated, with the artistic extremely constructed dishes coming from an ultra modern kitchen that in his day served the simplest of tavern foods.

But time, and culinary arts, march on.

The Society dining room features exposed English Bond brickwork, a handcrafted and embossed tin ceiling, and rich hardwood floors. At rear is the Chef's Table dining room, with seating for 14 under a Baccarat crystal chandelier.

Braised and Grilled Octopus with Coriander, Fennel, and Variegated Lemon

~ SERVES 6 ~

SAUTÉED FENNEL

2 tablespoons extra-virgin olive oil

1 fennel bulb, trimmed, cored, and julienned

3 drops fennel extract (see Note)

Kosher salt

OCTOPUS

1 (4- to 6-pound) octopus

8 cups extra-virgin olive oil, plus more for coating

2 variegated lemons, halved, plus ¼ cup freshly squeezed variegated lemon juice, for serving (see Note)

1 large fennel bulb, trimmed, cored, and cut into large dice

2 tablespoons toasted coriander seeds

15 fresh thyme sprigs

Salt

1 cup chopped fresh cilantro

For the sautéed fennel: In a small, heavy saucepan, heat the olive oil over medium heat and sauté the julienned fennel for 3 to 5 minutes until wilted and crisp-tender. Add the fennel extract and kosher salt to taste. Set aside.

For the octopus: Preheat the oven to its lowest setting (ideally, 80°F, but no more than 200°F). Place the octopus in a Dutch oven and add the 8 cups olive oil to cover. Add the lemons, diced fennel, coriander seeds, and thyme. Cover and cook for 7 hours, or until very tender. Using tongs, transfer the octopus to a plate and let cool to the touch. Remove the suckers and outer skin; it should slide off easily.

Prepare a hot fire in a charcoal grill or preheat a gas grill to high. Cut the octopus tentacles into serving size pieces (2 to 3 inches in length), toss the octopus in a little olive oil to coat, and season with salt. Place on the grill and cook until charred, about 3 minutes on each side.

Place the octopus on serving plates. Garnish with the cilantro and toss with the sautéed fennel, a little olive oil, and the variegated lemon juice.

NOTE: *Without a doubt, this is the most complicated recipe in this book, and if cooked the way they do in a restaurant, would require special equipment, such as an immersion circulator and a Cryovac sous vide unit, to accomplish properly. This recipe is adapted to be cooked in a conventional oven.*

Fennel extract is available from specialty foods stores. Variegated lemons have distinctive green and yellow variegated stripes and a pink blush to the skin. These lemons have pink flesh, clear juice, and a wonderful lemon flavor, and can be ordered online or found in produce sections of upscale markets.

Varallo's Chile Parlor & Restaurant
NASHVILLE, TN ~ EST. 1907

Frank Anthony Varallo, a concert violinist, was on a concert tour of South America and was taught how to make a bean soup while staying with a family in that country. When Frank was injured in a hunting accident many years later and had to give up his musical career, he remembered that recipe and tried it out for some friends and his family. When they all gave it a double thumbs-up, he decided to try his hand as a cook and began serving up his version of the South American dish at the Climax Saloon downtown, calling in "chile" and selling it for fifteen cents a bowl.

Four years later, in 1907, he opened Varallo's Restaurant on Broadway, which he ran until 1929. After he died, his son Frank, who was only fourteen, took over and managed the restaurant for

another seventy years, passing on the business to his grandson Todd when he retired at eighty-five.

"I had worked in the restaurant since I was a kid, so it kind of fell my way," Todd says. "I remember going up there when I was four or five, don't remember what I did, but eventually I worked every job in the place. I got married young and was going to school part time, and my grandfather came to me and he asked me to give it a try, and I said, 'Sure, I'll try,' and the rest is history."

Dining at Varallo's is an informal experience. Everything is served on plastic plates with plastic utensils, but no one complains. The emphasis is on hearty and filling breakfasts and lunches. The interior is basic fifties diner: tables are covered with red-and-white checked plastic tablecloths, and historic pictures and clippings cover the walls. The menu is on a board at the back of the restaurant, and you can see the various side dishes behind glass as you walk along the cafeteria-style counter with your plastic tray.

Varallo's calls their food "soul food," but I think of it as "comfort food." Turkey and stuffing, macaroni and cheese, fried catfish, barbecued pork, beef stew, country-fried steaks and gravy, meat loaf and meatballs, fried chicken, and banana pudding are all on the menu. They serve twenty side dishes on a rotation of ten each day.

And then there's the "3 Way," the most popular dish on the menu, and an invention of Great-Grampa Frank. It combines three unlikely foods: a hearty helping of spaghetti is topped with a large tamale, which is smothered in their century-old beans and meat chili. Most folks order a side dish with the 3 Way—such as a grilled cheese sandwich. Talk about your carbs!

The 3 Way comes in two sizes: the svelt and trim Regular Size, and the I'm-not-sure-I-can-

Varallo's Restaurant and the family-owned jewelry store next door in 1934.

Varallo's Banana Pudding

∾ SERVES 10 ∾

6 large egg yolks

1½ cups sugar

Pinch of ground nutmeg

⅓ cup all-purpose flour

2 cups whole milk

1 teaspoon vanilla extract

3 bananas

½ box vanilla wafers

Whipped cream, for topping

In a medium saucepan, whisk the egg yolks, sugar, and nutmeg together. Gradually whisk in the flour until smooth. Gradually whisk in the milk until blended.

Set the pan over medium-low and cook, stirring frequently, until thickened and creamy. Remove from the heat and stir in the vanilla. Peel and slice the bananas. In a 9 by 12-inch baking dish, alternate layers of the pudding, wafers, and sliced bananas. Repeat to use all the ingredients.

Cover and refrigerate until ready to serve. Top with whipped cream.

Owner Todd Varallo with portrait of his grandfather, Frank Varallo, Sr., the first owner.

finish-this King Size. I ordered the smaller version, but server Cheryl McKnight, who's worked here for more than thirty years, giggled as she handed me what she called the "manly" version. I couldn't finish it. And you can always just order a bowl of chili. Even in summer, they sell an average of sixty gallons a day, both to eat-in customers and as take-out (in pint and quart sizes). The only change to the recipe since 1907 is that they've reduced the red pepper. "It used to be pretty spicy, but we took the cayenne out," says Todd.

"It's funny though," he continues. "In the winter, there are tons of customers who order chili of some sort, but in the summer I don't see those customers in here at all. Guess chili to some is a winter kind of thing. But we have a regular customer base; some come in every day, some two to three times a week, and some maybe every other week. They make up 75 to 80 percent of our business and have for as long as I can remember."

With an eleven-year-old daughter showing interest in the restaurant, and two grandsons in the family, Todd is pretty sure Varallo's will stay in the family for another generation or so.

Menger Hotel
SAN ANTONIO, TX ~ EST. 1859

In 1950, Army Specialist fourth class Shearn Moody, a lowly enlisted man stationed at Ft. Hood, Texas, discovered the regulation that soldiers who owned local property were allowed to live off post. He didn't want to stay in the smelly, drafty, hot army barracks and asked his company commander if he could live at the luxurious Menger Hotel instead. The captain laughed and patiently explained to him that you had to own the property that you lived in to take advantage of this regulation, and he doubted Moody was the owner of a world-famous hotel.

Moody moved in later that day. It seems that his grandfather W. L. Moody had purchased the hotel in 1943, and when he died the ownership passed to his son, then to grandson Shearn. For

the rest of his stay in the Army, Moody lived in the most luxurious hotel in Texas.

The original two-story limestone building stood on a street corner about one hundred yards north of the Alamo; with expansion over the years, the hotel now takes up the entire block. William Menger, a German immigrant and owner of a successful brewery, decided to expand his boardinghouse business by having a fifty-room hotel built next to his brewery in 1859. It was so successful that even before the building was completed, work started on constructing a three-story addition.

For many years, the Menger was the most famous and luxurious hotel west of the Mississippi. Ulysses S. Grant, William Sydney Porter

∽ Menger Facts ∽

• The first public demonstration of barbed wire was held outside the hotel in 1876, after which interested ranchers trooped inside to order up some of the newfangled fencing.

• In its early days, chefs used a system of ropes and pulleys on an old cottonwood tree in the garden to hang buffalo, venison, elk, and other wild game to age the meat until they were ready to prepare it for guests.

• Until 1950, the hotel kept several alligators in the garden; later they were moved to a pool in the main lobby. Unfortunately they are long gone.

• When Menger built the hotel, he had a system of tunnels dug under the front of the building so the brewery next door could roll barrels of his beer into the hotel.

(better known as O. Henry), Robert E. Lee, Dwight Eisenhower, Mae West, Babe Ruth, Sarah Bernhardt, Oscar Wilde, and Western opera star Lillie Langtry all frequented the bar and hotel. Another famous guest, Gutzon Borglum, designer and sculptor of Mt. Rushmore, kept a studio in the hotel for many years and reportedly created two statues that were displayed in the courtyard.

Teddy Roosevelt first visited when he was twenty-nine years old while in Texas to hunt javelina. Years later, he returned with Army Colonel Leonard Wood to organize the volunteer cavalry that became known as the Rough Riders. The hotel bar proudly displays images of Roosevelt and memorabilia of his military adventures.

An exact replica of London's House of Lord's Pub, the Menger Bar, Roosevelt's unofficial Rough Rider's recruiting station, was built in 1887. It has a paneled ceiling of dark cherrywood, beveled mirrors from France, and the original brass spittoons provided for the convenience of its early customers. Once the site of more cattle deals than any place in Texas, the bar has been voted one of the Top Ten Most Historic Bars in the United States.

The Colonial Room Restaurant is an elegant Greek Revival style room featuring white Corinthian columns, wooden dentils, decorative scrollwork, arched windows, and romantic period lighting. I felt guilty about not wearing a tuxedo, or at least a suit and tie, but was comforted to see my fellow diners attired in everything from shorts to silk suits.

In use continuously since 1859, the restaurant kitchen was initially headed by chefs brought in from Europe, hence the German and French touches to the menu. Many of the dishes have been offered here for decades, but influences from Mexico and the Southwest have added flavor to the Old World style of cooking. As early as 1960, the restaurant had firmly established a reputation for superb cuisine, often featuring wild game.

I was surprised to see that one of their signature dishes was wiener schnitzel, this being Texas steak country, but the veal is better than just about any schnitzel I've ever enjoyed, even in Germany. The light, golden brown crisp breading guards the moisture and tenderness inside. Every mouthful is a treat.

The red cabbage was exactly on target, a bit sweet, a bit tangy, a bit crunchy, and a perfect mate for the veal and the spaetzle, which was tender, flavorful, and buttery. My server insisted that I try their mango ice cream. It was creamy and loaded with mango tartness. I highly recommend you leave room for this treat.

I was sad to leave this historic hotel, which is an important part of the history of both Texas and the American West, but somewhere down the trail I'll point my horse in their direction to visit the grand old lady of San Antonio again.

Above: The "Babe" standing outside the hotel in 1930.
Right: The three-story Victorian lobby is simply spectacular, with its beautiful skylight, period antiques, and imported tile floor.

Top: Voted "One of the Top Ten Historic Bars in the US," the Menger
Bar is loaded with Teddy Roosevelt and Rough Rider memorabilia.
Above: The hotel in 1882.
Right: The luxurious Colonial dining room with its Corinthian
columns, arched windows, and starched tablecloths.

Wiener Schnitzel with Red Cabbage

∞ SERVES 4 ∞

BUTTER SAUCE

4 tablespoons clarified unsalted butter

2 tablespoons freshly squeezed lemon juice

¼ teaspoon minced garlic

1 teaspoon chopped fresh flat-leaf parsley

RED CABBAGE

1 red cabbage, halved and cored

1 red onion, halved

3 tablespoons bacon grease

2 red apples, peeled, cored, and diced

1 cup dry red wine

½ cup red wine vinegar

2 bay leaves

4 (4-ounce) veal scallops, ¼ inch thick, trimmed of excess fat

Salt

⅔ cup all-purpose flour

1 large egg, beaten

⅔ cup dried bread crumbs

4 cups canola oil, for frying

4 teaspoons unsalted butter

Spaetzle, for serving

For the butter sauce: In a small saucepan, combine all of the ingredients, then heat over medium heat while stirring constantly until the sauce is well mixed. Keep warm and set aside.

For the red cabbage: Cut the cabbage and onion into thin shreds. In a large, nonreactive sauté pan, heat the bacon grease over medium heat and sauté the red cabbage, red onion, and apples until tender. Stir in the wine, vinegar, and bay leaves. Reduce the heat to low, cover, and cook, stirring occasionally, for about 25 minutes, or until the liquid is almost completely reduced. Set aside and warm while you prepare the Wiener schnitzel.

Flatten the veal scallops with a meat pounder or a heavy skillet to an even thickness of about ⅛ inch. Pat the veal dry with paper towels, then salt the meat and let it stand for about 10 minutes.

Dip the veal scallops in the flour, then the beaten egg, then the bread crumbs. Transfer to a baking sheet for 15 minutes to set the breading.

In a large, heavy sauté pan, heat the oil to 355°F on a deep-fat thermometer, add the butter, then fry each veal scallop until golden brown, about 1 minute on each side.

Remove and drain the schnitzels and then top each with a tablespoon or so of the lemon butter sauce and serve with spaetzle and warm red cabbage.

Southside Market & Barbeque
ELGIN, TX ~ EST. 1882

Bryan and Billy Bracewell.

In 1882, Texas butcher William J. Moon began processing beef and pork on a small ranch near Elgin, Texas. This was before refrigerators were in common use, in rural states anyway, so he loaded his sausages onto a wagon and drove into town to deliver the tasty links door to door. He originated the phrase "butcher today, delivery today," and his goods were popular in a part of the state where immigrant Germans loved their wursts and sausages.

Four years later, he tired of the daily trek and figured he could sell more sausages if he opened a storefront in town. So in 1886, he started the Southside Market. He smoked meat that was left over, grinding his beef and pork trimmings, seasoning them with salt, red pepper, and other spices, then stuffing them in natural casings. You could buy the sausages raw and cook them yourself or purchase them already smoked.

In early 1908, Lee Wilson bought the company. The legendary sausages, called "hot guts" by locals and fans, just kept getting famous and gathering a local, then statewide, then nationwide following of sausage aficionados. There was simply no other sausage as popular in the country.

Over the next twenty-five years, a succession of owners kept the smokehouse running, but added refrigeration, a sales counter, and chairs and tables in a small dining room. In 1968, Ernest and Rene Bracewell bought the market and began cementing the legend that was the Southside Market. They added a second dining room, took the "hot" out of the "hot guts" by cutting back on the cayenne, instead using it to spice up the barbecue sauce they bottled for customers to use at the table.

In 1983, a fire set off by a bottle rocket on the roof caused Ernest to look at relocating, and ten years later the business moved into the huge present-day location just outside town on Highway 290. With two huge modern dining rooms seating over three hundred, the market came into the twenty-first century in a big way. The location also has ample space for sausage production, a butcher shop, a shop that sells their famous sauce and spice rubs as well as souvenir shirts and hats, and an ice cream parlor.

The powerful aroma of barbecue will grab you as soon as you get out of your car in front of the restaurant. When you make your way to the

counter, you order either meat by the pound or various plates and combination plates of meats and side dishes.

There's a nice snap when you bite into the sausage, then the moist smoky texture of the subtly spiced meat. If it's not hot enough for you, use the barbecue sauce, or try the original 1882 hot sausage. They also have four other varieties: Polish, country style, jalapeño Cheddar, and pork and garlic.

The sausage is great, but the standout on the sample platter is the brisket, the best I've ever eaten in any restaurant. The meat is fork-tender with a slight pull when you bite into it, dripping with moisture, with the perfect blend of spice and smoke flavors.

Bryan Bracewell, the CEO, says the beauty of barbecue is its individuality and hand-me-down

Ernest Bracewell and his hot sausages, 1968.

Southside Market Sausage Meat Loaf

∾ SERVES 4 TO 6 ∾

2 pounds ground beef

1 cup finely chopped carrots and celery

2 cloves garlic

1 large egg

⅓ cup dried bread crumbs

1 teaspoon salt

1 teaspoon freshly ground black pepper

1 pound Southside Market Original Smoked Beef Sausage

1 pound Longhorn Cheddar cheese

2 to 3 green jalapeños, sliced (seeded, if you like less of a kick)

Preheat the oven to 350°F. In a large bowl, combine the ground beef, chopped vegetables, garlic, egg, bread crumbs, salt, and pepper. Stir until fully incorporated.

In a 9 by 5-inch loaf pan, spread one-third of the ground meat mixture. Slice the smoked sausage links lengthwise down the middle and lay them in the center of the pan, pressing them into the meat mixture. Cut the Cheddar into sticks ¼ inch thick and 6 to 8 inches long. Lay the Cheddar on top of the sausage links. Lay the jalapeños on top of the cheese, down the length of the pan. Spread the remaining beef mixture in the pan to completely cover the sausage, Cheddar, and jalapeños. Bake for 1 hour, or until the internal temperature reaches 170°F.

Remove from the oven and let cool for 15 to 20 minutes. Pour off as much of the hot grease from the pan as possible. Carefully unmold the meat loaf onto a carving board. Let cool slightly, then slice, serve, and enjoy!

ancestry. "When everyone goes home to do their barbecue in their backyards, it's their style of barbecue, and that's how their kids are going to do it. And that's cool. It doesn't mean it's right or wrong. And that's why barbecue appeals to so many people."

And, by the way, if you're hankerin' for their smoked sausages or mouth waterin' brisket, you can go to their website and order smoked brisket and either smoked or fresh sausage with two-day delivery. But be sure to order some sauce too. Their two blends are perfect for their sausage or brisket, and quite unlike other sauces you may have run into on the barbecue trail.

Stagecoach Inn
SALADO, TX ~ EST. 1861

Salado, Texas, is today a mere shadow of its glory days in the 1880s. At that time, the town, which is located forty-nine miles north of Austin, boasted seven churches, fourteen stores, two hotels, two blacksmiths, and three cotton gins. After the railroads were built to the north and east of Salado, the new towns along the route drew most of the trade from here and Salado steadily declined. The population dwindled from 900 in 1882 to 400 by 1914 and only slightly over 200 in 1950.

Amanda and William Armstrong built and opened the Shady Villa Hotel in Salado in 1861; at that time it was a rustic Overland Stage and Pony Express stop along the Old Chisholm Trail. The trail came right up Main Street, and the stage lines that served central Texas included Salado among their stops. Cattle drives and cavalry, stagecoach passengers and cattle barons, heroes and desperadoes all found a welcome resting place on the banks of Salado Creek, an ancient crossroads where centuries-old Comanche campgrounds and buffalo hunters' log cabins gave way to vast herds of longhorn cattle being driven north to the Kansas City stockyards.

After its Shady Villa years, the inn was known as the Buckles Hotel, then the Lone Star. In the 1940s, Ruth and Dion Van Bibber bought and restored the building, giving it its current name, and the fame of its dining room began to spread. Today, the inn's restaurant has a national reputation for its hospitality and the quality of the food served.

The inn is a good example of frontier domestic and functional architecture, and features the original limestone fireplaces and a two-story galleried porch with a second-story balustrade. If there is a template for an Old West stagecoach stop, surely the Stagecoach Inn is its inspiration.

Military figures George Armstrong Custer and Robert E. Lee, cattle baron Shanghai Pierce, and Sam Houston, who was twice elected president of the Republic of Texas, all stayed here in the early years. But some bad guys loved this place as well; Jesse and the James Brothers and outlaw Sam Bass signed the register, under different names to be sure, and enjoyed respite here under the shade-giving burr oaks.

The Van Bibbers, especially Ruth, developed the menu and many of the Southern-style dishes she created, such as hush puppies, catfish, and Southern fried chicken, are still on the menu today. Eventually, the restaurant became so popular that the inn stopped taking overnight guests, instead adding two more dining rooms.

Sam Houston

The menu features other classic down-home dishes such as chicken-fried steak, baked ham, shrimp, beef Stroganoff, burgers, salmon or chicken salad, and various steaks. They even serve tomato aspic, something I haven't seen on a restaurant menu in years. Since my mother instilled in me a love of this astringent jellied tomato concoction, I gleefully tried it and the taste took me back to the Thanksgivings and Christmases of my childhood. Thank you, Mrs. Van Bibber!

The Stroganoff is good, and the green beans and steamed potatoes are a nice complement, but the bell-ringer is the signature banana fritters, which are crisp, hot, and dusted with confectioners' sugar, though it was unexpected to find them served with an entree.

The inn today has eighty-two guest rooms. I was there in June, and it was a haven of shade, with a cooling pool, and most rooms are a mere hundred yards or so from the restaurant—and those yummy, yummy, only slightly fattening fritters.

Banana Fritters

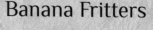

∾ SERVES 4 TO 6 ∾

2 cups all-purpose flour, plus about ¼ cup for dredging

¼ teaspoon salt

1 tablespoon baking powder

½ cup granulated sugar

2 large eggs, beaten

½ cup whole milk

Peanut or canola oil, for frying

6 to 8 large bananas, peeled and cut into 2-inch pieces

Confectioners' sugar, for dusting

Halved maraschino cherries, for garnish

In a large bowl, combine the 2 cups flour, the salt, baking powder, and granulated sugar and stir with a whisk to blend. Add the eggs and milk and beat until smooth.

In a large sauté pan, heat 3 to 4 inches of oil to 325°F on a deep-fat thermometer. Roll each piece of banana in the flour and then into the batter. Remove with a toothpick and slip into the oil. Fry until golden, turning often. Using a wire-mesh skimmer, transfer to paper towels to drain.

Serve hot, dusted with confectioners' sugar and garnished with maraschino halves.

Rabbit Hill Inn
LOWER WATERFORD, VT ~ EST. 1834

Tucked away in a quiet corner of Vermont, Rabbit Hill Inn, which began life as the Samuel Hodby Tavern in the late 1700s, is one of the most popular places to stay in the eastern United States. It's so popular, in fact, that during "the foliage," the magical fall season when leaves turn the hills into living murals of fiery reds and oranges and brilliant yellows, there is not the hint of an available room. It seems that repeat customers book every room in the house up to two years ahead of time.

The inn stands overlooking the tiny village of Lower Waterford (population 1,204), a miniscule gathering of houses, a church, and a small building, which holds the town clerk, the library, and the post office. The inn began when

Samuel Hodby realized that the village was midway between Montreal and the busy harbors of Boston and Portland, Maine, an eighteen-day round trip, and that the loggers, tradespeople, and adventurous travelers who passed by needed to refill their water barrels, get a hot meal, and have a civilized place to stay. Overnight lodgers stayed in dorms or in small, bare rooms on simple beds.

By comparison, the rooms today are exquisite. In fact, *Yankee Magazine* calls the inn the "Best Romantic Place" in New England, and the *Zagat Survey* says "the meals are amazing, and this just might be the most romantic place on the planet."

In the early nineteenth century, the meals served in the inn were simple but in large portions; venison, pheasant, squirrels, rabbits (from the

Owners Leslie and David Mulcahy.

hillside warrens surrounding the village), beef or lamb, chicken, corn and cooked grains, root vegetables, and various hearth-baked breads were the main comestibles.

Today, the inn's meals are a nonstop culinary adventure, as executive chef John Corliss and his staff offer a sophisticated menu that you'd normally expect in a four-star New York or San Francisco restaurant. Like many chefs today, John practices a farm-to-table regimen, relying as much as he can on local farmers for his produce.

Breakfasts are included in your stay and include freshly baked pastries, homemade granola, yogurts, fresh fruit, and several kinds of juices. Guests are also offered the choice of two breakfast entrees: Apple Cheddar Crepes in a caramel sauce, served with a spinach-orange-pecan salad, or a Cheddar and Roasted Red Pepper Egg Napoleon drizzled with sun-dried tomato anglaise, and accompanied with a rosemary potato galette.

The Rabbit Hill Inn (lower right) on a foggy fall day.

Afternoon tea is also served, complete with a dozen or so different pastries and several varieties of tea. Guests who prefer a colder, more bracing beverage amble twenty feet across the parlor to the Snooty Fox Pub, where they can relax, play a board game, or work on one of the inn's beautiful wooden jigsaw puzzles. In summer, there's always a pitcher of ice-cold lemonade on the front porch.

Dinner entrees include Sage-Dusted Maine Halibut, Braised Kurobuta Pork Belly and Cheek, Kangaroo Loin, Duck Breast with Foie Gras, and Black Beluga Lentil-Stuffed Delicata Squash, as well as more traditional fare, such as Chicken and Biscuits, Maine Clam and Seafood Chowder, and Grilled Rib Steak. Their Seared Guinea Hen is tender pink in the middle, buttery tender, and rich with flavor. The stuffed squash could best be described as an 11 on a scale of 1 to 10. And don't pass on dessert—not

The Inn in the 1870s – carriage house at right now houses 5 guest suites. Below is the Cedar Glenn suite.

with offerings such as Whiskey Pear Cake and Grand Marnier Chocolate Cobbler.

Perhaps the unheralded star of their dinners is the small loaf of Oatmeal Molasses Bread served to each table. Made fresh every day from a recipe that's over one hundred years old, this small loaf is rich with molasses flavor, has a firm, chewy texture, and has been a favorite since it was first served in the tavern. We share the recipe here, but you'll have to cut the butter into rabbit shapes on your own.

Speaking of rabbits, Rabbit Hill Inn has a whole lot of them scattered around the rooms—over 270 at last count. Small bunny salt and pepper shakers, each set different, live on the dining room tables. Ironically, innkeepers Leslie and David Mulcahy have never had to purchase a single bunny—all of them were given to them by guests.

Leslie tells me they are "corporate dropouts" who both left jobs in Rhode Island to work as assistant innkeepers here until they took over in 1997. "We love it here and consider the staff and guests our family." I highly recommend that you find a way to spend a few days here, but I caution you, you'd better call for a reservation yesterday! And please, even if it's your first visit, bring a bunny.

Oatmeal Molasses Bread

∾ MAKES 2 LOAVES ∾

2 cups cold water, plus ½ cup warm (105° to 115°F) water

1 cup quick-cooking oats

1½ tablespoons unsalted butter, plus more for serving

1 package active dry yeast

½ cup dark molasses (not blackstrap)

2 teaspoons salt

4⅔ cups all-purpose flour

In a small saucepan, bring the 2 cups water to a boil. Remove from the heat and stir in the oats and the 1½ tablespoons butter. Let stand for 1 hour.

In a large bowl, sprinkle the yeast over the ½ cup warm water and let stand until foamy, about 5 minutes. Stir until dissolved. Stir in the molasses, salt, and the oatmeal mixture. Stir in the flour, ½ cup at a time, to make a stiff dough. Transfer to a floured board and knead for 8 minutes, or until elastic, adding more flour if needed to prevent sticking.

Place the dough in an oiled bowl, turn to coat, cover with a damp cloth, and let rise in a warm place until doubled in volume. Divide into 2 pieces and form into loaves. Oil two 9 by 5-inch bread pans and place the loaves in them, seam side down. Cover with a towel and let rise in a warm place until doubled in volume.

Preheat the oven to 375°F. Bake the loaves for 35 minutes, or until nicely browned on top and hollow sounding when thumped on the bottom. Serve warm, with butter for spreading.

The Dorset Inn
DORSET, VT ~ EST. 1796

The travelers dismounted their carriage and tied the team of horses to the hitching posts in front of the inn. Inside, they were directed to the fireside lounge, where the men took off their boots, the women removed their fancy hats, and they all relaxed. An hour or so later, at the invitation of the innkeeper, they moved into the dining room for a hearty meal of venison stew, corn cakes, braised corn, and fresh lima beans. Their mugs were kept filled with a sweet-bitter cider made in the shed behind the inn. The women refused dessert, but the tall, lanky gentleman and his short, round friend eagerly accepted thick pieces of cold apple pie with a wedge of Cheddar cheese.

Following dinner, the four retired to the lounge and the waiting fire. The men broke out their clay pipes and began puffing away, while their wives took up a deck of cards and began a spirited but quiet game of whist. As the clock struck nine, both women headed off to their bedrooms, but the men settled deeper into their chairs with small pewter cups of Barbados rum. The innkeeper knew how to keep a good table.

An hour later, they drained their cups and headed off for a night of rest. Tomorrow they would have twenty miles to go before they reached their destination. Now the prospect of a sound sleep was the best thing they could think of, except for a few thoughts about the inn's famous breakfast scones, a steaming pot of newly imported Twining tea, and some fatback bacon that the round gent had seen hanging in the kitchen.

A scene from a movie about Colonial America? No, just a typical group of travelers journeying from Boston to Albany in the late 1700s, stopping at a popular inn in the hamlet of Dorset that was known for its comfortable lodgings and large and delicious meals.

Decades of owners, hundreds of hours of reconstruction and renovation, and thousands of guests later, the Dorset has regained its reputation as one of the finest inns in a part of the country where great inns are the rule, not the exception. Owners Steve and Lauren Bryant have created a near-perfect hostelry in a picture-perfect Vermont town.

The inn experience begins when you walk up the marble steps between soaring white columns overlooking the town green. Inside, period furnishings, new carpeting, and Colonial-style paisley wallpaper fully complement the polished wide pine floors and the subtle lamp- and candle-lit rooms with their tartan and floral accents. Multiple original fireplaces warm the lounge, lobby, and dining rooms on crisp fall or bitter winter days and nights.

The Dorset is considered one of the best restaurants in the region. A member of the Vermont Fresh Network, many of its herbs, spices, vegetables, fruits, and cheeses are the freshest available and are from local farms and businesses, meaning the menu is ever changing. The sign out front says that the inn is open for lunch and dinner, but guests are thankful to learn that there is a morning menu and a sunny breakfast room. Vermont maple syrup and local cheeses are served at breakfast, as they are at lunch and dinner.

Dinner begins with a shared sampling of local cheeses accompanied with house-made crackers, honeycomb, maple walnuts, fresh fruit, a

roasted garlic bulb topped with melted Brie and chèvre, and red onion jam. Splendid! Entrees include Chicken Pappardelle Pasta with cremini mushrooms, roasted tomatoes, red pepper, sweet onion, spinach, and Grana Padano cheese, as well as Roast Turkey Croquettes with pan gravy and cranberry sauce. The crisp, golden breading embraces the lusciously moist turkey, and every forkful is enriched with a touch of rich gravy and bitter-sweet cranberry sauce. They are perfect.

My dessert was Chocolate Dreams, a rich dark chocolate cake filled with Belgian chocolate mousse, generously ladled with hot fudge sauce and cocoa cream. Also delicious was the Classic Bread Pudding with warm bourbon sauce and whipped cream. After dinner, you can enjoy Eden Vermont Ice Cider while sitting by the fireplace, sans the pipe smoking. And like our fictional eighteenth-century round friend, who may have been one of the nation's first foodies, you may have fleeting thoughts of the blueberry scones, a piping hot mug of hot cocoa, and some maple-smoked bacon you'll have for breakfast. Hmm. Guess not much has changed in two hundred years after all.

The Inn in the early 1900s.
Photo courtesy of Dorset Historical Society.

Turkey Croquettes with Cranberry Sauce

∼ Serves 6 to 8 ∼

CRANBERRY SAUCE

2 cups sugar

2 cups water

1 pound fresh cranberries

1 large orange, peeled and chopped

TURKEY CROQUETTES

2 cups diced cooked turkey

1 cup cooked favorite homemade or boxed stuffing mix

¼ cup canola oil, plus more for frying

1 yellow onion, sliced

1 stalk celery, chopped

½ leek, white part only, sliced and rinsed

½ teaspoon dried sage

½ teaspoon dried thyme

½ teaspoon dried tarragon

1 cup turkey gravy

1 cup all-purpose flour

4 large eggs, beaten with a little water

2 cups fresh bread crumbs

For the cranberry sauce: In a small, heavy saucepan, combine the sugar and water and bring to a boil over medium-high heat, stirring to dissolve the sugar. Add the cranberries and orange. Simmer until the cranberries just begin to split open. Let cool to room temperature, then refrigerate.

For the croquettes: In a large bowl, combine the turkey and stuffing. Set aside. In a medium, heavy saucepan, heat the ¼ cup oil over medium heat and sauté the onion, celery, leek, sage, thyme, and tarragon until the onion is tender, about 5 minutes. Remove from the heat and let cool, then add to the turkey and stuffing mixture. Toss with your hands. Put the entire mixture in a food processor and pulse to chop coarsely; do not puree. The croquettes are best with some texture. Return the mixture back to the mixing bowl and add the gravy. This will bind the mixture, so you will now be able to form it into golf ball sized croquettes.

In a large cast-iron skillet or Dutch oven, heat 2 inches of canola oil to 350°F on a deep-fat thermometer.

Put the flour, eggs, and bread crumbs into three separate shallow bowls. Roll each croquette in the flour, shaking off the excess. Dip each croquette in the egg mixture, and then roll in the bread crumbs until evenly coated. In batches if necessary to prevent crowding, drop the croquettes, one at a time, into the oil. (Be careful because the hot oil will boil and splatter.) Cook until golden brown, about 5 minutes. Using a slotted spoon, transfer to paper towels to drain and cool briefly.

Serve the croquettes hot, with the cranberry sauce on the side, accompanied by mashed potatoes and gravy and sautéed corn or peas.

Michie Tavern
CHARLOTTSVILLE, VA ~ EST. 1784

Miranda Dean, Tavern Docent

The Michie (pronounced Mickey) Tavern has the distinction of being the only establishment in this book that has been moved, lock, stock, and barrel. In 1927, it was packed up and transported from its location on Buck Mountain Road in Earlysville to its present site near Charlottsville.

John Michie bequeathed his eleven-thousand-acre estate to his wife and his eleven children, including William Michie, once a corporal in the First Artillery Regiment, Virginia Continental Troops, who served with General Washington. Much of the land was planted with wheat and tobacco, which William continued to farm. The following year, he decided to build a tavern on the side of a well-traveled stagecoach road adjoining his land. A natural spring on the property would provide water, and the local forests the building material.

He began operating the tavern a year later. When he wasn't running the tavern, William functioned as town sheriff and later as a justice of the peace. His second wife, Ann, was praised for the simple but delicious meals she prepared for hungry travelers.

The large tavern rivaled the most elaborate accommodations of the day. The big Assembly Room upstairs served as a community gathering spot for meetings, dances, and church services and was also a post office and a school. Local doctors and dentists rented out space in the inn to ply their services.

But after stagecoach travel stopped, the means by which most travelers had arrived at the inn, the huge building reverted to a private home for the growing Michie family. After being in the Michie family for 130 years, the home was sold at an estate auction to another family. Then in 1927, Mrs. Mark Henderson, who loved history and saw a great opportunity, bought the deteriorating building. She had it dismantled and the pieces numbered, and then moved everything sixteen miles by horse, wagon, and truck to its present location, where it was painstakingly reassembled. No longer in an isolated location, it proudly sits today one-half mile from Monticello, Thomas Jefferson's legendary home.

A year later, the Michie Tavern opened as a museum filled with many of Mrs. Henderson's own personal collection of Colonial antiques, and is now designated a Virginia Historic Landmark. Visitors can take an interactive tour of the Tavern Museum or visit the Metal Smith Shop, the Tavern Gift Shop, the Clothier Shop, or the nearby General Store—all housed in historic buildings on the property. At the stores and online you can purchase miniature Revolutionary and Civil War soldiers; small presidential busts; clever Revolutionary and Civil War chess sets; T-shirts; assorted jams, jellies, and fruit butters; cameo jewelry; Colonial clothing; reproduction flintlock and repeating pistols; Civil War bullets; pewter dinnerware; crockery jugs and bowls; clay pipes; and all manner of books about the Revolutionary War, Civil War, presidents, and hardbound copies of the Constitution and the Declaration of Independence. They even sell packages of the fried chicken breading used in the tavern itself.

The Ordinary, as the dining wing is called, is open only for lunch, but it's open 363 days a year. They serve Midday Fair in a fixed-price buffet (cafeteria style). There is table service for seconds,

Right: Brittnay Ferguson makes sure the serving line is well stocked.

drinks, and desserts, but otherwise you stand in line, fill your own plate, and find a table in one of their three dining rooms. In the summer months, you can also dine in the covered courtyard. Try to sit in the dining room fashioned from the hand-hewn logs and beamed ceilings from the original Tavern.

The menu hasn't changed in thirty-five years, and the food is based on eighteenth-century recipes and is simple, ample, and delicious. The entrees are Southern Fried Chicken, Hickory Smoked Pulled Pork Barbecue, and Marinated Baked Chicken, with side dishes of black-eyed peas, stewed tomatoes, mashed potatoes with gravy, sautéed green beans, whole baby beets, coleslaw, yeast biscuits, and corn bread. Beverages include beer and wine, cider, soft drinks and coffee or tea. The fried chicken is crisp on the outside and juicy inside; the vegetables (especially the stewed tomatoes) are cooked just right, the gravy heavenly, and the biscuits and corn

bread will likely make you ask a bonneted server for seconds.

Overnight guests and day visitors can experience a day in the life of an eighteenth-century tavern keeper or weary traveler by visiting the Michie Tavern. Come in for a chilled cider or local brew, grab your pewter plate, and load up with some fried chicken and fixin's. Ann Michie would be so proud.

Stewed Tomatoes

∽ SERVES 6 ∽

4 cups canned tomatoes, quartered

½ cup sugar

2 tablespoons unsalted butter, melted

Salt and freshly ground pepper to taste

6 Murphy's Biscuits (recipe follows)

In a large, nonreactive saucepan, combine the tomatoes, sugar, and butter. Add salt and pepper to taste. Crumble the biscuits and add to the mixture. Cover and cook over medium heat for 15 minutes. Serve warm as a side dish.

Murphy's Biscuits

∽ MAKES 10 TO 12 BISCUITS ∽

2 cups all-purpose flour

2 teaspoons baking powder

¼ teaspoon salt

3 tablespoons vegetable shortening or cold unsalted butter

⅔ cup whole milk

Preheat the oven to 450°F. Lightly butter a baking sheet.

Sift the flour, baking powder, and salt into a medium bowl. Using a pastry cutter or two dinner knives, cut in the shortening until the mixture resembles small peas. Using a fork, quickly stir in the milk to make a light and fluffy but not sticky dough. Form into a ball and transfer to a lightly floured board. Knead just until the dough is smooth, about 10 times. Roll the dough out to a ½-inch thickness. Cut into biscuits with a biscuit cutter. Place well apart on the prepared pan and bake until golden, 8 to 10 minutes. Remove from the oven and transfer the biscuits to wire racks.

The Tavern
Abingdon, VA ~ Est. 1779

This small gray building with its moss-covered roof in the center of picturesque Abingdon looks and is very old. But despite its advanced years, it is still functioning as the center of the town, just as it did 232 years ago.

Today, the tavern is a popular restaurant and bar, but it has also functioned at various times in the past as a bank, a bakery, a general store, a cabinet shop, a barbershop, a private residence, an antiques shop, and a post office. You can still see the mail drop slot from the street on the left side of the building, just underneath the American flag.

The building also served as a hospital for both Union and Confederate troops (we assume at different times). And, during its many years as a tavern with a few small rooms for guests, Henry

Clay; Louis Philippe, the King of France; President Andrew Jackson; and Pierre Charles L'Enfant ate, drank, and slept here. You may not recognize Mr. L'Enfant, but he was the man President Washington called on to design Washington, D.C.

For over one hundred years, the tavern was owned by the Thaddeus Harris family and was briefly a general store. Many years later, local attorney Emmitt Yeary took over and began bringing the crumbling antique back to its Colonial glory, ghosts and all. Donnamarie Emmert, who has led ghost tours in Abingdon for fifteen years, says the tavern is the most haunted building in town and that among the many resident ghosts is the "Tavern Tart," a young prostitute murdered at the tavern by a client. Emmert says that the Tart

Above: The tiny kitchen is about 9 by 12 yet puts out 100+ dinners every night.
Below: The main dining room and (right) the Tavern in 1941.

Raspberry Duck with Melba Sauce

∼ SERVES 4 ∼

MELBA SAUCE

1 (10-ounce) package frozen
  raspberries in syrup, thawed

1 tablespoon brown sugar

½ tablespoon freshly squeezed
  lemon juice

1 teaspoon cornstarch

¼ teaspoon ground cinnamon

¼ teaspoon salt

2 (12-ounce) boneless Moulard
  duck half breasts, with skin

1 tablespoon olive oil

½ cup chicken broth

½ cup veal demi-glace

Rice, pasta, or mashed potatoes,
  for serving

Preheat the oven to 375°F.

For the sauce: Press the raspberries through a medium mesh sieve into a bowl using the back of a large spoon. Stir in the brown sugar, lemon juice, cornstarch, cinnamon, and salt. Transfer to a heavy, medium nonreactive saucepan and cook over medium-low heat, stirring frequently, until slightly thickened. Remove from the heat and let cool.

Using a sharp knife, score the skin and underlying fat on the duck breasts. In a large, heavy ovenproof skillet, heat the oil over medium-high heat and add the duck breasts, skin side down. Cook until golden brown, about 10 minutes, without turning. Turn the breasts over and transfer the pan to the oven. Cook until an instant-read thermometer inserted into the thickest part of the breast registers 135°F (medium-rare), about 8 minutes. Using tongs, transfer the breasts to a carving board and tent with aluminum foil for 10 minutes.

Add the chicken broth to the skillet and stir to scrape up the brown bits from the bottom of the pan. Add ½ cup of the Melba sauce and stir. Add the demi-glace and stir to incorporate. Cook over medium-high heat until reduced to the consistency of syrup.

Cut the duck breasts into ¼-inch-thick diagonal slices, skin and all. Fan the meat on a large platter or on individual serving plates. Reserve the meat juices from the carving board and stir into the sauce. Taste and adjust the seasoning.

Generously drizzle the sauce over the sliced duck meat and serve over rice, pasta, or mashed potatoes.

still has an eye for men and loves to pinch or grab their backsides. She'll also watch out the window and stare at men as they cross the street.

I asked the chef if he'd ever had a ghostly experience, but a laugh and the rolling of his eyes told me he probably hadn't. As I entered the tiny kitchen, and I do mean tiny, I realized why. There isn't room. It is the smallest restaurant kitchen I've ever entered, and I don't know how two chefs can turn out 130 meals a night in this cramped space. One works the grill and fryers on one side of the closet-sized kitchen, the other works in the food-prep area on the other side.

But they must have their act together. The meals fly out of the kitchen and the waitstaff grab plates by the armful and head to one of two dining rooms, the bar, the back porch, or the shaded terrace. During most of the year, the tavern serves a local cadre of customers, but in the summer tourists flock there.

Entrees are where the tavern really shines. With an owner who was born in Germany (Max Hermann, who bought the place in 1994), it's not surprising that there are a number of German dishes. Three schnitzels, a dish of German-style smoked pork loin, and spaetzle and red cabbage side dishes are popular. But so too is their jambalaya, ahi tuna, Italian-style stuffed filet mignon, and several duck dishes.

The pan-roasted duck breast with raspberry puree (blueberry in summer) is delicious. The raspberry melba reduction sauce in which the duckling swims will send your taste buds to the moon. After dinner, you can sit on the terrace as the sun is tucked in for the night and the fireflies emerge, and be at peace in the world. Or at least for as long as your snifter of apple and pear brandy lasts.

Wayside Inn
MIDDLETOWN, VA ~ EST. 1797

Jacob and Lois Charon must be the Superman and Wonder Woman of innkeepers. This couple smoothly run a huge inn in the Shenandoah Valley of Virginia. The historic Inn, which first saw the light of day in 1797, today consists of six meeting rooms, seven dining rooms, a tavern, and twenty-two guest rooms, staterooms, and suites. And they do it all virtually by themselves, employing just three kitchen staff, two housekeeping staff, and one part-time maid.

Jacob began his culinary training first at his father's restaurant in Israel, and then in his own restaurants there. After immigrating to the United States, he opened another one, and both he and Lois previously owned a hotel/restaurant in Richmond, Virginia, before moving to the Shenandoah Valley.

So, this is not their first rodeo. Together they form the dynamic duo that is keeping the Wayside Inn afloat, despite a bad economy, high gas and food prices, and historically low occupancy at inns and hotels across the country.

In its first years the inn was known as Wilkenson's Tavern and welcomed guests who were traveling through the Shenandoah Valley. Two decades later, the Valley Pike was carved through the rolling hills, and the inn became a stagecoach stop, where fresh horses were hitched to the coaches and the passengers could rest and refresh themselves.

In that era, a servant boy, most often a slave, would be sent to the top of a nearby hill to watch for approaching coaches, and when he sighted one would run to the inn to announce its imminent arrival. By the time the coach and four pulled up to the carriage entrance, the innkeeper would have a hot meal and cold beverages waiting.

Jacob Larrick bought the inn before the Civil War and changed the name to Larrick's Hotel. The hotel survived the ravages of the Civil War by serving officers and soldiers of both sides at different times. Other places weren't so lucky or clever, as many buildings were destroyed when Stonewall Jackson carried out his valley campaign in the spring of 1862 against three Union armies. A memorial sign outside the inn makes note of the Battle of Middletown, which took place two miles to the east.

In the early 1900s, owner Samuel Rhodes added a third floor, wings on each side, and a new name: the Wayside Inn. In the next few years, as the bumpy dirt pikes were transformed into paved roads and automobiles began touring the valley, the inn proclaimed itself "America's First Motor Inn." It was bought again in the 1960s and lovingly refurbished by a Washington, D.C., financier and Americana collector. Fifty years later, the present owners set about maintaining the quality of the rooms, hospitality, and meals.

As with many historic inns, countless famous personages have stayed at the Wayside and enjoyed its cuisine. Proudly displayed in the

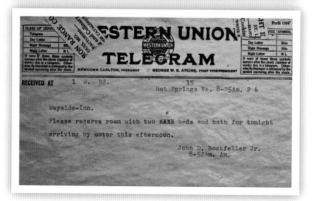

hallway is a telegram from John D. Rockefeller, Jr., asking the inn to set aside a room with two beds and a bath for his arrival.

The seven dining rooms include the Lord Fairfax Room (named for the only resident peer in Colonial America), the Old Servant Kitchen, the Coachyard Lounge, Larrick's Tavern, and the Carriage and Portrait rooms. In all, the dining rooms can seat two hundred people. The Carriage Room was once outside the main building where carriages unloaded their passengers. The old slave quarters have been turned into a small, intimate dining room.

Settling down for some of their famed hospitality, I ordered the signature Rack of Lamb, six large meaty chops grilled and glistening on a plate, with sautéed potatoes, green beans, and the most intriguing dipping sauce. Jacob combines balsamic vinegar with several kinds of oil, honey, and mint to make a sauce so good you'll want to sop up the last drops with one of their yeast rolls.

If you love spoon bread, or if you've never tried it, the inn's version is a can't miss. As you dip into the golden brown crust of this mélange of cornmeal, eggs, butter, and milk, you'll know why it's been on the menu for two hundred years!

I consider this dish the best use of corn in the history of man. I left not a bite of it. Another treat not to miss: Jacob's rightly celebrated fresh fig pie, lovingly topped by two mounds of fresh whipped cream.

The inn is a delightful place, situated in a lovely part of the Shenandoah Valley, and superbly operated by a talented and hard-working couple, who should top any list of super-hero innkeepers.

Right: the Jubal Early State room.
Below: The Carriage dining room and former slave quarters behind.

Wayside Inn Spoon Bread

∞ SERVES 4 ∞

4 cups whole milk

1½ cups cornmeal

⅓ cup sugar

½ cup (1 stick) unsalted butter, cut into 8 pieces

4 large eggs, separated

Salt and freshly ground black pepper

¼ teaspoon ground nutmeg

Preheat the oven to 375°F. Butter a medium-sized soufflé dish or a 9 by 9-inch baking pan.

In a large saucepan, bring the milk, cornmeal, and sugar to a low boil, stirring constantly. Cook, stirring frequently, until thick and smooth. Remove from the heat and stir in the butter. Let cool slightly and add the egg yolks one at a time, stirring constantly. Season to taste with salt and pepper and add the nutmeg.

In a large bowl, beat the egg whites into stiff, glossy peaks and fold into the cornmeal mixture. Spoon into the prepared dish and bake for 18 to 20 minutes, or until golden brown.

Let cool slightly, then serve.

*Above: Owners Jacob and Lois Charon own and run the inn.
Below: the guest register from 1915.*

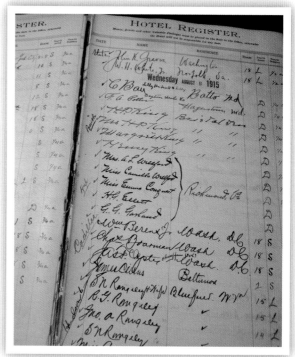

Maneki
SEATTLE, WA ~ EST. 1904

Maneki, the oldest Japanese restaurant in America, opened in 1904 Seattle's Japantown to serve the large Japanese community that had put down roots in the Pacific Northwest. At the time, the restaurant featured Seattle's first sushi bar, could seat up to five hundred customers in several private tatami rooms joined together with sliding doors, and also had one of the country's first karaoke bars. The three-story building, described as looking like a Japanese castle or pagoda, also served as a community center for plays, weddings, family gatherings, and funerals.

The name Maneki is taken from the maneki neko, or "Beckoning or Welcoming Cat," a china round-bodied cat with one paw raised that is found everywhere in Asia. Placed near the front door of a place of business, it is said to promote hospitality, attract new patrons, and bring good

fortune. One story of its origin is that a shogun in Japan once stopped during his travels to admire a cat that appeared to be waving to him, and in doing so just missed being struck by lightning.

"The restaurant was the center of Japantown," says current owner Jeanne Nakayama, "until the Second World War, that is." That was when all the Japanese who worked at the restaurant, and most of the community itself, were given two weeks' notice to "sell or store everything you own," then were hustled off to internment camps for the duration of the war. So between 1941 and 1946, Maneki stood empty and was ransacked and ruined. The employees had each been provided a small amount of floor space in the nearby NP Hotel to store their personal goods.

After the war, Joe Ichikawa and his wife, Virginia, were next to assume ownership and had to move the restaurant from the "castle" because of the destruction of the building. In 1974, Joe set up shop in Maneki's current location near Chinatown. His chef, Kozo, eventually bought the restaurant in 1993 and ran it with his wife, Jeanne. During those years, they hired a young University of Washington student, Takeo Miki, as a dishwasher. After graduation, Takeo went back home, where he was elected Japan's sixty-sixth prime minister, and probably never had to wash dishes again.

Jeanne, who has run the restaurant since her husband died in 1998, and Fusae, or "Mom," who began working here in 1960 as a waitress and cashier and now is a part-time bartender and co-hostess, are a chirping and pleasant duo who greet guests as if they were long-absent but adored relatives. The menu could be right from a top Tokyo restaurant, featuring both nigiri and maki sushi, a full page of à la carte dishes, and yet another full page of appetizers.

Some offerings you won't find at most Japanese restaurants in America include a donut hole filled with octopus and topped with a special sauce, bonito shavings, and nori sprinkles; burdock root and carrot cooked in soy sauce and dashi with a hint of chile pepper; and deep-fried soft-shell crab in tempura batter, with cucumber, avocado, radish sprouts, and flying fish eggs. The culinary hit of my visit was an entree not on the menu but gleaned from handwritten notes listing "specials" on the main wall of the dining room. Broiled Black Cod Collars in Miso Marinade features a generous helping of the dense lobster-like meat with a phenomenal sweet, smoky, and savory miso sauce, tinged with a beer-like, hoppy taste.

As Jeanne says, "Any ingredients we can't get fresh here in Seattle are shipped overnight from Japan. Global delivery makes it all much easier now—so you can pretty much experience all you get in Japan right here at

Black Cod Collars in Miso marinade is one of the most popular dishes.

Maneki. We've discovered that our customers are more global now, and have the palates to prove it."

The crowded restaurant is a quiet eating place. The only buzz is from the tiny bar and the small dining room; the only audible sign that the two tatami rooms are occupied is the gentle click of chopsticks and the clink of sake cups.

When asked about the secret of Maneki's longevity, Jeanne has a simple answer: "When we're not at home and are hungry we need somewhere to sit down, converse, and eat food. It's that simple," she said with a smile.

Perhaps it was just my imagination that the dozens of "welcoming cats" perched around the place seem to brighten as guests arrive and almost wave their lifted paws, but assume a sad, hope-you-come-back-soon look when guests get up to leave.

Bartender/hostess Fusae "Mom" Yokayama and owner Jeanne Nakayama.

Maneki's Black Cod Collars in Miso Marinade

∽ SERVES 2 ∽

2 (8-ounce) pieces black cod collars

1 cup white or yellow miso

½ cup sugar

½ cup sake

½ cup mirin

Steamed rice, for serving

Grilled carrots, green beans, and red pepper strips, for serving

Scale and trim the black cod collars. Place in a sealable plastic bag or a medium bowl.

In a small bowl, mix together the miso, sugar, sake, and mirin and stir to blend. Pour the marinade into the plastic bag or into the bowl completely covering the fish. If using a bowl, cover with plastic wrap. Refrigerate for 3 days, then remove the cod and rinse.

Prepare a medium fire in a charcoal grill, preheat a gas grill to medium, or preheat a broiler. Grill the fish or broil it on an oiled broiling rack for 5 to 7 minutes on each side, until grill-marked on the outside and opaque throughout. Do not burn.

Serve at once, with steamed rice and grilled vegetables.

Horseshoe Café
BELLINGHAM, WA ~ EST. 1886

Some have said that the historic Horseshoe Café is a West Coast version of Cheers, the famed Boston Bar where "everybody knows your name" (at least according to the TV series). It's a popular bar, lounge, diner, and Internet café all rolled into one, and it claims to be the oldest continually operating restaurant west of the Mississippi.

There is not much historical information available about the early days of the Horseshoe, but in 2003 the local newspaper interviewed Bonnie Jean Foster, a waitress who told how she was called on to work the graveyard shift and ended up serving the prostitutes who were working on the second floor above the café. Ladies of the night plying their trade above a bar was not an unusual occurrence in taverns and saloons of that era. Little else is known of how the place made it through two

wars, Prohibition, and the Depression and survived in a town that has seen better days.

For most of its history, the Shoe has been open twenty-four hours a day as a gathering, drinking, and eating spot for an eclectic group of customers—everyone from bankers to lawyers, policemen and firemen to students, travelers, and wanderers. It is not fancy. The plastic-covered booths are reminiscent of a 1950s diner, and the bright and whimsical Western-themed wall mural, with a painted blue sky and puffy clouds extending across the ceiling, is the only decoration.

Outside, the café looks like a classic "greasy spoon" restaurant, but that couldn't be further from the truth. Since Travis Holland bought the place in 2000, everything they serve is made from scratch with fresh ingredients. The beef is from a local butcher and is fresh, not frozen; the sauces and gravy, pancake batter, and salad dressings are all made fresh every day in the kitchen. The bacon, important in a restaurant where breakfast is often the business meal, is good quality and extra thick. Holland explains, "I love good-quality bacon, and as a pilot who flies all over the world I appreciate how difficult it is to get, so for the customers who come here we think it is something special and worth the extra money."

The lounge/bar in an adjoining room looks as if it belongs in a Dashiell Hammett novel. It's dark, small, worn, and frequently populated from the time the bar opens at 9 a.m. until the place shuts down for the night at 2 a.m. It is popular with a group of locals, who frequent the Horseshoe the way that Norm and Cliff spent much of their days at Cheers. It doesn't hurt the bar's popularity that they offer a

"happy hour" from 9 a.m. to 6 p.m., promote selected appetizers at half-price from 6 to 10 p.m., and throw in "nighttime specials" from 8 p.m. until midnight.

On one wall of the bar is a unique original oil painting by Western artist Fred Oldfield. The cowboy portrait fits the Old West–themed bar and lounge perfectly, but if you look at it very closely, especially from a 45-degree angle, there appears a ghost image of a cowgirl, her red lips clearly seen over the cowboy's nose. Oldfield also painted the mural behind the bar, which also supposedly contains a ghost image, although this one is much harder to see.

The menu practically defines "comfort food." Breakfasts include hotcakes, biscuits and gravy, omelets, and six kinds of hash browns. Lunch items include meat loaf, mac and cheese, hot turkey sandwiches, fish and chips, and steak

Country Chicken-Fried Steak

∽ SERVES 4 ∽

4 (8-ounce) cube steaks

2 cups all-purpose flour

2 teaspoons baking powder

1 teaspoon baking soda

1 teaspoon freshly ground black pepper

¾ teaspoon salt

1½ cups buttermilk

1 large egg, beaten

1 tablespoon Tabasco sauce

2 cloves garlic, minced

3 cups vegetable shortening or canola oil, for deep-frying

8 ounces bulk pork sausage

With a meat mallet or heavy skillet, pound the steaks to about a ¼-inch thickness. Put the flour in a shallow bowl. In another shallow bowl, combine the baking powder, baking soda, pepper, and salt; stir in the buttermilk, egg, Tabasco sauce, and garlic. Dredge each steak first in the flour, then in the batter, and again in the flour. Pat the flour onto the surface of each steak so it is completely coated with flour. Reserve the remaining flour and the remaining buttermilk mixture.

In a large cast-iron skillet, heat the shortening to 325°F on a deep-fat thermometer. In batches if necessary to prevent overcrowding, fry the steaks until evenly golden brown, 3 to 5 minutes per side. Using a slotted metal spatula, transfer the steaks to a plate lined with paper towels to drain. Drain all but ¼ cup of the fat and as much of the solids as possible from the skillet.

Return the skillet to medium-low heat with the reserved fat. Add the sausage and cook, stirring to break it up, until browned. Stir the reserved flour into the fat and scrape the bottom of the pan with a spatula to release the solids into the gravy. Add the reserved buttermilk mixture, increase the heat to medium, and bring the gravy to a simmer. Cook until thick, 6 to 7 minutes. Taste and adjust the seasoning. Spoon the gravy over the steaks to serve.

burgers. The dinner menu lists chicken-fried steak, ground chuck steak, spaghetti, and grilled chicken. It's all good home-cooked food at low prices, and the portions for all their dishes are more than generous.

The Country Chicken-Fried Steak, one of their most popular dishes, is a hand-breaded chicken-fried cube steak topped with their signature sausage gravy, served with three eggs, hash brown potatoes, and toast, and will keep you going for the rest of the day.

This Bellingham landmark has been an important part of the community for over one hundred years. As Travis says about his competition, "There used to be two Denny's and a Pancake House here. Used to be is the operative phrase. First one of the Denny's closed, then the Pancake House folded, and now there's only one competitor and us. I know we're not a four-star restaurant, but that's gotta tell you something."

It tells me the Shoe will be around for many more years to come.

The Greenbrier
WHITE SULPHUR SPRINGS, WV ~ EST. 1778

In the mid-1700s, Native Americans "took the waters," bathing and drinking the hot sulphur spring water that bubbled up from the ground in the forested Allegheny Mountains of what would become West Virginia. Soon, pioneers showed up seeking relief from their rheumatism and stomach ailments. Some came because the two-thousand-foot elevation and cool mountain air offered escape from the heat and humidity in the lowlands to the east.

A number of cottages were built to house the many visitors, and the White Sulphur Springs Resort was born. The "village in the wilderness" began to attract people of prominence. Soon thereafter, an influential Baltimore family, the Calwells, took over the resort and began selling cottages to well-off Southern families. Before the Civil War, five sitting U.S. presidents had enjoyed

staying in the cabins, thus cementing the resort's reputation as a gathering place for influential and powerful folks.

In 1858, the owners constructed the Grand Central Hotel, also called the Old White Hotel, a soaring three-story white palace that sported porches on all three levels. The Grand continued to gain a reputation as America's most fashionable social resort, and was given the nickname the "Queen of Southern Spas."

During the Civil War, the hotel was closed to the public as the property changed hands between the Confederate and Union armies, the latter almost burning the hotel to the ground. Both sides used the spacious building as both a hospital and headquarters. It survived the travails of the war and reopened at war's end. The setting for many post war reconciliations, the Grand was

where Robert E. Lee issued the famous White Sulphur Manifesto, advocating the merging of Southerners and Northerners.

The completion of the Chesapeake & Ohio Railway vastly increased the ease of reaching the remote hotel, and for the next century it became one of the premier railroad resorts in America. Then in 1910, the C&O bought the resort and built the Greenbrier Hotel (the central building of today's resort), added a building to house the mineral pool, and constructed the first golf course.

In 1922, the obsolete Old White Hotel was torn down and a larger building was constructed, with five hundred rooms. The designer mixed elements of the hotel's Southern roots with motifs from the Old White. During World War II, the military once again took over the hotel and this time used the luxury resort as a place to house German, Italian, and Japanese diplomats until they could be exchanged for American diplomats being held in those countries. The army then bought the hotel and converted it into a two-thousand-bed surgical and rehabilitation hospital called

Left: Smoked salmon and the chef's "control tower" high above the huge kitchen. Above: A small portion of the staff doing lunch prep in the massive kitchen.

the Ashford General Hospital. When the war ended, the army closed the hospital.

The railroad repurchased the property and made the famous decision of hiring designer Dorothy Draper to work her magic, bringing in colors, fabrics, and furnishings that are still the signature of the hotel's design today. Later improvements included two new golf courses, one headed by legendary golfer Sam Snead; a neighborhood of custom homes called the Greenbrier Sporting Club; exercise facilities, tennis courts, a forty-thousand-square-foot spa, and an infinity pool; plus a dozen more restaurants, exclusive shops, a casino, and more recreational venues than most small cities. There is simply nothing like the Greenbrier anywhere else in the United States.

There are now thirteen restaurants here, so no matter what you want to eat, they probably have it. Their breakfasts are well known and are served the way you would expect them to be served at Buckingham Palace. Mirrored glass tables are covered with fresh fruit, lox, bagels, and more fancy pastries and breads than a small bakery, and a cheery chef waits beside a grand piano to cook huge omelets. White-jacketed waiters attentively take care of your every need, setting platters of Eggs Benedict and Breakfast Trout before you only minutes after you order them.

The Greenbrier is not for anyone on a tight budget. But visiting this luxury resort is a worthwhile once-in-a-lifetime experience. If you can possibly stay or dine at this amazing place on the western slopes of West Virginia, you will never forget your visit. And just think, it all began with smelly, bad-tasting hot water bubbling up in a forest.

Greenbrier Eggs Benedict

~ SERVES 2 ~

HOLLANDAISE SAUCE

3 large egg yolks

Juice of ½ lemon

1 tablespoon water

1 cup (2 sticks) unsalted butter, melted and cooled

Kosher salt

Dash of cayenne pepper

Splash of cider vinegar

4 large eggs

2 English muffins, split and toasted

4 (¼-inch-thick) slices Canadian bacon

Oil, for frying

1 to 2 tablespoons minced fresh flat-leaf parsley, for garnish

For the sauce: In a stainless-steel bowl set over a saucepan of barely simmering water (and not touching the water), whisk the egg yolks with the lemon juice and 1 tablespoon water. Continue to whisk briskly, scraping the sides of the bowl with the whisk, until the mixture has thickened.

Remove from the heat and gradually whisk in the melted butter to yield a thick sauce. Season with salt and cayenne. Add additional lemon juice if needed. Cover and keep warm over a bowl of lukewarm water.

In a deep sauté pan, combine 2 inches of water with a splash of vinegar. Bring to a low simmer. Crack each egg into a shallow dish and gently add the egg to the water at the surface. Do not pour the egg in the water. Cook until the eggs look set, about 4 minutes. Using a slotted spoon, rinse under hot water, then drain, in the spoon, on paper towels. Transfer to a plate and keep warm.

Toast the English muffins and fry the Canadian bacon in a little oil. To assemble, place the muffin on a warm plate and place the bacon on top. Place an egg on top of each muffin half and top with warm hollandaise sauce. Sprinkle with the parsley and serve at once.

One end of the huge Main Dining Room has an atrium-garden view.

Wilmot Stage Stop
WILMOT, WI ~ EST. 1848

Many centenarian restaurants serve special dishes that people drive miles to eat. Some feature unique soups or salads, others show off gargantuan steaks or prime rib cuts, while some present fancy desserts or unique side dishes that people rave about. But the Wilmot Stage Stop, a place that started life as a stagecoach stop, is famous for a very common, ordinary, you-can-get-these-anywhere item: a baked potato.

It's not how the potato is prepared or how it's cooked or baked that has helped the lowly spud achieve regional fame. It's what's in it. Look closely at the picture. See the masses of yellow squares inserted into the open potatoes? They're hunks of butter. And although the menu says "served with heaps of butter," you don't expect a full quarter-pound per spud. Plus, it's served with sour cream as well!

Despite their wide selection of steaks, one of the most popular entrees on the menu is (remember, we are in the middle of Wisconsin, miles from any saltwater) lobster, which, of course, is served with melted butter.

Just to be clear, the cream of lobster bisque is delish as is the lobster spread loaded with crustacean flavor and spread on toast points. I did eat all of the lobster tail (delicious) dipped in drawn butter, as well as ⅓ of the well-marbled steak (delicious and perfectly cooked), but removed the brick of butter from the potato (again perfectly cooked—the potato, not the butter). And to top it off, you can order up a

The third floor of the Wilmot features six of the original hotel rooms, each about seven by seven feet in size.

special dessert/drink called the Brandy Ice for dessert: an astounding half gallon of vanilla ice cream mixed with brandy and crème de cacao. All of this goes to prove that Wisconsin really is "America's Dairyland."

The building was once called the Wilmot Hotel during Wisconsin's Territory days, when farmers headed to town to use the local mill to grind their wheat and found it convenient to bunk here overnight. Convenient, but not comfortable, as a visit to the third floor of the current building will reveal. Six or seven of the original hotel room doors have been fitted with windows so one can peek in and see the luxurious accommodations. Each room is about seven by seven feet, has a wooden commode right next to the bed, and

provided a rope support system for a small mattress filled with hay.

The second floor of the restaurant is a museum with displays of various memorabilia, household goods, old furniture and farm tools, and aged newspaper clippings and period photographs preserved so today's generation can learn about the way the pioneers lived in the mid-nineteenth century.

Travelers in those days got a room, a meal, and feed for their horses. Some nights there were musicians and other forms of entertainment; some nights the bar was the entertainment. During the day, the hotel also functioned as a general store selling fruit trees, cigars, tobacco, liquor, simple provisions, oysters, and ice—all very important in those days.

The Hegeman family has owned and operated the Stage Stop since its first days, surviving the privations of two wars, the Depression, and the hated Prohibition. One of the lighter moments came when the Ringling Brothers and Barnum & Bailey Circus stopped by on their way to one of their circuits around the country. Those tiny rooms must have been a tight fit for the acrobats, clowns, and ringmasters, not to mention the "Fat Lady." The elephants, horses, lions, and tigers we assume were stabled in a lot across the street.

The fourth generation of owners, Rolland and Mariann Winn, did more remodeling, widening the staircases to the second and third floors, creating the open grill in the center of the dining room, and spotlighting six different steaks on their menu and adding shrimp, lobster, lamb, and pork to the offerings as well. Rolland is also the gent who came up with the idea of adorning the baked potatoes with the aforementioned "heaps of butter." For this, the Wisconsin dairy industry, and perhaps regional cardiologists, are forever in his debt.

Fifth- and sixth-generation family members have continued the task of serving guests, modernizing, and at the same time retaining the charm and ambiance of the past. And the seventh generation is waiting in the wings to continue the long tradition of this classic old place.

Brandy Ice

∽ SERVES 2 TO 4 ∽

5 ounces brandy

2 ounces crème de cacao

½ gallon vanilla ice cream

In a separate mixing container, add 2½ ounces of brandy with 4 generous scoops of vanilla ice cream.

Hand churn the brandy, crème de cacao, and ice cream till it's very thick but pliable. Pour the remaining 2½ ounces of brandy into a martini or red wine glass.

Using a spoon, slowly and carefully scoop the hand-churned ice cream into the glass, stacking until it towers 3 to 4 inches above the rim of the glass.

Big Horn Smokehouse & Saloon
BIG HORN, WY ~ EST. 1882

Many restaurants in this book started out as saloons, bars, or taverns. But this is the only one we know of that started life as a livery stable.

It was 1882, and the town of Big Horn had just been founded, smack dab on the historic Bozeman Trail. John W. Custis, a direct descendant of Martha Custis Washington, the wife of the first U.S. president, decided to build a livery stable in the new town, but less than six months later he realized that with five livery stables already, perhaps a saloon was needed more. After all, you can tie up your horses in front of a saloon, right? So the stables were, hopefully, cleaned out, and became the Last Chance Saloon.

The Last Chance went through several owners, including an Italian man who turned the place into a restaurant in the early 1900s, but soon sold it to new owners who turned it back into a bar and kept the popular billiards table as well.

After a few years, John Henry Sackett, who was a hunter and guide for the Buffalo Bill show in the 1800s, decided to change careers and move his family to Big Horn, where he bought the Last Chance. He partnered with Charles Skinner, and they started transporting goods to Big Horn from the wagon trains in Cheyenne. They sold provisions out of their wagons until they eventually built the Big Horn Mercantile, which is still owned and operated by the Skinner family today.

In 1892, the railroad moved its tracks to nearby Sheridan and Big Horn began to fall apart, but the Last Chance soldiered on, morphing back into its billiards parlor and saloon role. The next owner, Brownie Sensel, formerly the town blacksmith, was found one morning, quite dead, sitting on the outhouse toilet. Being a stubborn cuss, he decided to stick around and haunt the place. Since then more than twenty people have heard strange noises in the kitchen that they attribute to old Brownie.

The name of the saloon was changed to the Bozeman Trail Inn in 1969, and twenty-eight years later, Jeri and Don Sheperd bought the inn. When Don suddenly passed away, their son Clint stepped in to co-own and manage the restaurant with his mother. Parts of the building were rapidly wearing out—after all it was 115 years old the day the Sheperds bought it, but they were hoping it could last a while longer before needing expensive repairs. Then fate, and a possible arsonist, stepped

in, and a "non-accidental, humanly caused" fire destroyed part of the roof and much of the kitchen, and caused extensive smoke damage throughout the building.

Clint and Jeri, after consulting with engineers, had the building completely reframed, a concrete foundation poured (before, there was no foundation at all), a new kitchen built, and a security and sprinkler system added. They had managed to save the restaurant, and in fact the original barroom was virtually untouched by the fire.

The wooden bar has its own story. As Jeri told it, "It was purchased from an Elks Club back east and was shipped to Miles City, Montana, by train. Then it was loaded aboard a wagon and driven here over two hundred miles of dirt roads. It's the most historic thing in the building."

The food was above and beyond what you'd expect in a small country town, and could even be called big-city sophisticated. The evening I was there, chef Clint was offering a special of skirt steak stuffed

Ernest Hemingway and friend Bunny in Big Horn, Wyoming, sit on the running board of his Model T in 1928.

with wild mushrooms. The steak was seared in a hot skillet, then popped into the oven to finish. Served medium-rare and loaded with mushrooms, it is the perfect end to a long day of travel.

In honor of one of the inn's most famous customers, I also indulged in a couple of mojitos, which couldn't have been better if they'd been made in Havana. Jeri told me this story: "One summer, an author who regularly stayed in one of the nearby mountain lodges came here every day and was often seen sitting at the end of the bar editing a book that his publisher had sent to him for corrections. Perhaps you've heard of his book?"

I asked if she knew the title. "Let me think, yes, it was called Farewell to something . . . yes, *Farewell to Arms*." Choking and almost falling out of my chair, I stammered, "Do you mean Hemingway. Ernest Hemingway?" "Yes," she exclaimed after a momentary pause to think it over, "that's it, Hemingway. Do you know him?"

It turns out that Hemingway, one of America's greatest authors, had sat on a barstool in that very bar, finishing work on what many consider the greatest novel ever written about World War I. Papa spent almost the entire month of August 1928 in Wyoming, either staying at the Spear-o-Wigwam Ranch or at the Sheridan Inn, both ten miles from the Bozeman Inn, because he liked the solitude of the Wyoming back country when writing. He made a few trips to the Bozeman to work on proofs of the novel, which was published in 1929.

Perhaps this small historic bar in tiny Big Horn, Wyoming, inspired Hemingway's famous quote: "Never sit at a table when you can stand at a bar."

Editor's Note: In late 2012, the Bozeman Trail Inn became Big Horn Smokehouse & Saloon under new ownership, but they continue serving the public just as they have during their long and storied history.

Duxelles-Stuffed Sirloin

∽ SERVES 4 ∽

1½ tablespoons unsalted butter

¼ cup minced shallots

12 ounces wild mushrooms, finely diced

2 teaspoons minced fresh flat-leaf parsley

1 teaspoon kosher salt

1 teaspoon freshly ground black pepper

⅓ cup heavy cream

½ cup panko (Japanese bread crumbs)

4 (8-ounce) sirloin steaks, ½ inch thick

Preheat the oven to 425°F. In a medium sauté pan, melt the butter over medium heat and sauté the shallots for 2 to 3 minutes, or until translucent. Add the mushrooms and sauté until the mushrooms release their liquid and then absorb it. Stir in the parsley, salt, pepper, cream, and panko until blended.

Using a meat mallet or a heavy skillet, flatten the steaks to a thickness of about ⅓ inch. Spoon a line of one-quarter of the mushroom mixture down the center of each steak, leaving a 1-inch margin at top and bottom, and roll into the shape of a log. Tie closed in several places with kitchen twine.

Heat a large grill pan over medium-high heat and oil the grids. Sear the steaks on both sides, then transfer the pan to the oven and roast for about 15 minutes for medium-rare.

Remove the kitchen twine and cut into thick slices. Serve hot.

Bellingham
Seattle
Coeur d'Alene
Ft. Benton
Portland (3)
Butte
Boise
Sheridan
Winnemucca
Salt Lake City
Piedmont
Denver
San Francisco (2)
Aspen
Pescadero
Santa Barbara
Santa Fe
Los Angeles (2)
Prescott

Traveling the lower 48 states was intended to be a two-month mission, but as is the case with most things in life, grew by scale as it gained momentum, and turned into a two-year project. I made seven separate journeys, four by car and three by plane, and got to learn more history of the U.S. through restaurants than most people get in a history class. I feel very privileged to have been able to experience American history through some of the best and most historic restaurants in the country.

Rick

Photos by Kate Browne (top), Bob Buckley (three, left to right), and Steve Lane (far right).

46,066 Miles Through History

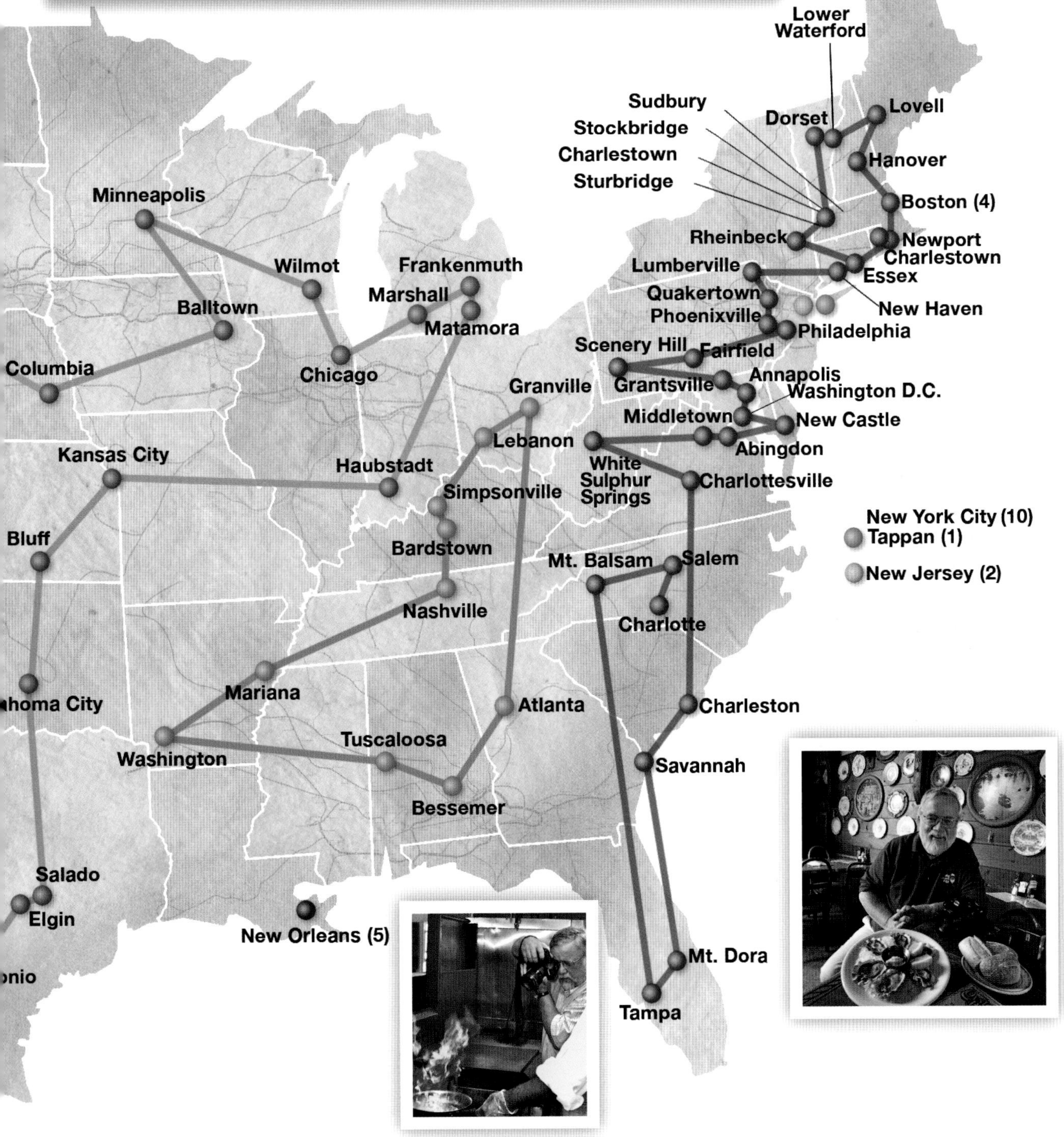

Lower Waterford

Sudbury
Stockbridge
Charlestown
Sturbridge

Dorset

Lovell

Hanover

Boston (4)

Minneapolis

Wilmot

Frankenmuth

Marshall

Matamora

Rheinbeck

Lumberville

Newport
Charlestown
Essex

Balltown

New Haven

Columbia

Chicago

Quakertown
Phoenixville

Philadelphia

Scenery Hill

Fairfield

Granville

Grantsville

Annapolis
Washington D.C.

Kansas City

Haubstadt

Lebanon

Middletown

New Castle

Bluff

Simpsonville

White
Sulphur
Springs

Abingdon

Charlottesville

New York City (10)
Tappan (1)

New Jersey (2)

Bardstown

Mt. Balsam

Salem

homa City

Nashville

Charlotte

Mariana

Atlanta

Charleston

Washington

Tuscaloosa

Savannah

Bessemer

Salado

Elgin

New Orleans (5)

Mt. Dora

onio

Tampa

Acknowledgments

THANK YOUS

I literally couldn't have done this book without the help of dozens of wonderful people all over the country. If I inadvertently left someone off the list I tender my deepest apologies. Thank you all for your support, encouragement, enthusiasm, thoughtful insights, and, most especially, fantastic meals. Special thanks go to the folks at TomTom who provided me with one of their superb GPS units to find my way around the country. I would still be lost in South Jersey looking at an old map if it wasn't for this wonderful device.

Rick Browne

Acme Oyster House: Paul Rottner, Monique Rodrigue, Anne & Kary Goodwin

Antoine's: Andrew J. Crocchiolo, Randy Guste, Chef Michael Regua, Wendy Chatelain

Balsam Mountain Inn: Kim & Sharon Shailer, Chef K. Boyd

Barbetta: Laura Maiolio, Gunter Blobel

The Bell in Hand Tavern: Debbie Kessler

Black Bass Hotel: Grant Ross, Bob & Linda Buckley

Breitbach's Country Dining: Mike & Cindy Breitbach

Bridge Café: Adam Weprin, Chef Joseph Kunst, Bruce & Pam Paris, Cathie & Bill Goodwin

Cattleman's Steakhouse: Dick Stubs, Brendan Hoover, Erick Johnson

CentralChef.com: Michael Eisenberg

Century Inn: Megin Harrington, Chef Steve Thompson

Charlotte's Eats & Sweets: Charlotte Bowls

City Tavern: Walter Staib, Diana Wolkow, Molly Yun, Kristofer Mehaffey, Jim Messlier, Sylvia Burnell

Cold Spring Tavern: John Locke, Wayne Wilson

Cole's: Dave Freeman, Paul Yrastorza, Chef Jason Cancedo

Collection of Old Salem Museums & Gardens, Winston-Salem, NC: Gary Albert, Michele Doyle

Columbia: Richard Hernandez, Casey Hernandez, Jim Garris, Chef Geraldo Bayona, Angela Geml, Joe Roman

Commander's Palace: Chef Tory McPhail, Lovely Wakefield

Dan & Louis Oyster Bar: Doug & Keni Wachsmuth

Delmonico's: Corrado Goglia, Chef William Oliva, Jennifer Roth, Dennis Turcinovic, Dick Saar

Duarte's Tavern: Ron, Kathy & Tim Duarte

Durgin Park: Seana Kelley

Fairfield Inn: Saul & Joan Chandon

Fenton's Creamery: Gregory Scott Whidden

Ferrara: Ernest Lepore, Nancy Rodriguez

Fior d'Italia: Bob & Jinx Larive, Chef Gianni Audieri

Fraunces Tavern: Chef Billy Barlow, John Mutovic

Fraunces Tavern Museum: Suzanne Prabucki, Jessica Baldwin, Fran Coolman

Galatoire's: David Barr Gooch, Melvin Rodrigue, Chef Brian Landry, Carrie DeVries, Imre Szalai, Charles Grimaldi, Dorris Sylvester, Garrett Bess

Gluek's Restaurant: Linda Holcomb

Glur's Tavern: Todd & Carrie Trofholz

Grand Union Hotel: Kernan Myers, Cheryl Gagnon, Chef Scott Meyers

Grande Finale: Vicki Raymond, Virginia Chambers, Greg & Susan Gilbert

Hays House: Chef Doug & Sheri Wilkerson, Stuart Collier

Horseshoe Café: Travis & Alicia Holland

Hotel Jerome: Chef Rich Hinojosa, Belinda Oster

Huber's Café: James & David Louie

Hudson's Hamburgers: Todd Hudson, Jack & Cheryl Lawrence

Jake's Famous Crawfish: John Underhill, Chef Billy Hahn, James C. Pappas, Jamieson & April Fuller, Jennifer Tidwell

Jessop's Tavern: Richard Day

Jones' Bar-B-Q Diner: James Jones

Katz's Delicatessen: Alan & Jake Dell, Chef Kenneth Kohn

Keens Steakhouse: James Conley, Bonnie Jenkins, Chef Bill Rodgers

Kimberton Inn: Jeff Effgen, Rick Smyth

La Fonda: John Rickey, Chef Lane Warner, Shawn Murphy

Lakeside Inn: Chef Patrick Deblasio, James Barrgren, Jay Banfal-Feather, Jason Fiegel, Kim Chambers

Longfellow's Wayside Inn: John Cowden, Jr., Guy LeBlanc, Marvin Cohen, John O'Brien (Carriage House)

Louis' Lunch: J. W. Lassen, Jenn Myers

M & M Cigar Store: Sam Jankovich, Kacie Raybould, Shana Fortune, Jerry Issacson, Brian McLeod, Crystal Albrecht, Wendy Hoar

Maneki: Jeanne Nakayama, Fusae "Mom" Yokoyama

McCoole's at the Historic Red Lion Inn: Jan Hench, Megan Limbert, Chef Clyde Bradford

McCrady's: Adi Noe, Chef Sean Brock

Menger Hotel: Ernesto Malacara

Michele's Pies: Michele Albano

Michie Tavern: Gregory MacDonald, Sam Morris, Miranda Dean, Cindy Conte, Brittnay Ferguson

Middleton Tavern: Chrissy Nokes, Chef Arthur Gross Miette & Lance Wasson

Mike's Pies: Michael Martin, Courtney Anderson

Mirabelle Cheese Shop: Andrea Itin

Mr. B's Bistro: Chef Michelle McRaney

Museum of the City of New York: Carin S. User, Marah Newman, Robbi Siegel

New Orleans Convention & Visitors Bureau: Noreen Tibbets

Norman Rockwell Museum: Corry Kanzenberg, Mary Melius

Old Ebbitt Grill: Christopher Godown, Chef R. McGowan

Old Homestead Steakhouse: Michael D. Florea, Carol Troche, Steve Mangione, Chef Oscar

Old Salem Tavern: Gayle Winston

Old Stone Inn: Shelley Thompson, Chef Jerrett Berry

Omni Parker House: Chef Gerard Tice, Kali Horton, Toui Tran, Kerri McCulloch

Pete's Tavern: Gary Egan

Peter Luger Steakhouse: Pam Stroch

Phillippe The Original: Julie Tauscher, Mark Massengill

Pleasant Point Inn: Sue & Alan Perry

Rabbit Hill Inn: Leslie & Brian Mulcahy, Chef M. Sechich

Rhinebeck Historical Society: Michael Frazier

Savoy Grill: Donald Lee, Mary McDonald, Curtis Haugh, Ron Garris

Southside Market & Barbeque: Bryan Bracewell, Ernest Bracewell, Ed Weiss, Dustin Manhart, Alexa Hazelton

Stagecoach Inn: Terry Potts, Susan & Greg Gilbert

The Old '76 House: Robert Norden

The Berghoff: Carolyn Berghoff, Amy Ricchiuto

The Bozeman Trail Inn: Clint Sheperd, Jeri Sheperd

The Bright Star: Nick Koikos, Jim Koikos, Ross Daidone

The Buckhorn Exchange: Bill Dutton

The Buxton Inn: Audry & Orville Orr

The Casselman Inn: Merv Brenneman, Heather Bova, Marcia Brenneman, Christi Orendorf

The Dorset Inn: Steve & Lauren Bryant

The Golden Lamb: DeDe Bailey

The Golden Rule: Michael Matsos, Bernice Kelly, Michael Booker, Peggy Martin

The Greenbrier: James Justice, Lynn Swann

The Griswold Inn: Alan Barone, Chef Jim Gallagher, Joan Paul, Geoffrey Paul, Douglas Paul, Gregory Paul

The Hanover Inn: Chef Justin Dain

The Historical Society of Washington County, Virginia

The Log Inn: Gene, Rita, Kathy, Daryl & Trish Elpers

The Martin Hotel: John Arant

The Old Talbott Tavern: James Kelley

The Palace Restaurant & Saloon: Dave Michaelson, Chef Gary Creamer

The Pirate's House: John Pierse, John Chaplin, Megan Cox

The Publick House: Michael Glick, Chef Michael Heenan

The Red Lion Inn: Chef Brian Alberg, Julie Rodriguez, Carol Bosco Baumann

The Stockton Inn: Fred & Janet Stackhouse, Chef Berisha

The Tadich Grill: Rick Powers

The Tavern: Max & Kelly Herman, Carrie Baxter

The Tavern at the Beekman Arms: Denise Cvijanovich

The Warren Tavern: John Harnett

The White Horse Tavern: Megan Kenney, Paul Hogan, Erica Emerson, Chef Richard Silvia, Gary Swanson

The Wyoming Room, Sheridan County Fulmer Public Library: Judy Slack

TomTom: Lea Armstrong

Tujague's: Paul Gustings, Chef Rhett Byrd, Mark Latter

Union Oyster House: Mary Ann Milano-Picardi, Joseph A. Milano, Jr., Jim Malinn, John Ferrari, Anton Christen, Valerie & Dash Roberts

Varallo's Chile Parlor & Restaurant: Todd & Tiphoney Varallo

Wayside Inn: Lois & Jacob Charon

Wilcox Tavern Restaurant: Susan Loiselle, Chef Jamie Grider

Wilmot Stage Stop: Jill Hackett, Kevin Krueger

Williams Tavern: Joyce Graves, Linda Keen, Terri Ryan, George Staples, Abraham Block

Win Shuler's: Larry, Win & Hans Schuler, Julie Staab

White Horse Inn: Tim & Lisa Wilkins

Ye Olde Centerton Inn: Joanne & Brian Goode

Zehnder's: John & Albert Zehnder

Index

C

Metric Conversions and Equivalents

METRIC CONVERSION FORMULAS

TO CONVERT	MULTIPLY
Ounces to grams	Ounces by 28.35
Pounds to kilograms	Pounds by 454
Teaspoons to milliliters	Teaspoons by 4.93
Tablespoons to milliliters	Tablespoons by 14.79
Fluid ounces to milliliters	Fluid ounces by 29.57
Cups to milliliters	Cups by 236.59
Cups to liters	Cups by .236
Pints to liters	Pints by .473
Quarts to liters	Quarts by .946
Gallons to liters	Gallons by 3.785
Inches to centimeters	Inches by 2.54

APPROXIMATE METRIC EQUIVALENTS

VOLUME

¼ teaspoon	1 milliliter
½ teaspoon	2.5 milliliters
¾ teaspoon	4 milliliters
1 teaspoon	5 milliliters
1¼ teaspoons	6 milliliters
1½ teaspoons	7.5 milliliters
1¾ teaspoons	8.5 milliliters
2 teaspoons	10 milliliters
1 tablespoon (½ fluid ounce) .	15 milliliters
2 tablespoons (1 fluid ounce) .	30 milliliters
¼ cup	60 milliliters
⅓ cup	80 milliliters
½ cup (4 fluid ounces)	120 milliliters
⅔ cup	160 milliliters
¾ cup	180 milliliters
1 cup (8 fluid ounces)	240 milliliters
1¼ cups	300 milliliters
1½ cups (12 fluid ounces) . . .	360 milliliters
1⅔ cups	400 milliliters
2 cups (1 pint)	460 milliliters
3 cups	700 milliliters
4 cups (1 quart)	0.95 liter
1 quart plus ¼ cup	1 liter
4 quarts (1 gallon)	3.8 liters

WEIGHT

¼ ounce	7 grams
½ ounce	14 grams
¾ ounce	21 grams
1 ounce	28 grams
1¼ ounces	35 grams
1½ ounces	42.5 grams
1⅔ ounces	45 grams
2 ounces	57 grams
3 ounces	85 grams
4 ounces (¼ pound)	113 grams
5 ounces	142 grams
6 ounces	170 grams
7 ounces	198 grams
8 ounces (½ pound)	227 grams
16 ounces (1 pound)	454 grams
35.25 ounces (2.2 pounds) . .	1 kilogram

LENGTH

⅛ inch	3 millimeters
¼ inch	6 millimeters
½ inch	1¼ centimeters
1 inch	2½ centimeters
2 inches	5 centimeters
2½ inches	6 centimeters
4 inches	10 centimeters
5 inches	13 centimeters
6 inches	15¼ centimeters
12 inches (1 foot)	30 centimeters

OVEN TEMPERATURES

To convert Fahrenheit to Celsius, subtract 32 from Fahrenheit, multiply the result by 5, then divide by 9.

DESCRIPTION	FAHRENHEIT	CELSIUS	BRITISH GAS MARK
Very cool	200°	95°	0
Very cool	225°	110°	¼
Very cool	250°	120°	½
Cool	275°	135°	1
Cool	300°	150°	2
Warm	325°	165°	3
Moderate	350°	175°	4
Moderately hot	375°	190°	5
Fairly hot	400°	200°	6
Hot	425°	220°	7
Very hot	450°	230°	8
Very hot	475°	245°	9

COMMON INGREDIENTS AND THEIR APPROXIMATE EQUIVALENTS

1 cup uncooked white rice = 185 grams

1 cup all-purpose flour = 140 grams

1 stick butter (4 ounces • ½ cup • 8 tablespoons) = 110 grams

1 cup butter (8 ounces • 2 sticks • 16 tablespoons) = 220 grams

1 cup brown sugar, firmly packed = 225 grams

1 cup granulated sugar = 200 grams

Information compiled from a variety of sources, including Recipes into Type *by Joan Whitman and Dolores Simon (Newton, MA: Biscuit Books, 2000);* The New Food Lover's Companion *by Sharon Tyler Herbst (Hauppauge, NY: Barron's, 1995); and* Rosemary Brown's Big Kitchen Instruction Book *(Kansas City, MO: Andrews McMeel, 1998).*